NEW STEPPING STONES 1

TEACHER'S GUIDE

Julie Ashworth   John Clark

Syllabus	2
Introduction	7
Lesson Notes	14
Resource File	162
Wordlist	172
Test Cards	174

LONGMAN

Syllabus

Unit		Main Structures	Vocabulary	Main Communicative Functions	Tasks and Activities
Colours and Numbers		Stand up. Sit down.	boys girls everybody black blue brown green red white yellow NUMBERS: 1 – 7	Respond to simple oral instructions.	Action Games. Make word stones. Song. Make colour flashcards. Rhyme.
Pets	**1a**	Who's this? Turn around. Walk. Stop. I'm … Point to … What's your name? Make …	pet hi hello goodbye number Julie Butch Kev Kate Sam name badge NUMBERS: 8, 9, 10	Greet other people. Identify other people by name. Ask someone their name. Say goodbye.	Make a name badge. Action Game.
	1b	Touch … This is … Are you ready?	table chair colour Suzy Duffy Slow Wow Yes No Bingo	Identify pets.	Action Games. Make Bingo cards. Bingo. Role play.
	1c	Sit on … Stand on … What's this? What's that? Draw a … Look!	door floor cat dog mouse snake tortoise computer	Ask for/Give the identity of people.	Action Game. Draw animals. Colouring activity. Crossword. Make word stones. Word stones games. Character card games.
	1d	Walk to … Pick up … Put down … Is this a … ? It's a … Is it a … ? What colour is … ? Your turn.	book pen pencil cow duck hen monkey sheep you your	Identify a picture. Identify animal noises. Give simple descriptions using colour.	Action Games. Character card games. Song.
	1e	Open … Close … Is this your … ? Have you got a pet? Your turn. My turn.	window cake hat house box bird fish frog hamster rabbit rat	Play a board game.	Action Games. Make word stones. Games with word stones. The Stepping Stones Game. Add speech bubbles to a cartoon strip. Stepping Stones Action Game 1.
	1f	I've got (a) …	bird plane Supersnake puppet	Ask someone if they have a pet.	Project: *Pets* Make a snake. Evaluation.

	Unit	Main Structures	Vocabulary	Main Communicative Functions	Tasks and Activities
School	2a	Don't … WORD ORDER: *a blue bag* What colour's … ?	bag book pencil chair table grey orange pink purple spinning top	Identify objects.	Action Game. Song. Make word stones. Make a spinning top. Spinning top word games.
	2b	Write number 1 on the blackboard. I don't know. WORD ORDER: *three purple books*	blackboard chalk pen pencil case pencil sharpener rubber ruler my your	Ask/Answer about colour of objects.	Action Game. Pairwork. Colouring. The Blackboard Game. Make word stones.
	2c	How many … can you see? Where's … ?	on under NUMBERS: *11 – 20* right wrong	Saying a calculation is right or wrong. Ask about location using *Where's*. Ask/Answer questions about quantity.	Action Game. Bingo. Crossword. Rhyme. Maths questions. Make number flashcards. Play number flashcard games. Number Bingo
	2d	Where's the … ? There! Guess! Put your … on/in/under … Where's the pen in picture 6? WORD ORDER: *The blue pencil is under the chair.* His/Her name is … There's … There are …	in teacher Mr Mrs	Ask/Say where things are. Gather information about the colour of everyday objects. Give someone's name.	'Where's the rubber?' game. Groupwork: Questionnaire. Action Game. Personal file: Draw your teacher.
	2e	My/Your … is in/on/under …	bed glue kite sink bin clock compass cupboard desk paint paintbrush scissors	Describe the position of objects in a picture.	Action Game (Simon Says). Make word stones. Word stones games. The Stepping Stones Game. Draw and describe a picture. Add speech bubbles to a cartoon strip. The Stepping Stones Action Game. Solve anagrams. Kim's Game.
	2f	What's four and five? That's very difficult. Thanks.	dice winner counter start finish chancer coin heads tails number school worm	Revision of questions and instructions.	Groupwork: Dice game. Project: Games of chance. Evaluation.

Syllabus

Families

Unit	Main Structures	Vocabulary	Main Communicative Functions	Tasks and Activities
3a	... is called ... How many people live at your house? Who's this? What's his/her name?	family sister brother father mother grandfather grandmother	Identify family members.	Action Game. Character card game. Personal file: My family tree.
3b	It's my birthday today. How old are you? I'm five (years old). How old is Maria?	birthday NUMBERS: 30 – 100 snake ladder up down	Ask someone their age. Tell someone your age.	Song. Character card game. Personal file: Me. Action Game. Snakes and Ladders.
3c	How are you? Fine thanks. POSSESSIVE 's I've got ...	friend quickly slowly	Ask/talk about families.	Character card game. Make word stones. Fill in a form. Crossword. Action Game. Personal file: My family.
3d	I've got ... How many? PLURAL s	uncle aunt cousin dad mum grandad grandma	Describe your family.	Quiz. Make and play word stones. Stepping Stones Game. Classwork: Survey. Add speech bubbles to a cartoon strip. Stepping Stones Action Game. Draw a Mother's Day card. Crossword.
3e	I haven't got any ...	age family tree	Write about your family.	Project: Families. Evaluation.

	Unit	Main Structures	Vocabulary	Main Communicative Functions	Tasks and Activities
Body	4a	What colour is Julie's hair? What colour are Julie's eyes? How tall is Suzy? How tall are you? Is Suzy thin? Guess who!	body tall short small big fat thin blonde hair nose mouth eyes ears metre centimetre black blue brown green grey	Describe people's appearance.	Action Game. Groupwork: Questionnaire. Groupwork: Survey.
	4b	She's got long, blonde hair. He's got blue eyes. He's got a big nose.	head shoulders knees toes hand arm leg foot/feet tooth/teeth children yellow purple orange ugly	Ask questions about people's appearance.	Song. Make a cut-out face. Write quiz questions. Action Game. Make word stones.
	4c	... hasn't got ... It's got no ...	ghost spider crocodile friendly hairy bad angry	Describe a monster.	Board game. Draw a monster. Action Game. Write a magic spell.
	4d	Keep moving. Who's got the ball? How big is your hand/foot? How many arms has your monster got?	finger thumb happy today nod	Ask people about their height etc.	Bingo. Crossword. Song. Playground Game. Measure your hands a feet. Invent and write about a monster.
	4e	This is me and my sister. I've got brown hair.	toe shoe lips teeth glasses moustache beard new curly	Describe people's appearance.	Word stones game. The Stepping Stones Game. Describe a family photo. Add speech bubbles to a cartoon strip. The Stepping Stones Action Game.
	4f	He's/She's got ... What a big nose you've got! What big teeth you've got!	mask button wool string	Describe a famous person.	Face collage. Describe a famous person. Identify a famous person from a description. Project: Make masks. Evaluation.
Festivals		Merry Christmas Happy New Year Season's Greetings	Christmas Easter egg roll hill painted	Exchange Christmas greetings. Help someone find a hidden object.	Christmas carol. Make a Christmas card. Plan a Christmas party. Find objects in a picture. Make a painted egg. Egg hunt. Easter project.

New Stepping Stones

is a four-year English course for young learners beginning English at Primary level. The course is carefully constructed around a conceptual framework in which the tasks, activities and language points reflect the interests and development of young learners.

The key features of **New Stepping Stones** are as follows:

A syllabus geared to the child's development
The *New Stepping Stones* syllabus has been designed to meet the specific needs of young learners, providing four achievable years of English. The syllabus takes into account the cognitive development of children this age. The choice of themes therefore reflects children's developing awareness. For example, in Year 1 of the course, the topic about animals focuses on pets. In Year 2, the same topic relates to wild animals.

The syllabus also grades the tasks and activities in which children participate. This is related to a thorough coverage of appropriate structures, functions, words and pronunciation. All the language points are regularly revised and reviewed to ensure maximum progress for all learners.

Topic-based learning
Level 1 of *New Stepping Stones* is divided into four topics. Within each topic, the language items are carefully selected and graded. Pupils are presented with language which allows them to communicate in a genuinely meaningful way about each topic. The topic-based syllabus also offers maximum opportunity for project work.

Personalisation
Children get great motivation and satisfaction from talking and writing about themselves. *New Stepping Stones* offers many opportunities for pupils to do this in English.

Variety of learning styles
It is generally acknowledged that all children learn in slightly different ways. To accommodate this, *New Stepping Stones* exploits a wide range of tried and tested techniques and activities to allow all pupils to fulfil their maximum potential.

Teaches positive learning habits
One of the purposes of learning English at Primary level is to provide positive motivation for future studies. This includes not only laying foundations in terms of language and enjoyment but also developing positive learning habits in young learners.

New Stepping Stones teaches pupils organisational skills; the importance of co-operation; referencing skills; and the need to use language for real purposes. The Activity Book contains innovative learner-training sections with self-assessment activities.

Comprehensive coverage of skills
The syllabus in *New Stepping Stones* is carefully graded in order to ensure comprehensive coverage of all four skills. Within each lesson pupils are engaged in listening, speaking, reading and writing in English, with listening and speaking having prime importance in the early years. The Coursebook and Activity Book feature clear rubrics, signposts and progression.

Interdisciplinary
The topics and activities in *New Stepping Stones* provide an interdisciplinary approach to language learning, enabling teachers to link the study of English with work in other areas of the curriculum. The projects, which are built into the Coursebook, actively encourage such links.

Simple to use
The teaching notes to *New Stepping Stones* include a step-by-step guide to every activity in every lesson. Reproduction of both the Coursebook and Activity Book alongside the teaching notes provides an immediate reference for teachers.

Pupils learn by doing
The activities in *New Stepping Stones* require the active participation of the pupils. There are games which practise the language through physical involvement, tasks which involve making things and emphasis upon learning through concrete activities. The unique new 'word stones' sections involve pupils in active vocabulary development.

Learning is fun
New Stepping Stones is based on the belief that learning is most effective when it is fun and moreover that enjoyment provides motivation and encourages pupils to continue in their studies.

Introduction

ORGANISATION

Contents of the course

Level 1 of *New Stepping Stones* consists of:

Coursebook

64 lively, full-colour pages, featuring stories, cartoon strips, vocabulary and project work, games, songs and rhymes and numerous activities for presenting and practising the language.

Cut-outs

Each Activity Book comes complete with its own centre pull-out section of cut-outs. These include playing cards and story bubbles for use in a wide variety of games and activities.

Activity Book

80 pages, providing practice in all the skills, with questionnaires, puzzles, games, tests and self-assessment activities to fully involve pupils in the learning process.

Teacher's Guide

A simple to use, lesson-by-lesson guide giving instructions on all activities. Reproductions of both Coursebook and Activity Book pages greatly simplify preparation and classroom use, while the **Resource File** at the back of the book provides a wealth of additional ideas. Photocopy masters are provided to support pupils' self-assessment work in the Activity Book.

Cassettes

The cassettes feature both adults and children and provide a wide range of natural listening material including dialogues, songs, rhymes and listening tasks.

Objectives of the course

The main objectives of *New Stepping Stones* are as follows:
- To instil the idea that learning languages is enjoyable.
- To encourage pupils to want to go on learning English in secondary school.
- To enable pupils to talk and write about themselves.
- To lay the foundations for future study in terms of basic structures, lexis, language functions and basic study skills.
- To enable pupils to use English for a purpose and to regard English as a means of communicating real information.

Organisation of the course

New Stepping Stones Level 1 is made up of four topics:
  PETS
  SCHOOL
  FAMILIES
  BODY
Pupils explore each topic in sufficient depth to enable them to talk and write about themselves, their family, their classmates and their possessions. Each topic contains an introductory story, four or five units and project and evaluation work.
There is also an introductory unit on Colours and Numbers and two 'Festivals' lessons at the end of the Coursebook, for use as appropriate. Each unit is divided into three lessons (of approximately one hour) which, together with story, project and evaluation lessons, provides a total of 72 lessons. Further suggestions for projects, work on festivals and a wealth of ideas in the Resource File supplement the core material. There is constant revision throughout the course, four progress tests and four self-assessment sections.

Adaptability of the course

New Stepping Stones is designed to be as flexible as possible: the Coursebook and Activity Book are divided into units rather than lessons because the time available will vary from situation to situation, according to factors such as class size and age of pupils.
Simply work through the material in the order shown in the Lesson Notes. The topic-based structure and in-built revision make it possible to begin a lesson at any point.
The extra ideas in the **Resource File** also give the teacher greater flexibility in managing time.

Organisation of the Coursebook and Activity Book

Each unit consists of two pages in the Coursebook and three pages in the Activity Book. The text of the introductory story is reproduced in the cut-out story bubbles in the Activity Book.
Key vocabulary and classroom language is given in wordlists at the back of the Coursebook.
Colour games material is provided in the centre pull-out section of the Activity Book.

Organisation of the Teacher's Guide

Each two-page spread is devoted to one lesson, i.e. approximately one hour's worth of material. There is a step-by-step guide giving detailed teaching instructions for each activity. Reproduced pages from both the Coursebook and the Activity Book allow teachers to see instantly which exercises are being referred to. Tapescripts and answers are also included. The symbol // is used in some tapescripts. This is an indication that the teacher should either stop the tape temporarily or use the 'pause' button.

Resource File

The Resource File is at the back of the Teacher's Guide. It contains suggestions and ideas for extra games, activities and projects. Many of these activities can be used at any stage; others are more applicable to particular lessons. Suggestions as to when extra activities are appropriate are given in the syllabus box at the top of each page of Lesson Notes. The numbers of appropriate activities from the Resource File are given here.

Main Language Items		Resource File	Materials Needed
Stand up!	everybody		cassette/cassette player
Sit down!	boys	6	materials to make and store word stones
	girls		coloured pencils

These extra ideas will also be helpful in dealing with mixed-ability groups, since they include suggestions for remedial work and expansion activities.

TEACHING PROCEDURES

The following notes deal with how to use *New Stepping Stones* in the classroom. Pupils are required to learn only a limited number of techniques, which can be applied to a wide range of activities in the Coursebook (called CB in the Lesson Notes) and the Activity Book (AB). All variations upon these techniques are given in the Lesson Notes.
The activities in *New Stepping Stones* can be loosely divided into those which concentrate on one of the four skills (SPEAKING, LISTENING, READING and WRITING) and those which practise two or more skills simultaneously.

Speaking activities

Pair Work

The **Pair Work** exercises provide much of the initial presentation and practice of new language and range from very controlled exercises (i.e. drills in which both questions and answers are given) to free exercises based on picture prompts.
For controlled exercises the following procedure is recommended, although as a first step it may be useful to demonstrate exercises with one pupil, or get more able pupils to show the rest of the class.

a   Divide the class into pairs and give each pair question and answer roles (for suggestions on organising pupils into pairs see **Classroom Management**).
b   Each pair uses only one book, placed between them, open at the appropriate page. The words should *always* be covered. Pupils must not read while listening.
c   Pupils repeat after the tape. All pairs work simultaneously. P1 repeats the questions, pointing and referring to pictures as appropriate to contextualise the questions. (This is necessary since, for example, 'What's this?' is meaningless unless it is clear what is being referred to.) P2 answers.
    As the course progresses, pupils can be encouraged to test themselves by trying to answer before the tape.

d   Practise without the help of the tape. P1 now uses the words in his book as prompts to ask the questions. (NOTE Simply reading the question aloud destroys natural rhythm and pronunciation, so encourage pupils to adopt a 'Look and Say' method here, i.e. pupils read the question silently before looking up at their partner and asking the questions.)

P2's book should remain on the table with the words covered. He/she answers the questions using the pictures as prompts and help from P1, if required.

e Change roles and repeat step d.
f Practise until the whole exercise can be done using only the pictures as prompts. (This stage will be reached gradually as skill and confidence increase.)
g During the practice phase the teacher's task is to circulate and help the pupils where necessary. Praise and encourage natural speed and intonation; the use of 'Look and Say' techniques; co-operation between pupils – helping and checking etc.

The above procedures are goals to be worked towards. Pupils will take time to get used to working in pairs. Therefore during **Pair Work** it is important to keep a few points in mind:

Take your time ...

All pupils vary in ability; some will instantly grasp the technique while others may still be getting used to it in Topic 2.

Communication before correctness ...

Don't expect instant perfection. Communication is more important initially: correctness will come gradually.

Timing ...

Controlled **Pair Work** will usually take about fifteen minutes. Pupils will vary in terms of what they can achieve in this time. More able pupils will be able to produce both questions and answers without the help of the words, while less able pupils should at least know key vocabulary items and question words.

Noise levels ...

Pupils working simultaneously in pairs will inevitably generate some noise. The sound of a class working is a healthy learning environment but only tolerate noise that relates to the task in hand.

These techniques are invaluable in maximising the involvement of all pupils. Individual capabilities vary, but even less able pupils will be more active and involved in their own learning than if the teacher is asking all the questions. Initially **Pair Work** may be time-consuming, but a little initial patience in using the above techniques will be greatly rewarded.

In freer **Pair Work**, the basic practice procedures are the same from the teacher's point of view although the model questions and answers are not on the tape. Demonstrate by asking appropriate questions to the whole class until pupils understand the nature of the exercise and the language forms needed.

Groupwork: Questionnaire

Questionnaires provide pupils with a real purpose for communication and an opportunity to talk about themselves. Always demonstrate **Questionnaires** to the class first, so that pupils know exactly what they have to do. Quickly draw a grid on the blackboard. Select one or two pupils. Write their names on the grid. Then ask the questions to be practised and write each pupil's answers alongside their name.

Name	dog	cat	other	no pet
Alex				
Anna				

a Divide the class into groups of three or more, depending upon the nature of the questionnaire. Ensure that pupils are not always in the same groups, so that Questionnaires are less predictable. (For suggestions on the organisation of groups see **Classroom Management**.)
b Then pupils complete their own questionnaires. Set a 5–10 minute time limit for the task.
c The teacher's task is to circulate, giving assistance if required. Ensure that pupils are using English and that they are asking questions and not simply copying each other's answers. Communication is more important than correctness here.
d When pupils have completed their questionnaires, ask the class questions about the information they have collected.

Role Play

Two types of **Role Play** are used in *New Stepping Stones*; conventional Role Plays and Role Plays using puppets.

Both can be used to bring more life to the language. The following points offer guidance on procedure:

a   Set the scene by telling pupils to look at the pictures and then asking questions about who and what they can see.
b   Play the tape. Pupils listen to the whole dialogue, looking at the pictures at the same time.
c   Give roles. Name badges or character cards from the cut-outs can be used to clarify the concept of playing a role.
d   Role Plays usually involve two characters. All pairs work simultaneously. Pupils should be standing or sitting, according to the relative positions of the characters in the picture.
e   Pupils then repeat the dialogue two or three times after the tape.
f   During the repetition phase insist upon intonation and gesture. Demonstrate to pupils by 'overacting' yourself, if necessary. Alternatively, to focus attention upon gestures, pupils can act out the dialogue using mime.
g   Pupils then act out the dialogue without the help of the tape. All pairs practise simultaneously. Allow pupils between five and ten minutes to practise the Role Play.
h   Volunteers can then be allowed to act out the Role Play in front of the class. However, it is best to restrict such activity to enthusiastic volunteers.
i   If time allows, pupils can change role and repeat the Role Play.

Listening Activities

Story presentation

The **Presentation** phases of lessons usually relate to the story cartoon strips in the Coursebook, all of which are recorded on the tape. These are used to contextualise all the language to be practised and provide Listening and Reading practice.

The full text appears in the cut-out Story Bubbles. Later in the Topic, pupils will get the chance to place the bubbles on the cartoons – a form of disguised reading comprehension practice.

Draw pupils' attention to the pictures and ask some simple questions to set the scene before playing the tape.

The focus of the **Supersnake** strips is on reading and listening. Encourage pupils to read silently to themselves before listening to the tape.

Listening (Task)

These exercises provide a contrasting type of listening exercise to the **Presentation** strips. Rather than listening for general meaning, pupils are now required to listen for specific detail and carry out a set task. The activities themselves vary from simple, directed colouring and drawing in the early units, to chart-filling activities as the book progresses. Procedures for individual activities are given in the Lesson Notes. All **Listening (Task)** exercises are on tape.

Reassure pupils that they do not have to understand all the words, but only listen for specific information.

Action Game

The **Action Games** are an adaptation of Asher's Total Physical Reponse method. The aim is to improve listening comprehension through the active involvement of the pupils.

The teacher gives instructions in English. Demonstrate the meaning by acting out the instruction with the pupils, not by translation.

Detailed guidance on the language to be used is given in the Lesson Notes. Obviously the physical layout of the classroom will determine to what extent instructions can be used with the whole class simultaneously or only with individual pupils. Most of the games can be adapted to suit the environment and those instructions which require pupils to 'Walk' can be practised with individuals. The **Action Games** are very important since they introduce a great deal of functional classroom English which is later recycled in the CB itself. (The written forms of the language introduced in the **Action Games** are given in the AB.)

The following points offer guidance as to procedure:

a   Pupils should not repeat the instructions. **Action Games** are silent listening games!
b   Always demonstrate all new words by acting them out with two or more pupils at the front of the class. It is not sufficient to show the meaning by demonstrating yourself. Pupils must do each action.
c   Continue to act out each new instruction until pupils can do it without your help. To check pupils are comfortable with a new instruction, delay your own response slightly to give them a chance to act on their own.
d   Always practise a new instruction with the whole class at some stage. All pupils should be active as much of the time as possible.
e   Combine words previously introduced with new words to make your own original instructions. Perhaps note these down before the lesson.
f   Do not try to progress too fast. It may take a little time for pupils to understand some instructions.
g   Speak at natural speed and do not split sentences to make it easier for pupils. Simply repeat the instruction, if necessary.
h   Do not try to trick pupils. Your aim is that they should always succeed.
j   **Action Games** should last about ten minutes, depending on the particular game. Games will work

better if they are repeated and extended in a subsequent lesson.

Reading Activities

Reading (Task)

With the **Reading (Task)** exercises, pupils are directly involved in performing a task, this time based upon a written passage. They may be asked to 'Read and colour' or 'Read, then write.' Once again, the pupils do not have to understand all the words, but only that information which will enable them to complete the task.

Pupils should work individually and the ability of the group will dictate the amount of time each activity takes. The cut-outs also can be used to provide extra practice for faster pupils.

Encourage pupils to compare their work when they have finished. Round off the activity by going over correct solutions on the blackboard.

Stepping Stones Game

This is a simple sentence-making game. The object of the game is to make as many sentences as possible. Pupils work from left to right and select a word, or words, from each column. Each sentence must be a correct description of a picture or pictures in the CB. Pupils may choose not to select a word from a column if they wish, but must still work across from left to right. One pupil from each pair should write their answers on a piece of paper. Demonstrate the game by constructing a similar grid on the blackboard and asking pupils to make sentences. Write these on the board.

Set a time limit of ten minutes. Then ask each pair how many sentences they have made. Check that all sentences are correct and appropriate to the picture. Correct any mistakes. Pupils must deduct incorrect sentences from their total. The pair with the most sentences are the winners. Pupils' answer sheets can be collected to assess progress.

Writing Activities

Word stones

The 'Word Stones' section is another example of pupil-centred work in *New Stepping Stones*. Pupils start their own collection of 'word stones' either by writing words as directed on real stones or on stone-shaped pieces of card. The 'word stones' are an exercise technique to extend vocabulary and to practise phonics and rhyme. They can be stored in a box (such as an old shoe box) or in a large, strong envelope. Pupils use them in matching activities and games in later lessons, and they can also be used for revision and self-testing. Pupils should be encouraged to add their own words and build up their own collection of word stones for future reference.

Puzzles

A variety of **Puzzles** provide valuable revision and reinforcement of vocabulary and structures in an enjoyable way.

Personal File

The **Personal File** gives pupils the opportunity to write about themselves. These exercises are always based upon models in the CB and pupils' attention should be drawn to these models both before, during and after the exercise, to allow them to monitor their own work.

The **Personal File** involves pupils drawing and colouring pictures and then describing them. It is often helpful if the teacher provides a model on the blackboard first, giving personal information about herself as an example.

The **Personal File** makes excellent wall displays, providing motivation and the opportunity for follow-up work involving the whole class. (See **Resource File** for suggestions.) Pupils derive satisfaction from seeing their own work displayed, despite differences of ability.

Other writing exercises

Most of the other **Writing** exercises in *New Stepping Stones* are there to provide reinforcement of the spoken word. These include answering questions in writing and simple sentence-completion exercises. It is important to encourage pupils to monitor and check their own written work. Models are always given in the CB and pupils should be referred to these to compare their own answers, rather than having their work corrected by the teacher. Pupils can also be encouraged to check each other's work. This adds a game-like element to such correction.

Freer writing exercises, in which pupils write questions or messages for their partners to answer, are an effective way of dealing with mixed-ability classes, since they ensure faster pupils always have something to do (see **Resource File**).

Integrated skills

Cut-outs

The cut-out material is located in the centre pull-out section of the AB. The cut-outs consist of two colour pages and two black-and-white pages. There are 15 colour playing cards linked to PETS and FAMILIES, featuring all the characters, and four sets of story bubbles, containing the text to accompany the introductory stories in each topic.

The playing cards and story bubbles have to be cut out before they can be used. (See **Classroom Management** below.) They provide an added element of physical manipulation in practising the language.

A wide variety of games and activities using the cut-outs are described in the Lesson Notes. The cut-outs can be used at any time to provide extra practice of words and structures, and are particularly useful as a source of extra activities for faster pupils, in mixed-ability classes.

Games

The games in *New Stepping Stones* provide variety in the presentation and practice of the language. Although they are there to be enjoyed, they all have a linguistic purpose. Some of the games are traditional children's playground games and introduce an element of cultural study.

Songs & rhymes

All the songs and rhymes in *New Stepping Stones* are traditional English songs, providing an important element of authenticity in the course.[1]

They are activities for the whole class. Always use the pictures to clarify meaning and use actions wherever appropriate.

The Lesson Notes indicate when the song is to be first presented, but once pupils know the tune and words they can be repeated in any lesson.

Phonics (Listen and match)

These exercises, which appear in the AB, have a dual function. They present the most common sound-letter correspondences in English, particularly the vowels, and they provide valuable pronunciation practice. The following procedure is recommended:
a Play the tape, one phrase at a time. Pupils listen and draw a line to match the phrase and picture.
b Listen to the presentation phrase on the tape again and pause for pupils to repeat.
c Play the tape again. Pupils repeat the phrases as quickly as they can.
d Pupils practise saying the phrases as quickly as they can. Volunteers then say the phrases as fast as they can in front of the class.
e Pronunciation will develop systematically through the use of these exercises and the teacher should not over-correct pupils.

[1] With the exception of *Colours*, which is sung to the tune of *Mary had a little lamb*.

Projects

Project work calls upon the pupils to work independently or in small groups. It allows them to explore their immediate environment, tailor the task to their learning style and personal preferences, use their prior knowledge and experiences, and integrate the four skills. Pupils should state their objectives before they begin, or at least have a clear idea of what they intend to do. Once they have chosen their own work, they should also be encouraged to continue it outside their English class. Display as much of the work as possible.

Other activites

All other activities in *New Stepping Stones* are fully explained in the Lesson Notes. These include: **Bingo**, **Number Dictations**, **Find more words**, **Quizzes**, **'Making' Activities** and **Surveys**.

Evaluation

Although evaluation in **New Stepping Stones** is continuous, there is a teacher-administered test and a self-assessment activity at the end of each of the four topics.

Teacher-administered tests

The teacher-administered test is useful in that it signals some stages in the learning process and allows both teacher and pupils to look back on what they have achieved up to that moment.

Some pupils are easily discouraged by their mistakes; avoid using red ink to correct tests and try to focus on the improvement in their work rather than on their deficiencies. In this way, they will be able to appreciate the positive aspects of their school experience.

Test yourself

The self-assessment activities help centre pupils' attention on what they have learned and the score which they must circle at the bottom of the page gives them instant feedback on their performance. To test themselves, pupils use a set of cards with words and pictures on them. (Photocopy masters for these are at the end of the Teacher's Guide.)

Self-assessment is essential in that it allows pupils to become more aware of their own strengths and weaknesses. Point out to them that errors are a natural part of the learning process and remind them that you can be sure of avoiding mistakes only if you learn nothing.

Classroom management

The organisation of your classroom is very important.
Always ensure pupils know exactly what they are doing before they start an activity. A demonstration is often more satisfactory than an explanation. Although this can be time consuming with new activities, a little time spent before an activity can save a lot of time and effort later.
Organising pupils into pairs and groups is another important job for the teacher. Pair pupils with the person sitting next to them, if possible. This can be done if pupils are sitting around tables:

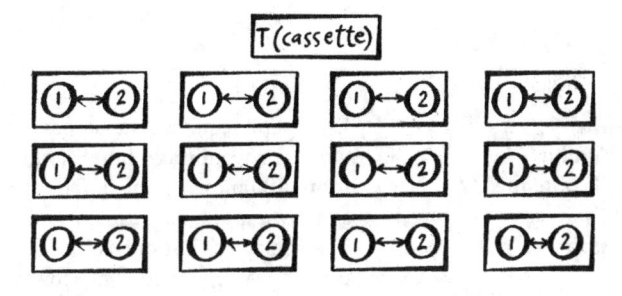

or in rows:

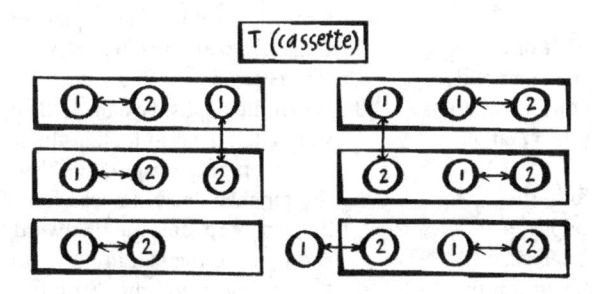

Pupils can always turn to work with the person behind them:

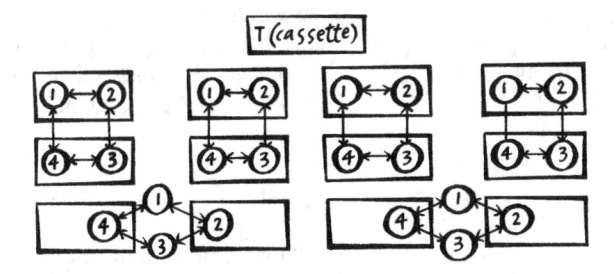

Give pupils roles. Since the questions and answers in *New Stepping Stones* are colour-coded, this can be used as a prompt when giving roles. Say to each pupil in turn '**You are blue. You are red.**' Next ensure pupils understand the roles they have been given. Say '**Blue stand up!**' etc. Then write the first two questions on the blackboard in coloured chalk. Initially use these as prompts while pupils repeat. (Cards with the word '**QUESTION**' and '**ANSWER**' or the letters '**Q**' and '**A**' can be given to all pupils to clarify roles, if necessary.) Pupils will quickly learn to get themselves into pairs and this procedure can soon be abandoned. Above all, be patient during early exercises and give pupils time to learn the procedures.

For **Groupwork**, ensure that pupils are facing one another and not spread out in a line, making communication impossible.

Organisation of equipment is another important responsibility for the teacher. A list of items required for each lesson is given in the syllabus box in the Lesson Notes. Encourage pupils to be responsible for bringing their own coloured pencils etc., but try to have a class set available to avoid time wasting.

It is probably a good idea for the teacher to look after the cut-outs and word stones, if they are to be used most effectively. Collect the cut-outs and word stones and store them in envelopes or boxes in the classroom. They can be returned to pupils at the end of term. (See **Resource File** for further ideas on the storage of cut-outs.)

Language in the classroom

Using English in the classroom is a very good way of both introducing and constantly recycling language. *New Stepping Stones* encourages this in two particular ways:
a   Through the Action Games.
b   Through the teacher's script, which is given in the Lesson Notes.

Extensive piloting has shown that **New Stepping Stones** can be used equally effectively with or without the mother tongue. The mother tongue may be useful for classroom management, although a demonstration is often an equally effective substitute. Use English wherever possible and encourage pupils to do the same. Pictures or actions can usually be used instead of translation to explain meaning. As pupils become familiar with English expressions and classroom language, such phrases should always be used.

The following expressions may be useful. Pupils should be able to recognise these expressions by the end of Year 1.

Hello.	Goodbye.
Give me ...	Thank you.
Come here, please.	Listen.
Read.	Write.
Draw.	Colour.
Repeat.	Cover the words.
Good.	Well done.
Quiet.	Hands up.
You ask the questions.	You give the answers.
Get into pairs.	Get into groups.
Good morning/afternoon/evening.	

Starter lesson 1

Main Language Items		Resource File	Materials Needed
Stand up!	everybody		
Sit down!	boys	6	cassette/cassette player
	girls		materials to make and store word stones
			coloured pencils

This opening unit, which covers basic instructions, colours and numbers, is a simple introduction to skills such as listening to the tape recorder, pair work, referencing and classroom games. Use of the tape recorder is recommended even for the simplest exercises.

Step 1 Discussion (L1)

a Ask pupils to name any countries where English is spoken (e.g. England, USA, Canada, Australia, etc.).
b Explain that English is an international language and is used in their own countries too. Ask pupils if they can name any examples of where English is used in their country.
c Ask pupils if they know any English words.

Step 2 Listen and point

a Say 'Open your books at page 2' and hold up your CB to show pupils. Point to the picture at the top of the page and say 'Look at the picture.'
b Say 'Listen to the tape.' Listen to the introduction and the first word ('taxi').
c Point to the taxi in the picture. Pupils find the word **taxi** in their own books.
d Pupils listen to the rest of the words one at a time and point to them in their books.
e Play the words again. Emphasise the English pronunciation.

Tapescript:
taxi // hotel // restaurant // burger bar // football // tennis // supermarket // fast food // airport // sport // stop //

Step 3 Action Game

a Bring five chairs to the front of the classroom. Sit on the centre chair and motion four pupils to sit on the others. Use two boys and two girls on either side.
b Say '**Stand up!**' and perform the action. Motion the four pupils to follow. Then '**Sit down!**' Repeat.
c Continue until pupils can perform the actions. Say '**Everybody, stand up!**' then '**Everybody, sit down!**' Repeat.
d Then turn to the two girls and say '**Girls, stand up!**' Then '**Boys, stand up!**', '**Boys, sit down!**', etc.
e Repeat with the whole class using **boys**, **girls** or **everybody**. To check on comprehension, try '**Sit down!**' when pupils are already seated.

Step 4 Word stones

a Pupils start their own collection of 'word stones' either with real stones stored in a box (such as an old shoe box) or stone-shaped pieces of card stored in a large strong envelope. NB As well as making the word stones shown in each topic, pupils can add their own words to their collection individually, for example when doing project work.
b Each pupil requires four 'stones'. Pupils write one word (**taxi, hotel, tennis, football**) on each stone in felt-tip pen, as shown in the pictures.
c Pupils may use just one colour felt-tip pen or a variety of colours. However, if pupils all colour their stones each time in the same colours as shown in their CBs, they will be able to play a variety of games, putting stones into colour sets, later on.
d When the pupils have made their four stones, tell them to look at the picture at the top of the page. Say '**Listen to the tape**' and play the tape from Step 2 again. Stop after the first word 'taxi' and point to the taxi in the picture. Pupils should find the word 'taxi' in their own books and place the appropriate word stone on top. Demonstrate.
e Continue in the same way with the other words.
f Pupils then store their stones for future use. You may like to keep their boxes or envelopes in the classroom.

Step 5 Find the words

a Say '**Open your Activity Books at page 4.**' Point to the picture in activity 1. Pupils find the words in the picture and colour them in any colour they wish. They tick the words in the list as they find and colour them.

Colours and Numbers

Step 2

🎧 Listen and point

🎧 Sing

Colours

Red and yellow, blue and green,
blue and green, blue and green, red and yellow,
blue and green, black and white and brown.

🎧 Say the rhyme

One Potato

One potato, two potatoes, three potatoes, four,
Five potatoes, six potatoes, seven potatoes, MORE!

Step 4

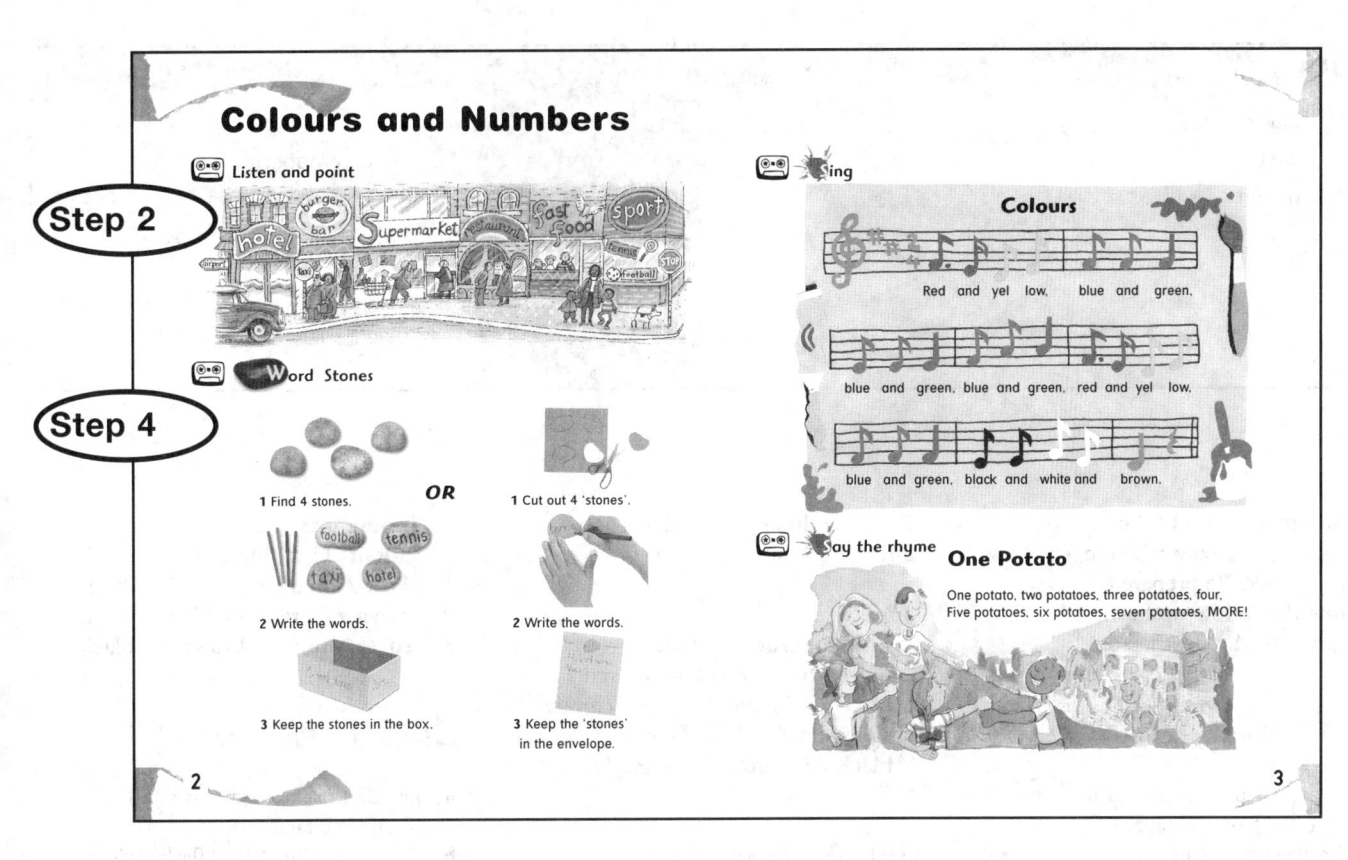

🎧 Word Stones

1 Find 4 stones.   OR   1 Cut out 4 'stones'.
2 Write the words.   2 Write the words.
3 Keep the stones in the box.   3 Keep the 'stones' in the envelope.

2   3

Colours and Numbers

Step 5

1 Find the words. Colour.

sport	airport	football
stop	hotel	restaurant
supermarket	fast food	taxi
basketball	tennis	

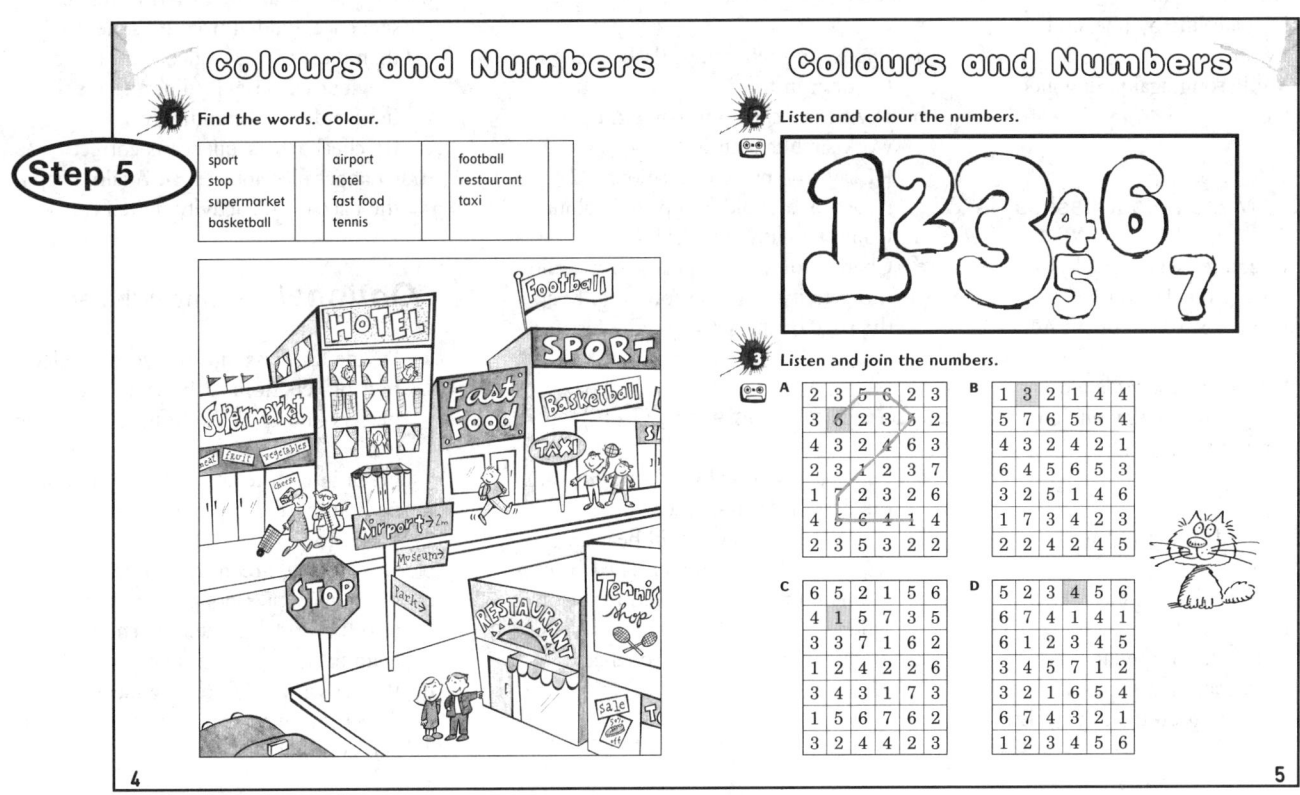

Colours and Numbers

2 Listen and colour the numbers.

1 2 3 4 6 5 7

3 Listen and join the numbers.

A
2	3	5	6	2	3
3	6	2	3	5	2
4	3	2	4	6	3
2	3	1	2	3	7
1	2	2	3	2	6
4	5	6	4	1	4
2	3	5	3	2	2

B
1	3	2	1	4	4
5	7	6	5	5	4
4	3	2	4	2	1
6	4	5	6	5	3
3	2	5	1	4	6
1	7	3	4	2	3
2	2	4	2	4	5

C
6	5	2	1	5	6
4	1	5	7	3	5
3	3	7	1	6	2
1	2	4	2	2	6
3	4	3	1	7	3
1	5	6	7	6	2
3	2	4	4	2	3

D
5	2	3	4	5	6
6	7	4	1	4	1
6	1	2	3	4	5
3	4	5	7	1	2
3	2	1	6	5	4
6	7	4	3	2	1
1	2	3	4	5	6

4   5

15

Starter lesson 2

Main Language Items		Resource File	Materials Needed
red	black		card/paper
yellow	white	5	coloured pencils
blue	brown	6	cassette/cassette player
green			

The song in Step 1 and the making activity in Step 2 may take longer than you think. Be prepared to postpone the follow-up flashcard activities until the next lesson.

Step 1   Song

a Look at page 3 of the CB and listen to the whole song on the tape.
b Listen to the song again.
c Then listen again line by line, and repeat the words.
d Play the whole song again. Sing along with the tape.

Step 2   Make colour flashcards

a Each pupil requires seven small pieces of card or paper for flashcards (approximately 8 x 10 cm or $\frac{1}{8}$th A4 paper).
b Pupils colour their flashcards red, yellow, blue, green, black, white and brown, as in the song.

Step 3   Listening (Task)

a Pupils lay their colour flashcards on the desk in front of them.
b Play the first word on the tape (i.e. 'red'). Demonstrate that pupils should respond by holding up the appropriate card.
c Continue through the colours as directed by the tape.

Tapescript:
Colours Listening task 1
red // blue // yellow // red // black // brown // blue // green // white // black // blue // black // yellow // green //

Step 4   Pairwork

a Pupils lay their colour flashcards on the desk in front of them.
b Divide the class into pairs. All pairs work simultaneously.
c P1 says the name of a colour. P2 responds by holding up that colour.
d Continue with other colours.
e Change roles and repeat. Do not allow this activity to go on too long. Keep the pace of the activity quite fast.

Step 5   Listening (Task)

a Pupils lay their colour flashcards on the desk in front of them.
b Play the tape. Pupils will hear a sequence of four colours. The object is to line up their flashcards in the correct order.
c Repeat with the other sequences.

Tapescript:
Colours Listening task 2
1 black // red // green // white
2 brown // green // blue // yellow
3 red // white // brown // black

Step 6   Pair work

a Divide the class into pairs. All pairs work simultaneously
b P1 places four colour flashcards in a sequence, hidden from P2's view. P1 then dictates the sequence as in the previous exercise. P2 lines up his/her flashcards correspondingly.
c P1 checks the sequence is correct.
d Change roles and repeat. Again, keep the pace of the activity quite fast.

Optional   Game (Whole class)

a Divide the class into two teams. Select four players from each team. The players line up at the front. Each player is given a colour: red, blue, yellow, green in each team. Each player should be holding the appropriate coloured flashcard.
b Say '**yellow, green, red, blue**'.
c The pupils must organise themselves into the correct sequence. The first team to do so wins a point.
d Repeat with a different sequence.
e Select four new pupils from each team and continue.

Colours and Numbers

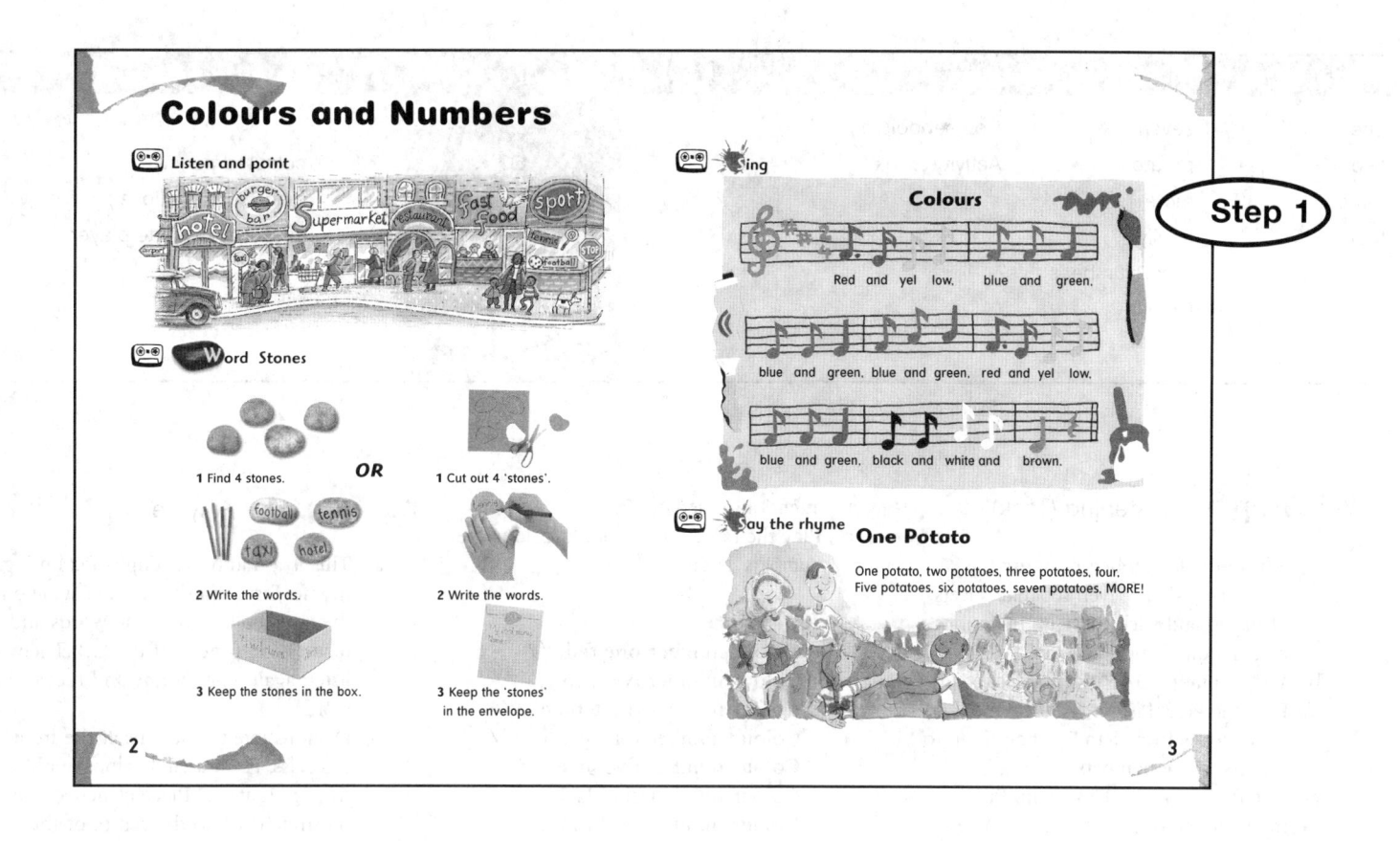

Listen and point

Word Stones

1 Find 4 stones.
2 Write the words.
3 Keep the stones in the box.

OR

1 Cut out 4 'stones'.
2 Write the words.
3 Keep the 'stones' in the envelope.

Sing

Colours

Red and yellow, blue and green,
blue and green, blue and green, red and yellow,
blue and green, black and white and brown.

Say the rhyme

One Potato

One potato, two potatoes, three potatoes, four,
Five potatoes, six potatoes, seven potatoes, MORE!

Step 1

2

3

Starter lesson 3

Main Language Items		Resource File	Materials Needed
one	seven		
two	potato	Coursebook	coloured pencils
three	more	Activity Book	magazines (optional)
four	family	5	cassette/cassette player
five	What number's this?	6	
six	Colour …	31	

Step 1 Listening (Task)

a Before the lesson begins, write the numbers 1–7 on seven separate sheets of paper, and stick these up in various places around the classroom.
b Write numbers 1–7 on the blackboard. Play the tape. Listen to all the numbers in sequence from 1 to 7. Then listen to the first three numbers.
c Listen to numbers 1–3 again. Pupils repeat in chorus. Do this three times.
d Say the numbers at random. Pupils hold up the right number of fingers.
e Now play the first series of nine numbers. These are in random order. Pupils listen and point to the numbers that you have stuck around the room.
f Then dictate further random series of numbers 1–3 to the pupils.
g Repeat the procedure for numbers 4–7. Pupils listen and repeat.

Tapescript:
Numbers Listening task.
1 // 2 // 3 // 4 // 5 // 6 // 7 //
Listen and repeat.
1 // 2 // 3 //
Listen and point.
2 // 1 // 2 // 3 // 2 // 2 // 1 // 3 // 1 //
Listen and repeat.
4 // 5 // 6 // 7 //
Listen and point.
4 // 6 // 5 // 6 // 4 // 7 // 5 // 6 // 7 //

Step 2 Listen and colour

a Say 'Open your Activity Books at page 5.' Demonstrate. Direct pupils' attention to activity 2.
b Play the tape. Pupils should colour the numbers as directed.

Tapescript:
Colour number one red. //
Colour number two brown. //
Colour number three blue. //
Colour number four yellow. //
Colour number five green. //
Colour number six black. //
Colour number seven blue. //

Step 3 Listen and draw

a Direct pupils' attention to activity 3.
b Point to the first numbered grid, 'A'. Then play the tape. Draw a line between each square as directed on the tape. This will produce the number 2, as the example in the book shows. Pupils then answer the question 'What number's this?' on the tape.
c Once pupils understand the nature of the exercise, play the tape for the other grids. Explain that they should always start with the shaded square. Pupils draw lines in their own grids and answer the question.

Tapescript:
a 6 // 5 // 6 // 5 // 4 // 1 // 7 // 5 // 6 // 4 // 1 //
b 3 // 2 // 1 // 6 // 3 // 2 // 6 // 1 // 3 // 7 //
c 1 // 2 // 1 // 3 // 1 // 4 // 4 // 5 // 6 // 7 // 6 //
d 4 // 3 // 2 // 7 // 1 // 2 // 7 // 6 // 4 // 7 //

Step 4 Rhyme

a This is a traditional English counting rhyme. Listen to the whole rhyme on the tape. Follow with the words and pictures on page 3 of the CB. Then listen again line by line and repeat the words.
b Demonstrate the actions at the front of the class. Form a circle along with three volunteers. Place clenched fists outstretched into the centre of the circle. Count each fist in turn, chanting the rhyme on each beat. The fist that is tapped on 'More!' (i.e. every eighth fist) is 'out' and must be placed behind the back. When both fists are counted out, that player leaves the game.
c Play the counting game in small groups.

Step 5 Read and colour

a Say 'Open your Activity Books at page 6.' Point to activity 4. Colour the pictures according to the number code.

Step 6 Words and pictures

a Point to the pictures in activity 5. Use them to demonstrate the meaning of the following instructions.
b Say 'Stand up.' Pupils stand up. Say 'Sit down.' Pupils sit down. Say 'Boys stand up. Girls stand up' etc.
c Pupils then draw lines connecting the words to the pictures.

Colours and Numbers

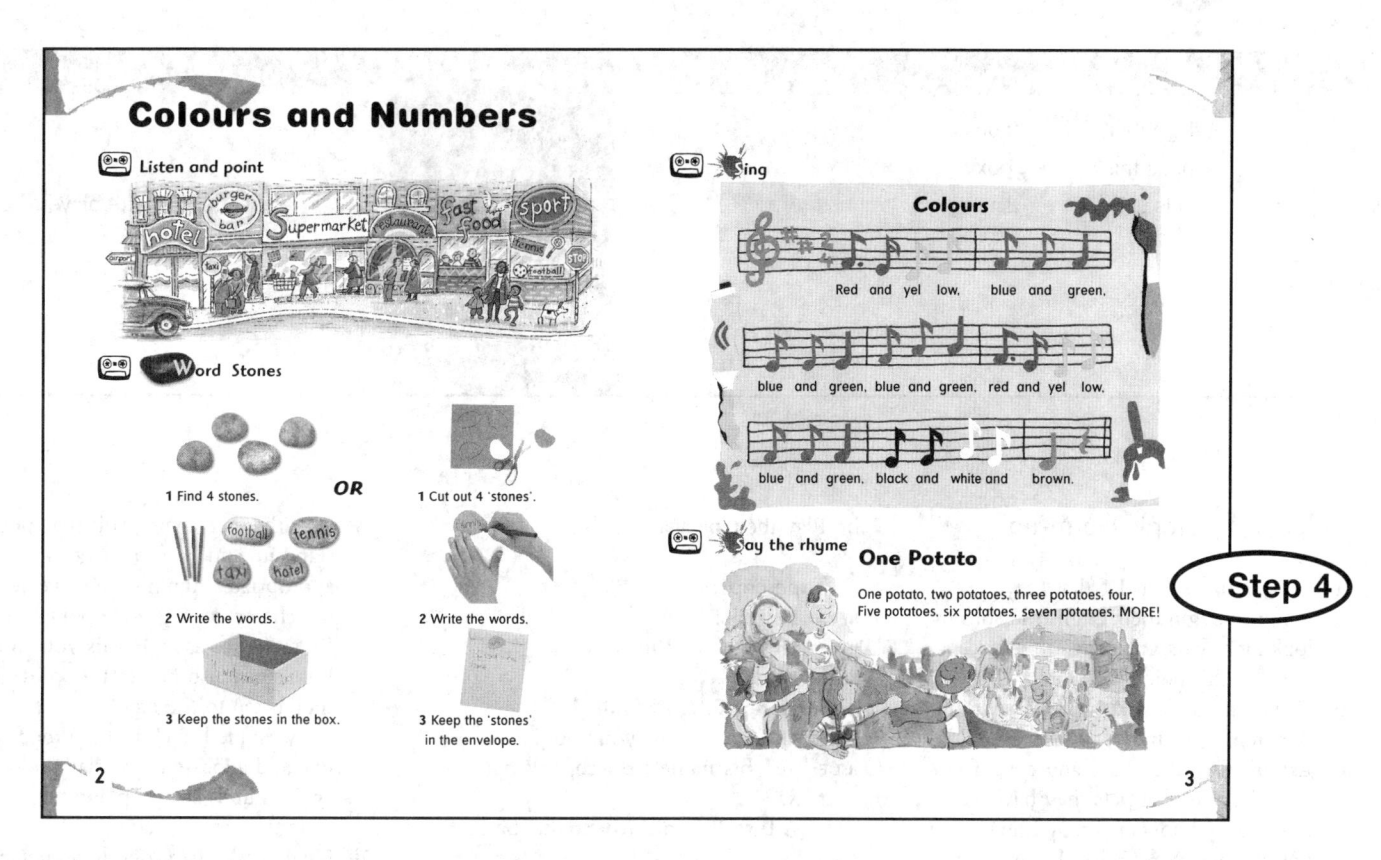

Listen and point

Word Stones

1 Find 4 stones. OR 1 Cut out 4 'stones'.
2 Write the words.   2 Write the words.
3 Keep the stones in the box. 3 Keep the 'stones' in the envelope.

Sing

Colours

Red and yellow, blue and green,
blue and green, blue and green, red and yellow,
blue and green, black and white and brown.

Say the rhyme — **One Potato**

One potato, two potatoes, three potatoes, four,
Five potatoes, six potatoes, seven potatoes, MORE!

Step 4

Colours and Numbers

Listen and colour the numbers.

1 2 3 4 5 6 7

Step 2

Listen and join the numbers.

Step 3

A
2	3	5	6	2	3
3	6	2	3	5	2
4	3	2	4	6	3
2	3	1	2	3	7
1	7	2	3	2	6
4	5	6	4	1	4
2	3	5	3	2	2

B
1	3	2	1	4	4
5	7	6	5	5	4
4	3	2	4	2	1
6	4	5	6	5	3
3	2	5	1	4	6
1	7	3	4	2	3
2	2	4	2	4	5

C
6	5	2	1	5	6
4	1	5	7	3	5
3	3	7	1	6	2
1	2	4	2	2	6
3	4	3	1	7	3
1	5	6	7	6	2
3	2	4	4	2	3

D
5	2	3	4	5	6
6	7	4	1	4	1
6	1	2	3	4	5
3	4	5	7	1	2
3	2	1	6	5	4
6	7	4	3	2	1
1	2	3	4	5	6

Colours and Numbers

Read and colour.

Step 5

1 = blue   2 = white   3 = yellow   4 = green
5 = black 6 = brown   7 = red

Match the words and the pictures.

Step 6

stand up
girl
boy
sit down

1 Story lesson

Main Language Items			Resource File	Materials Needed
pet	Who's this?	dog		
Hi!	What's this?	box	12	cassette/cassette player
Hello	Is this ...?	snake	35	
Bye!				
Goodbye				

Step 1 Topic warm-up

a Tell pupils in their L1 that they are going to begin their English lessons by looking at pets. Introduce the word 'pets' at this point.

b Then ask pupils what words they think they might learn.

c Ask pupils if they have any pets. If they do, ask what pets they have.

d Ask if they know anyone with an unusual pet. What is it? Discuss what we can keep as pets and what we can't.

e Ask pupils if they think children in other countries keep the same pets. Why do they think they do/don't?

Step 2 Story prediction

a Say 'Open your Coursebooks at page 4. Look at the pictures.' Demonstrate what you mean by holding up your CB and pointing to the pictures.

b Ask pupils in their L1 what they can see. Who do they think the children might be and what is their relationship?

c Ask what they think is going to happen in the story.

d Ask pupils if they can see anything in the pictures they can name in English.

Step 3 Story listening

a Say 'Listen to the tape.' Pupils look at the pictures and listen to the tape at the same time.

b Play the tape again.

Tapescript:
KEV: Hi Julie!
JULIE: Hello Kev! Who's this?
KEV: Kate.
JULIE: Hello Kate. I'm Julie.
KATE: Hello ... Is this your dog?
JULIE: Yes, his name's Butch ... What's this?
KATE: A box ... Look! My snake, Sam.
SAM: Ssss!
JULIE: Aagh!
KATE: Goodbye!
JULIE: Bye.

Step 4 Story task

a Play the first part of the dialogue and point to Kev as he is speaking.

b Play the complete story on tape again and demonstrate the task to pupils: point to each character in turn as he or she is speaking. Pupils listen to the tape and watch the demonstration.

c Then play the complete story again. Pupils listen, look at the pictures and point to each character in turn as he or she is speaking.

Step 5 Story mime

a Allocate the roles of Kev, Julie, Kate, Butch and Sam to volunteers. Ask them to stand up as their character speaks. Play the tape.

b Play the tape again. This time pupils stand up and perform actions as appropriate, miming the movements of the characters, e.g. Kate points to Butch as she says 'Is this your dog?' Pupils can also mouth the words as they listen to the tape.

c Now divide the class into groups of five and allocate roles. Play the tape again. Pupils stand up and perform actions as appropriate.

d Finally, ask one group to volunteer to come to the front of the class and perform, listening to the tape.

1 Pets

STORY

Kate's Snake

Step 2
Step 3
Step 4

1ᴬ Lesson 1

Main Language Items			Resource File	Materials Needed
Who's this?	Julie	Make a name badge		
Walk!	Butch			
Stop!	Kev		24	materials to make a name badge
Turn around!	Kate			cassette/cassette player
	Sam			

Step 1   Presentation

a   Say 'Open your Coursebooks at page 4 and look at the pictures.' Play the whole story on tape.
b   Then say 'Open your Coursebooks at page 6' and ask pupils to look at the first two frames of the story. Ask pupils to tell you in their L1 what the language in the speech bubbles means.
c   Play the story extract and point to the characters.
d   Divide the class into pairs. All pairs work simultaneously. Play the tape again. P1 repeats Kev's words and P2 repeats Julie's words.
e   Change roles and repeat the procedure.

Tapescript:
KEV: Hi Julie!
JULIE: Hello Kev! Who's this?
KEV: Kate.

Step 2   Make a name badge

The Action Games require the teacher to know the names of all pupils so they can be called on individually to perform actions. (You may like to give pupils an English equivalent of their names.)

a   Say 'Open your Coursebooks at page 6.' Draw pupils' attention to the activity headed *Make a name badge*.
b   Each pupil should make a badge with their own name on, using the materials illustrated. The names should be written boldly enough to be read at a distance. (If safety pins are unavailable, the badges can be worn around the neck on a piece of string.)

Step 3   Action Game

a   Bring five chairs to the front of the classroom. The teacher should sit in the centre chair and instruct four pupils, by name, to 'Sit down!' alongside.
b   Quickly revise instructions 'Stand up!', 'Sit down!' and 'boys' and 'girls.' Briefly command individuals by name.
c   Then working only with the four pupils (by name), say 'Stand up!, Walk!' and walk forwards yourself, motioning pupils to follow. Then say 'Stop!, Turn around!, Walk!, Stop!, Sit down!' Perform all actions as you give the commands. Check the four pupils are copying. If not, repeat the instruction and the action.
d   Repeat above sequence. Then, using the same commands, vary the sequence. When the four pupils can perform the actions without your help, call on individuals to respond.
e   Then use the same instructions with the words **boys**, **girls** and **everybody**, to involve individuals and the whole class.
NOTE: If '**Walk!**' is impractical due to constraints of classroom size, have pupils walk on the spot.

Step 4   Hello Game

a   Introduce yourself to a pupil by saying '**Hello, I'm** *(your name)*' to elicit the response '**Hello** *(your name)*' Point to another pupil (P2) and ask '**Who's this?**' to elicit their name from P1 and then say '**Hello …**'
b   Repeat the procedure around the class with different pupils.

Step 5   Write

a   Tell pupils to open their Activity Books at page 7. Pupils choose the appropriate phrase from the box and write the dialogue in the speech bubbles provided.

Hi, Julie!

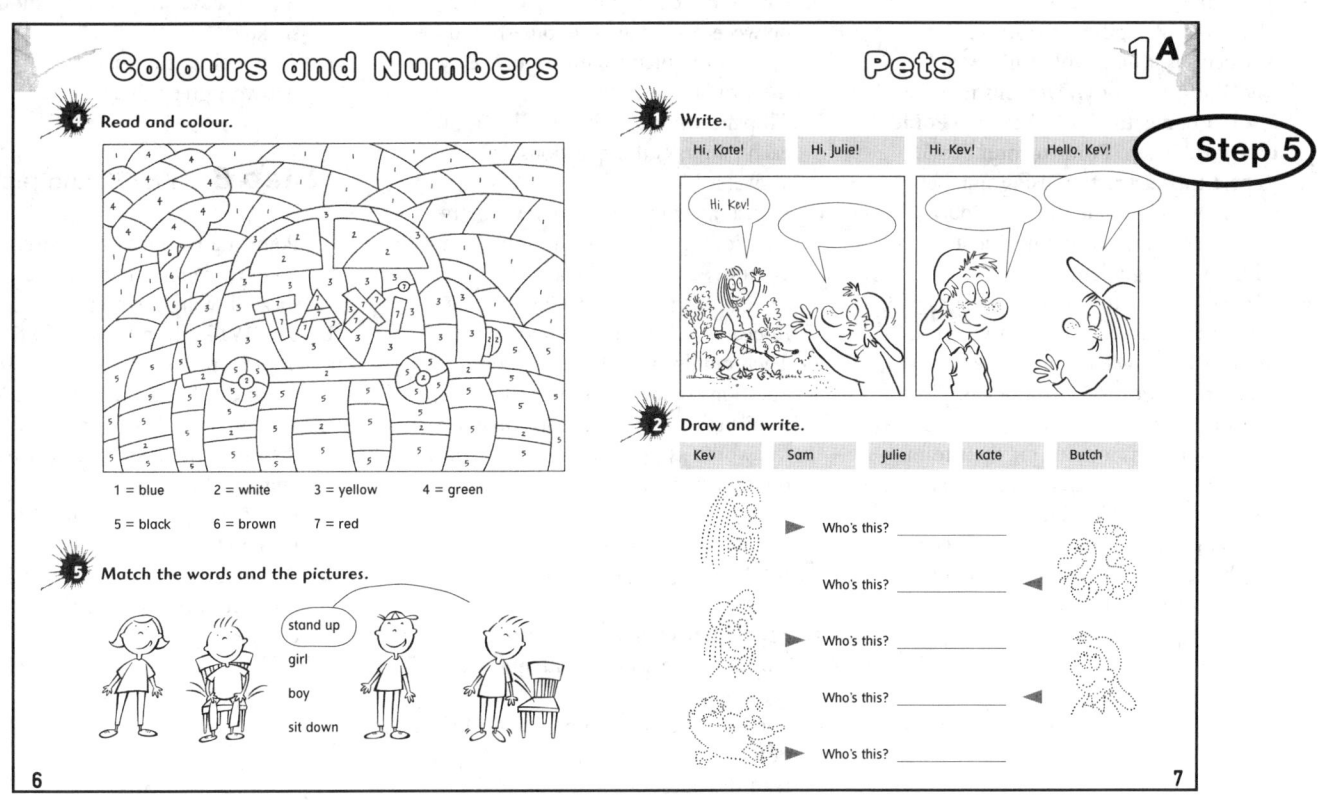

Pets 1A

Step 1 — Listen

"Hi, Julie!" "Hello, Kev!" "Who's this?" "Kate."

Step 2 — Make: A Name Badge

You need:
1 Write your name.
2 Stick the pin on.
3 A name badge.

Ask and answer

Who's this?	Julie.
Who's this?	Butch.
Who's this?	Kate.
Who's this?	Sam.
Who's this?	Kev.

Answer

"Hello! I'm Kate. What's your name?" "Hi! I'm Julie. What's your name?"

6 · 7

Colours and Numbers

Pets 1A

4 Read and colour.

1 = blue 2 = white 3 = yellow 4 = green
5 = black 6 = brown 7 = red

5 Match the words and the pictures.

stand up
girl
boy
sit down

Write.

Hi, Kate!   Hi, Julie!   Hi, Kev!   Hello, Kev!

Hi, Kev!

Step 5

2 Draw and write.

Kev   Sam   Julie   Kate   Butch

Who's this? _____
Who's this? _____
Who's this? _____
Who's this? _____
Who's this? _____

6 · 7

23

1A Lesson 2

Main Language Items		Resource File	Materials Needed
Point to…	number		
Hello	eight	12	number flashcards
Hi!	nine	26a	cassette/cassette player
	ten		coloured pencils
	colours (revision)		
	numbers 1–7 (revision)		

Step 1 Action Game

a Number flashcards are required for this game. The numbers 1–10 should be written, one number on each card. Display the cards around the classroom. (Alternatively, write the numbers well apart on the blackboard.)

b Introduce numbers 8–10 here. First point to the cards and say the numbers. Then ask pupils to point to the numbers.

c Motion four pupils to the front. Use instructions '**Stand up! Walk! Stop!**'

d Say '**Point to a boy.**' Demonstrate. Motion pupils to copy. Then say '**Point to a girl.**' Then '**Point to number 3.**' Repeat this instruction using numbers at random. Continue until the four pupils can carry out the instruction without your guidance.

e Repeat step **d** with the whole class.

f Divide the class into teams. One player from each team stands up. Give an instruction. '**Point to number 6.**' The first player to correctly carry out the instruction wins a point for their team. Then the second player in each team takes their turn. Continue until all players have had at least one go. The number of rounds will be dictated by the size of the class.

Step 2 Story listening

a Say '**Open your Coursebooks at page 4. Look at the pictures. Listen to the tape.**' Pupils look at the pictures and listen to the tape at the same time.

b Play the tape again.

Step 3 Pair work

A Divide the class into pairs. One CB between each pair of pupils should be open at the pictures on page 7. Cover the words.

b All pairs work simultaneously. P1 in each pair asks the questions, P2 answers.

c Repeat after the tape. P1 repeats the questions, pointing at the appropriate picture. P2 repeats the answers.

d Repeat this procedure. Change roles. Repeat twice more.

e Then pupils ask and answer the questions without the help of the tape. Pupils asking the questions may use the words as prompts and must check their partners' answers.

Step 4 Draw and write

a Say '**Open your Activity Books at page 7.**' Direct pupils' attention to activity 2.

b For each character, pupils first join the dots to complete the picture. They then read the questions and choose the correct answer from the names in the boxes. They write the answer in the space provided.

b Pupils should then check their answers against the model on page 7 of the CB.

Step 5 Trace and colour

a AB, page 8. Pupils trace through the maze beginning from each colour until they discover the correct colours of the snake.

b Then colour the snake.
Answer: green/blue.

Step 6 Words and pictures

a Point the pictures in activity 4. Use them to demonstrate the meaning of the following instructions.

b Say '**Walk.**' Pupils walk on the spot. Say '**Stop.**' Pupils stop. Say '**Turn around.**' Pupils turn 180°. Do the actions yourself to demonstrate at first, then give the instructions without helping the pupils.

c Repeat for girls and boys if you have a mixed class.

d Pupils then return to their ABs and draw lines connecting the words to the pictures.

Hi, Julie!

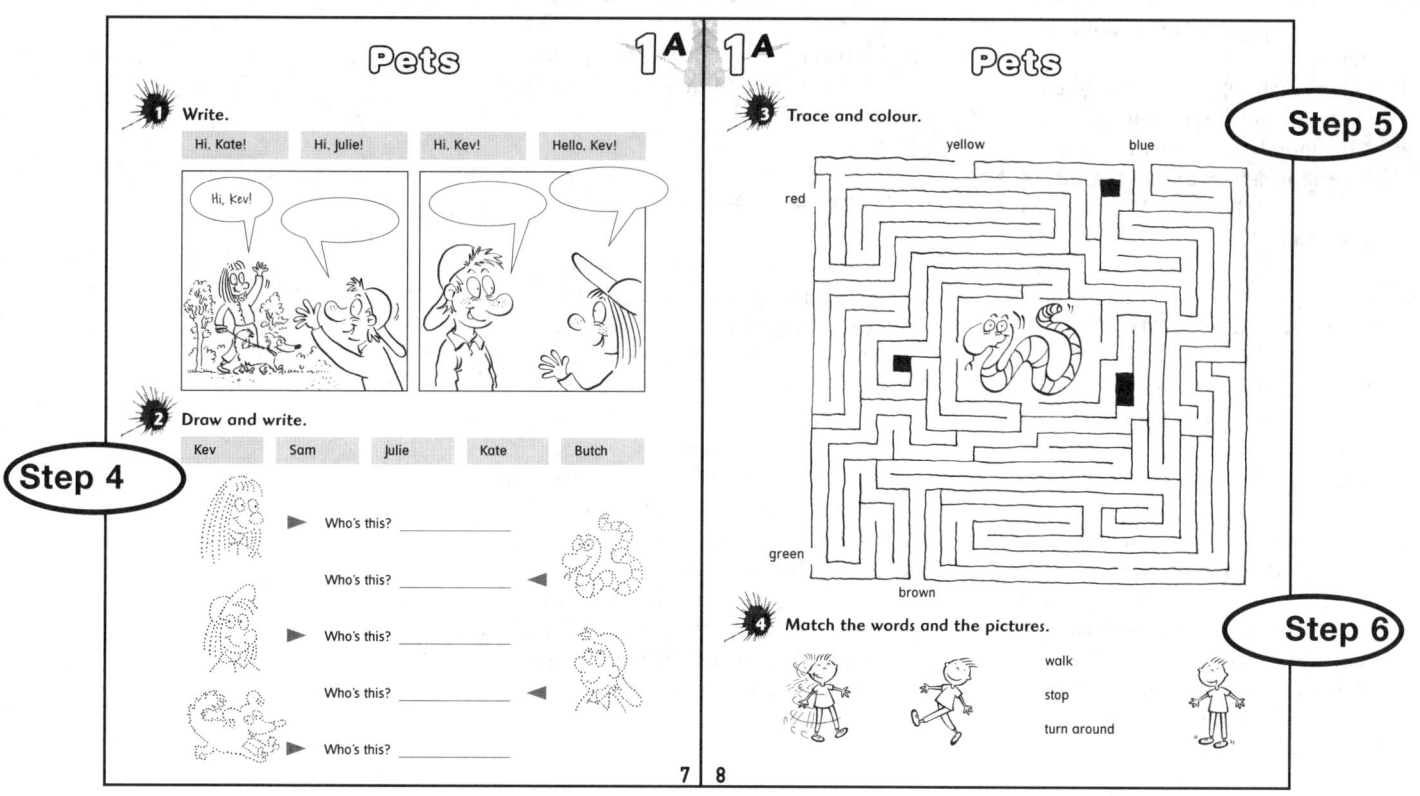

Listen

Make — A Name Badge

You need:
1 Write your name.
2 Stick the pin on.
3 A name badge.

Pets — 1A

Ask and answer

	Who's this?	Julie.
	Who's this?	Butch.
	Who's this?	Kate.
	Who's this?	Sam.
	Who's this?	Kev.

Answer

Hello! I'm Kate. What's your name?
Hi! I'm Julie. What's your name?

Step 3

6 · 7

Pets — 1A

1 Write.
Hi, Kate! Hi, Julie! Hi, Kev! Hello, Kev!

Hi, Kev!

2 Draw and write.
Kev Sam Julie Kate Butch

- ▶ Who's this? _____
- Who's this? _____ ◀
- ▶ Who's this? _____
- Who's this? _____ ◀
- ▶ Who's this? _____

Step 4

Pets — 1A

3 Trace and colour.
red   yellow   blue
green   brown

Step 5

4 Match the words and the pictures.
walk
stop
turn around

Step 6

7 · 8

25

1A Lesson 3

Main Language Items	Resource File	Materials Needed
I'm … What's your name? Goodbye Bye!	12	ball/bean-bag/piece of rolled-up paper cassette/cassette player

This lesson gives further practice in asking and giving names, and introduces the question 'What's your name?' Pupils should not wear their name badges.

Step 1 Presentation

a Say 'Open your Coursebooks at page 7.' Direct pupils to the picture of Kate and Julie at the bottom of the page. Play the tape. Pupils read at the same time.
b Play the tape again. Encourage pupils to answer Julie's question.
c Now introduce yourself to a pupil. Repeat quickly with other members of the class. 'Hello, I'm Mr(s) … What's your name?'

Step 2 Classwork

a When pupils are familiar with the above form, encourage them to introduce themselves to the person sitting next to them and ask the same question.
b When pupils have answered their partners' question they can introduce themselves to another pupil, creating 'chains' of questions and answers around the class.
c Pupils could then be divided into groups to try and speed up the chain.

Step 3 Ask and answer

a Say 'Open your Activity Books at page 9.' Direct pupils' attention to activity 5.
b Pupils draw or stick a picture of themselves in the space provided and write their names in the speech bubble.
c Pupils then introduce themselves to other members of their group saying 'Hello, I'm … What's your name?' They write the answers in the grid provided.
d All pupils work simultaneously and swap groups until they have filled their chart.

Step 4 Game

a Pupils stand in a circle. A ball or piece of rolled up paper is required. P1 begins by greeting any other player 'Hello *Alex*' and simultaneously throwing the ball. P2 must catch the ball and return the greeting. P2 then becomes the thrower.
b If a player drops the ball, they must say '**Goodbye**' and turn and face out of the circle. Whole group says '**Goodbye** *Anne*.' This pupil remains out of the game until the ball is dropped again, when they may return saying '**Hello.**' Whole class replies. Only one player is out of the game at any one time.

Step 5 Write

a Pupils look at activity 6 on AB page 9. They select the appropriate question from the box and write it in the space provided.

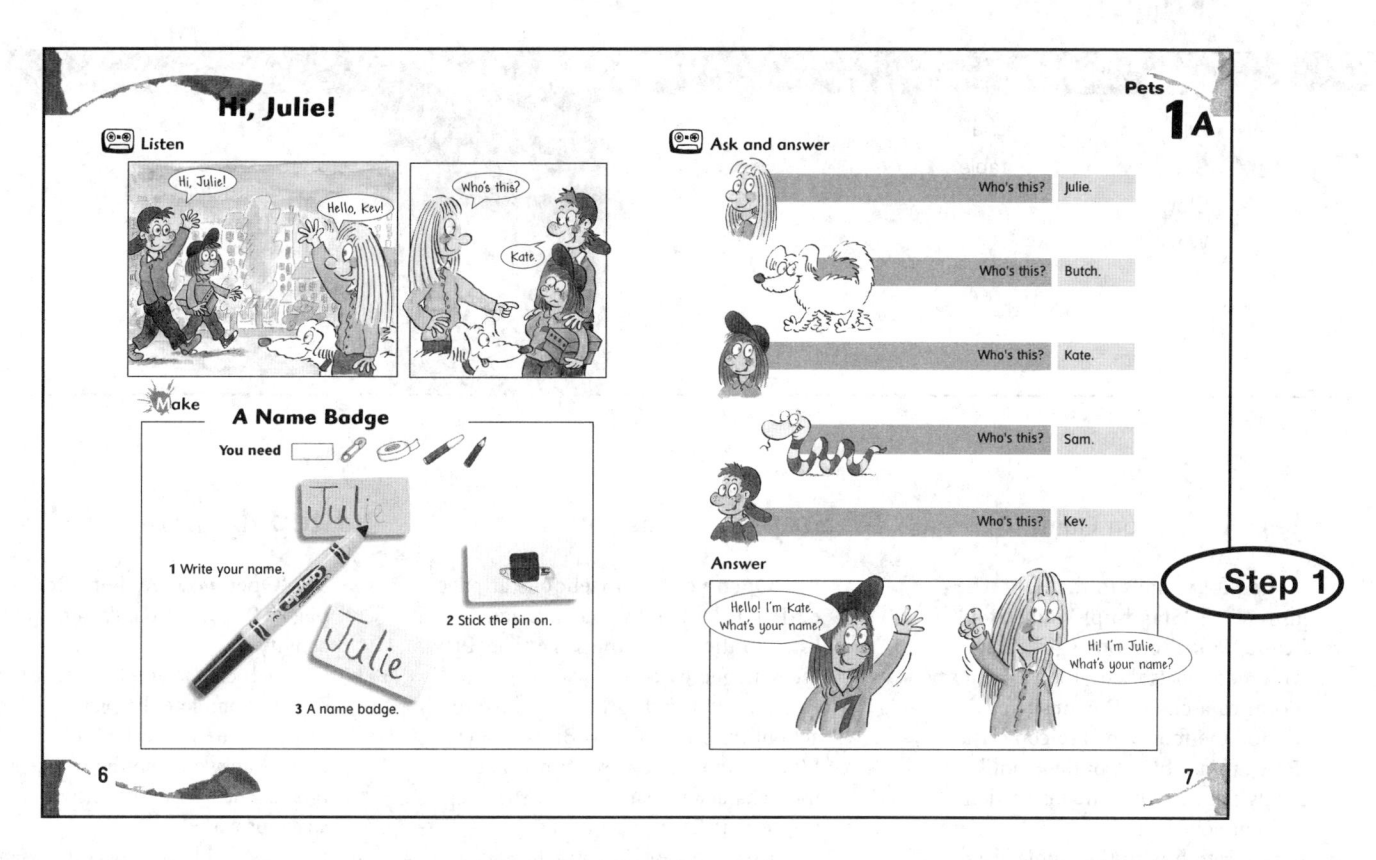

Hi, Julie!

Listen

Make — A Name Badge

You need:
1 Write your name.
2 Stick the pin on.
3 A name badge.

Ask and answer

	Who's this?	Julie.
	Who's this?	Butch.
	Who's this?	Kate.
	Who's this?	Sam.
	Who's this?	Kev.

Answer

Hello! I'm Kate. What's your name?
Hi! I'm Julie. What's your name?

Pets — 1A

Step 1

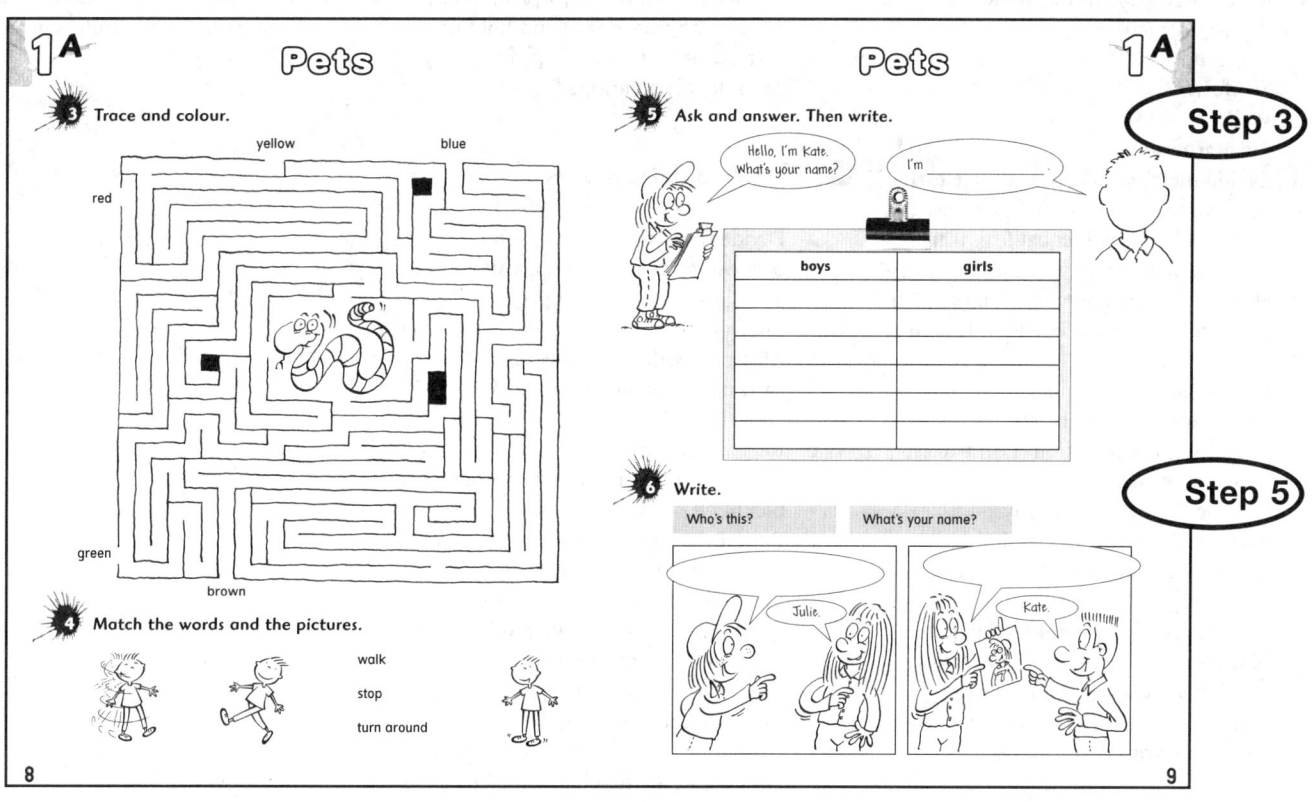

1A Pets

3 Trace and colour.

yellow, blue, red, green, brown

4 Match the words and the pictures.

walk
stop
turn around

Pets 1A

5 Ask and answer. Then write.

Hello, I'm Kate. What's your name?
I'm _____

boys	girls

6 Write.

Who's this?   What's your name?

Julie.   Kate.

Step 3

Step 5

1B Lesson 1

Main Language Items		Resource File	Materials Needed
Who's this? Bill	chair	24	character cards
Suzy	table	29	cassette/cassette player
Slow		52	
Wow			
Duffy			

Step 1 Action Game

a Motion four pupils to the front. Use instructions **'Stand up! Walk! Stop!'**
b Revise **'Point to a boy/girl.'** Repeat with individuals then groups. Then say **'Point to a chair.'** Demonstrate. Motion the four pupils to copy. Then **'Point to a table.'** Continue until pupils can carry out the instruction without your help.
c Repeat step b with the whole class. Revise instructions:
Stand up
Sit down
Walk
Turn around
d Divide the class into teams. Give each pupil a number from 1 to 6. Teams need not be exactly equal (e.g. if there are more than six pupils in each team, allocate the same number to more than one team member). Give each team the name of a colour.
e Check pupils have understood. Say **'Stand up Number 1!'** etc.
f Then use the instruction **'Point to …'** in a team game, i.e.
Number 3, point to a boy.
Number 5, point to a table.
Point to a chair, number 4, etc.
The first player to carry out the instruction wins a point for his team. However if the wrong player carries out the command his team loses a point. In case of a split decision, give another instruction.

Step 2 Presentation

a Say **'Open your Coursebooks at page 8.'** Pupils look at the pictures and listen to the tape at the same time. Play the dialogue twice.
b Put the pupils into groups of three to act out the roles of Kev, Bill and Suzy. Play the tape. They use mime to act their character's part without speaking.
c (Optional) Each pupil uses the character cards of Kev, Bill and Suzy. They listen to the tape and hold up the correct card when each of the characters is mentioned.

Step 3 Pair work

a Divide the class into pairs. One CB between each pair of pupils should be open at the pictures on page 8. Cover the words.
b All pairs work simultaneously. P1 in each pair asks the questions. P2 answers.
c Repeat after the tape. P1 repeats the questions, pointing at the appropriate picture. P2 repeats the answers.
d Repeat the procedure then change roles and repeat twice more.
e Pupils then ask and answer the questions without the help of the tape. Pupils asking the questions may use the words as prompts and must check their partners' answers.
f Change roles and repeat the procedure until pupils are familiar with the names.

Step 4 Draw and write

a Say **'Open your Activity Books at page 10.'** Direct pupils' attention to activity 1.
b For each character, pupils first join the dots to complete the picture. Then they read the questions and choose the correct answer from the names in the boxes. They write the answer in the space provided.
c Pupils should then check their answers against the models on page 8 of the CB.

Bill's Tortoise

Step 2

Listen

- Who's this? / Slow.
- Who's this? / Wow.
- Slow, this is Wow.
- Who's that? / It's Suzy.
- Hello! / Hi, Suzy!
- Who's this? / Duffy.

Step 3

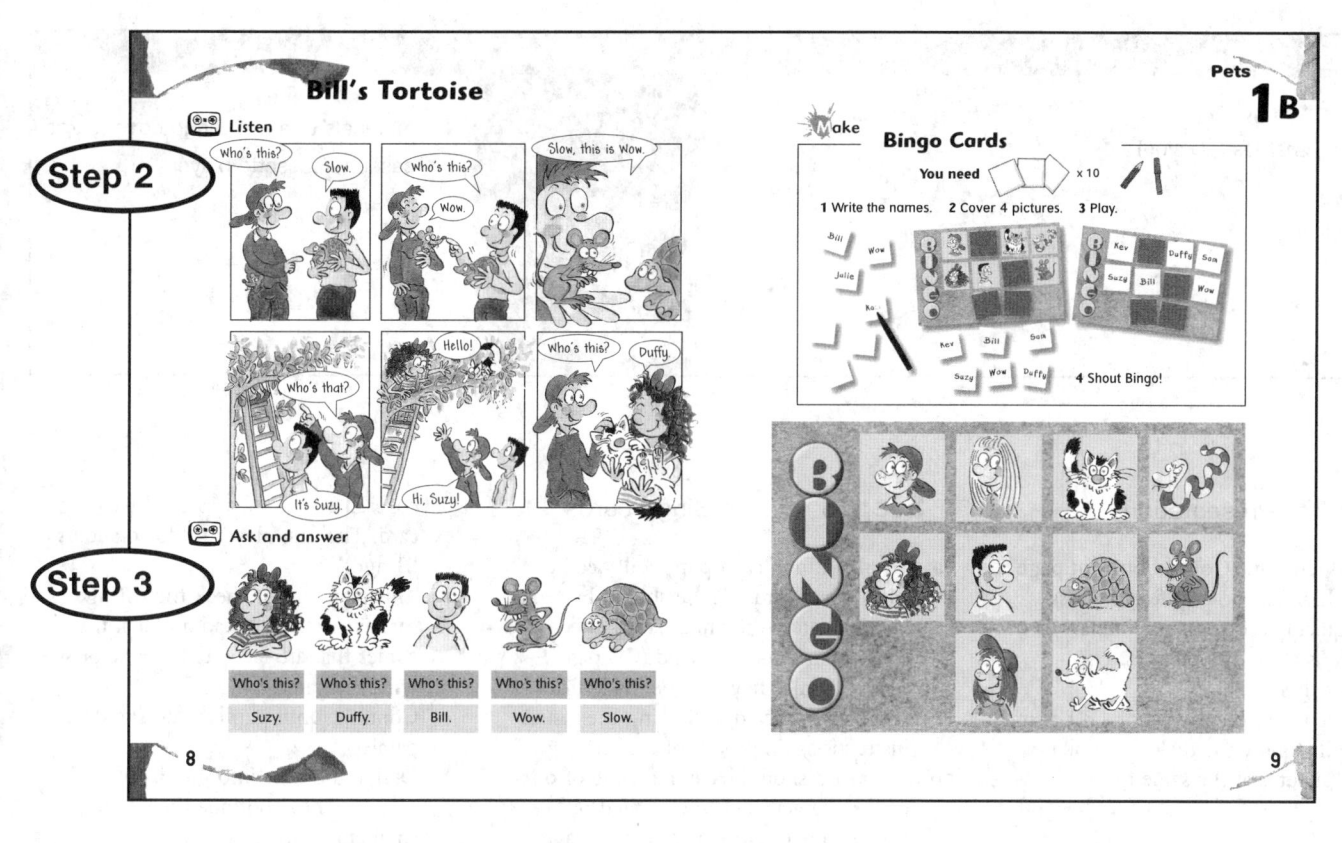

Ask and answer

Who's this?	Who's this?	Who's this?	Who's this?	Who's this?
Suzy.	Duffy.	Bill.	Wow.	Slow.

Pets 1B

Make Bingo Cards

You need ▭▭ x 10

1 Write the names. 2 Cover 4 pictures. 3 Play.

4 Shout Bingo!

1B Pets

Step 4

1 Draw and write.

Suzy   Duffy   Wow   Bill   Slow

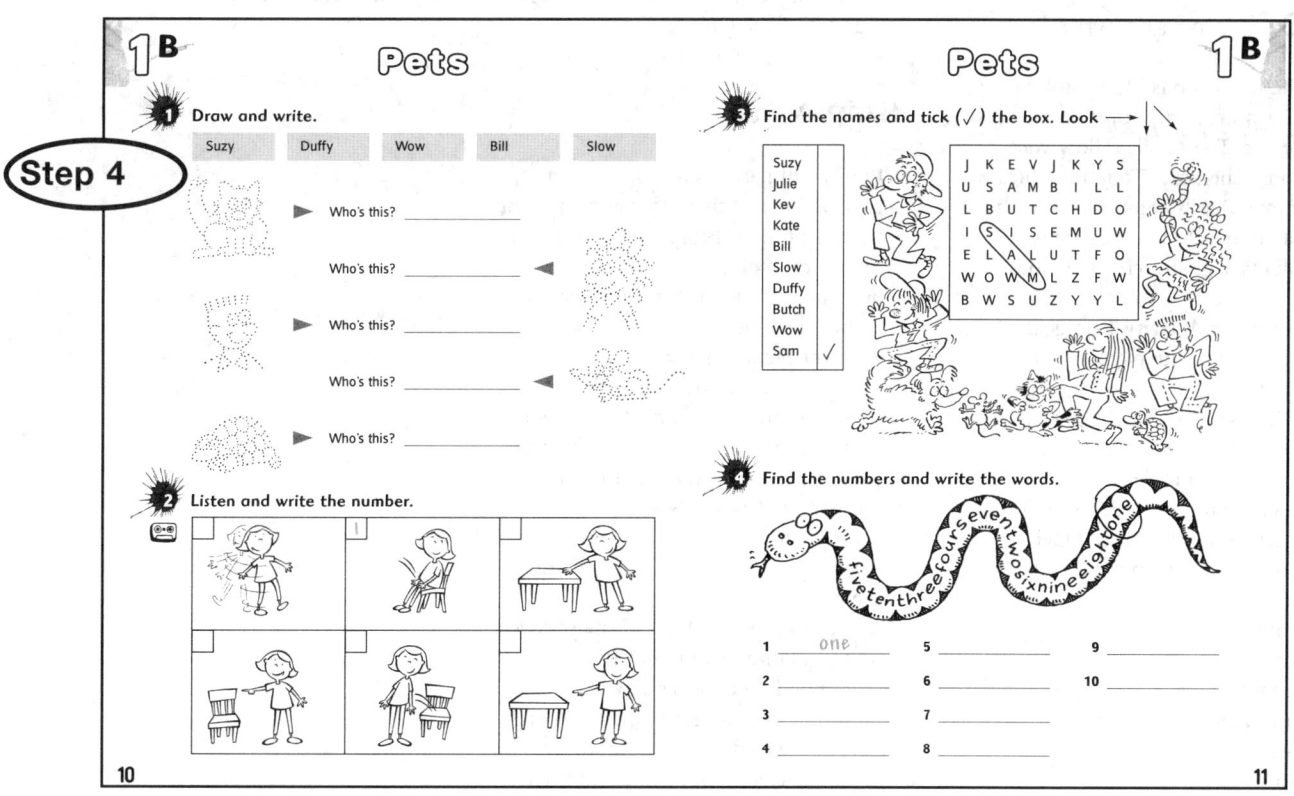

▶ Who's this? _____
Who's this? _____ ◀
▶ Who's this? _____
Who's this? _____ ◀
▶ Who's this? _____

2 Listen and write the number.

Pets 1B

3 Find the names and tick (✓) the box. Look →↓

Suzy
Julie
Kev
Kate
Bill
Slow
Duffy
Butch
Wow
Sam ✓

J	K	E	V	J	K	Y	S
U	S	A	M	B	I	L	L
L	B	U	T	C	H	D	O
I	S	I	S	E	M	U	W
E	L	A	L	U	T	F	O
W	O	W	M	L	Z	F	W
K	S	U	Z	Y	Y	Y	L
B	W	S	U	Z	Y	Y	L

4 Find the numbers and write the words.

fivetenthreefoursevent wosixnineeightone

1 one   5 _____   9 _____
2 _____   6 _____   10 _____
3 _____   7 _____
4 _____   8 _____

1ᴮ Lesson 2

Main Language Items		Resource File	Materials Needed
Touch …	Bingo	34	materials to make Bingo cover cards
Are you ready?	*names* (revision)	52	cassette/cassette player
Yes/No			

Step 1 Presentation

a Say 'Open your Coursebooks at page 8.' Hold your book up for the class. Very quickly ask some preliminary questions about the pictures. Use 'Who's this?'

b Play the tape from Step 2 of 1B Lesson 1. Pupils follow the dialogue looking at the pictures at the same time.

Step 2 Listen and write

a Revise the instructions **Stand up!**, **Sit down!**, **Turn around!**, **Point to a girl/boy**, etc. The pupils follow your instructions. Then say '**Touch a table.**' Demonstrate. Pupils copy. Repeat with '**Touch a chair.**' Do more examples using colours, e.g. '**Touch the colour red.**'

b Say '**Open your Activity Books at page 10.**' Point to the pictures at the bottom of the page.

c Play the first sentence as the pupils listen and look at the pictures. This answer has been completed.

d Play the six sentences three times. The pupils listen and write the number in the box on the correct picture.

Tapescript:
1 Sit down.
2 Touch a table.
3 Point to a table.
4 Turn around.
5 Stand up.
6 Point to a chair.

Step 3 Make Bingo cards

a To play Bingo each pupil will need ten small cover cards. These should be approximately the same size as the squares on the Bingo card (CB page 9, 3cm x 3cm). They may be made from paper or thin card, following the visual instructions on page 9 of the CB.

b Each card should have the name of one of the characters clearly printed on it. Pupils can copy the names from pages 7 and 8 of the CBs.

Step 4 Bingo

a Pupils will need their CBs open at page 9. Instruct them to cover any four squares on their Bingo card by placing the appropriate cover card face down over the picture. In this way each pupil's card should now have six different pictures showing.

b The Bingo Caller (teacher) will also need a set of name cards. Shuffle your cards. Lay them face down in front of you. Say '**Are you ready?**' Encourage the answer '**Yes**' or '**No**', as appropriate.

c Select a card. Read out the name on the card.

d If you read out '**Bill**' pupils must cover up the picture of Bill with the corresponding cover card. Cover cards must now be laid name up. If Bill is already covered, pupils do nothing.

e Continue calling out names from your cards until one of the pupils has covered all the squares on their Bingo card. The first player to do so shouts '**Bingo!**'

f This player must check their Bingo card is correct by reading back the names that are face up. If so, he or she wins the game.

g Continue until pupils understand the game.

h Divide the class into groups of 4–6 players. They continue the game simultaneously in groups.

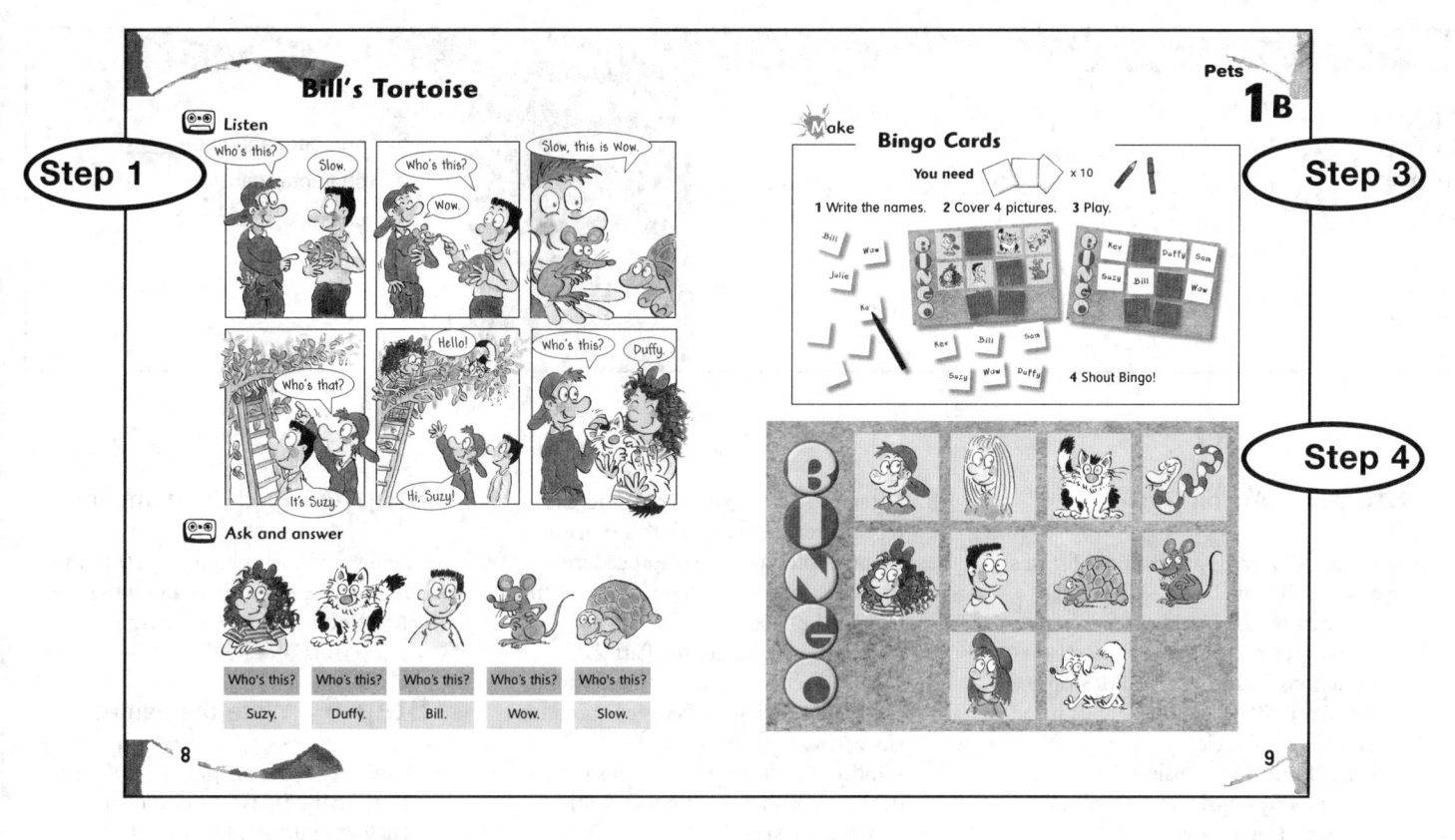

Bill's Tortoise

Listen

Who's this? — Slow.
Who's this? — Wow.
Slow, this is Wow.
Who's that? — It's Suzy.
Hello! — Hi, Suzy!
Who's this? — Duffy.

Ask and answer

Who's this?	Who's this?	Who's this?	Who's this?	Who's this?
Suzy.	Duffy.	Bill.	Wow.	Slow.

Pets 1B

Make Bingo Cards

You need ▢ ×10

1 Write the names. 2 Cover 4 pictures. 3 Play.

4 Shout Bingo!

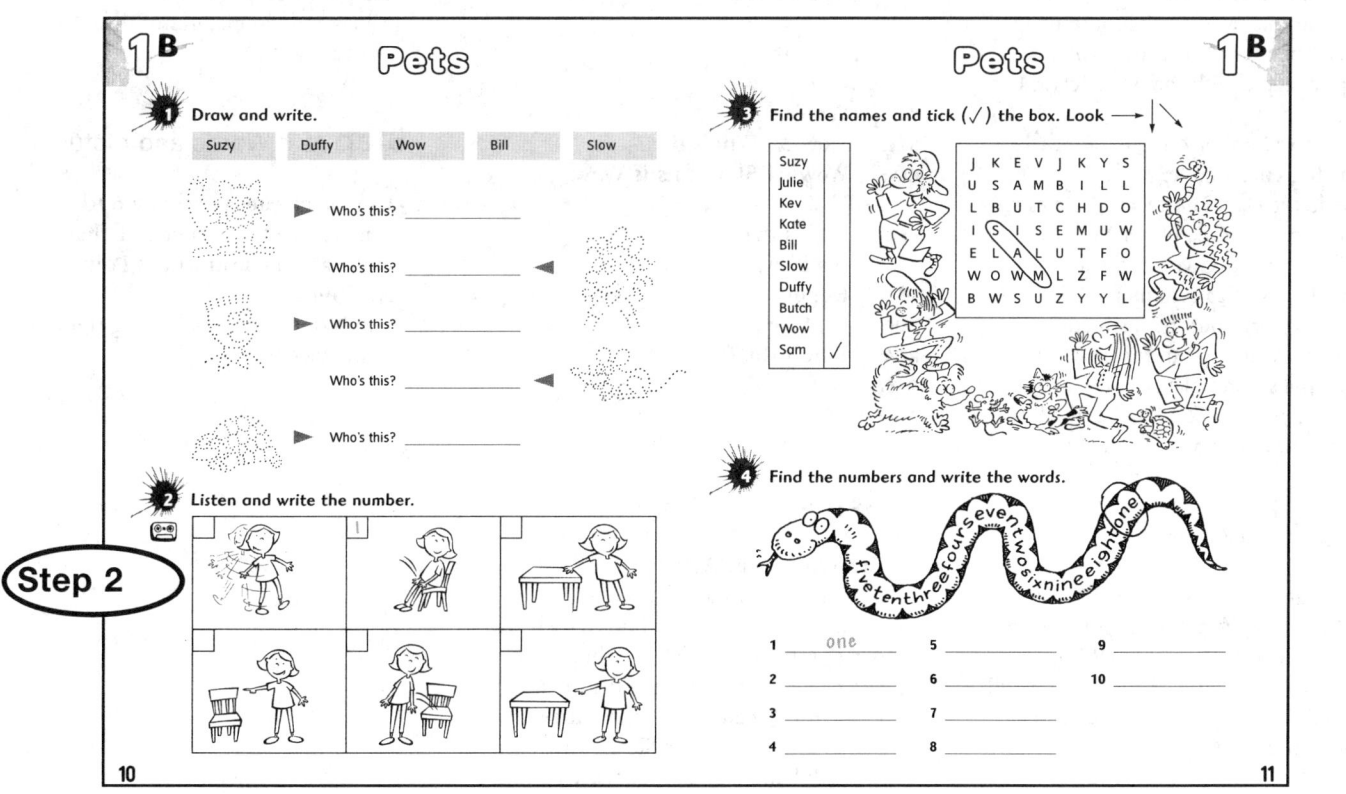

1B Pets

1 Draw and write.

Suzy   Duffy   Wow   Bill   Slow

▶ Who's this? _____
  Who's this? _____ ◀
▶ Who's this? _____
  Who's this? _____ ◀
▶ Who's this? _____

2 Listen and write the number.

Pets 1B

3 Find the names and tick (✓) the box. Look → ↘

Suzy
Julie
Kev
Kate
Bill
Slow
Duffy
Butch
Wow
Sam ✓

```
J K E V J K Y S
U S A M B I L L
L B U T C H D O
I S I S E M U W
E L A L U T F O
W O W M L Z F W
B W S U Z Y Y L
```

4 Find the numbers and write the words.

fivetenthreefoursevent wosixnineeightone

1 one   5 _____   9 _____
2 _____   6 _____   10 _____
3 _____   7 _____
4 _____   8 _____

1B Lesson 3

Main Language Items	Resource File	Materials Needed
This is … *names* Who's this? Who's that? Touch … Point to …	34	number flashcards character cards cassette/cassette player

Step 1 Action Game

a Number flashcards are required for this game, or the numbers 1–10, written well apart on the blackboard.

b Motion four pupils to the front. Use instructions '**Stand up! Walk! Stop! Turn Around! Sit down!**' Pupils sit on chairs facing the class.

c Revise '**Point to …**' using the numbers, **boys**, **girls**, **chairs** and **tables**. Then say '**Touch Number 1.**' Demonstrate. Motion the four pupils to copy. Then try '**Touch the table.**'

d Repeat step c with the whole class. Use instructions:
Point to Number 4 etc.
Touch a chair/table.

e Divide the class into teams. Give each team a colour. One player from each team stands up. Give an instruction. '**Touch/Point to Number 8.**' The first player to carry out the instruction correctly wins a point for their team. Then the second player in each team takes their turn. Continue until all players have had at least one turn.

Step 2 Role play

a Use character cards of Kev, Bill, Suzy and Duffy to help explain role-playing. Divide the class into pairs. Within each pair, say who will be Kev and who will be Bill. Listen to Part 1 of the dialogue from CB page 8.

b Listen to Part 1 again. This time pupils repeat after the tape. Do this twice. Change roles and repeat procedure.

c Pupils act out the dialogue without the help of the tape.

d Repeat the procedure for Part 2.

e Using the character cards, pupils act out similar dialogues between the other characters.

f (Optional) Alternatively, pupils can use drawings of their own pet and role-play themselves.

Tapescript:
PART 1
KEV: Who's this?
BILL: Slow … Who's this?
KEV: Wow … Slow, this is Wow.
PART 2
KEV: Who's that?
BILL: It's Suzy.
SUZY: Hello!
REV: Hi, Suzy!
REV: Who's this?
SUZY: Duffy
DUFFY: Miaow!

Step 3 Find the names

a Say '**Open your Activity Books at page 11.**' Pupils look at the word square in activity 3 and find the ten names listed on the left. As they find and circle the names, they tick them off in the list. (There are actually fifteen names in the square as Slow, Wow, Suzy, Bill and Sam appear twice.)

Step 4 Find the numbers

a Pupils find the numbers 1–10 in the word snake (activity 4) and write them next to the figures on the right.

Step 5 Write the names

a Pupils solve the anagrams on AB page 12 (activity 5) and write the names.

b They then draw a line to link the names and the pictures of the characters.

Step 6 Words and pictures

a Use the pictures in activity 6 to demonstrate the meaning of **chair** and **table**, and the instructions **Point to** and **Touch**.

b Pupils draw lines connecting the words to the pictures.

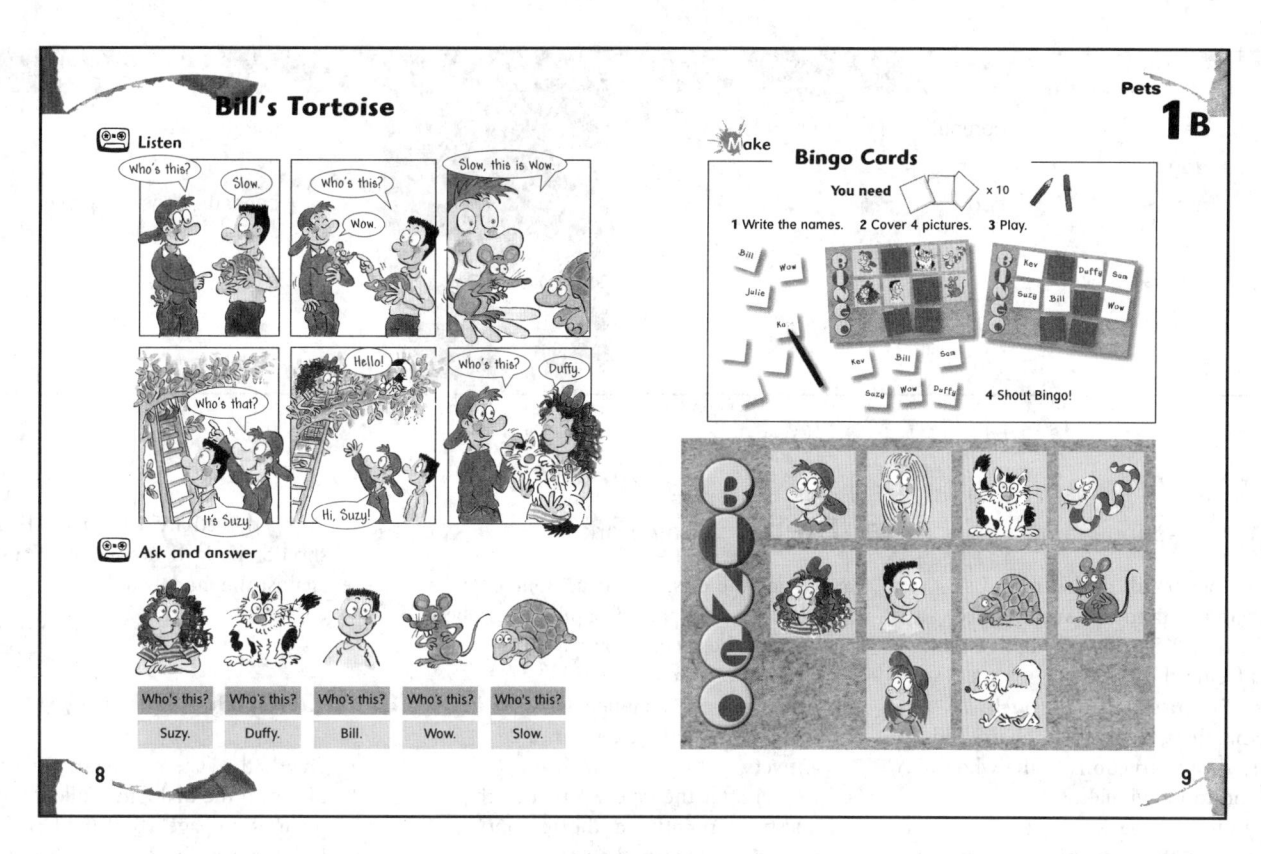

Bill's Tortoise

Listen

- Who's this? / Slow.
- Who's this? / Wow.
- Slow, this is Wow.
- Who's that? / It's Suzy.
- Hello! / Hi, Suzy!
- Who's this? / Duffy.

Ask and answer

Who's this?	Who's this?	Who's this?	Who's this?	Who's this?
Suzy.	Duffy.	Bill.	Wow.	Slow.

Pets 1B

Make Bingo Cards

You need □□ x 10

1 Write the names. 2 Cover 4 pictures. 3 Play.

4 Shout Bingo!

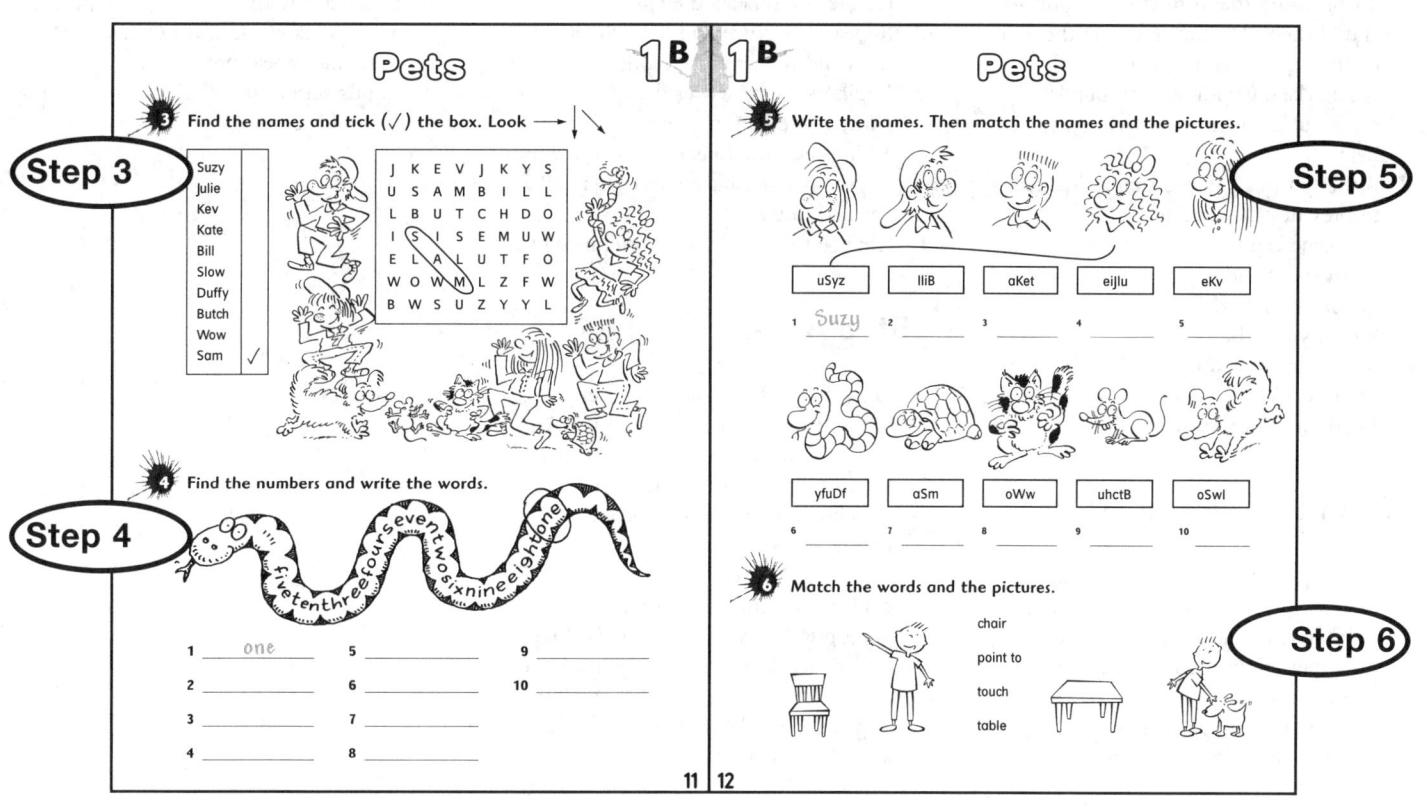

Pets 1B

Step 3 — Find the names and tick (✓) the box. Look →↓

Suzy
Julie
Kev
Kate
Bill
Slow
Duffy
Butch
Wow
Sam ✓

```
J K E V J K Y S
U S A M B I L L
L B U T C H D O
I S I S E M U W
E L A L U T F O
W O W M L Z F W
B W S U Z Y Y L
```

Step 4 — Find the numbers and write the words.

fivetenthreefoursevententwosixnineeightone

1 one   5 ____   9 ____
2 ____   6 ____   10 ____
3 ____   7 ____
4 ____   8 ____

Pets 1B

Step 5 — Write the names. Then match the names and the pictures.

uSyz	lliB	aKet	eijlu	eKv
1 Suzy	2 ____	3 ____	4 ____	5 ____

yfuDf	aSm	oWw	uhctB	oSwl
6 ____	7 ____	8 ____	9 ____	10 ____

Step 6 — Match the words and the pictures.

chair
point to
touch
table

1c Lesson 1

Main Language Items			Resource File	Materials Needed
What's this?	cat	computer		
What's that?	dog	door	34	cassette/cassette player
Stand on …	mouse	floor		
Sit on …	snake			
Draw a …	tortoise			

Step 1 Action Game

a Motion four pupils to the front. Use instructions '**Stand up! Walk! Stop! Turn around! Sit down!**' Pupils sit on chairs facing the class.

b Revise '**Point to …**' and '**Touch …**' using numbers, **boys**, **girls**, **chairs** and **tables**. Give instructions to the whole class and to individuals.

c Then introduce the words '**door**' and '**floor**' using the instructions '**Point to**' and '**Touch**'. Demonstrate and the four pupils copy. Then practice with the whole class. Continue until pupils can carry out the instructions without your help.

d Although this game is simply intended to present new vocabulary for later use, the game can be livened up with some novel commands:
Sit on the floor!
Sit on your chair!
Stand on the floor!
Stand on your chair!
Keep the action brisk at all times.

Step 2 Presentation

a Say '**Open your Coursebooks at page 10.**' Hold your book up for the class. Very quickly ask some preliminary questions about the pictures. Use '**Who's this?**'

b Play the tape. Pupils listen to the dialogue looking at the pictures at the same time.

Step 3 Pair work

a Divide the class into pairs. One CB between each pair of pupils should be open at the pictures on page 10. Cover the words.

b All pairs work simultaneously. P1 in each pair asks the questions. P2 answers.

c Repeat after the tape. P1 repeats the questions, pointing at the appropriate picture. P2 repeats the answers.

d Repeat this procedure then change roles and repeat twice more.

e Pupils ask and answer the questions without the help of the tape. Pupils asking the questions may use the words as prompts and must check their partners' answers.

f Change roles and repeat the procedure.

Step 4 Read and draw

a Draw four large squares on the blackboard, as on page 13 of the AB. Write the instructions at the top of each square. '**Draw a snake**' etc.

b Quickly draw a snake in box 1. Ask pupils '**What's this?**'

c Ask for volunteers to '**Draw a cat/mouse/tortoise**' in the appropriate box. Write '**What's this?**' under each box. Request volunteers to write the answers: '**A snake**' etc. Other pupils should determine whether these answers are correct.

d Then erase work from the blackboard.

Pupils do activity 1 in their AB. They should check their completed answers against the models on page 10 of the CB.

Optional Role play

a Divide the class into pairs. Give roles. Listen to the dialogue. Follow with the pictures on page 10 of the CB.

b Listen again, this time pupils repeat after the tape. Do this twice. Change roles and repeat procedure.

c Pupils act out the dialogue without the help of the tape.

Kev's Computer

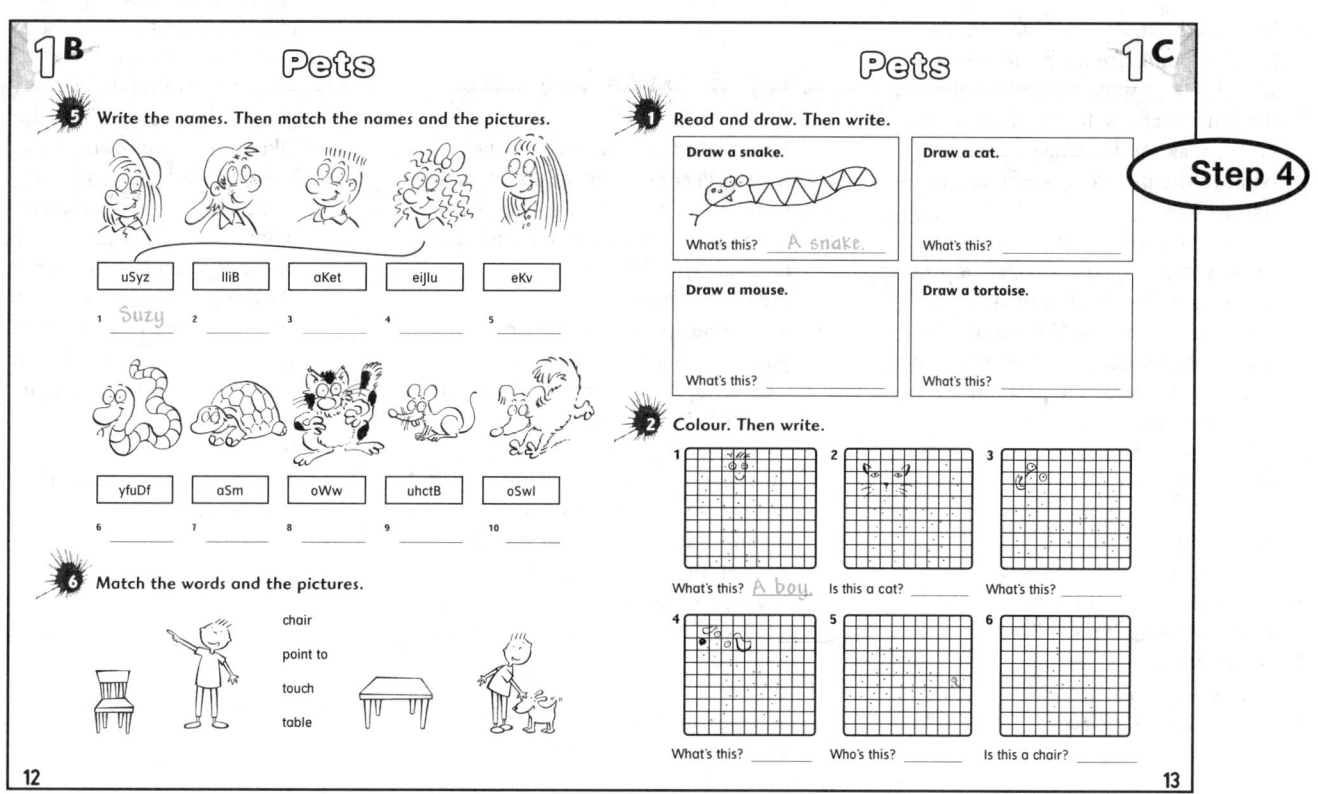

Listen

"What's this?" "A computer."
"What's that?" "A dog."
"What's that? Is it a snake?" "Yes, look!"

Ask and answer

What's this?	What's this?	What's this?	What's this?	What's this?
A dog.	A cat.	A mouse.	A tortoise.	A snake.

Step 2

Ask and answer

1. Is this Kev? Yes.
2. Is this Sam? No.

Ask and answer

Who's this?
What's this?
Is this …?

Pets 1C

Step 3

1B **Pets**

5 Write the names. Then match the names and the pictures.

uSyz	lliB	aKet	eijlu	eKv
1 Suzy	2	3	4	5

yfuDf	aSm	oWw	uhctB	oSwl
6	7	8	9	10

6 Match the words and the pictures.

chair
point to
touch
table

12

Pets 1C

1 Read and draw. Then write.

Draw a snake.	Draw a cat.
What's this? A snake.	What's this?

Draw a mouse.	Draw a tortoise.
What's this?	What's this?

Step 4

2 Colour. Then write.

1. What's this? A boy.
2. Is this a cat? ____
3. What's this? ____
4. What's this? ____
5. Who's this? ____
6. Is this a chair? ____

13

35

1c Lesson 2

Main Language Items		Resource File	Materials Needed
What's this?	cat	5	coloured pencils
What's that?	dog	7	materials to make word stones
Is this …?	mouse		cassette/cassette player
Look!	snake		
	tortoise		

Step 1 Presentation

a Say 'Open your Coursebooks at page 10.' Pupils look at the pictures and listen to the tape at the same time.

Step 2 Pair work

a Say 'Look at the pictures at the top of page 11.' Hold up your book to show pupils.
b Point to the first picture. Ask 'Is this Kev?' If pupils are unable to respond, say 'Yes.' Ask similar questions about the other pictures. Revise the answer No by making deliberate mistakes, e.g. point to the picture of Duffy and ask 'Is this Sam?'
c Divide the class into pairs, with one book between each pair, open at page 11. All pairs work simultaneously. Repeat after the tape. P1 repeats the questions, pointing at the appropriate picture. P2 answers. Repeat four times, changing roles.
d Pupils ask and answer questions without the tape.

Tapescript:
1 Is this Kev? // Yes. //
2 Is this Sam? // No. //
3 Is this Kate? // Yes. //
4 Is this Wow? // Yes. //
5 Is this Suzy? // Yes. //
6 Is this Duffy? // No. //

Step 3 Colour. Then write

AB page 13, activity 2. Pupils colour the dotted squares only to reveal a picture. They then write the answers to the questions.

Step 4 Crossword

Pupils complete the crossword on page 14 of their AB.

Step 5 Make word stones

a Pupils add five more word stones to their collection following the visual instructions on page 14 of the AB (activity 4). They should already be familiar with these words from the previous lesson.
b Say 'Open your Activity Books at page 14.' Point to the word stones. Check pupils are familiar with their meaning. Pupils point to the appropriate word stone in their books.
c To make the word stones, each pupil requires five 'stones' (either real stones or stone-shaped pieces of card as before). Pupils write one word (**dog, snake, cat, mouse, tortoise**) on each stone in felt-tip pen, as shown in the pictures.
d When pupils have made all five stones, ask them to look at page 10 of their CB and put their stones on top of the same word or on top of a picture of the appropriate animal.
e Pupils then store their stones for future use.

Optional

a Working in pairs, pupils play a simple memory game with their word stones. P1 lays out one full collection of word stones, face up. Both pupils spend a minute trying to memorise the stones. They then turn them face down.
b The other collection of word stones is put in a box, from which the pupils take turns to draw one stone, without looking inside the box. They read the word and try to find the same word among the upside-down stones. They may only turn over one stone. If their choice is correct, they keep the two matching stones for scoring purposes. If they are incorrect, the other player has a try. If neither is able to find the correct stone, then the 'clue' stone goes back into the box
c At the end of the game, the player with most word stones is the winner.

Kev's Computer

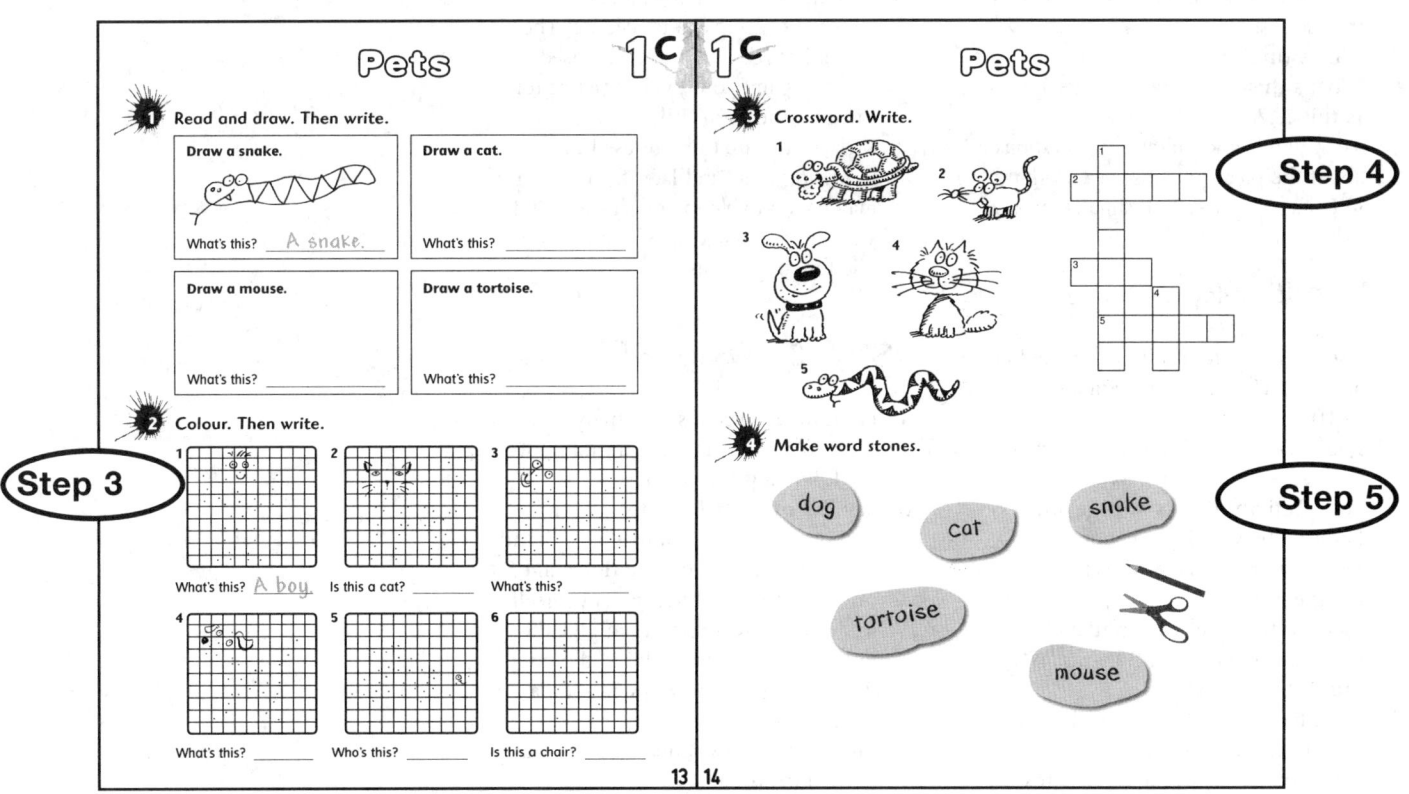

Listen

- What's this? — A computer.
- What's that? — A dog.
- What's that? Is it a snake?
- Yes, look!

Ask and answer

What's this?	What's this?	What's this?	What's this?	What's this?
A dog.	A cat.	A mouse.	A tortoise.	A snake.

Pets 1c

Ask and answer

1. Is this Kev? — Yes.
2. Is this Sam? — No.

Ask and answer

- Who's this?
- What's this?
- Is this …?

Step 1 *Step 2*

10 · 11

Pets 1c

1 Read and draw. Then write.

- Draw a snake. — What's this? A snake.
- Draw a cat. — What's this? _____
- Draw a mouse. — What's this? _____
- Draw a tortoise. — What's this? _____

2 Colour. Then write.

1. What's this? A boy
2. Is this a cat? _____
3. What's this? _____
4. What's this? _____
5. Who's this? _____
6. Is this a chair? _____

1c Pets

3 Crossword. Write.

4 Make word stones.

dog, cat, snake, tortoise, mouse

Step 3 *Step 4* *Step 5*

13 | 14

37

1c Lesson 3

Main Language Items		Resource File	Materials Needed
Who's this?	*names* (revision)		
What's this?	No	45a	character cards (see AB centre cut-outs section)
Is this …?		46	scissors
What's your name?		52	envelopes

Step 1 Pair work

a Using the large group picture on page 11 of the CB revise structures introduced to date. Ask pupils what questions they can ask in English about the picture. Write the questions on the blackboard. Ask for a volunteer to come to the front and ask the class random questions. Expect the following questions from the pupils and provide those they do not suggest themselves:
Who's this?
What's this?
Is this …?

b Then pupils ask and answer questions about the picture themselves, working in pairs. All pairs work simultaneously.

Step 2 Play the game

a Use the character cards of the children and pets. Use only cards numbered 1–10.

b Pupils work in pairs. They require one pack of ten cards each. Say '**Open your Activity Books at page 15.**' Look at the visual instructions.

c Demonstrate the game in activity 5 using two pupils. Both pupils shuffle their cards. P1 selects a card and, without showing it to P2, asks '**Who's this?**' P2 guesses.

d Then P1 reveals the card. If the answer is correct, P2 wins the card; if incorrect, P1 keeps the card. Cards won in this way should be kept separate from the cards in the pupils' hands, for scoring purposes.

e Continue in this way, with pupils taking alternate turns to ask and answer the questions.

f When the class understands the procedure, all pupils play the game simultaneously in pairs. The player to collect the most cards is the winner.

g The game can be simplified by using only the five children character cards, which speeds up the procedure. The five animal cards can then be used in a separate game to provide practice for the question form '**What's this?**'
NOTE Cards are to be re-used in the following units and later for revision. It may be advisable to collect them and store them in envelopes. See Resource File for suggestions.

Step 3 Words and pictures

a Point to the pictures in activity 6. Use them to demonstrate the meaning of the following instructions.

b Say '**Sit on a chair**' and sit down. Pupils copy you. Continue with **Stand on a chair**, **Stand on the floor** and **Sit on the floor**. Do the actions yourself to demonstrate at first, then give the instructions without helping the pupils.

c Repeat for girls and boys, if you have a mixed class.

d Pupils draw lines connecting the words to the pictures in activity 6.

38

Kev's Computer

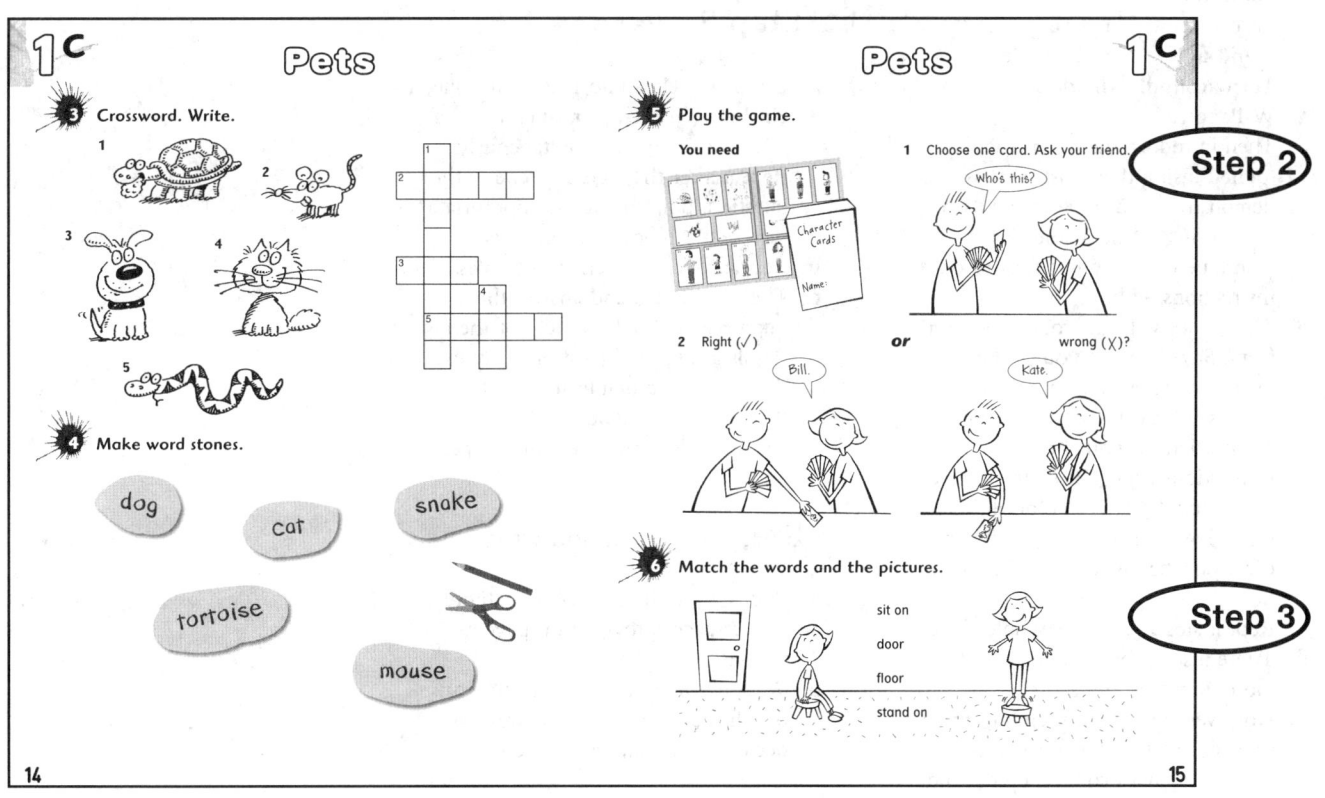

Pets 1c

Listen

What's this? — A computer.
What's that? — A dog.
What's that? Is it a snake? — Yes, look!

Ask and answer

1. Is this Kev? Yes.
2. Is this Sam? No.

Ask and answer

What's this?	What's this?	What's this?	What's this?	What's this?
A dog.	A cat.	A mouse.	A tortoise.	A snake.

Ask and answer

Who's this?
What's this?
Is this ...?

Step 1

1c Pets

3 Crossword. Write.

1. 2. 3. 4. 5.

4 Make word stones.

dog   cat   snake   tortoise   mouse

Pets 1c

5 Play the game.

You need: Character Cards

1. Choose one card. Ask your friend.
   Who's this?
2. Right (✓) — Bill.   *or*   wrong (✗)? — Kate.

Step 2

6 Match the words and the pictures.

sit on
door
floor
stand on

Step 3

1D Lesson 1

Main Language Items			Resource File	Materials Needed
Is this a …?	you	door	5a	cassette/cassette player
It's a …	no	floor	8a	
Stand on …	monkey	pen		
Sit on …		pencil		

Step 1 Action Game

a Motion four pupils to the front. Use instructions '**Stand up! Walk! Stop! Turn Around! Sit down!**' Pupils sit on chairs facing the class.
b Revise the following instructions with the four individuals and the whole group:
Point to …   a boy
Touch …   a girl
Stand on …   the floor
Sit on …   a chair
Stand up!   a/the table
Turn around!   the door
Walk to …
c Then introduce the words '**pen**' and '**pencil**' using these instructions. You demonstrate and the four pupils copy. Then bring in the whole class. Continue until pupils can carry out the instructions without your help.
d Then work with the four pupils at the front. Say '**Pick up your pencil.**' Demonstrate. Motion pupils to copy. Then say '**Put down your pencil.**' Then '**Pick up your book.**' Repeat instructions using '**Pick up/Put down**' and '**pencil**', '**pen**' and '**book.**' Continue until the four pupils can carry out the instruction without your help.
e Repeat step d with the whole class.
f These instructions may take a little more time than the earlier ones. However, it is worth spending the time now since a number of the more enjoyable games coming up depend upon these instructions.

Step 2 Presentation

a Say '**Open your Coursebooks at page 12.**' Hold your book up for the class. Very quickly ask some preliminary questions about the pictures. Use '**Who's this?**' '**Is this …?**'
b Play the tape. Pupils follow the dialogue looking at the pictures at the same time.

Step 3 Pair work

a Divide the class into pairs, with one CB between each pair, open at page 12. All pairs work simultaneously. Repeat after the tape. P1 repeats the question, pointing at the appropriate picture. P2 repeats the answers.
b Repeat four times, changing roles.
c Then pupils ask and answer the questions without the help of the tape. Pupils asking the questions may use the words as prompts and must check their partners' answers.
d Change roles and repeat the procedure.

Step 4 Look and write

a Pupils write the answers to activity 1 in the spaces provided on page 16 of the AB.
b Working in pairs, pupils try to work out the content of the pictures and decide if their answers are correct.

Step 5 My drawings

a Pupils draw pictures of their choice in the boxes provided. One picture must be of their partner.
b Pupils act out a similar dialogue to the one between Suzy and Bill on page 12 of the CB, this time using their own pictures.

Suzy's Drawings

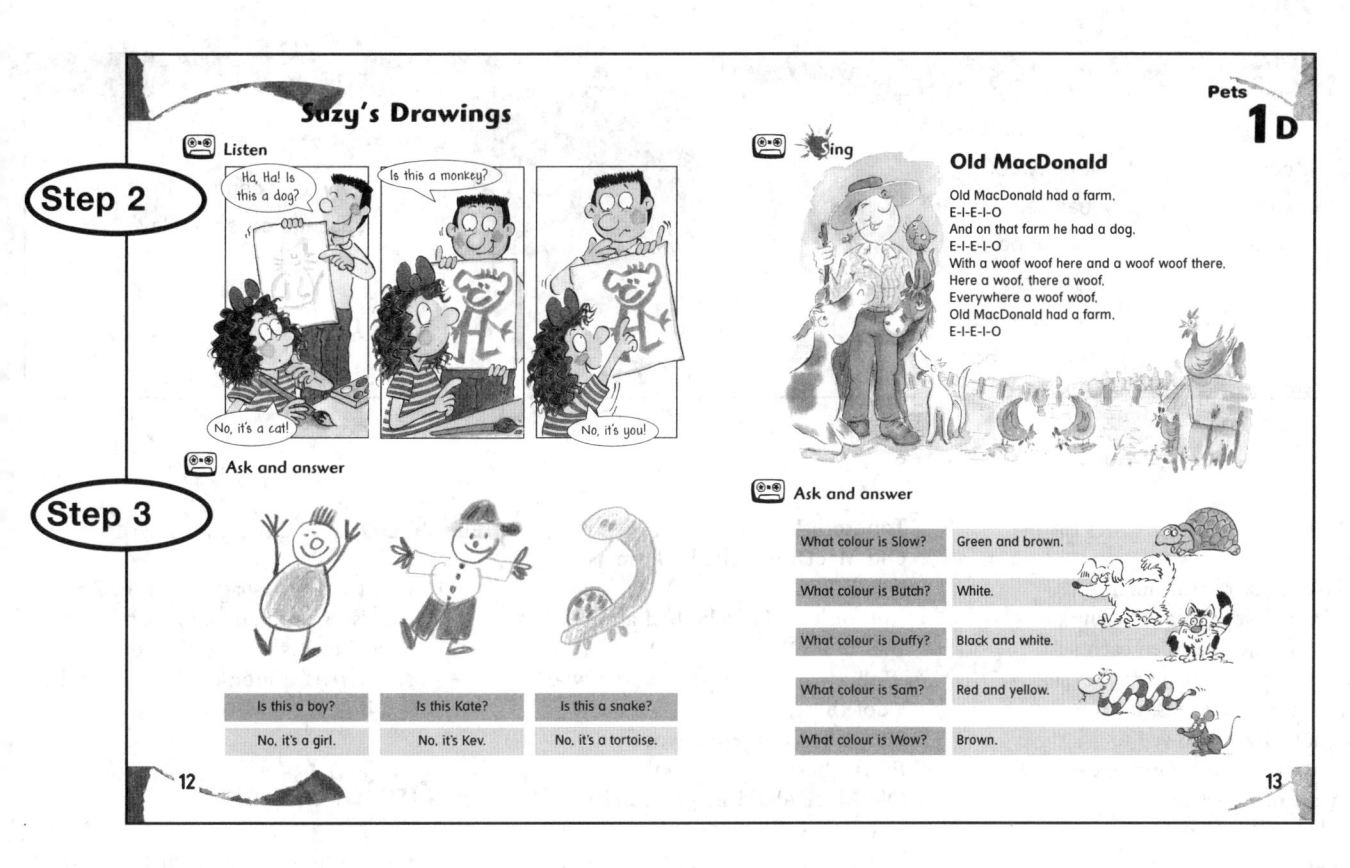

Pets 1D

Step 2

Listen

Ha, Ha! Is this a dog?
No, it's a cat!
Is this a monkey?
No, it's you!

Sing

Old MacDonald

Old MacDonald had a farm.
E-I-E-I-O
And on that farm he had a dog.
E-I-E-I-O
With a woof woof here and a woof woof there.
Here a woof, there a woof.
Everywhere a woof woof.
Old MacDonald had a farm.
E-I-E-I-O

Step 3

Ask and answer

| Is this a boy? | Is this Kate? | Is this a snake? |
| No, it's a girl. | No, it's Kev. | No, it's a tortoise. |

Ask and answer

What colour is Slow?	Green and brown.
What colour is Butch?	White.
What colour is Duffy?	Black and white.
What colour is Sam?	Red and yellow.
What colour is Wow?	Brown.

12 / 13

Pets 1C

5 Play the game.

You need: Character Cards

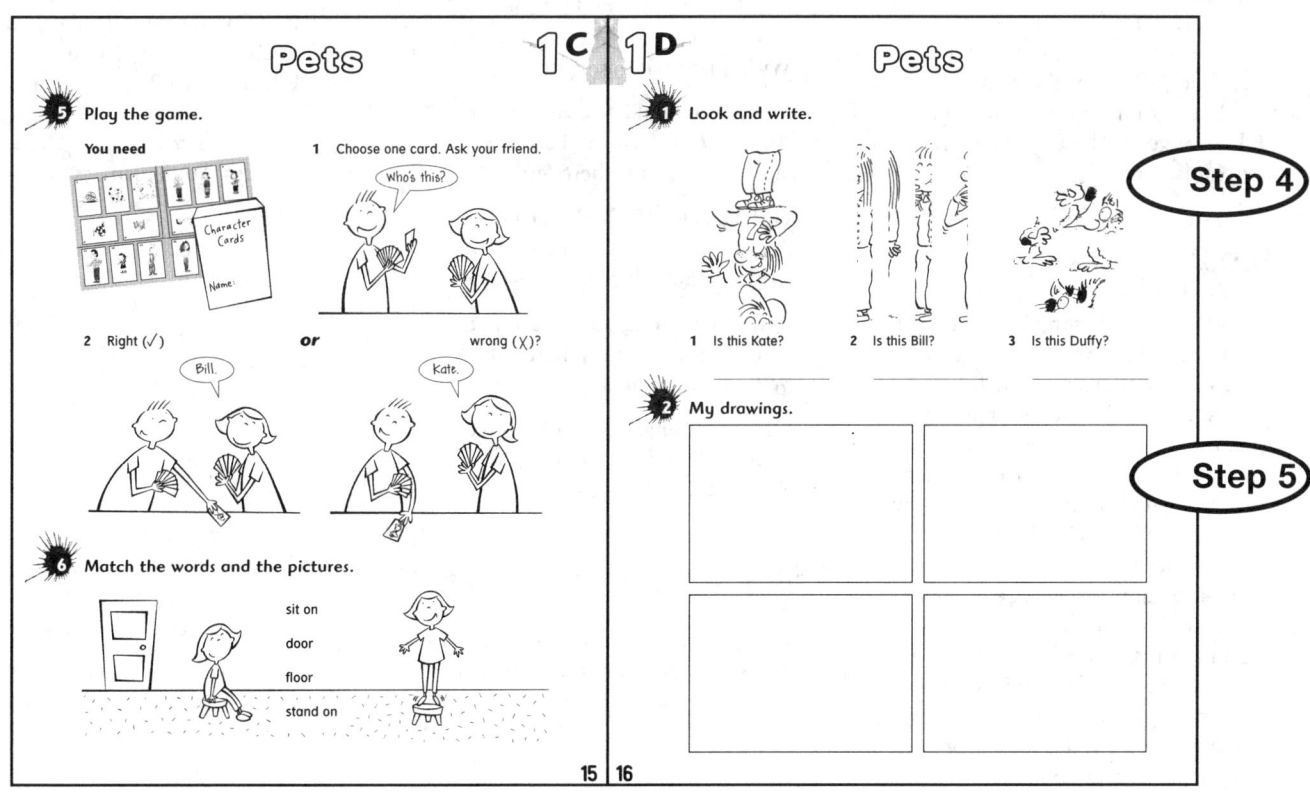

1 Choose one card. Ask your friend.
Who's this?

2 Right (✓) or wrong (✗)?
Bill.
Kate.

6 Match the words and the pictures.

sit on
door
floor
stand on

Pets 1D

Step 4

1 Look and write.

1 Is this Kate? _____
2 Is this Bill? _____
3 Is this Duffy? _____

2 My drawings.

Step 5

15 / 16

41

1D Lesson 2

Main Language Items			Resource File	Materials Needed
I don't know	sheep	*animal noises:*	5a	character cards 1–10
Is it a ...	cow	woof woof	8a	cassette/cassette player
	hen	baa baa	23	
	duck	moo moo		
		cluck cluck		
		quack quack		
		miaow miaow		

Step 1 Character card game

a Use the character cards numbered 1–10. Pupils work in pairs using one pack of ten cards between each pair.

b Lay the cards face down on the table. P1 picks a card. P2 must try to guess the identity. P2 is allowed to ask three questions of the 'Yes/No' type, but can only make one guess, e.g.
Is it a boy? Yes/No
Is it a pet? Yes/No
Is it a cat? Yes/No etc.
If P2 guesses correctly, they win the card. If not, P1 keeps the card. Then P2 selects a card. Continue until all the cards have gone. The player with the most cards wins.

Step 2 Song

a Listen to the whole song on the tape. Follow with the words on page 13 of the CB. Draw animals on the board or use flashcards to help understanding. Then listen to the first verse.

b Listen again taking one verse at a time. Encourage pupils to join in the song by humming the tune. Get them to do the animal noises.

c Without looking at their books, pupils hum, make the animal noises or even sing the words, if they can. If possible, display flashcards of the animals in a line to prompt pupils and to encourage them not to look at the words. Or draw simple sketches on the blackboard.

Tapescript:
Old MacDonald had a farm
E–I–E–I–O
And on that farm he had a dog
E–I–E–I–O
With a woof woof here and a woof woof there.
Here a woof, there a woof.
Everywhere a woof woof.
Old MacDonald had a farm
E–I–E–I–O

Old MacDonald had a farm, etc.
And on that farm he had a sheep.
With a baa baa here, etc.

Old MacDonald had a farm, etc.
And on that farm he had a cow.
With a moo moo here, etc.

Old MacDonald had a farm, etc.
And on that farm he had a hen.
With a cluck cluck here, etc.

Old MacDonald had a farm, etc.
And on that farm he had a duck.
With a quack quack here, etc.

Old MacDonald had a farm, etc.
And on that farm he had a cat.
With a miaow miaow here, etc.

Step 3 Words and pictures

a Look at activity 3 on page 17 of the AB. Pupils draw lines to connect the animals to the appropriate words.

Step 4 Listen and write

a In activity 4 on page 17 of the AB, the task is to write down the name of the animal that is making the noise.
Answers: 1 a monkey 2 a cat 3 a hen 4 a dog 5 a cow 6 a mouse

Optional Game

Pupils can play a game in small groups. P1 impersonates an animal, other pupils guess the identity, e.g.
P2: **Is it a cat?**
P1: No.
P3: **Is it a cow?**
P1: Yes. Your turn.

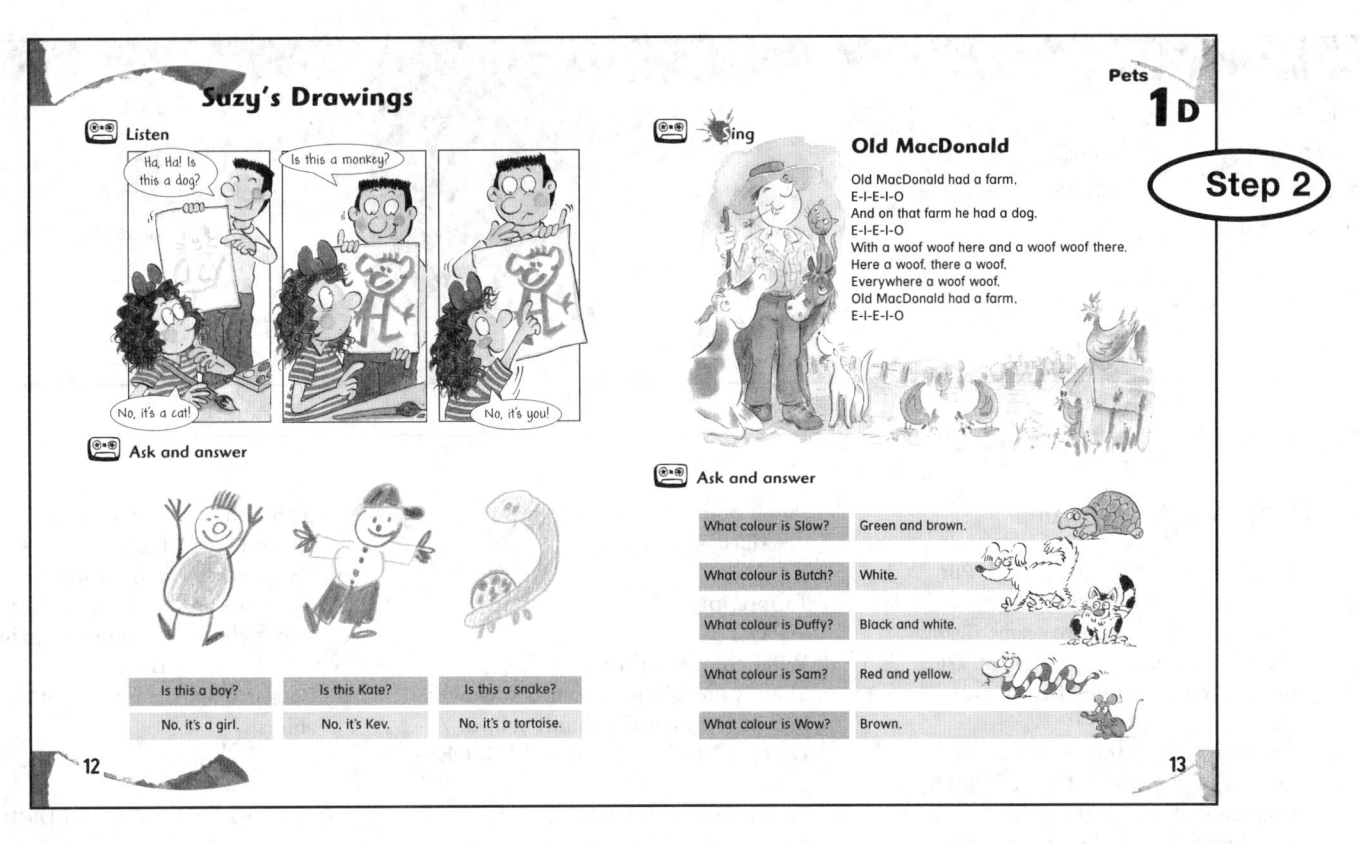

Suzy's Drawings

Listen

"Ha, Ha! Is this a dog?" "No, it's a cat!"
"Is this a monkey?" "No, it's Kev."
"No, it's you!"

Ask and answer

| Is this a boy? | Is this Kate? | Is this a snake? |
| No, it's a girl. | No, it's Kev. | No, it's a tortoise. |

Pets 1D

Step 2

Sing

Old MacDonald

Old MacDonald had a farm,
E-I-E-I-O
And on that farm he had a dog,
E-I-E-I-O
With a woof woof here and a woof woof there.
Here a woof, there a woof.
Everywhere a woof woof.
Old MacDonald had a farm,
E-I-E-I-O

Ask and answer

What colour is Slow?	Green and brown.
What colour is Butch?	White.
What colour is Duffy?	Black and white.
What colour is Sam?	Red and yellow.
What colour is Wow?	Brown.

12   13

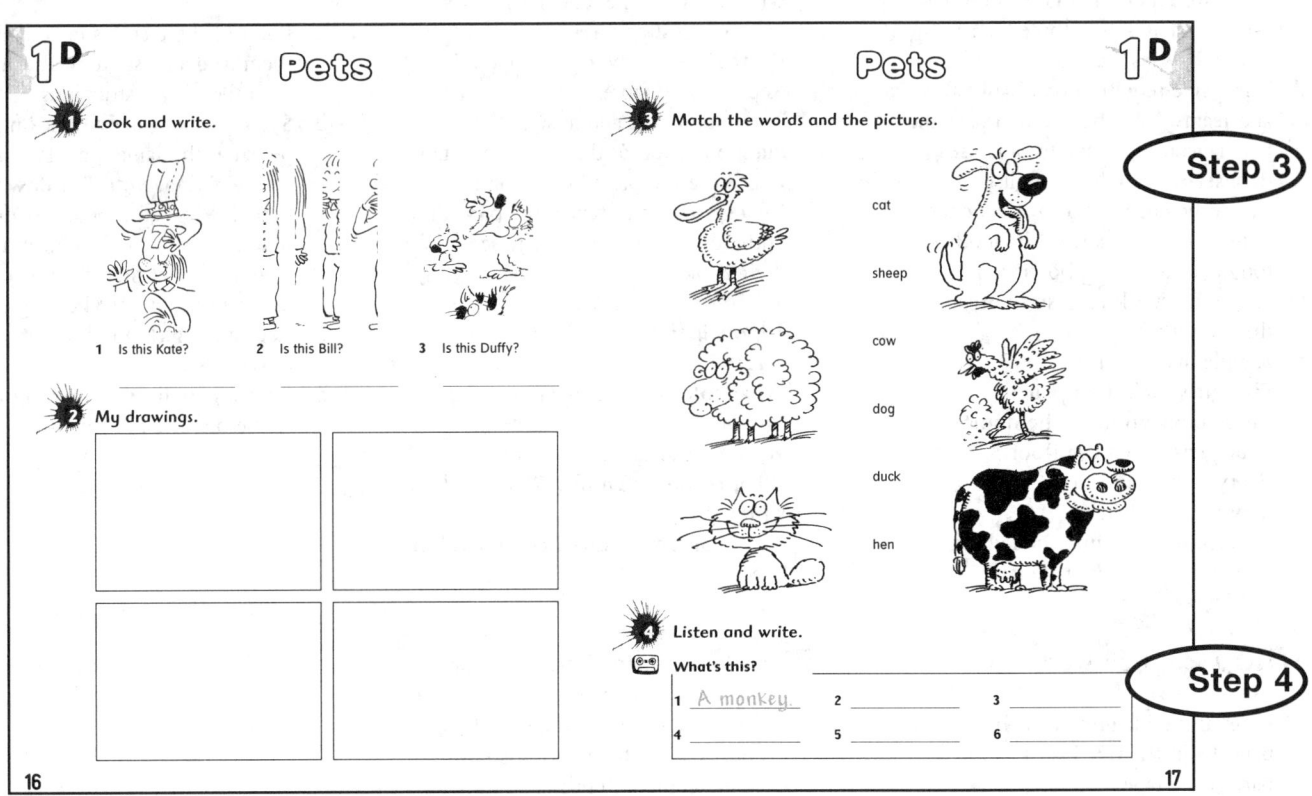

1D   Pets

1 Look and write.

1 Is this Kate?
2 Is this Bill?
3 Is this Duffy?

2 My drawings.

Pets   1D

3 Match the words and the pictures.

cat
sheep
cow
dog
duck
hen

Step 3

4 Listen and write.

What's this?

1 A monkey   2 _____   3 _____
4 _____   5 _____   6 _____

Step 4

16   17

43

1D Lesson 3

Main Language Items		Resource File	Materials Needed
Pick up ...	pen		
Put down ...	pencil		
What colour is ...?	*colours*	5a	coloured pencils
Slow is green and brown.			cassette/cassette player

Step 1 Action Game

a Briskly revise '**Pick up ...**' and '**Put down ...**' with the whole class.

b Divide the class into two teams. Teams should be as equal as possible in terms of size, and a mixture of boys and girls.

c The aim of this game is for the correct number of pupils to carry out a given instruction. E.g. if you say '**Three boys stand up**', then the first team to have three boys and only three boys standing, wins a point.

d This game requires organisational skills and teamwork. The children have the language at this stage to organise themselves entirely in English. This should be encouraged by deducting a point if pupils resort to the mother tongue or awarding bonus points to a team who speak English to organise themselves.

e Sample instructions:
Five girls pick up a pencil!
Three boys point to the door!
Four girls touch the floor!
Everybody stand up! ... One girl sit down!
Everybody pick up a pencil! ... Four boys put down your pencil!

Step 2 Pair work

a Look at the pictures at the bottom of page 13 in the CB. Listen to the first part of the tape.

b Pupils point to each pet as it is described.

Tapescript:
PART 1
What colour are the pets?
Slow is green and brown. // Wow is brown. // Sam is red and yellow. // Duffy is black and white. // Butch is white. //

c Pupils close their books. Play the second part of the tape. P1 repeats the questions. P2 answers.

d Do the exercise twice. Change roles. Repeat twice more.

e Then pupils ask and answer the questions without the help of the tape. Pupils use the pictures as prompts.

f Change roles and repeat the procedure until pupils can do the exercise without their books.

Tapescript:
PART 1
What colour is Slow? Green and brown.
What colour is Butch? White.
What colour is Duffy? Black and white.
What colour is Sam? Red and yellow.
What colour is Wow? Brown.

Step 3 Write. Then colour

a Look at the puzzle at the top of page 18 of the AB. The pets' leads have become tangled. Pupils must trace a path from each animal to the colour at the end of the lead.

b Pupils complete the sentences writing the correct colour for each animal.

c Pupils check their answers against the model in the CB on p13.

d Pupils colour the pictures of the animals.

Step 4 Words and pictures

a Point to the pictures in activity 6. Use them to demonstrate the meaning of the following instructions.

b Say **Pick up a pencil**, picking up a pencil at the same time. Pupils copy you. Continue with **Put down a pencil**, **Pick up a pen**, **Put down a pen**. Do the actions yourself to demonstrate at first, then give the instructions without helping the pupils.

c Repeat for girls and boys, if you have a mixed class.

d Pupils draw lines connecting the words to the pictures in activity 6.

Suzy's Drawings

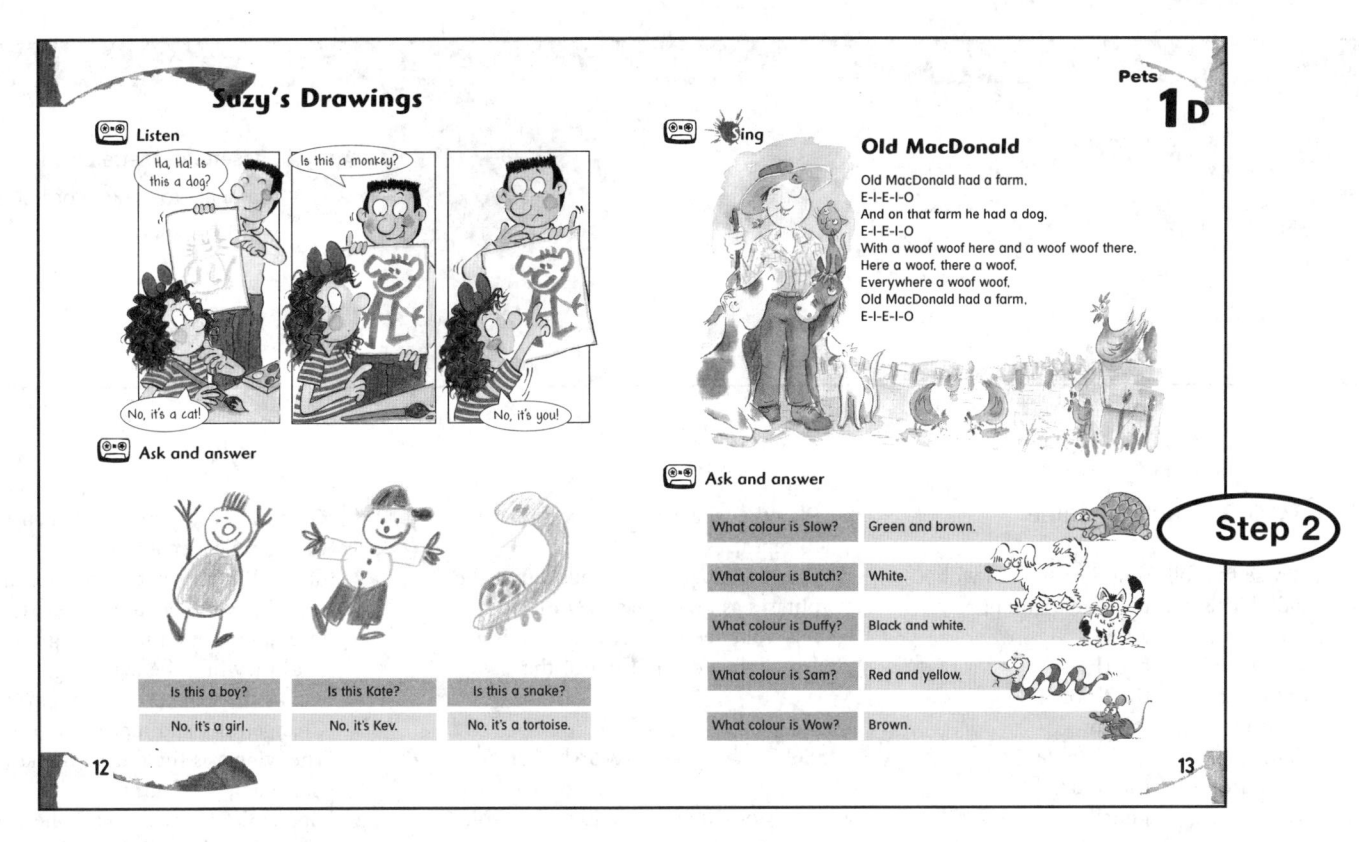

Listen

Ha, Ha! Is this a dog?
No, it's a cat!
Is this a monkey?
No, it's you!

Ask and answer

Is this a boy?	Is this Kate?	Is this a snake?
No, it's a girl.	No, it's Kev.	No, it's a tortoise.

Pets 1D

Sing — Old MacDonald

Old MacDonald had a farm,
E-I-E-I-O
And on that farm he had a dog,
E-I-E-I-O
With a woof woof here and a woof woof there,
Here a woof, there a woof,
Everywhere a woof woof,
Old MacDonald had a farm,
E-I-E-I-O

Ask and answer — Step 2

What colour is Slow?	Green and brown.
What colour is Butch?	White.
What colour is Duffy?	Black and white.
What colour is Sam?	Red and yellow.
What colour is Wow?	Brown.

12 / 13

1D Pets

Step 3

5. Follow the line. Write. Then colour.

black and white — red and yellow — white — green and brown — brown

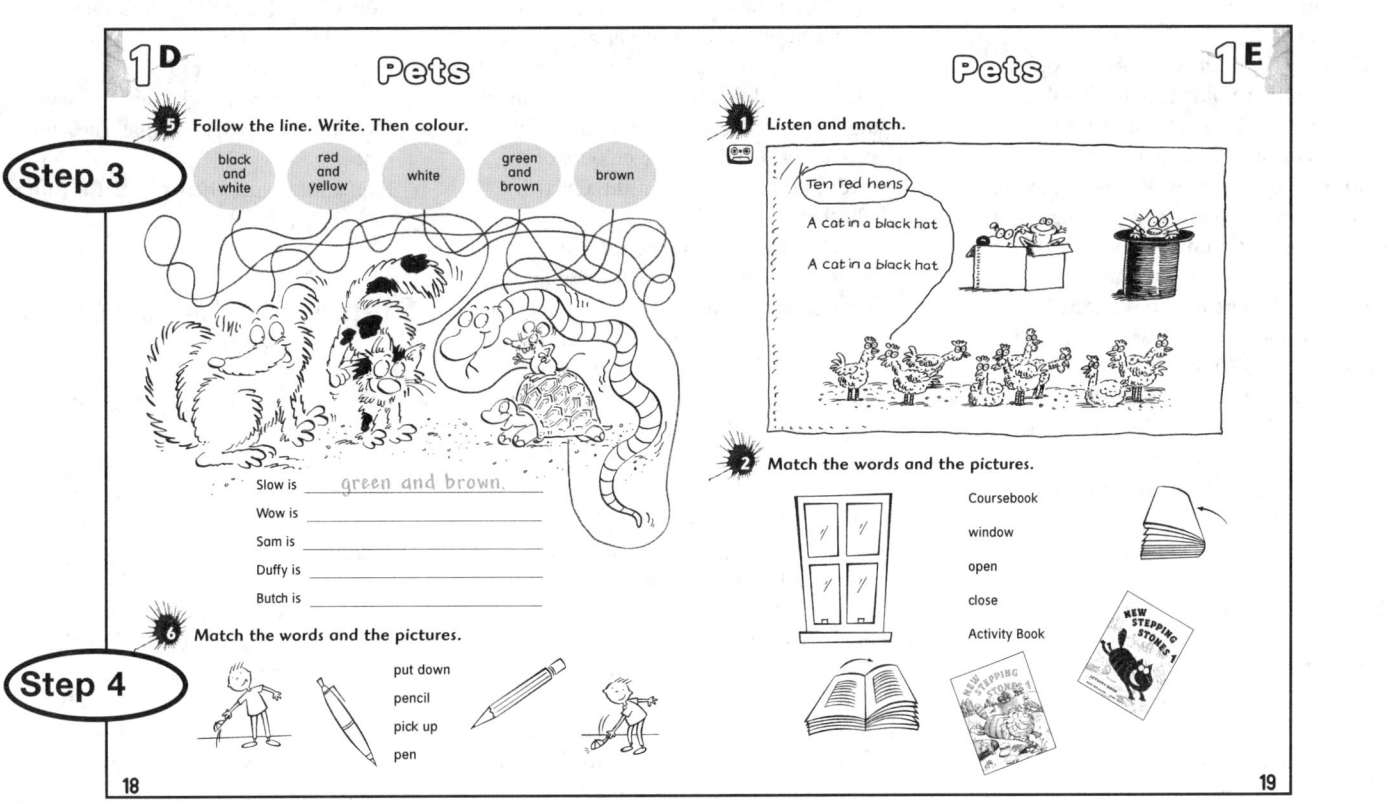

Slow is green and brown.
Wow is _____
Sam is _____
Duffy is _____
Butch is _____

Step 4

6. Match the words and the pictures.

put down
pencil
pick up
pen

Pets 1E

1. Listen and match.

Ten red hens
A cat in a black hat
A cat in a black hat

2. Match the words and the pictures.

Coursebook
window
open
close
Activity Book

18 / 19

45

1ᴱ Lesson 1

Main Language Items		Resource File	Materials Needed
Open your ...	hat	34	cassette/cassette player
Close your ...	hen	45a	materials to make word stones
Coursebook	frog	46	word stone collections
Activity Book	box		
window	house		

Step 1 Action Game

a Revise the following instructions with individuals and the whole group:
   Point to ...   a boy
   Touch ...   a girl
   Stand on ...   the floor
   Sit on ...   a chair
   Stand up!   a/the table
   Turn around!   the door
   Walk to ...   pencil
   Pick up ...   pen
   Put down ...

b Then say 'Pick up your Activity Book. Open your Activity Book. Touch your Coursebook. Open your Coursebook. Close your Activity Book.' Pupils may well understand the words **open** and **close** at this stage and so demonstration may be unnecessary. Continue with tasks at random.

c Then say '**Point to the window.**' Demonstrate with the whole class. Tell one pupil to '**Touch the window. Open the window. Close the window.**' Use the instructions **open** and **close** with the whole class, referring to the **door**, **window** and their books.

Step 2 Listen and match

a Say '**Open your Activity Books at page 19.**' Point to the phrases and pictures in activity 1.
b Play the tape, one phrase at a time. Pupils listen and draw a line to match the phrase and picture.
c Play the tape again, pausing for pupils to repeat.
d Play the tape again. Pupils repeat the phrases as quickly as they can.
e Ask volunteers to say the phrases as fast as they can in front of the class.

Step 3 Make word stones

a The word stones exercises, close to the end of each unit, are designed to expand pupils' vocabulary and help them to understand the relationship between spelling and pronunciation in English. Pupils will not know the new vocabulary items, but the colours of the words and the pictures in the CB will help them.
b Say '**Open your Coursebooks at page 14.**' Each pupil needs the following four stones from their collection: **cat**, **mouse**, **dog** and **snake**. Listen to the first part of the tape. Pupils place the appropriate stones on their desks or on the pictures in their CBs.
c To make new word stones, each pupil requires four 'stones'. Pupils write one word (**house**, **hat**, **cake**, **frog**) on each stone in felt-tip pen, as shown in the pictures. Play the second part of the tape. Pupils listen and repeat.
d Divide the class into pairs. Pupils then play the following games with their word stones.
e **Game 1:** Each pair uses one collection of stones face up. P1 says a word and P2 finds the correct stone. Change roles and repeat the procedure.
f **Game 2:** Each pupil in the pair places their own collection of stones face down. P1 turns one stone face up and says the word. P2 turns their stones face up one at a time, saying the words, until they find the matching one. P1 counts the number of turns this takes. Change roles and repeat the procedure. The winner is the one who takes the least number of turns.
g **Game 3:** P1 places their collection of stones face down. P2 places their collection face up. P1 turns one stone over and says the word, e.g. **dog**. P2 finds a stone which rhymes and says the word, e.g. **frog**. Change roles and repeat.
h Pupils then store their stones for future use.

Step 4 The Stepping Stones Game

a Direct pupils to the Stepping Stones Game on page 14 of the CB.
b Ask the class to make a sentence going from left to right across the stepping stones. They must begin in the first column and may take one word/phrase from each column/stone. Write two sample sentences on the blackboard.
c Divide the class into pairs. Give the class ten minutes to make as many sentences as possible from the words on the stones.
d Check the answers with the whole class. The pair to get the most correct and true sentences are the winners.

Words and Sentences

Word Stones

Use: cat, mouse, dog, snake

Make: house, cake, frog, hat

The Stepping Stones Game

Butch / Kate / Duffy / Suzy — is — a — dog / cat / black and white / girl

Step 3
Step 4

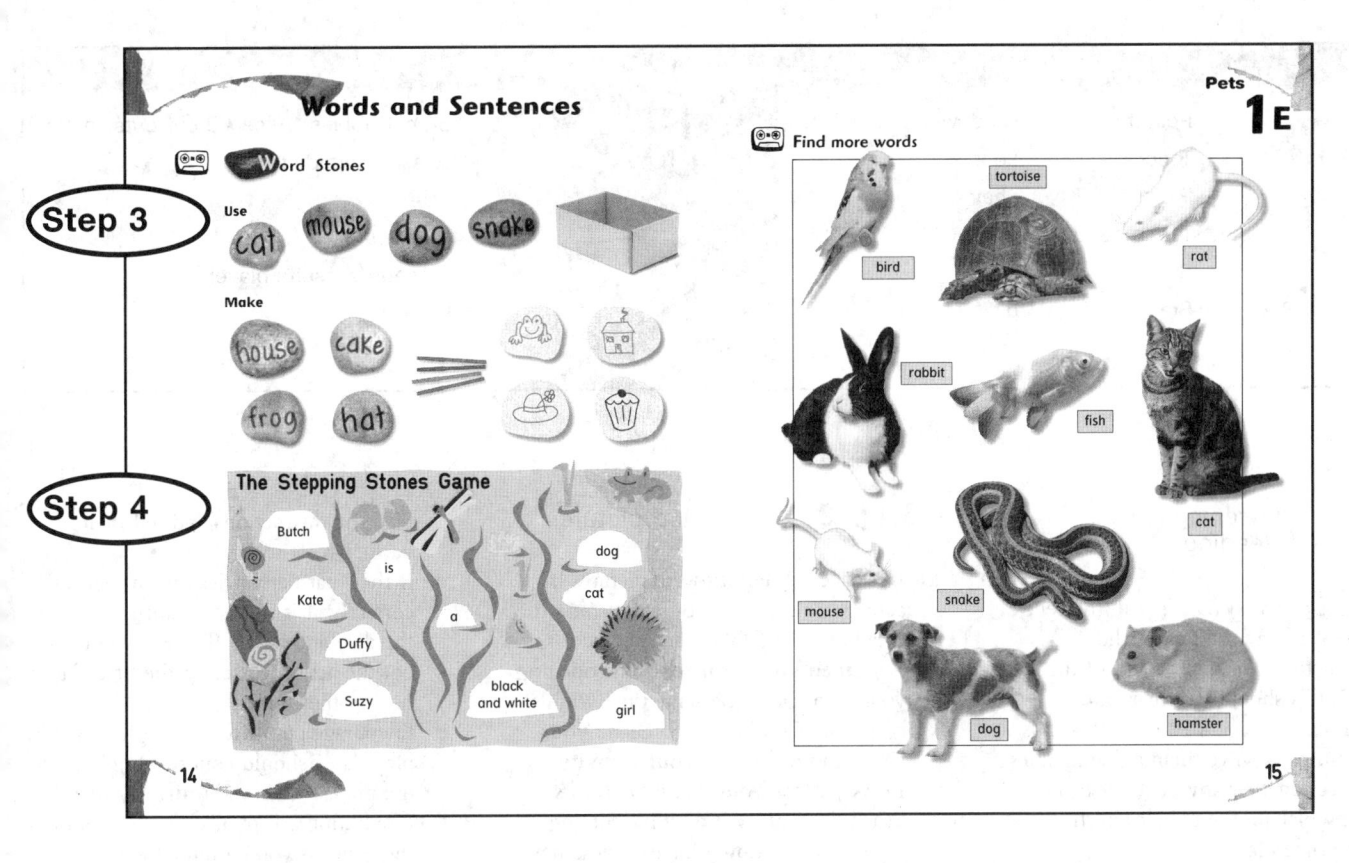

Find more words

bird, tortoise, rat, rabbit, fish, cat, mouse, snake, dog, hamster

Pets 1E

14 / 15

1D Pets

5. Follow the line. Write. Then colour.

black and white / red and yellow / white / green and brown / brown

Slow is _green and brown._
Wow is _____
Sam is _____
Duffy is _____
Butch is _____

6. Match the words and the pictures.

put down
pencil
pick up
pen

Pets 1E

1. Listen and match.

Ten red hens
A cat in a black hat
A cat in a black hat

Step 2

2. Match the words and the pictures.

Coursebook
window
open
close
Activity Book

18 / 19

47

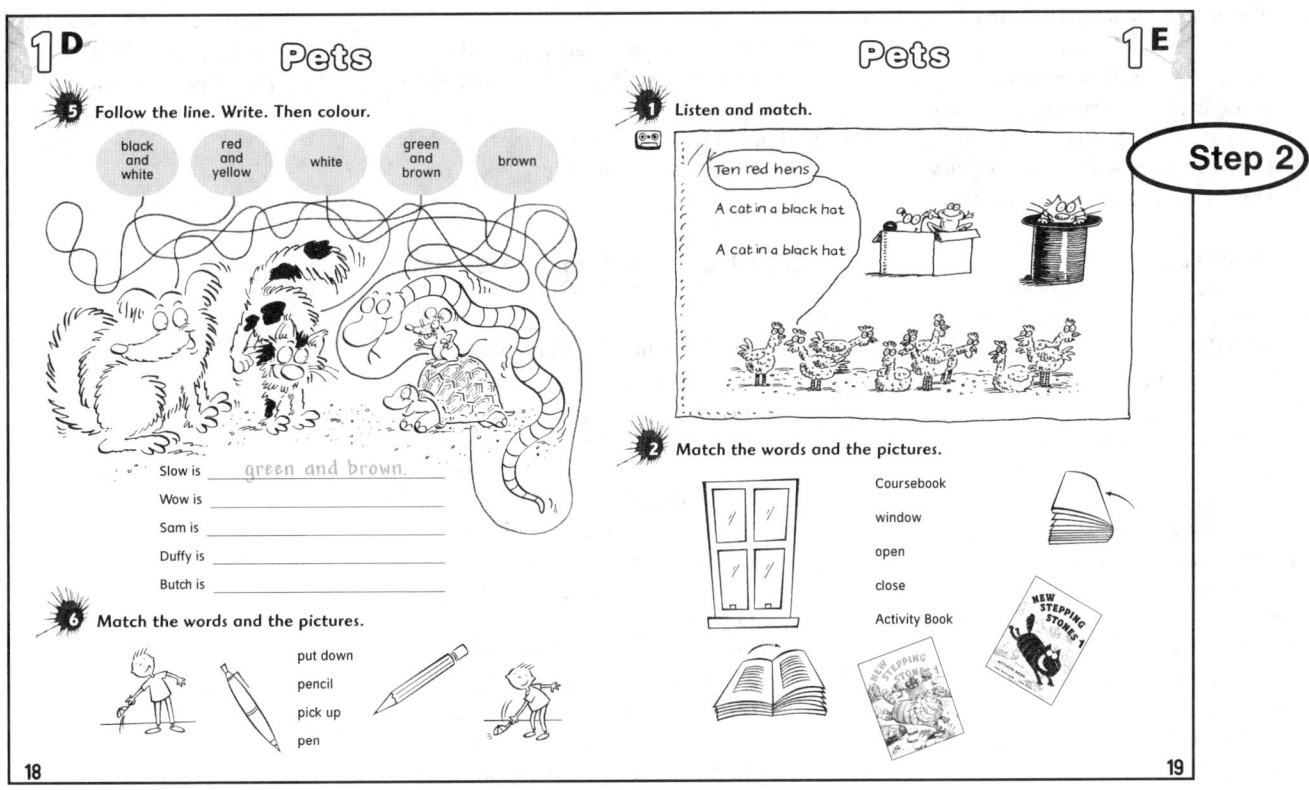

1ᴱ Lesson 2

Main Language Items			Resource File	Materials Needed
Who's this …?	Point to	window	pet	Story Bubbles 1 (see AB cut-outs section)
Is this your …?	Touch	floor	45	scissors (optional)
Look!	Pick up	chair		dice
What's this?	Turn around	door		counters
Open your Coursebook	Sit	boy		cassette/cassette player
Close your Activity Book	Stand	girl		

Step 1 Listening (Task)/Reading

a The cut-out *Story Bubbles 1* in the centre of the AB form the text to the introductory story on page 4 of the CB. Pupils should cut them out.

b Then turn to page 4 of the CB. Pupils work in pairs. Give them a few minutes to piece together any of the text they can, by placing the bubbles in the appropriate places.

c Play the whole text. Then play Part 1. Pupils check their answers to the first part and make changes where necessary. Give them two minutes to compare answers. Play Part 1 again. Check answers with the whole class.

d Do Parts 2 and 3 in the same way.

Tapescript:
PART 1
KEV: Hi Julie!
JULIE: Hello Kev!
JULIE: Who's this?
KEV: Kate.
JULIE: Hello Kate. I'm Julie.
KATE: Hello.
PART 2
KATE: Is this your dog?
JULIE: Yes, his name's Butch.
JULIE: What's this?
KATE: A box.
PART 3
KATE: Look! My snake, Sam.
SAM: Ssss!
JULIE: Aagh!
KATE: Goodbye!
JULIE: Bye!

Step 2 Words and pictures

a AB, page 19. Point to the pictures in activity 2. Use them to demonstrate the meaning of the following instructions.

b Say **Open your Coursebooks**, opening your own CB at the same time. Pupils copy you. Continue with **Close your Coursebooks, Open your Activity Books, Close your Activity Books**.

c Teach the word **window** by miming **Open the window**. Practise these new instructions at random. Do the actions yourself to demonstrate at first, then give the instructions without helping the pupils.

d Pupils draw lines connecting the words to the pictures in activity 2.

Step 3 The Stepping Stones Action Game 1

a Ideally the game should be played in pairs. Each pair needs one copy of the AB between them, open at page 20, a dice and two coloured counters. (If these items are unavailable small pieces of paper indicating each pupil's colour can replace the counters, and the numbers 1–6 can be written on each side of a six-sided pencil to replace the dice.)

b The object of the game is to make your way from the start to the finish.

c Players take it in turns to throw the dice and move around the board. When they land on a square they must read the instructions and tell their partner what to do.

d If their partner carries out the action correctly, it is then their turn to throw the dice and move. If they do not carry out the action correctly, the first player has another turn.

e Encourage pupils to use English as they play. They should count in English and use phrases such as 'Your/My turn.'

f In addition ask pupils questions about the game as you monitor their progress, e.g. '**Is it your turn?**', '**What's your colour?**'

g Play the game again.

1 Pets

STORY

Kate's Snake

Step 1

Pets

1. Listen and match.

   "Ten red hens"
   "A cat in a black hat"
   "A cat in a black hat"

2. Match the words and the pictures.

   Coursebook
   window
   open
   close
   Activity Book

Step 2

Pets

THE STEPPING STONES ACTION GAME 1

START
1. Point to the floor!
2. Touch a girl and point to the floor!
3. Point to a boy!
4. Sit on the floor!
5. Point to a chair!
6. Point to the door!
7. Turn around!
8. Touch the door and turn around!
9. Touch a girl!
10. Stand up and turn around!
11. Sit on the table!
12. Touch the floor!
13. Point to a girl!
14. Sit on the floor!
15. Touch a chair!
16. Point to a boy and touch the floor!
17. Stand up!
18. Stand on your chair!
19. Pick up a chair!
20. Touch a boy!
21. Point to the table!
22. Touch the door!
23. Stand up!
FINISH

Step 3

49

1E Lesson 3

Main Language Items			Resource File	Materials Needed
bird	rabbit	What's this?	19	
cat	rat	Is this a ...?	9	cassette/cassette player
dog	snake	Have you got a pet?	18	
fish	tortoise	Yes/No	18a	
hamster				
mouse				

This lesson provides preparation for the Project Lesson which follows. Pupils learn more words for animals and learn to ask their friends if they have got a pet.

Step 1   Find more words

a Say 'Open your Coursebooks at page 15' and look at the photos. Ask pupils in their L1 if any of them can see a picture of a pet they own.
b Play the tape and listen to the words while looking at the pictures.
c Play the tape again. This time pupils point to the pets as they hear the word.
d Play the tape again. Pupils listen and repeat the words.

Tapescript:
bird // cat // dog // fish // hamster // mouse // rabbit // rat // snake // tortoise

Step 2   Vocabulary games

a Game 1: Spell the name of one of the pets, e.g. 'D–O–G'. Pupils say the name of the pet, 'dog'. Repeat with other pets.
b Game 2: Stand at the front, clearly visible to the class, and silently 'say' the name of one of the pets. Pupils have to guess the pet, using the movement of your lips as their cue, and say the name of the pet aloud. Repeat with other pets.
c Game 3: Ask 'What's this?' and indicate the appropriate number of letters on the blackboard, e.g. – – – – – – – – . Pupils say the name of the pet (tortoise). Repeat with other pets.

Step 3   Find 10 pets

a Pupils look at the word square on AB page 21, find the names of the ten pets and circle them. Pupils can check back on page 15 of the CB if they are unsure of the names.
b Pupils tick the names of the pets on the list as they find them.

Step 4   Write

Pupils read the questions and write the answers in the spaces provided.

Step 5   Extension

a Ask various pupils 'Have you got a pet?' Pupils answer 'Yes' or 'No'.
b When pupils understand the question and can answer satisfactorily, encourage individuals to ask the person sitting next to them the same question.
c Set up a chain of such questions and responses going around the whole class, i.e. P1 asks P2 'Have you got a pet?' P2 answers 'Yes' or 'No', and then asks P3 'Have you got a pet?', etc.

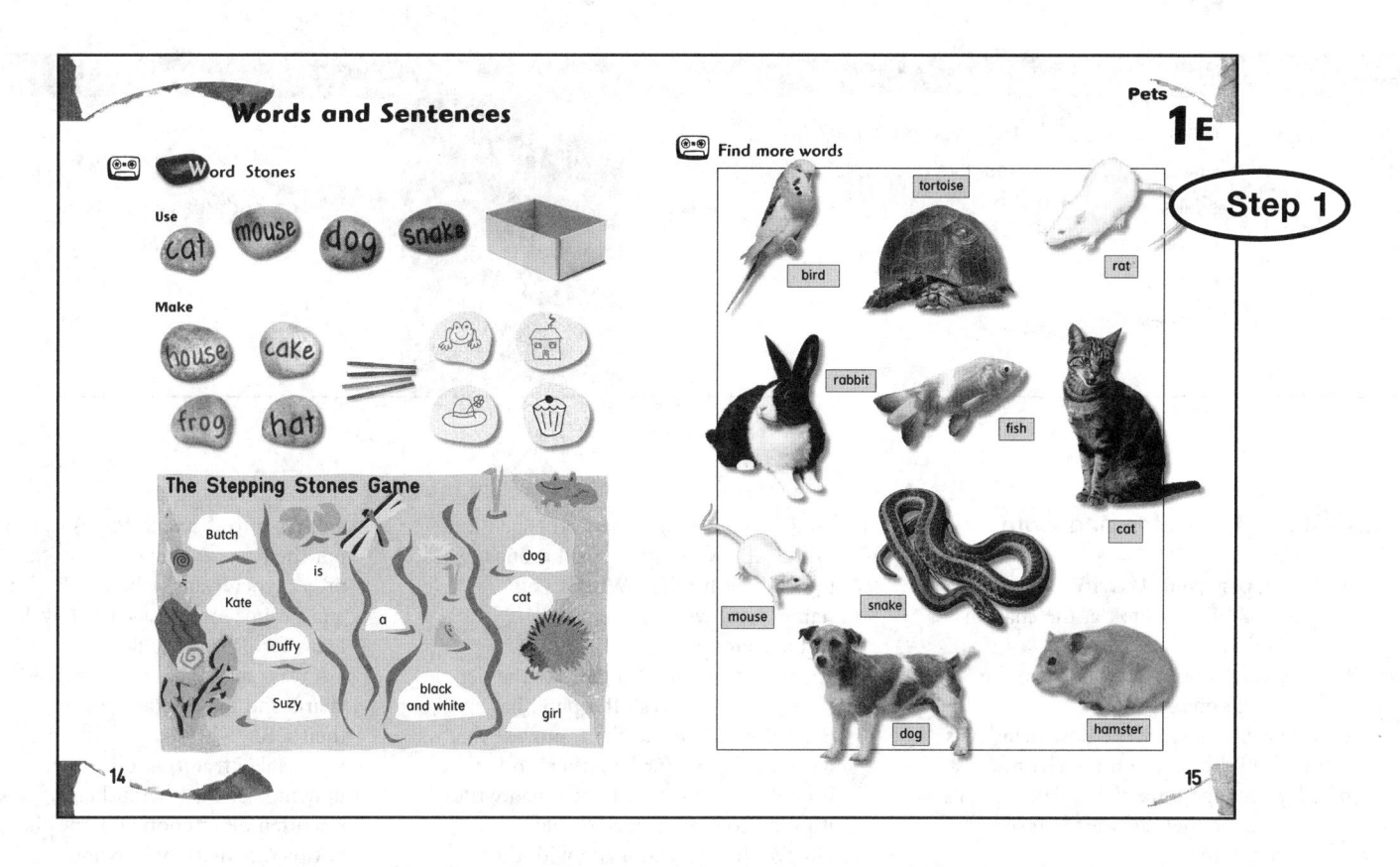

Words and Sentences

Word Stones

Use: cat, mouse, dog, snake

Make: house, cake, frog, hat

The Stepping Stones Game

Butch, is, dog, Kate, a, cat, Duffy, Suzy, black and white, girl

Pets 1E

Find more words

bird, tortoise, rat, rabbit, fish, cat, mouse, snake, dog, hamster

Step 1

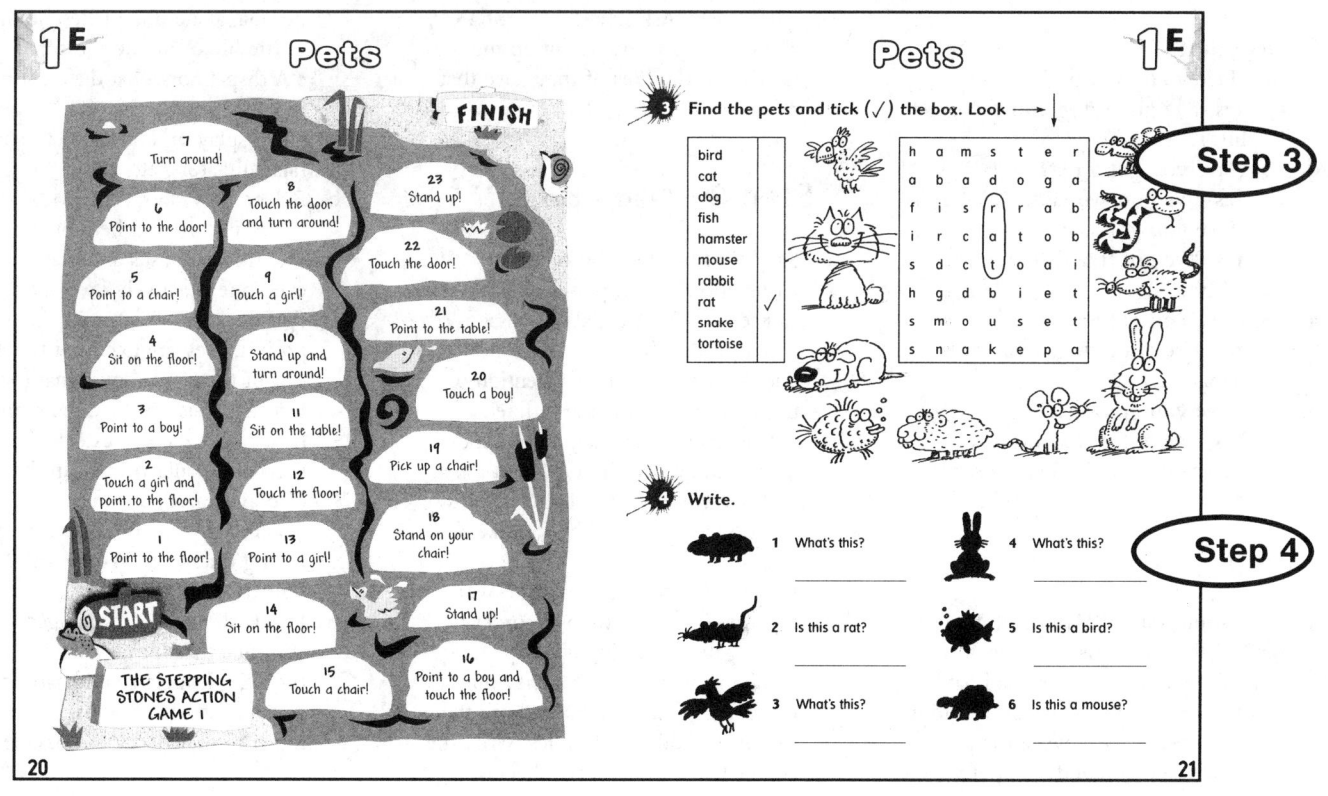

Pets 1E

THE STEPPING STONES ACTION GAME 1

START
1 Point to the floor!
2 Touch a girl and point to the floor!
3 Point to a boy!
4 Sit on the floor!
5 Point to a chair!
6 Point to the door!
7 Turn around!
8 Touch the door and turn around!
9 Touch a girl!
10 Stand up and turn around!
11 Sit on the table!
12 Touch the floor!
13 Point to a girl!
14 Sit on the floor!
15 Touch a chair!
16 Point to a boy and touch the floor!
17 Stand up!
18 Stand on your chair!
19 Pick up a chair!
20 Touch a boy!
21 Point to the table!
22 Touch the door!
23 Stand up!
FINISH

Pets 1E

3 Find the pets and tick (✓) the box. Look →↓

bird		h a m s t e r
cat		a b a d o g a
dog		f i s r r a b
fish		i r c a t o b
hamster		s d c t o a i
mouse		h g d b i e t
rabbit	✓	s m o u s e t
rat		s n a k e p a
snake		
tortoise		

Step 3

4 Write.

1 What's this? _____
2 Is this a rat? _____
3 What's this? _____
4 What's this? _____
5 Is this a bird? _____
6 Is this a mouse? _____

Step 4

51

1F Lesson 1 – Project

Main Language Items			Resource File	Materials Needed
bird	rabbit	Have you got a pet?		
cat	rat	Yes. I've got …/No.		
dog	snake		4	cassette/cassette player
fish	tortoise		38	project materials
hamster	*colours*			
mouse	*numbers*			

Step 1 Listen and write

a Say '**Open your Activity Books at page 22.**' Pupils look at the chart in activity 1.
b Play the five conversations pausing after each one.
c Pupils listen and write how many pets each child has got on the chart.
d Play the tape three times. Allow pupils to compare their answers before replaying the tape.

Tapescript:
1 A: Have you got a pet?
 C: Yes, I've got a dog and three birds.
2 A: Have you got a pet?
 C: Yes, I've got two cats.
3 A: Have you got a pet?
 C: Yes, I've got five fish and a rabbit.
4 A: Have you got a pet?
 C: Yes, I've got a dog, a cat and a hamster.
5 A: Have you got a pet?
 C: Yes, I've got three dogs, two cats, two rabbits and a hamster.

Step 2 Ask and answer

a Ask various pupils '**Have you got a pet?**' If the answer is '**Yes, I've got …**', write the pupil's name on the board and the name(s) of the pet(s) next to it. If the answer is '**No**', write the pupil's name on the board and '**No pet**'.
b Pupils complete the chart on page 22 of the AB. Working in small groups, they ask each other '**What's your name?**' and write the names.
c In their groups, pupils tick the appropriate column to indicate the pet, if the answer is '**Yes**'. If a pupil has a pet not listed on the chart, provide the name of the pet (or help them to look it up in a dictionary). Pupils then write it in the column headed '**other**'.
d Go over the questionnaire with the whole class. Ask '**Have you got a …?**' about each pet. Pupils put up their hands and say '**Yes**' if they have that pet.

Step 3 Start a project

a Say '**Look at page 16 of the Coursebook.**' Ask pupils what they can see and have a class discussion about pets in their L1. Ask them questions to focus their attention on the subject: What is the difference between a wild animal, a domestic animal and a pet? If you've got a pet, how are you responsible for it? How do you feed it, exercise it and keep it clean?
b Explain that they are going to work together in small groups in order to investigate something about pets. Give them a short list of ideas they might be interested in developing and ask them to suggest additional topics. Write the completed list on a large sheet of paper and fix it to the wall. Pupils can then put their names down next to the project they want to be involved in, and groups formed accordingly. Some ideas for projects could be:
• A class survey based on their AB charts and the display on page 16 of their CB.
• A display featuring photos or drawings of them with their pets, with a written description underneath.
• A picture diary of drawings or cut-out magazine photos describing a day in the life of my dog/cat/hamster etc.
• A display on what different pets like to eat.
• A display on unusual pets: snakes, rats, alligators, etc.
c Before they start, sit down with each group in turn and help pupils organise the different tasks and materials so that everyone is actively involved. Tell them that once they have completed their project, they are expected to tell the rest of the class about what they have learned. This can be done with the help of drawings, posters, photos, short texts and realia which can then be displayed around the room. Help them to talk about their work in English by asking questions. **What's this? Is this your dog, Maria?**
d Pupils should be encouraged to continue their project work outside their English class and share their discoveries with friends. Display as much of their work as possible.

Step 3

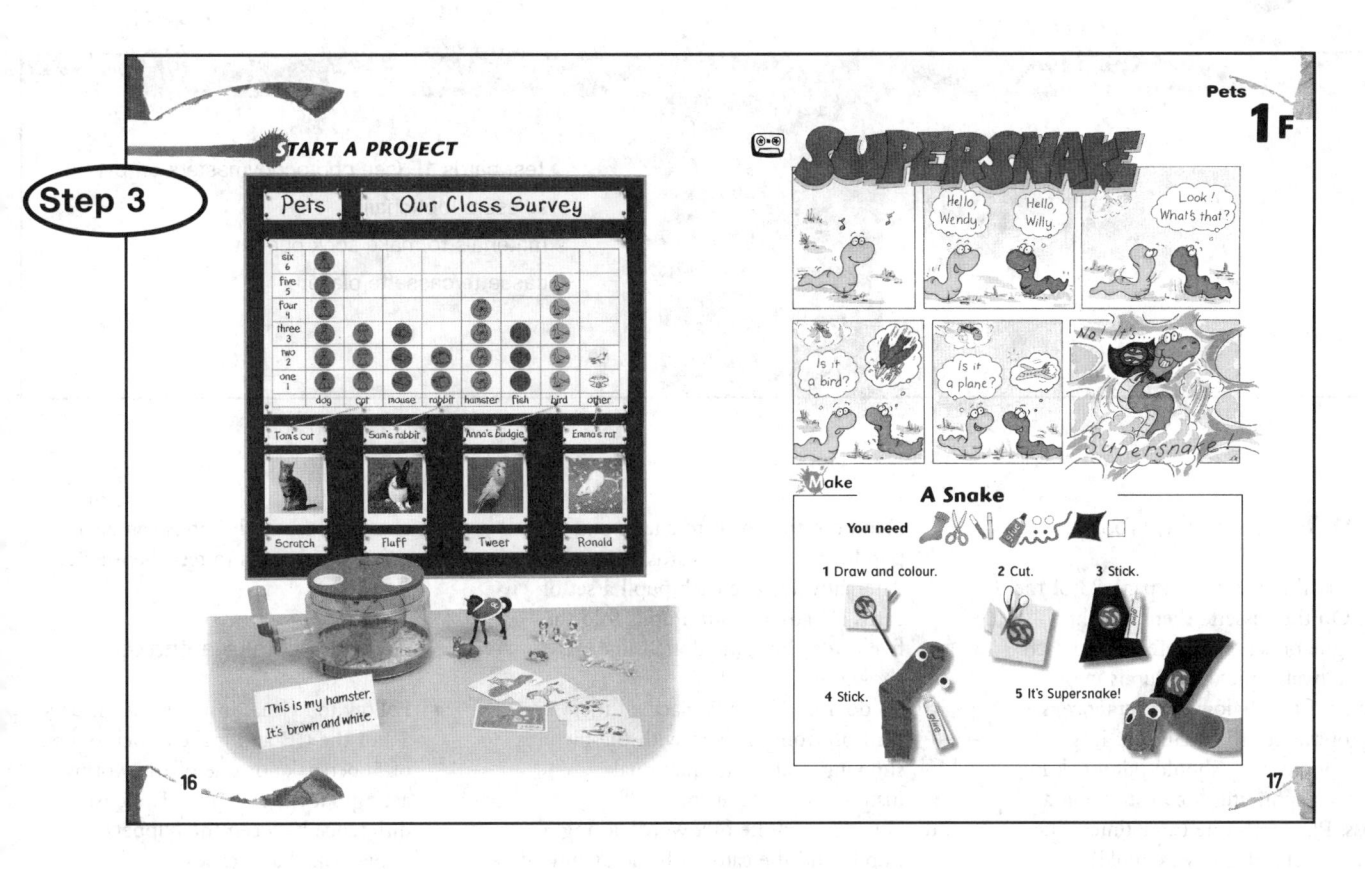

START A PROJECT

Pets | Our Class Survey

This is my hamster.
It's brown and white.

16

Pets

1F

SUPERSNAKE

Hello, Wendy
Hello, Willy
Look! What's that?
Is it a bird?
Is it a plane?
No, it's... Supersnake!

Make — **A Snake**

You need

1 Draw and colour.   2 Cut.   3 Stick.
4 Stick.   5 It's Supersnake!

17

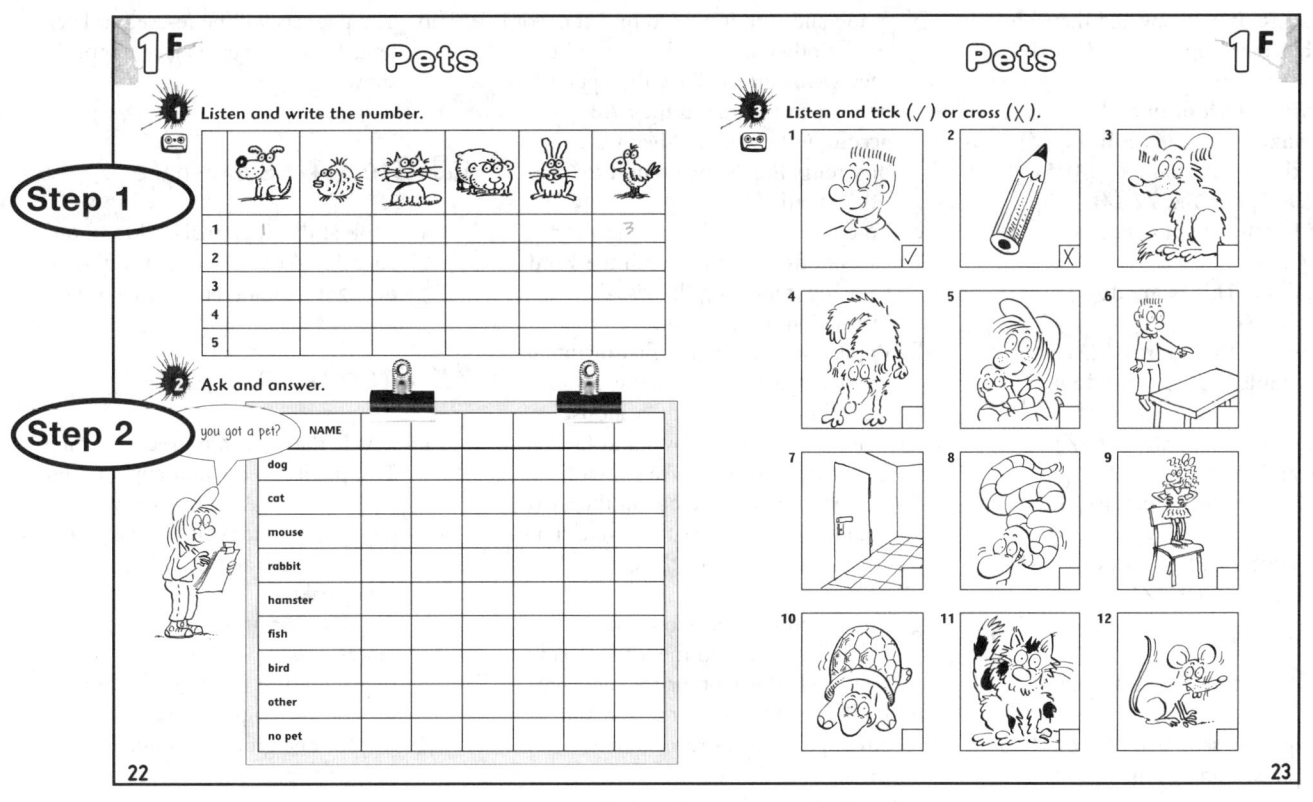

1F Pets

Step 1

1 Listen and write the number.

1	1					3
2						
3						
4						
5						

Step 2

2 Ask and answer.

you got a pet?

NAME		
dog		
cat		
mouse		
rabbit		
hamster		
fish		
bird		
other		
no pet		

22

Pets **1F**

3 Listen and tick (√) or cross (X).

1 ✓   2 X   3
4   5   6
7   8   9
10 11 12

23

53

1F Lesson 2 – Evaluation

Main Language Items	Resource File	Materials Needed
Is it a …? Make a … bird plane Supersnake puppet	33 49	Test cards 1F (see photocopymasters on p.174) scissors (optional) materials to make sock puppet cassette/cassette player

Step 1 Listening (Test)

a Look at the pictures on page 23 of the AB. On the cassette there is a short dialogue or sentence referring to each of the twelve pictures. Pupils must decide if the dialogue or sentence is appropriate to the picture. If it is appropriate, they should put a tick in the corresponding box; if not, put a cross. Play each one three times. The first two are given as examples.

b This exercise is a review and therefore is suitable as a simple test if desired.

Tapescript (with answers):
1 Is this Suzy? ~ No it's Bill. // (✓)
2 What's this? ~ A chair. // (✗)
3 Is this Duffy? ~ Yes. // (✗)
4 This is Butch. Butch is Julie's dog. // (✓)
5 I'm Kate. // This is my dog Butch. // (✗)
6 Bill, point to the door! // (✗)
7 Is this a table? ~ No it's a door. // (✓)
8 What's this? ~ A snake. // (✓)
9 Suzy, stand on a chair! // (✓)
10 Who's this? ~ Bill's tortoise, Slow. // (✓)
11 This is Duffy. Duffy is a dog // (✗)
12 Is this Wow? ~ Yes. (✓)

Step 2 Test yourself

a Photocopy one set of Test Cards 1F for each pupil (see photocopy master on TG page 174).

b Say 'Open your Activity Books at page 24 and look at the pictures.' Hand out the test card sheets and ask pupils to cut out the cards. Alternatively, give each pupil a set of cards already cut out. Pupils fold the five cards along the dotted line, as shown in the picture.

c To do Test 1, pupils place all their cards in front of them with the pictures showing, following the visual instruction. Demonstrate.

d You can read the first word, 'a dog'. Pupils find the card with the picture of a dog and turn it over to read the word on the other side, to check whether they were correct. They then put a tick or cross in the box in their AB according to whether they were right or wrong. Pupils then repeat for the other words.

e To do Test 2, pupils place all their cards in front of them with the words showing, following the visual instruction. Demonstrate.

f Pupils then look at the first picture in the list, which is of a mouse. Pupils must find the card with 'a mouse' written on it, turn it over and look at the picture to check. They then put a tick or a cross in the box in their AB according to whether they were right or wrong. Repeat for the other pictures.

g Pupils add up their scores out of five for each test to find the total. Finally, they circle the appropriate comment.

h Pupils can keep their test cards in an envelope to use as revision aids throughout the course.

i Pupils can further test themselves by placing the cards picture up, writing the word on a piece of paper and checking the card. Pupils can also create other cards to test themselves.

Step 3 Make a snake

a Follow the visual instructions on page 17 of the CB and make a sock puppet of Supersnake or one of the worms, for acting out the role play. The basic difference between the puppets is that Supersnake has a cape.

b The puppets will be re-used in later units for more Supersnake puppet shows.

Step 4 Supersnake

a Look at the Supersnake cartoon on page 17 of the CB. Listen to the dialogue, reading at the same time.

Step 5 Role play

a Divide the class into groups of three. Two pupils need worm puppets and one Supersnake. If pupils have no puppets, the index finger can be used for the worms and the whole arm for Supersnake.

b Play the tape again. This time pupils repeat.

c Pupils practise the puppet show without the help of the tape.

d Ask for one group to volunteer to act out the puppet show for the rest of the class.

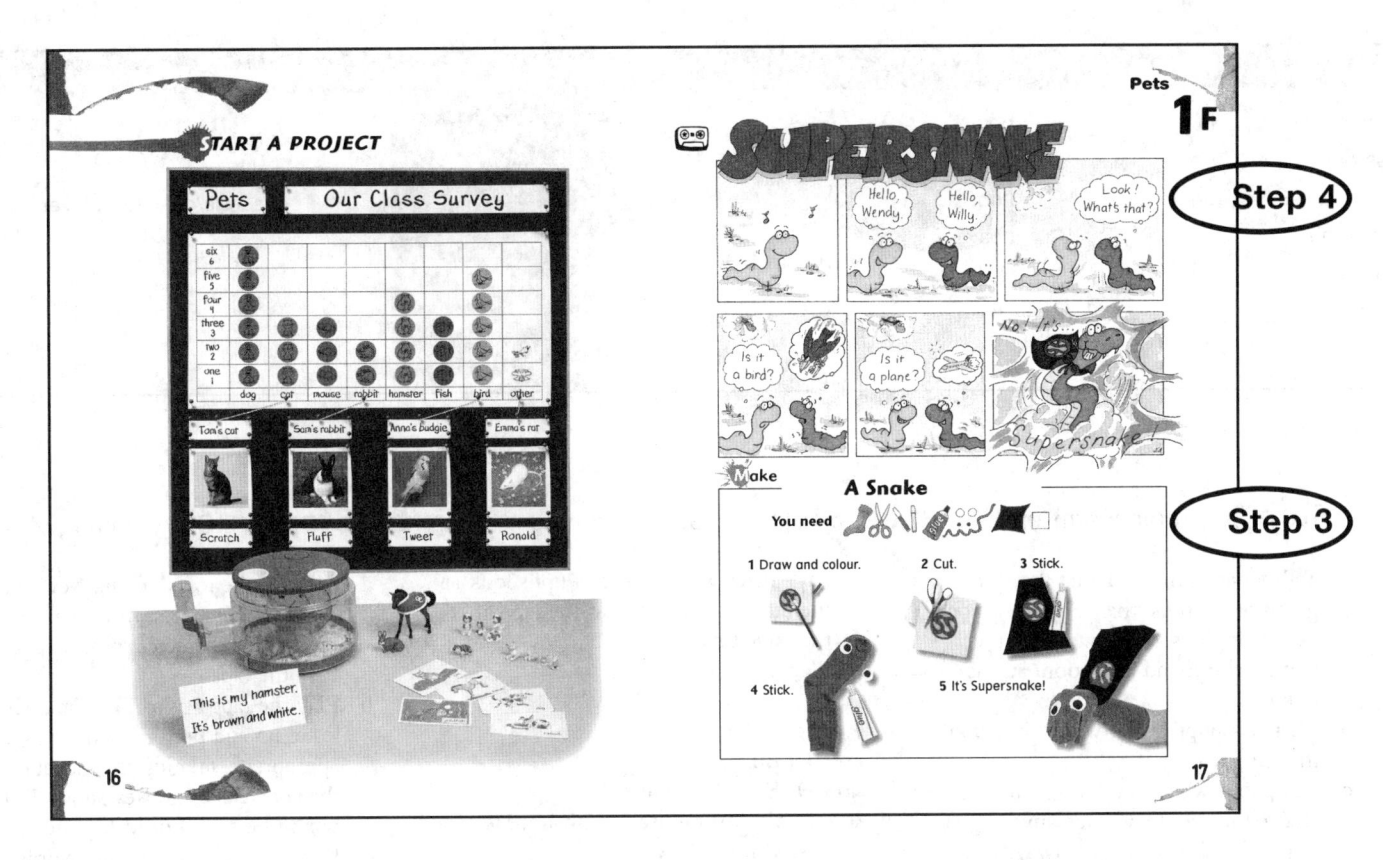

Pets 1F

START A PROJECT

Pets — Our Class Survey

Tom's cat — Scratch
Sam's rabbit — Fluff
Anna's budgie — Tweet
Emma's rat — Ronald

This is my hamster. It's brown and white.

Step 4

SUPERSNAKE

Hello, Wendy.
Hello, Willy.
Look! What's that?
Is it a bird?
Is it a plane?
No! It's... Supersnake!

Make A Snake

You need: ✂️ ✏️ 🖍️ paper

1 Draw and colour.
2 Cut.
3 Stick.
4 Stick.
5 It's Supersnake!

Step 3

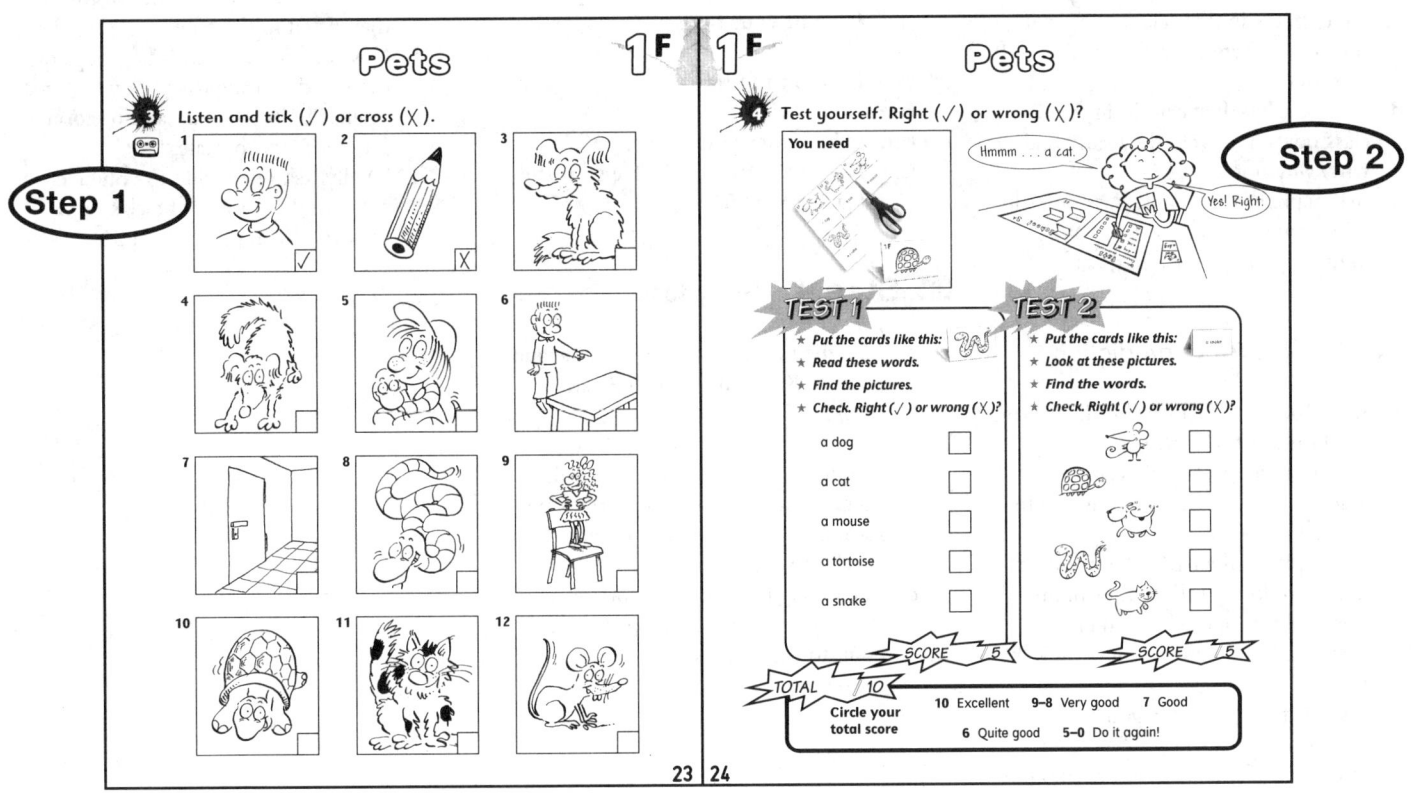

Step 1

3 Listen and tick (✓) or cross (✗).

1 ✓ 2 ✗ 3
4 5 6
7 8 9
10 11 12

4 Test yourself. Right (✓) or wrong (✗)?

You need ... Hmmm ... a cat. Yes! Right.

Step 2

TEST 1
★ Put the cards like this:
★ Read these words.
★ Find the pictures.
★ Check. Right (✓) or wrong (✗)?

a dog ☐
a cat ☐
a mouse ☐
a tortoise ☐
a snake ☐

SCORE /5

TEST 2
★ Put the cards like this:
★ Look at these pictures.
★ Find the words.
★ Check. Right (✓) or wrong (✗)?

☐ ☐ ☐ ☐ ☐

SCORE /5

TOTAL /10

Circle your total score:
10 Excellent 9–8 Very good 7 Good
6 Quite good 5–0 Do it again!

2 Story lesson

Main Language Items			Resource File	Materials Needed
school	in	box		
classroom	on	bag		
Hi!	under	floor	8a	cassette/cassette player
What's this?		chair	35	
Is he …?		table		
He isn't …				
's				

Step 1 Topic warm-up

a Tell pupils in their L1 that they are going to continue their English lessons by looking at school. Introduce the words **school** and **classroom** at this point.
b Then ask pupils what words they think they might learn.
c Ask pupils what they can see in their classroom. Can they name anything in English? Ask if there are always the same things in their classroom or if sometimes there are different things. If so, why?
d Discuss what they can do in their classrooms and what they can't and why/why not.
e Ask pupils if they think classrooms in other countries are the same. Why do they think they are/aren't?

Step 2 Story prediction

a Say '**Open your Coursebooks at page 18. Look at the pictures.**' Demonstrate what you mean by holding up your CB and pointing to the pictures.
b Ask pupils in their L1 what they can see. Who do they think the children are/might be and what is their relationship? Where do they think they are?
c Ask what they think is going to happen in the story.
d Ask pupils if they can see anything in the pictures they can name in English.

Step 3 Story listening

a Say '**Listen to the tape.**' Pupils look at the pictures and listen to the tape at the same time.
b Play the tape again.

Tapescript:
KEV: Hi Bill!
BILL: Hi Kev! … What's this?
KEV: Look! My mouse … Oh no! He isn't in the box!
BILL: Is he in your bag?
KEV: No.
BILL: Is he on the floor?
KEV: No.
BILL: Is he under your chair?
KEV: No … Oh no! Look! He's on the teacher's table!

Step 4 Story task

a Play the first part of the dialogue and point to Kev and Bill as they are speaking.
b Play the complete story on tape again and demonstrate the task to pupils. Point to each character in turn as he is speaking. Pupils listen to the tape and watch the demonstration.
c Then play the complete story again. Pupils listen, look at the pictures and point to each character in turn as he is speaking.

Step 4 Story mime

a Allocate the roles of Bill, Kev and Wow to volunteers. Ask them to stand up as their character speaks/appears. Play the tape.
b Play the tape again. This time pupils stand up and perform actions as appropriate, miming the movements of the characters, e.g. Kev shows Bill the box as he says '**Look! My mouse.**' Pupils can also mouth the words as they listen to the tape.
c Now divide the class into groups of three and allocate roles. Play the tape again. Pupils stand up and perform actions as appropriate.
d Finally, ask one group to volunteer to come to the front of the class and perform, listening to the tape.

2 School

STORY

Where's Wow?

Step 2

Step 3

Step 4

2A Lesson 1

Main Language Items		Resource File	Materials Needed
What's this?	pencil		
Is this a ...?	book		
It's a ...	chair	8a	cassette/cassette player
Don't ...?	table		
Open ...	bag		
Close ...	window		

Step 1 Action Game

a Briefly revise a variety of instructions used to date:

Point to ...	a boy/a girl
Touch ...	the floor
Stand on ...	a chair
Sit on ...	a/the table
Stand up!	the door
Turn around!	pen/pencil
Walk to ...	Activity Book
Pick up/Put down ...	Coursebook
Open/Close your ...	window

b Introduce 'Don't' as a prefix to some of these instructions, and demonstrate the meaning accordingly, e.g. 'Don't point to the door.'

c Practise with the whole class until they understand the meaning of 'Don't'.

d Explain that you are going to play a game. When you give an instruction the whole class should act it out. When you say 'Don't' the instruction should be ignored. Pupils who carry out the instruction when you say 'Don't' must leave the game. The last player remaining is the winner. Keep the action very brisk. If instructions are not obeyed immediately the pupils must also leave the game.

Step 2 Presentation

a Say 'Open your Coursebooks at page 18 and look at the pictures.' Play the whole story on tape.

b Then say 'Open your Coursebooks at page 20' and ask pupils to look at the first two frames of the story. Ask pupils to tell you in their L1 what the language in the speech bubbles means.

c Play the story extract and point to the characters.

d Divide the class into pairs. All pairs work simultaneously. Play the tape again. P1 repeats Kev's words and P2 repeats Bill's words.

e Change roles and repeat the procedure.

Tapescript:
KEV: Hi Bill!
BILL: Hi Kev! ... What's this?

Step 3 Pair work

a Divide the class into pairs, with one book between each pair, open at page 20. Say 'Cover the words. Look at the pictures.' All pairs work simultaneously.

b Pupils repeat after the tape. P1 repeats the questions, pointing at the appropriate picture. P2 repeats the answers. Repeat four times, changing roles.

c Then pupils ask and answer the questions without the help of the tape. Pupils asking the questions may use the words as prompts and must check their partners' answers.

d Change roles and repeat the procedure.

Step 4 Presentation

a Hold up or point to an object in the classroom such as a pencil, book, bag, table, etc. Ask 'Is this a pencil?' Pupils answer 'Yes' or 'No it's a ...' Write an example on the blackboard.

b Divide the class into pairs, with one CB between each pair open at page 20. P1 points to a picture and asks 'Is this a ...?' P2 answers 'Yes' or 'No, it's a ...'

c Change roles and repeat the procedure.

Step 5 Draw and write

a Say 'Open your Activity Books at page 25.' Look at activity 1. Pupils join the dots. Then they read the questions and write the answer in the spaces provided.

b Encourage pupils to check each other's answers when they have finished.

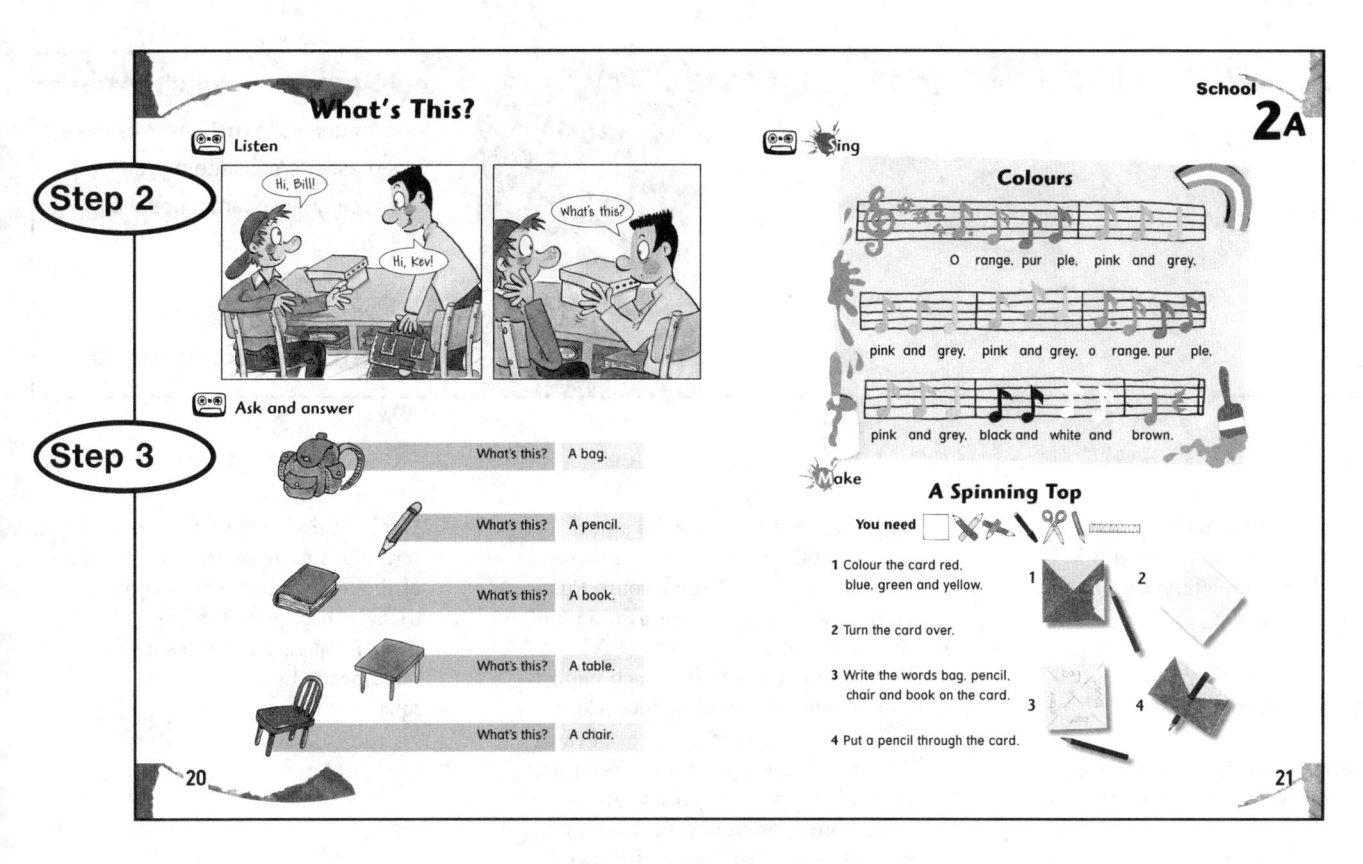

What's This?

Listen

> Hi, Bill!
> Hi, Kev!
> What's this?

Step 2

Ask and answer

Step 3

(bag)	What's this?	A bag.
(pencil)	What's this?	A pencil.
(book)	What's this?	A book.
(table)	What's this?	A table.
(chair)	What's this?	A chair.

School **2A**

Sing

Colours

O range, pur ple, pink and grey,

pink and grey, pink and grey, o range, pur ple,

pink and grey, black and white and brown.

Make

A Spinning Top

You need: [card] [crayons] [pencil] [scissors] [ruler]

1 Colour the card red, blue, green and yellow.

2 Turn the card over.

3 Write the words bag, pencil, chair and book on the card.

4 Put a pencil through the card.

20   21

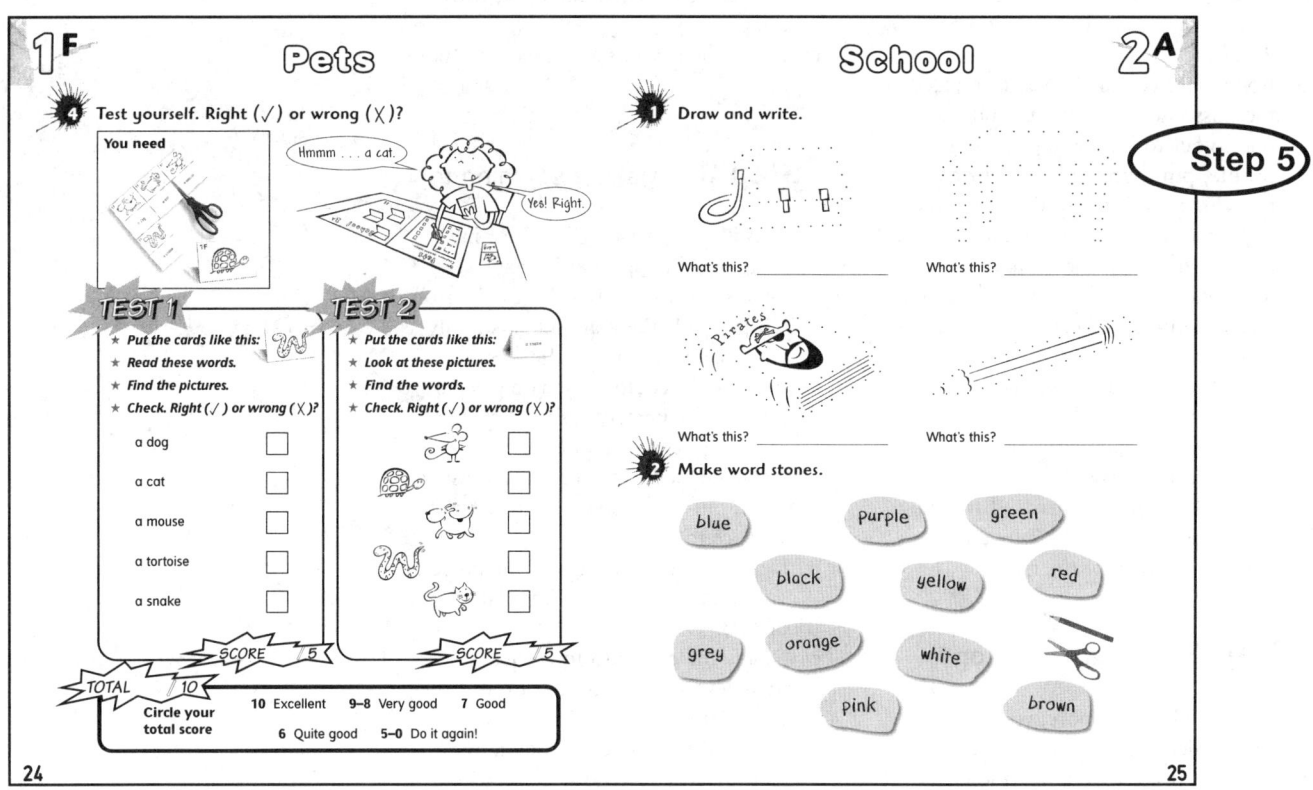

1F   Pets

Test yourself. Right (✓) or wrong (✗)?

You need: [scissors, cards]

> Hmmm ... a cat.
> Yes! Right.

TEST 1
- ★ Put the cards like this:
- ★ Read these words.
- ★ Find the pictures.
- ★ Check. Right (✓) or wrong (✗)?

- a dog ☐
- a cat ☐
- a mouse ☐
- a tortoise ☐
- a snake ☐

SCORE / 5

TEST 2
- ★ Put the cards like this:
- ★ Look at these pictures.
- ★ Find the words.
- ★ Check. Right (✓) or wrong (✗)?

- (mouse) ☐
- (tortoise) ☐
- (dog) ☐
- (snake) ☐
- (cat) ☐

SCORE / 5

TOTAL / 10

Circle your total score

10 Excellent   9–8 Very good   7 Good
6 Quite good   5–0 Do it again!

School   2A

Draw and write.

What's this? _____   What's this? _____

What's this? _____   What's this? _____

Step 5

Make word stones.

blue   purple   green
black   yellow   red
grey   orange   white
pink   brown

24   25

59

2A Lesson 2

Main Language Items		Resource File	Materials Needed
colours: orange purple pink grey	spinning top	29 39	materials to make word stones cassette/cassette player colour flashcards (optional) card scissors coloured pencils pencil/match/cocktail sticks

The song and the making activities may take longer than you think. Be prepared to complete Step 3 in the following lesson.

Step 1   Song

This is the second part of the song on page 3 of the CB and introduces four new colours.

a Listen to the song on the tape. Follow with the words and pictures on page 21 of the CB.
b If you have colour flashcards, divide the class into seven groups and assign one colour to each group (**orange, purple, pink, grey, black, white** or **brown**). Then listen to the song. The pupils in each group stand and hold up their flashcards as their colour is mentioned. Then they sit down again.
c Listen to the song again with the book closed.
d Then listen again line by line, and repeat the words.
e Now play the song again and sing along with the tape.
f Finally listen to both parts of the song. Try to sing parts 1 and 2 together, without the help of the tape.

Step 2   Make word stones

a Pupils add eleven more word stones to their collection.
b Say 'Open your Activity Books at page 25.' Point to the word stones. Check pupils are familiar with their meaning: say one of the colours. Pupils point to an object in the classroom of the same colour.
c To make the word stones, each pupil requires eleven 'stones' (either real stones, or stone-shaped pieces of card as before). Pupils write one word (**red, blue, black, purple, yellow, green, white, pink, orange, grey, brown**) on each stone in felt-tip pen, as shown in the pictures.
d Pupils then store their stones for future use.

Step 3   Make a spinning top

This is a teacher-led Task Reading exercise. Although pupils may understand the written instructions on CB page 21, these are intended only as reinforcement at this stage.

a Each pupil requires a square piece of card, approximately 10 x 10 cm. (Although paper can be used, it is not recommended.) You may find it useful to cut out and prepare the card in advance for pupils.
b Demonstrate each stage of the process on the blackboard or with a large sheet of card.
c Divide the card into four equal triangles by drawing lines from corner to corner.
d Colour the triangles as shown: red, blue, green and yellow.
e Similarly, divide the reverse side of the card into four triangles and write one of the following words in each triangle: **bag**, **pencil**, **book** and **chair**.
f Push a match, a cocktail stick or a small pencil through the centre of the square.

What's This?

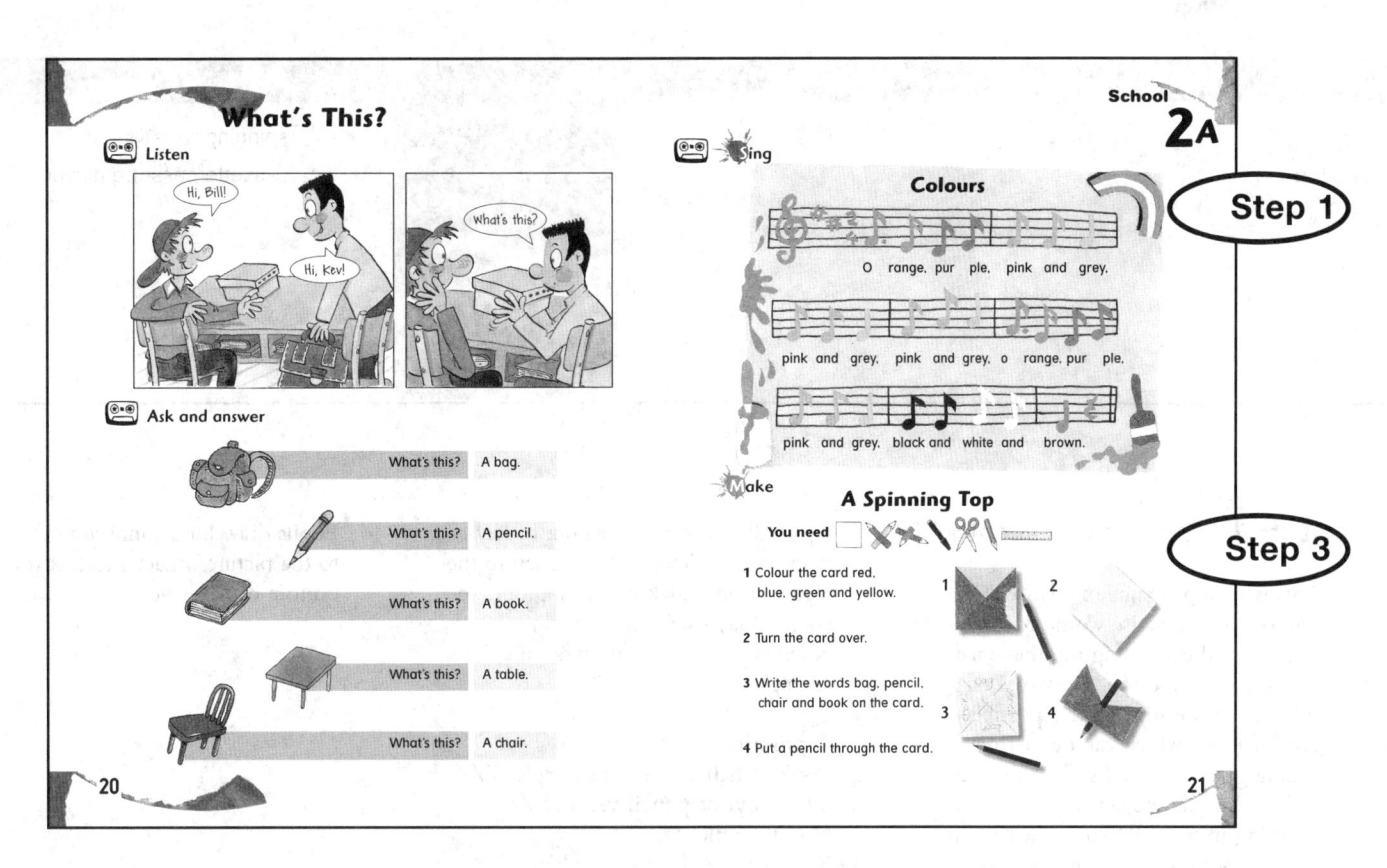

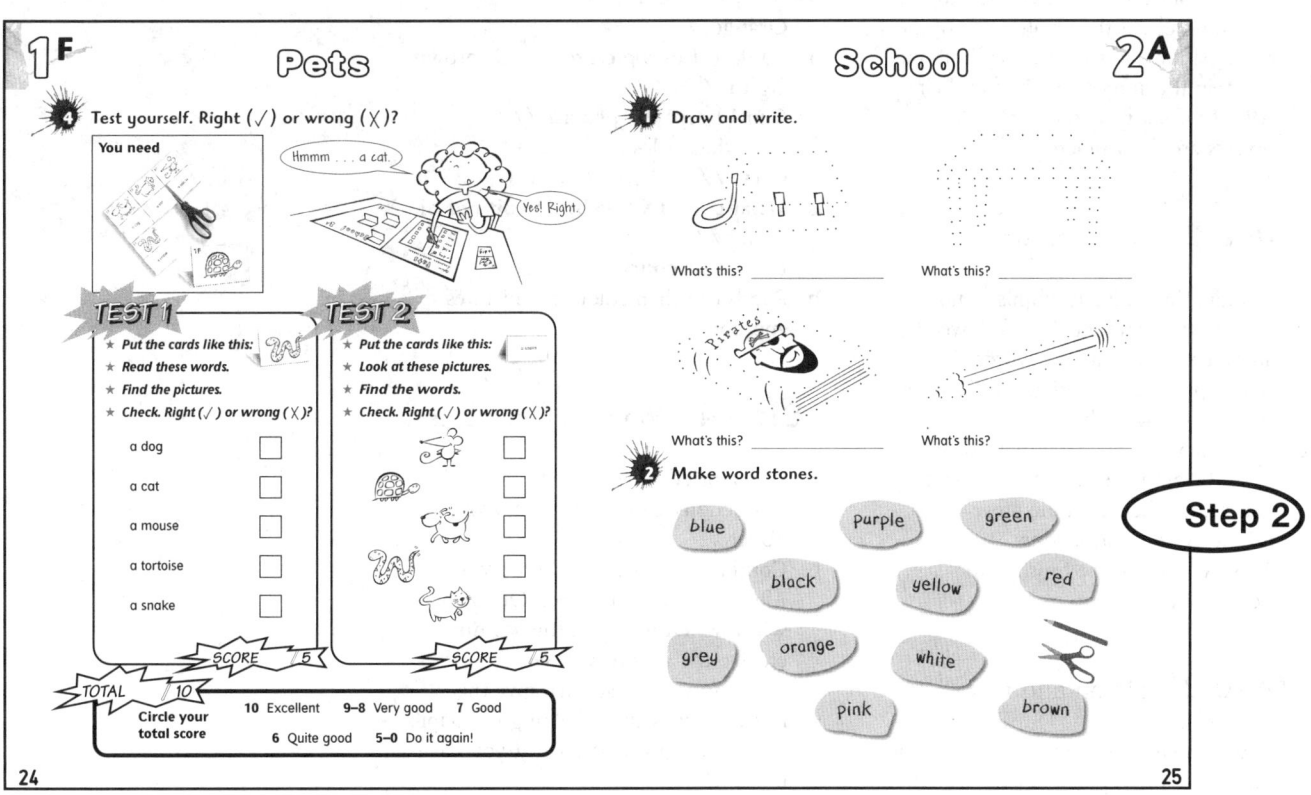

Listen

Hi, Bill! / *Hi, Kev!* / *What's this?*

Ask and answer

What's this? A bag.
What's this? A pencil.
What's this? A book.
What's this? A table.
What's this? A chair.

School 2A

Sing

Colours

O range, pur ple, pink and grey,
pink and grey, pink and grey, o range, pur ple,
pink and grey, black and white and brown.

Make

A Spinning Top

You need ...

1 Colour the card red, blue, green and yellow.
2 Turn the card over.
3 Write the words bag, pencil, chair and book on the card.
4 Put a pencil through the card.

Step 1

Step 3

1F Pets

4 Test yourself. Right (✓) or wrong (✗)?

You need / *Hmmm ... a cat.* / *Yes! Right.*

TEST 1
★ Put the cards like this:
★ Read these words.
★ Find the pictures.
★ Check. Right (✓) or wrong (✗)?

- a dog
- a cat
- a mouse
- a tortoise
- a snake

SCORE /5

TEST 2
★ Put the cards like this:
★ Look at these pictures.
★ Find the words.
★ Check. Right (✓) or wrong (✗)?

SCORE /5

TOTAL /10
Circle your total score

10 Excellent   9–8 Very good   7 Good
6 Quite good   5–0 Do it again!

School 2A

1 Draw and write.

What's this? _____   What's this? _____

What's this? _____   What's this? _____

2 Make word stones.

blue, purple, green, black, yellow, red, grey, orange, white, pink, brown

Step 2

2A Lesson 3

Main Language Items	Resource File	Materials Needed
spin spinning top	24	spinning tops cassette/cassette player

Step 1 Spin, match and tick

a This is a simple game of chance. The purpose is to practise word order. Pupils use the spinning top they made in the previous lesson. Activity 3 on page 26 of the AB lists five possible combinations which can occur from spinning the coloured side of the top followed by the object side.

b Working in pairs, P1 spins their top to get a colour then P2 spins their top to get an object. If they match one of the combinations on the list, they both put a tick in the appropriate box in their ABs. The first pair to tick all five objects are the winners.

Step 2 Spin and write

a Working individually, pupils again use their tops to spin a colour followed by an object, and write the words in the spaces provided in activity 4. Complete sentences 2–4 in this way.

b Pupils have now created their own Task Reading exercise and should draw and colour their own pictures following the instructions.

c This exercise can be finished for homework.

Step 3 Listen and tick

a Pupils listen to the tape and look at the pictures at the top of AB page 27. The tape will tell them the colour of key items in the pictures. They listen to the tape and put a tick by the appropriate colour. Play each one three times. Number 1 has been given as an example.

Tapescript:
1 Look at Bill's table. It's purple. //
2 Suzy, is your pencil yellow? //
 No, it's pink. //
3 Kate, what colour's your bag? //
 Orange. //
4 Look at Kev's picture. It's all brown. Ughh! //
5 Can I borrow a pencil? //
 Yes, what colour? //
 Grey. //
6 What colour's this bird? Is it red or pink? //
 It's red of course. //

b Pupils can then colour the pictures appropriately.

Step 4 Words and pictures

a Play a brief mime game to revise the instructions **Open**, **Point to**, and **Touch**.

b Continue, introducing the word **Don't**. Alternate rapidly between **Open the window**, **Don't open the window**, etc. Do the actions yourself to demonstrate at first, then give the instructions without helping the pupils.

c Repeat for girls and boys, if you have a mixed class.

d Pupils draw lines connecting the words to the pictures in activity 6 at the bottom of AB page 27.

2A School

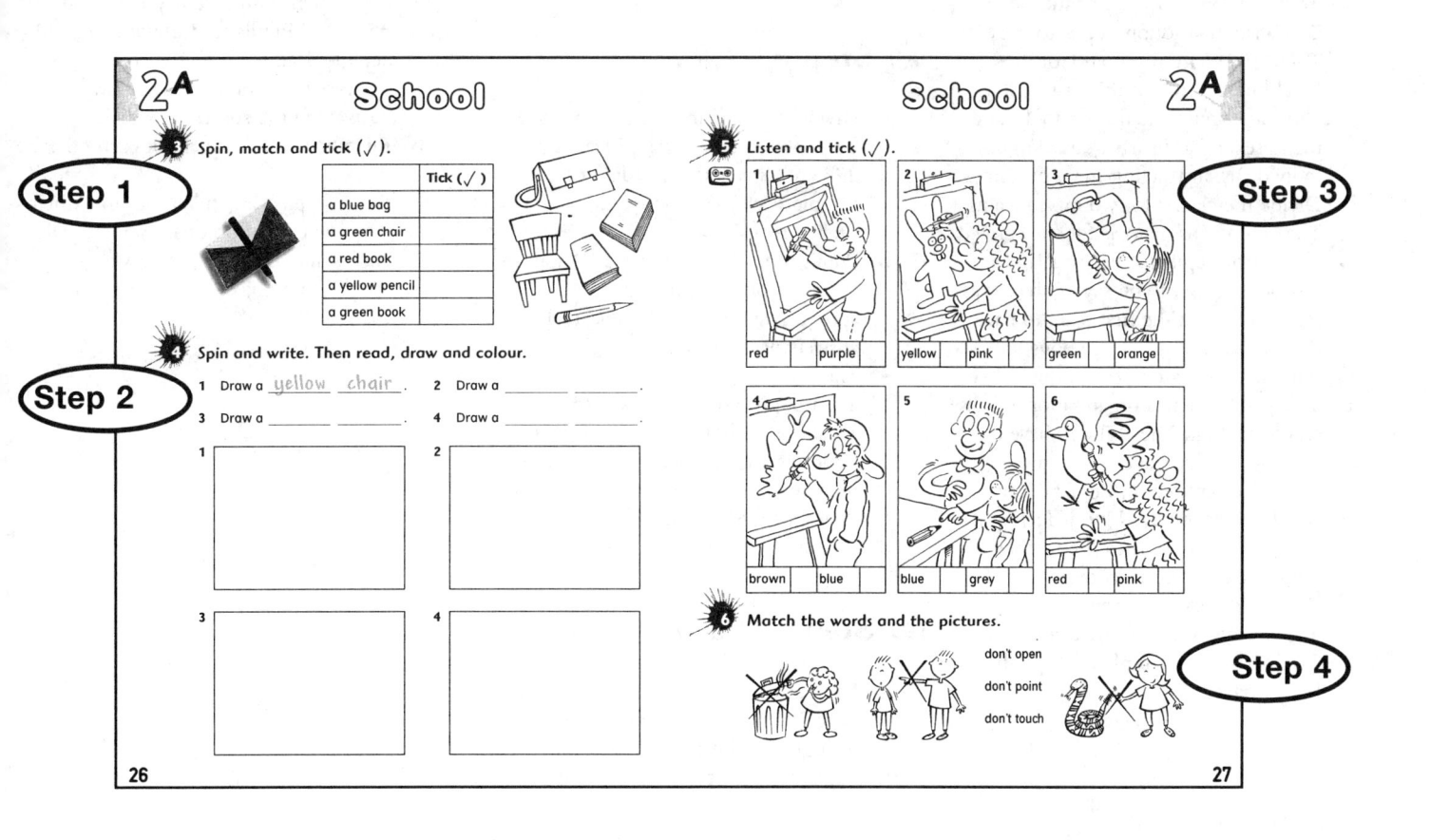

Step 1

3 Spin, match and tick (✓).

	Tick (✓)
a blue bag	
a green chair	
a red book	
a yellow pencil	
a green book	

Step 2

4 Spin and write. Then read, draw and colour.

1 Draw a <u>yellow chair</u>.
2 Draw a _____ _____.
3 Draw a _____ _____.
4 Draw a _____ _____.

1

2

3

4

26

2A School

Step 3

5 Listen and tick (✓).

| 1 red | purple | 2 yellow | pink | 3 green | orange |
| 4 brown | blue | 5 blue | grey | 6 red | pink |

6 Match the words and the pictures.

don't open
don't point
don't touch

Step 4

27

63

2B Lesson 1

Main Language Items			Resource File	Materials Needed
What is it?	pen	chalk	8a	
What's this?	rubber		17	cassette/cassette player
It's a …	ruler		22	
It isn't a …	blackboard			
Write …	pencil case			
No, it isn't …	pencil sharpener			

Step 1 Action Game

a Motion four pupils to the front. Use instructions **Stand up! Walk! Stop! Turn around!** Introduce the words **chalk** and **blackboard** using the instructions **Point to …** and **Touch …** Demonstrate and pupils copy. Then bring in the whole class.

b Then work with the four pupils at the front. Say '**Pick up the chalk.**' Demonstrate. Motion pupils to copy. Then say '**Write number 1 on the blackboard.**' Repeat this instruction with other numbers from 1 to 12 and then use similar instructions with other individuals, instructing them by name.

c Divide the class into two mixed teams.

d The aim of this game is for the correct number of pupils to carry out a given instruction, e.g. if you say '**Three boys stand up,**' then the first team to have three boys and only three boys standing, wins a point.

e This game requires organisational skills and teamwork. The children have the language at this stage to organise themselves entirely in English. This should be encouraged by deducting a point if pupils resort to the mother tongue. Sample instructions:
Five girls pick up a pencil.
Three boys point to the door.
Two girls write number 11 on the blackboard.

Step 2 Presentation

a Say '**Open your Coursebooks at page 22.**' Hold your book up for the class. Very quickly ask questions about the pictures. Use '**Who's this? What's this? Is this …?**'

b Play the tape. Pupils follow the dialogue looking at the pictures at the same time.

Step 3 Pair work

a Divide the class into pairs. Only one book between each pair, open at page 22. Say '**Cover the words. Look at the pictures.**' All pairs work simultaneously.

b Pupils repeat after the tape. P1 repeats the questions, pointing at the appropriate pictures. P2 repeats the answers. Repeat four times, changing roles.

c Then pupils ask and answer the questions without the help of the tape. Pupils asking the questions may use the words as prompts and must check their partners' answers.

d Change roles and repeat this procedure.

Step 4 Pair work

a Look at the pictures at the top of CB page 23 and listen to the model dialogue on the tape.

b Pupils work in pairs, asking and answering similar questions about the pictures. They may not produce exactly the same language as the model dialogue. This is perfectly acceptable, providing their attempts are meaningful.

Step 5 Write

a Say '**Open your Activity Books at page 28.**' Pupils read the questions in activity 1 and choose the correct answers from the boxes. They write the answers in the spaces provided.

b Encourage pupils to check each other's work.

c Faster pupils can attempt to draw their own pictures of objects from unusual angles and ask their partners to identify the object.

Step 2

What Is It?

🔊 Listen

"Look at number one. What is it?"
"It's a pencil."
"It's a pen!"
"It's a pencil!" "It's a pen!"
"It isn't a pencil or a pen. It's a ruler."

Step 3

🔊 Ask and answer

	What's this?	A pen.
	What's this?	A rubber.
	What's this?	A ruler.
	What's this?	A pencil sharpener.
	What's this?	A pencil case.

22

Step 4

School
2B

🔊 Ask and answer

What's number 1?
I don't know.
Is it a door?
Oh, yes!

1 2 3
4 5 6

💥 Play

The Blackboard Game

START Grey — START Pink
THROW THE DICE AGAIN
THROW THE DICE AGAIN
START Orange — START Purple

23

2B   School

Step 5

✏️ 1 Write.

A pencil.   A table.   No, it's a pencil sharpener.   Yes.

Is this a ruler? _____

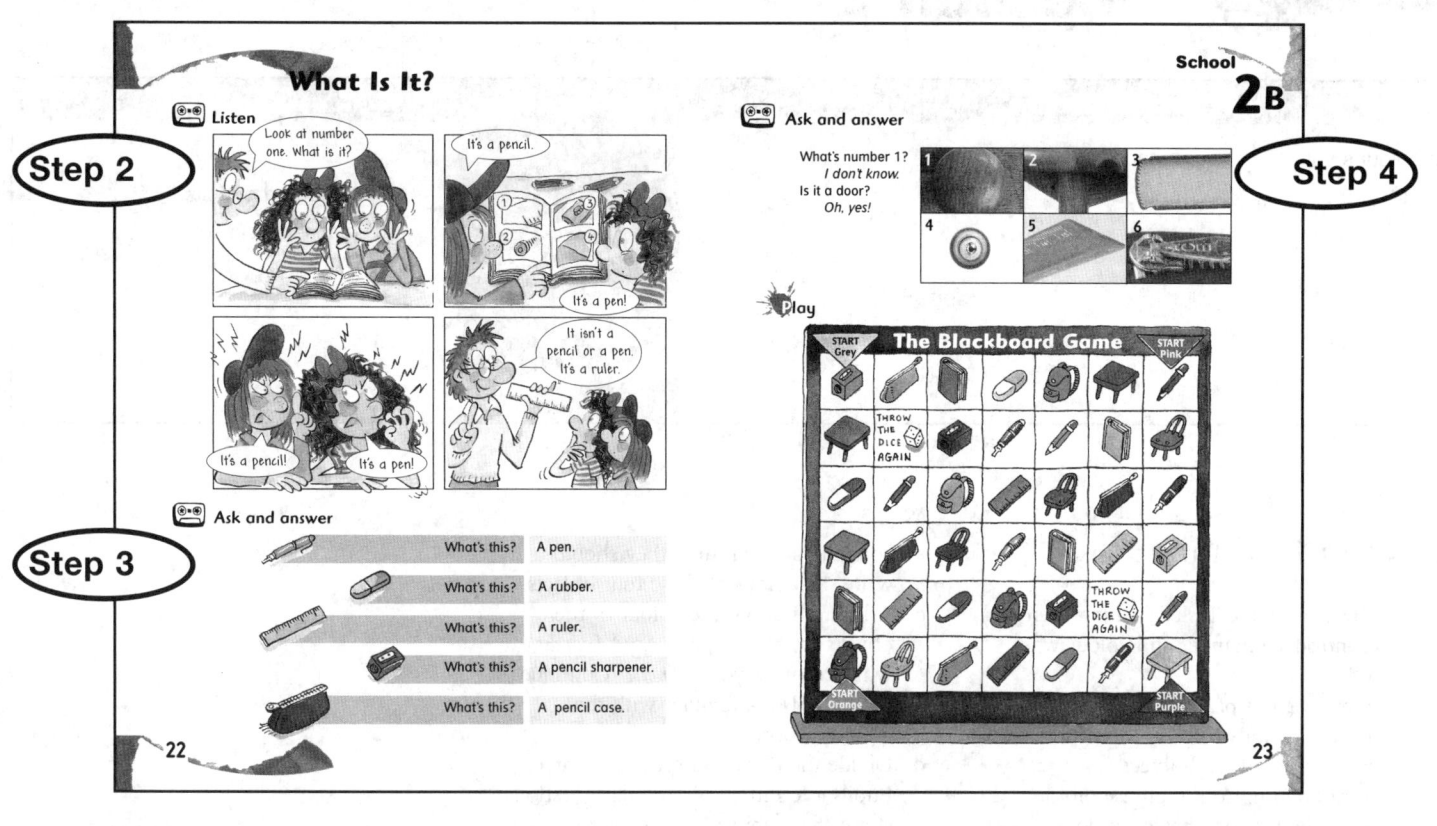

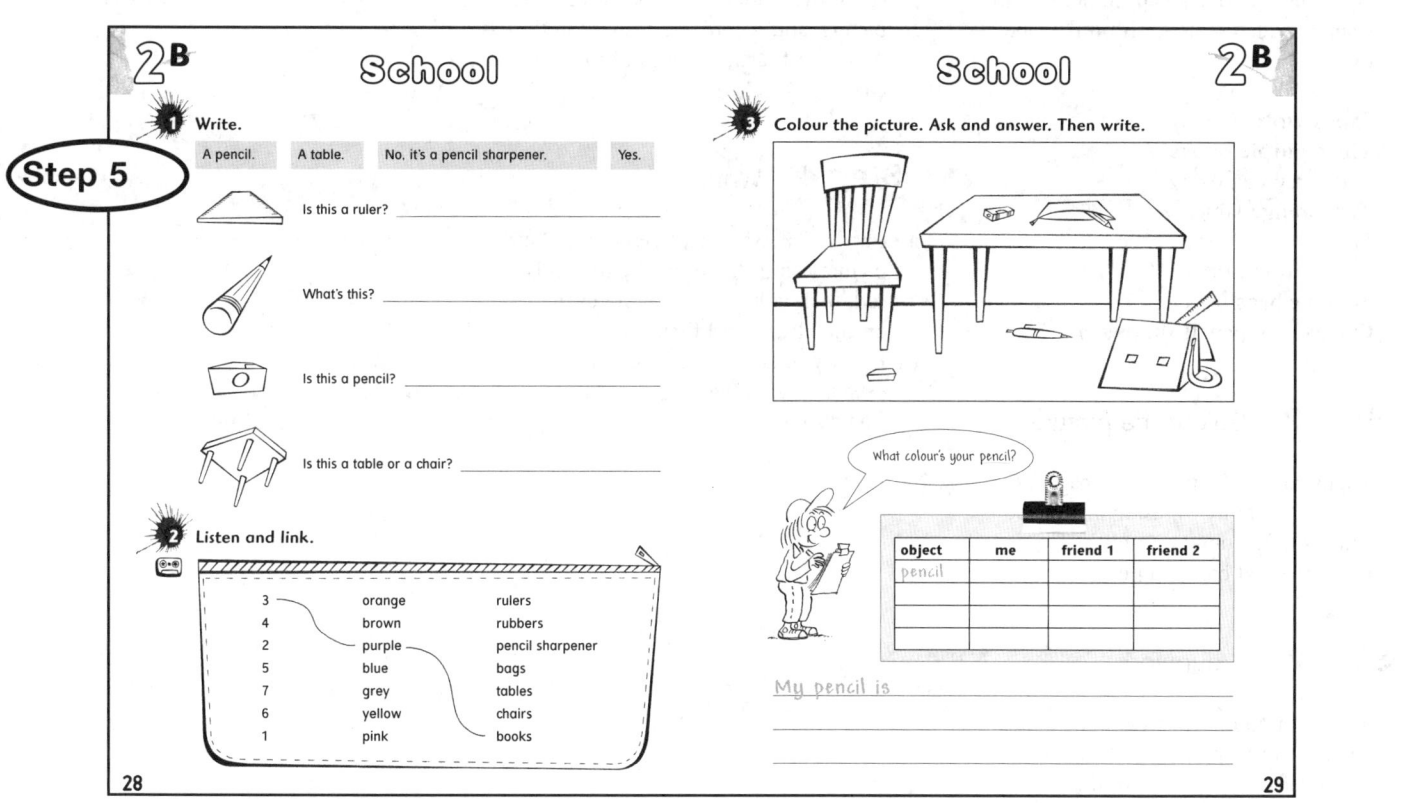

What's this? _____

Is this a pencil? _____

Is this a table or a chair? _____

💥 2 Listen and link.

3	orange	rulers
4	brown	rubbers
2	purple	pencil sharpener
5	blue	bags
7	grey	tables
6	yellow	chairs
1	pink	books

28

School   2B

💥 3 Colour the picture. Ask and answer. Then write.

"What colour's your pencil?"

object	me	friend 1	friend 2
pencil			

My pencil is _____
_____
_____

29

65

2B Lesson 2

Main Language Items		Resource File	Materials Needed
What colour's your ...?	friend	16	coloured pencils
My ... is ...	object	16a	cassette/cassette player

Step 1   Listen and link

This is a simple Task Listening exercise to introduce number and colour word order.

a Pupils look at page 28 of the AB. Play the tape. Pupils connect the appropriate number, colour and object corresponding to the phrase on the tape. The first one has been done as an example. Each sentence is on the tape twice.

Tapescript:
Three purple books. //
Four grey chairs. //
Two orange tables. //
Five pink rubbers. //
Seven brown rulers. //
Six blue bags. //
One yellow pencil sharpener. //

Step 2   Colour the picture

Pupils colour the picture on page 29 of their AB (activity 3), using any of the colours they know in English. This is not a directed colouring exercise.

Step 3   Groupwork

a This is based on the picture the pupils coloured in Step 2.
b In the left-hand column of the chart, pupils write the name of any four objects in the picture. In the second column, labelled 'me', they should write the colour of these four objects.
c Ask pupils about the colour of the objects in their picture, e.g. '*Andreas, what colour's your pencil?*' Continue until pupils are familiar with the question form.
d Divide the class into groups of three. Pupils ask and answer similar questions about the colour of the objects in their picture, and record the answers in the third and fourth columns of their charts.

Step 4   Write

a Pupils write sentences describing their picture using the form '**My pencil is red.**' Ask volunteers to write examples on the blackboard first.
b Faster pupils can continue in their exercise books, writing about their friend's picture.

66

2B School

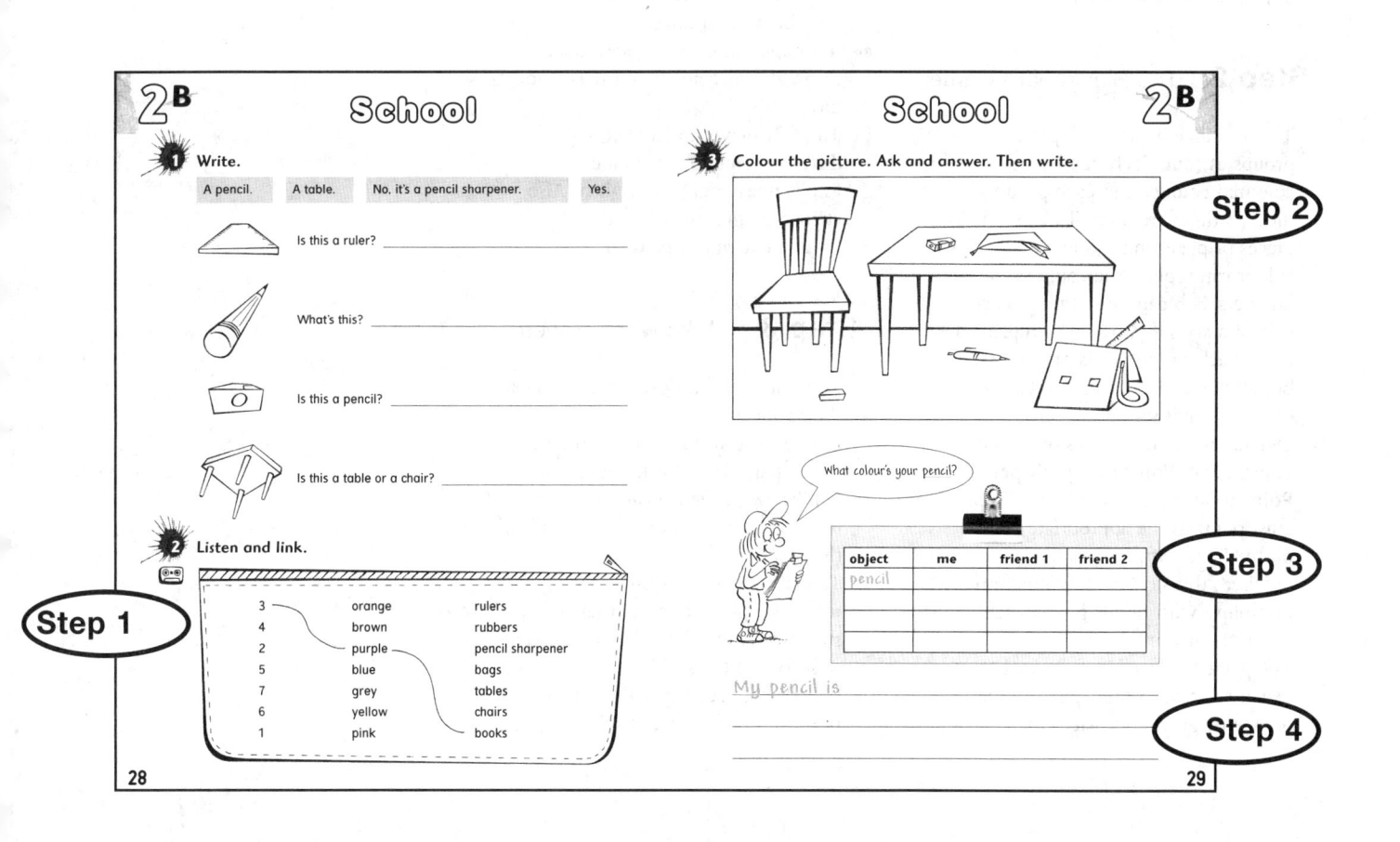

1 Write.

| A pencil. | A table. | No, it's a pencil sharpener. | Yes. |

Is this a ruler? _____

What's this? _____

Is this a pencil? _____

Is this a table or a chair? _____

2 Listen and link.

3	orange	rulers
4	brown	rubbers
2	purple	pencil sharpener
5	blue	bags
7	grey	tables
6	yellow	chairs
1	pink	books

School 2B

3 Colour the picture. Ask and answer. Then write.

What colour's your pencil?

object	me	friend 1	friend 2
pencil			

My pencil is _____

_____

_____

Step 1

Step 2

Step 3

Step 4

2B Lesson 3

Main Language Items		Resource File	Materials Needed
What colour's the …?	grey	17a	counters/dice
My/Your turn	pink	26	materials to make word stones
Point to a …	orange	27	
	purple		

Step 1   Pair work

a Say 'Open your Coursebooks at page 23 and look at the pictures.' Ask various pupils 'What colour's the pen?' etc., pointing at one of the objects in the board game.

b Then pupils ask and answer questions about the pictures themselves, working in pairs. All pairs work simultaneously.

c Alternatively, ask questions about objects in the classroom.

Step 2   The Blackboard Game

a This is a dice game to be played in groups of four. Each pupil needs a coloured counter and each group a dice. (If these are unavailable, small pieces of paper indicating each pupil's colour can replace the counters and the numbers 1–6 can be written on each side of a six-sided pencil to replace the dice.) Each group needs only one CB but all pupils should have their AB open at activity 4 on page 30.

b Quickly revise the names of all the objects. Say '**Point to a pink pencil. Point to an orange ruler.**' etc. Pupils must point to the appropriate picture on the board. If further practice is required, this may be continued briefly in groups, with pupils giving each other instructions.

c The game is played as follows. Each player selects a colour (pink, purple, orange or grey) and places their counter on the appropriate 'START'. All players throw the dice to decide who begins. Highest number goes first.

d Each player then takes turns to throw the dice and move around the board the appropriate number of squares. Players may move up, down or across, but not diagonally. The aim is to land on squares of their own colour. If successful they write the name of the given object on one of the lines on page 30 of their AB. Each object may only be written once.

e If a pupil lands on a 'dice' square they throw the dice again and have another turn.

f The first player to 'collect' eight different items is the winner.

g Pupils must count in English. Also encourage groups to use the phrases '**Your turn**' and '**My turn**'.

Step 3   Make word stones

a Pupils add eight more word stones to their collection.

b Point to the word stones at the bottom of AB page 30. Check pupils are familiar with their meaning: say one of the words. Pupils point to or hold up the object.

c To make the word stones, each pupil requires eight 'stones' (either real stones or stone-shaped pieces of card as before). Pupils write one word (**pen, pencil, bag, rubber, ruler, chair, table, book**) on each stone in felt-tip pen, as shown in the pictures.

d Working in pairs, pupils play a simple word-recognition game. Each pair uses one collection of stones, face-up. P1 says a word and P2 finds the correct stone. Change roles and repeat the procedure.

e Pupils then store their stones for future use.

68

What Is It?

Listen

- Look at number one. What is it?
- It's a pencil.
- It's a pen!
- It's a pencil!
- It's a pen!
- It isn't a pencil or a pen. It's a ruler.

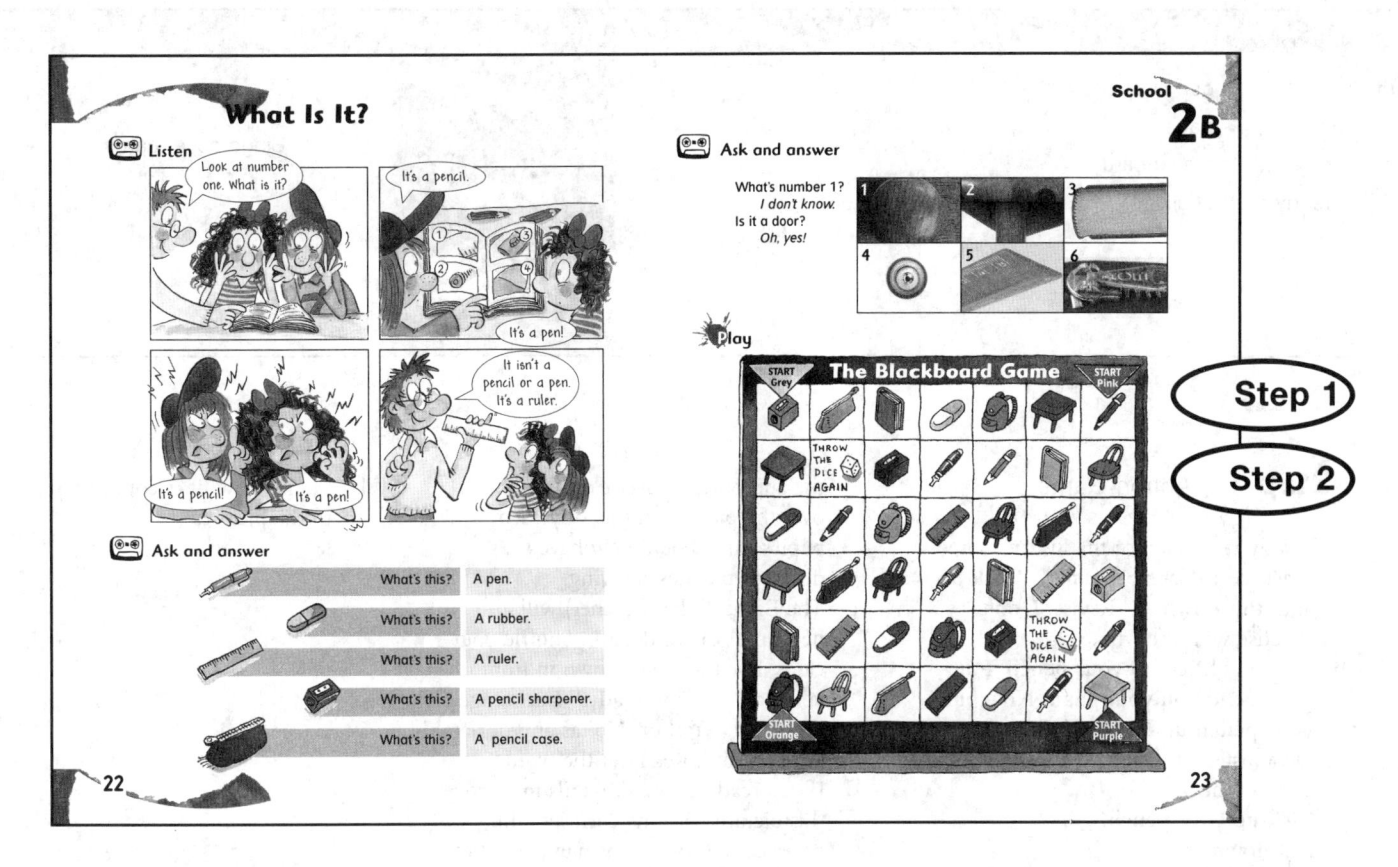

Ask and answer

	What's this?	A pen.
	What's this?	A rubber.
	What's this?	A ruler.
	What's this?	A pencil sharpener.
	What's this?	A pencil case.

22

School 2B

Ask and answer

What's number 1?
I don't know.
Is it a door?
Oh, yes!

Play

The Blackboard Game

START Grey — START Pink
THROW THE DICE AGAIN
START Orange — START Purple

23

Step 1
Step 2

2B School

Step 2

4 Play the game and write.
Look at the Blackboard Game on page 23 in your Coursebook.

My colour is _____ .

1 _____   5 _____
2 _____   6 _____
3 _____   7 _____
4 _____   8 _____

Step 3

5 Make word stones.

pen, ruler, table, bag, pencil, chair, rubber, book

30

School 2C

1 Crossword. Write.

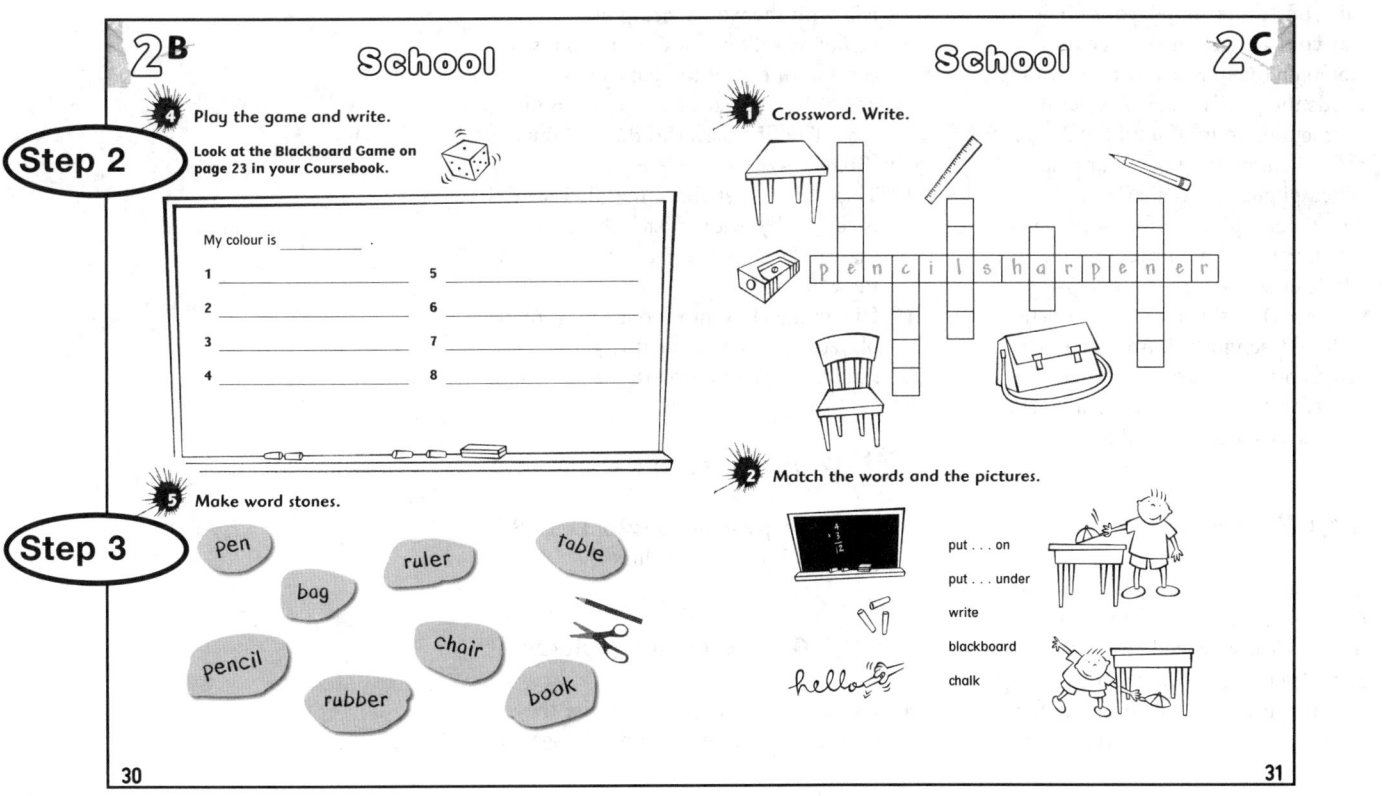

p e n c i l s h a r p e n e r

2 Match the words and the pictures.

put . . . on
put . . . under
write
blackboard
chalk

31

69

2c Lesson 1

Main Language Items		Resource File	Materials Needed
Write	game	26a	Bingo cover cards
Put ... on ...	page	49	
Put ... under ...	blackboard		
Are you ready?	chalk		

Step 1 Action Game

a Briefly revise any of the instructions practised to date, particularly '**Pick up**' and '**Put down ...**' Revise '**Don't**'. Practise with the whole class.

b Then say '**Pick up your pencil. Put your pencil on your chair. Now put your pencil under the chair.**' Demonstrate the new instructions as you say them:
Pick up your pencil.
Put down your pencil.
Put your book under your chair.
Put your pencil on your chair. etc.

c Combine the new instructions with any words the pupils know. Act out the instructions yourself until pupils can carry them out without your help.

d When pupils are familiar with the instructions, play the following game. When you give an instruction the whole class should act it out. When you say '**Don't**' before the instruction, it should be ignored. Any pupil who carries out the instruction when you say '**Don't**' must leave the game. The last player remaining is the winner.

Step 2 Bingo

a Each pupil will need nine small cover cards with the name of one of the objects clearly printed on each card.

b Say '**Open your Coursebooks at page 24.**' Instruct pupils to cover any four squares on their Bingo card by placing the appropriate cover card face down over the picture. In this way each pupil's card should now have six different pictures showing.

c The Bingo Caller (teacher) will also need a set of word cards. Shuffle your cards. Lay them face down in front of you. Say '**Are you ready?**' Encourage the answer '**Yes**' or '**No**' as appropriate. Select a card. Read out the word.

d If you read out '**pen**', pupils must cover this picture with the corresponding cover card. Cover cards must now be laid with the words facing up.

e Continue calling out objects from your cards until one of the pupils has covered all the squares on their Bingo card. The first player to do so shouts '**Bingo!**'

f This player must check that their card is correct by reading back the names that are face up. If correct, he or she is the winner.

g Divide the class into groups of 4–6 players. Pupils continue the game simultaneously in groups.

Step 3 Crossword

Pupils complete the crossword on AB page 31 using picture clues.

Step 4 Words and pictures

a Use a brief mime game to revise the expressions in activity 2 on AB page 31.

b Pupils draw lines connecting the words to the pictures.

Step 2

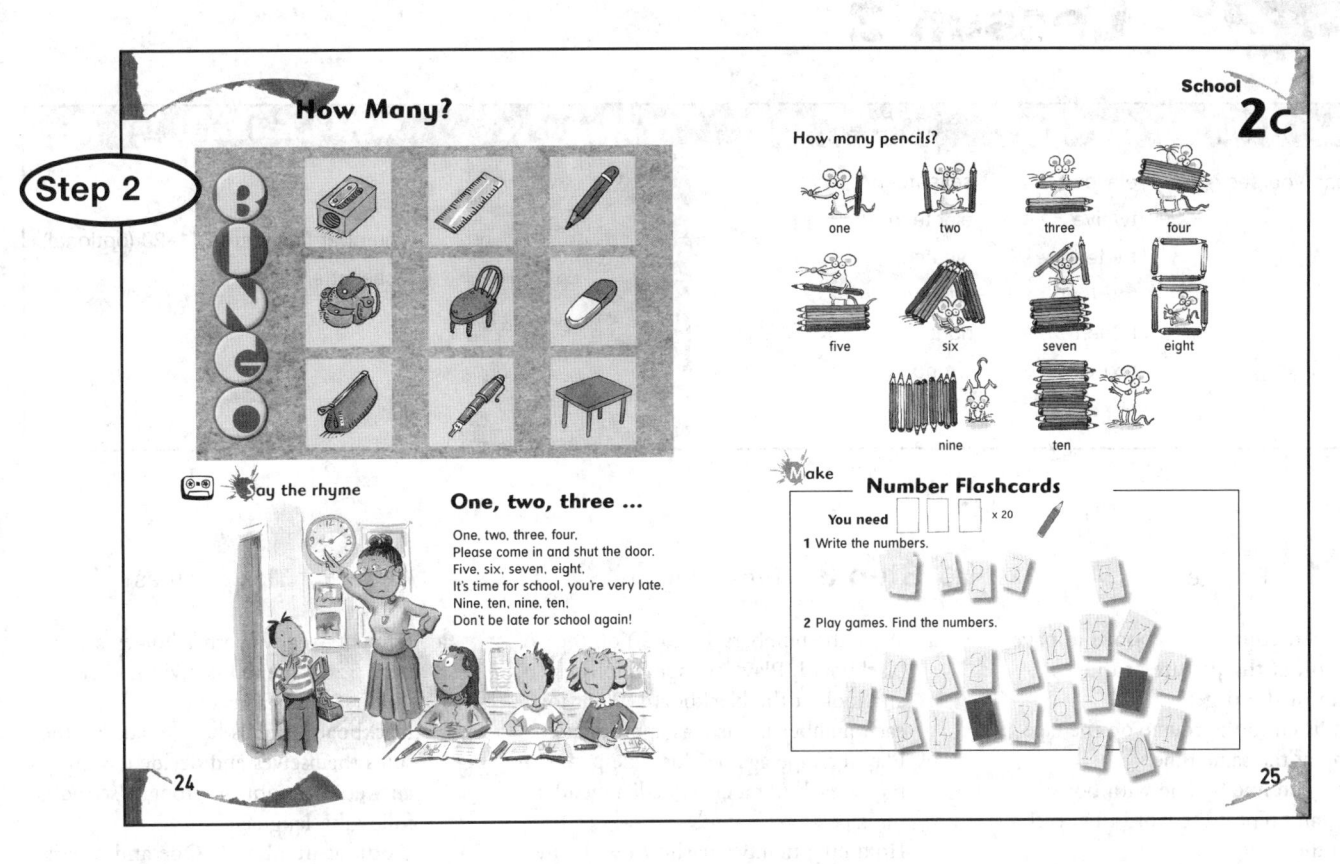

How Many?

BINGO

Say the rhyme

One, two, three ...

One, two, three, four,
Please come in and shut the door.
Five, six, seven, eight,
It's time for school, you're very late.
Nine, ten, nine, ten,
Don't be late for school again!

School
2c

How many pencils?

one two three four
five six seven eight
nine ten

Make **Number Flashcards**

You need ☐☐☐ x 20

1 Write the numbers.

2 Play games. Find the numbers.

24 25

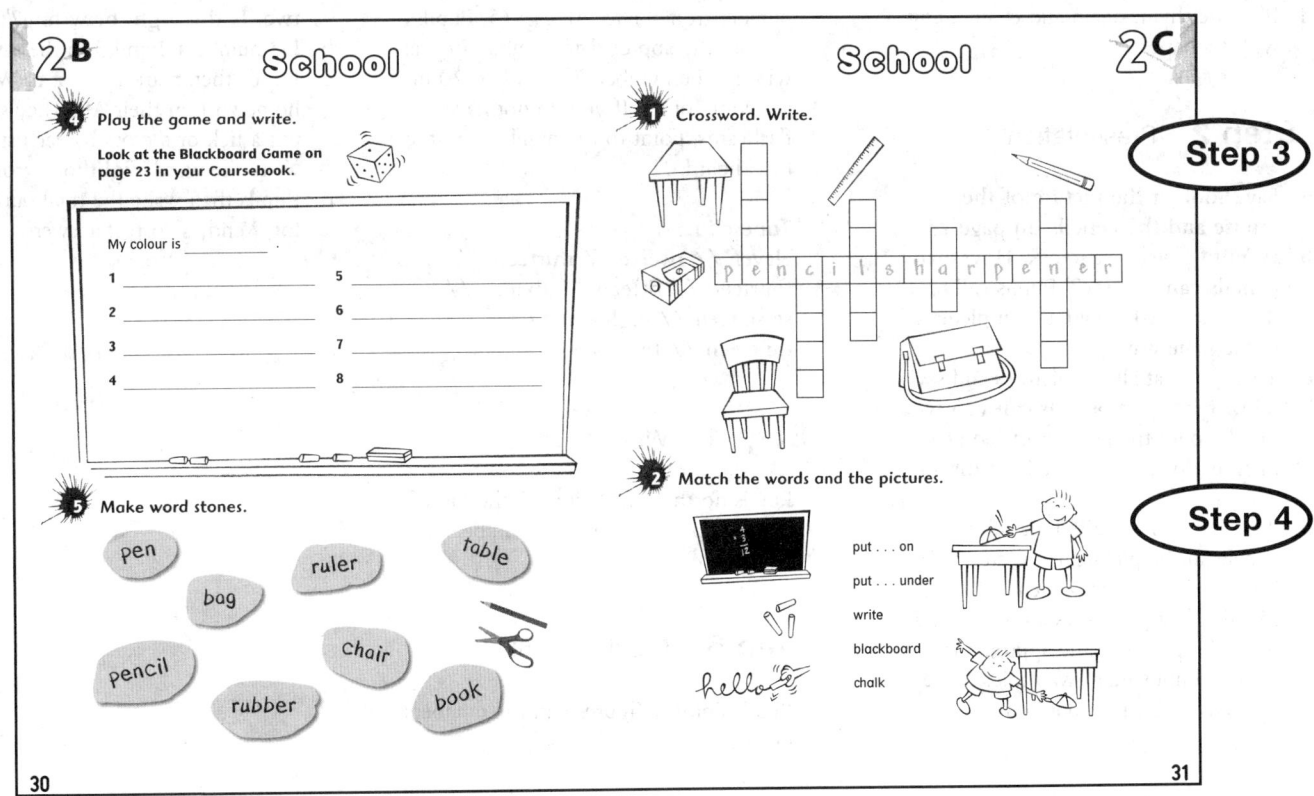

2B School

4 **Play the game and write.**

Look at the Blackboard Game on page 23 in your Coursebook.

My colour is _____

1 _____   5 _____
2 _____   6 _____
3 _____   7 _____
4 _____   8 _____

5 **Make word stones.**

pen   ruler   table
 bag
pencil   chair
 rubber   book

School **2c**

1 **Crossword. Write.**

p e n c i l s h a r p e n e r

2 **Match the words and the pictures.**

put ... on
put ... under
write
blackboard
chalk

Step 3

Step 4

30 31

71

2c Lesson 2

Main Language Items			Resource File	Materials Needed
How many … can you see?	eleven	seventeen	31	number flashcards 11–20 (optional)
1–10 (revision)	twelve	eighteen	32	cassette/cassette player
	thirteen	nineteen		
	fourteen	twenty		
	fifteen	right		
	sixteen	wrong		

Step 1 Rhyme

a Say 'Open your Coursebooks at page 24. Look at the picture at the bottom of the page.'
b Pupils listen to the rhyme on the tape, reading at the same time.
c Listen again line by line with books closed, and repeat the words. Do each line in the same way.
d Play the rhyme again and chant along with the tape.

Step 2 Presentation

a Say 'Look at the picture of the mouse and the pencils on page 25.'
b Point to a picture and ask 'How many pencils can you see?' Pupils call out the answer. Ask about all ten pictures in the same way.
c Then point at all the pictures and say 'How many red pencils can you see?' Pupils count the number of red pencils in all ten pictures and call out the answer.
d Ask about all the different coloured pencils in the picture. (This step may be played as a team game.)
e In pairs, one pupil says a number and the other points to the appropriate picture. Pupils than swap roles. Keep the activity brisk throughout.

Step 3 Presentation

a Write the numbers 11 to 20 on the blackboard. Play the tape. Pupils listen and look at the blackboard. Point to each number in turn, as appropriate.
b Play the tape again. This time pupils repeat each number immediately after the tape.
c Hold up a number flashcard with any number from 11 to 20, e.g. 15. Pupils call out the appropriate number. Repeat with all the numbers from 11 to 20 in a random order. If you do not have flashcards, point to the numbers on the blackboard.

Tapescript:
eleven // twelve // thirteen // fourteen // fifteen // sixteen // seventeen // eighteen // nineteen // twenty //

Step 4 Write

Pupils do the calculations at the top of AB page 32 and write the numbers in words.

Step 5 Read and link

Pupils link the figures and the numbers in words.

Step 6 Tick or cross

a Look at Wendy worm's homework on page 32 of the AB (activity 5). Copy the first three sums onto the blackboard. Pupils have to add up the sums themselves and decide if Wendy's answers are right or wrong. Use the following language:
'Look at number 1. One and one is two. Is this right or wrong?'
b Do numbers 2 and 3 in the same way.
c Pupils then mark the rest of Wendy's homework in their AB. They should put a tick or a cross by each sum and write the word '**right**' or '**wrong**'.
d Pupils then write the total our of ten for Wendy's correct answers.

How Many?

Say the rhyme

One, two, three ...

One, two, three, four,
Please come in and shut the door.
Five, six, seven, eight,
It's time for school, you're very late.
Nine, ten, nine, ten,
Don't be late for school again!

24

School 2c

How many pencils?

one two three four
five six seven eight
nine ten

Make — Number Flashcards

You need ☐☐☐ × 20 ✏️

1 Write the numbers.

2 Play games. Find the numbers.

25

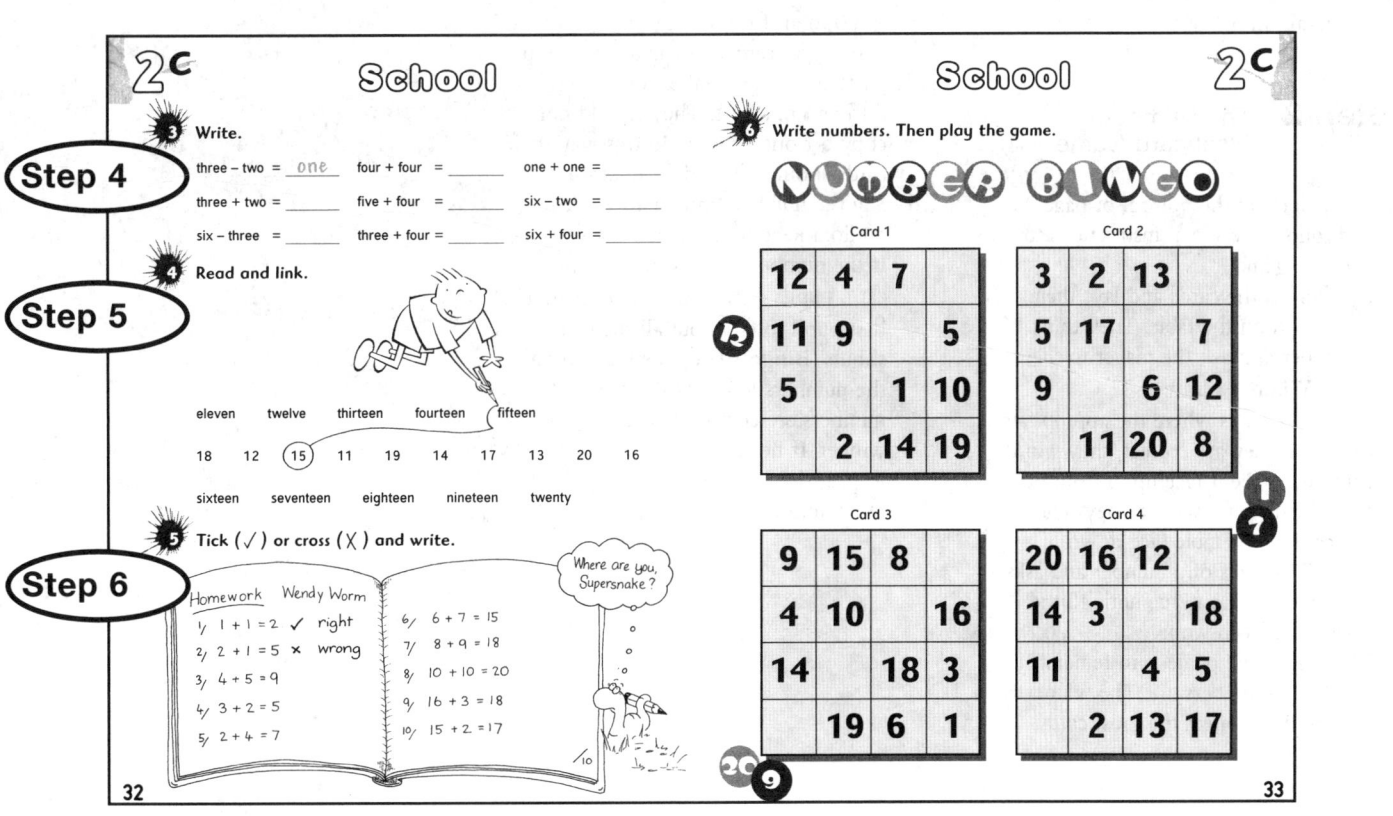

2c School

3 Write.

three − two = _one_   four + four = ____   one + one = ____
three + two = ____   five + four = ____   six − two = ____
six − three = ____   three + four = ____   six + four = ____

4 Read and link.

eleven   twelve   thirteen   fourteen   fifteen

18   12   (15)   11   19   14   17   13   20   16

sixteen   seventeen   eighteen   nineteen   twenty

5 Tick (✓) or cross (✗) and write.

Where are you, Supersnake?

Homework	Wendy Worm
1/ 1 + 1 = 2 ✓ right	6/ 6 + 7 = 15
2/ 2 + 1 = 5 ✗ wrong	7/ 8 + 9 = 18
3/ 4 + 5 = 9	8/ 10 + 10 = 20
4/ 3 + 2 = 5	9/ 16 + 3 = 18
5/ 2 + 4 = 7	10/ 15 + 2 = 17

/10

32

School 2c

6 Write numbers. Then play the game.

NUMBER BINGO

Card 1
12	4	7
11	9	5
5	1	10
	2	14	19

Card 2
3	2	13
5	17	7
9		6	12
	11	20	8

Card 3
9	15	8
4	10		16
14		18	3
	19	6	1

Card 4
20	16	12
14	3		18
11		4	5
	2	13	17

33

2c Lesson 3

Main Language Items	Resource File	Materials Needed
numbers 1–20 Where's ...?	31 32a	materials to make flashcards Bingo cover cards (optional)

Step 1 Make number flashcards

a Pupils look at the bottom of CB page 25 and follow the visual instructions to make the number flashcards, in preparation for the Number Flashcard Game.
b The game is to be played in pairs or in groups of three or four. Each pair or group will need twenty small pieces of paper or card (approximately 5–10 cm) on which to write the numbers 1–20 (numeral only).

Step 2 The Number Flashcard Game

a Pupils look at the bottom of page 25 and follow the visual instructions to play the game.
b P1 shuffles the cards and lays them face down on the table. They think of a number and ask the player to their right '**Where's number 3?**'
c P2 has to guess where the appropriate card is. If they are correct, they win the card and place it face up in front of them. If they are wrong, they return the card to the table face down.
d Then P2 thinks of a number and asks the question. Continue until all the cards have been won.
e The aim of the game is to remember where the numbers are. The winner is the pupil to collect the most cards.

Step 3 Number Bingo

a Say '**Open your Activity Books at page 33.**'
b Copy the first Bingo card onto the blackboard. Ask the pupils to give you any number between 1 and 20. Write the number in one of the blank squares. Continue until all blank squares in the first card have been filled. Erase your Bingo card from the blackboard.
c Tell pupils to write any number from 1–20 in all four blank squares on their first Bingo card. They may choose to write the same number four times, or different numbers. They should not copy off one another. In this way their cards should all be different.
d Say the numbers from 1 to 20 at random keeping note of what you say. If the number appears on their first card, pupils cross it out or cover it. The first pupil to cross out all their numbers shouts '**Bingo!**' They then call out all the numbers to check them. If the numbers are correct, that pupil is the winner. If not the game continues.
e Repeat the game with the three remaining cards.

How Many?

How many pencils?

one　two　three　four
five　six　seven　eight
nine　ten

Say the rhyme

One, two, three ...

One, two, three, four,
Please come in and shut the door.
Five, six, seven, eight,
It's time for school, you're very late.
Nine, ten, nine, ten,
Don't be late for school again!

Make **Number Flashcards**

You need ☐☐☐ x 20

1 Write the numbers.

2 Play games. Find the numbers.

Step 1

Step 2

2c School

3 Write.

three – two = one　　four + four = ___　　one + one = ___
three + two = ___　　five + four = ___　　six – two = ___
six – three = ___　　three + four = ___　　six + four = ___

4 Read and link.

eleven　twelve　thirteen　fourteen　fifteen

18　12　(15)　11　19　14　17　13　20　16

sixteen　seventeen　eighteen　nineteen　twenty

5 Tick (✓) or cross (✗) and write.

Homework　Wendy Worm
1/ 1 + 1 = 2 ✓ right
2/ 2 + 1 = 5 ✗ wrong
3/ 4 + 5 = 9
4/ 3 + 2 = 5
5/ 2 + 4 = 7

6/ 6 + 7 = 15
7/ 8 + 9 = 18
8/ 10 + 10 = 20
9/ 16 + 3 = 18
10/ 15 + 2 = 17

Where are you, Supersnake?

School 2c

6 Write numbers. Then play the game.

NUMBER BINGO

Card 1
12	4	7
11	9	5
5		1	10
	2	14	19

Card 2
3	2	13
5	17		7
9		6	12
	11	20	8

Card 3
9	15	8
4	10		16
14		18	3
	19	6	1

Card 4
20	16	12
14	3		18
11		4	5
	2	13	17

Step 3

2D Lesson 1

Main Language Items		Resource File	Materials Needed
Where's the …? there on		11	paper cups
on/under the table right in		49	pencil sharpeners
in the bag wrong under			rubbers
guess			cassette/cassette player

Step 1 Presentation

a Say 'Open your Coursebooks at page 26.' Look at the pictures of Suzy and Bill.
b Play the tape. Pupils follow, looking at the pictures.
c Now play the game at the front of the class. You need two paper cups and a rubber or pencil sharpener. Place the rubber under one of the cups. Shuffle the cups around then ask **'Where's the rubber?'** Ask for volunteers to come to the front and guess. Encourage pupils to say **'There'** when they point to the cups.
d If paper cups are not available simply show the class the object and place it in your hand. Put both hands behind your back and move the object from hand to hand. Then continue as above.
e Repeat the game a few times until pupils are familiar with the question.

Step 2 Game

a Working in pairs, pupils play the same game shown on page 26 of the CB.
b To encourage more realistic use of language, more than one object can be used to play the game, e.g. a rubber under one cup or in one hand and a pencil sharpener in the other. A choice of two questions can then be asked.

Step 3 Pair work

a Divide the class into pairs. One CB between each pair of pupils should be open at page 26.
b Look at the picture of the table and cover the words.
c Repeat after the tape. P1 asks the questions, P2 answers. Repeat again.
d Then change roles and repeat twice more.
e Pupils ask and answer the questions without the help of the tape. Pupils (P1) asking the questions should use the words as prompts and must check their partners' answers. P2 may use only the picture.
f Change roles and repeat the procedure. Continue until pupils can ask and answer questions about the picture without the help of the words.
g Do not expect questions and answers to be perfect at this stage. The main aim is that pupils attempt to ask questions without the book.

Step 4 Write

a Pupils read the questions and write the answers in the spaces provided on page 34 of the AB. CBs should be closed.
b Pupils should then check their answers against the model on page 26 of the CB.

Step 5 Groupwork

a The aim of the questionnaire in activity 2 is for pupils to investigate the colour of their friends' pencil, pen, bag and pencil case.
b Working in groups of three, pupils ask other members of their group, **'What colour's your pencil?'** etc.
c Write down the colour of each object in the appropriate columns.

Optional Write

This may be extended into a writing activity. Give examples on the blackboard. Use the form: *Maria's bag is blue.*

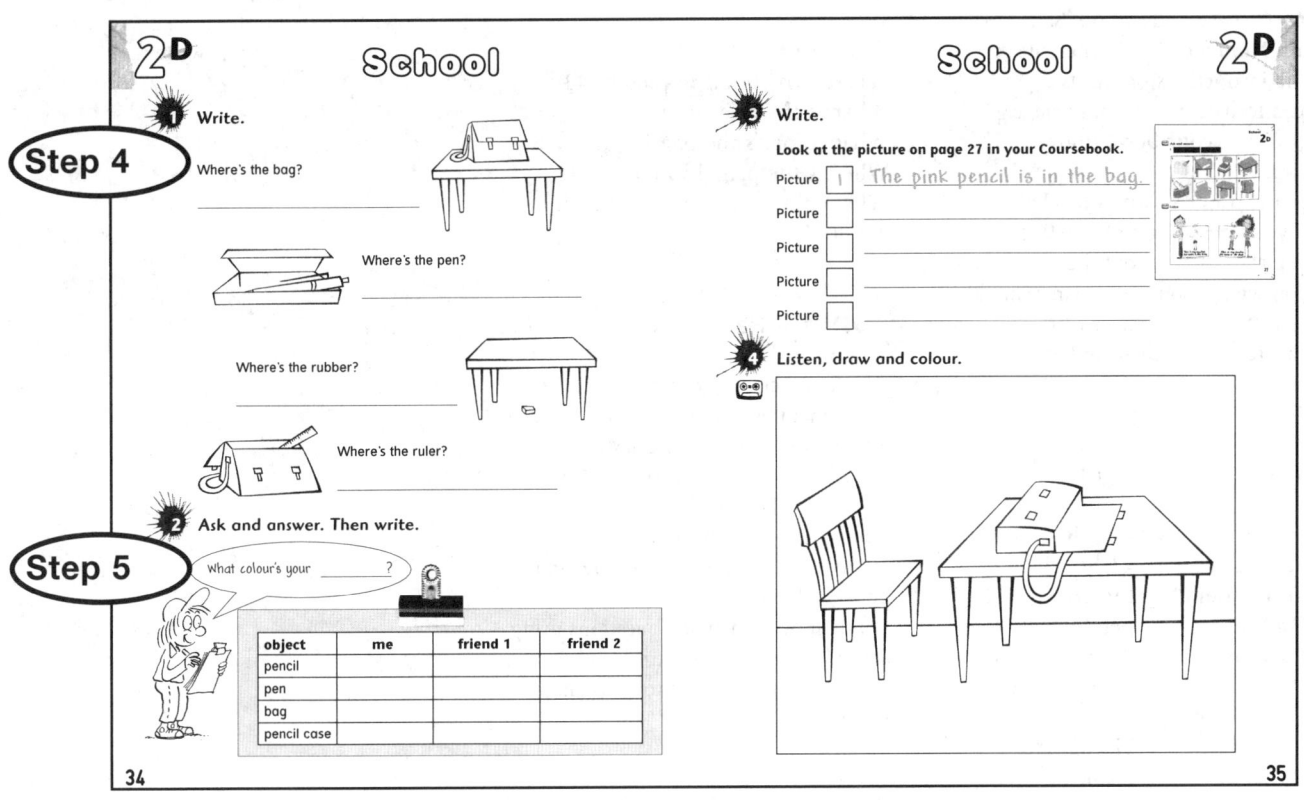

Where's the Rubber?

Step 1 — Play

"Suzy..."
"Where's the rubber?"
"I don't know"
"No, wrong!"
"Well, guess!"
"There!"
"OK, there!"
"Right!"

School 2D

Ask and answer

1 Where's the pencil?   It's in the bag.

1 2 3 4
5 6 7 8

Step 3 — Ask and answer

Where's the bag?	On the table.
Where's the pen?	In the box.
Where's the rubber?	Under the table.
Where's the ruler?	In the bag.

Listen

"This is my teacher. Her name is Mrs King."
"This is my teacher. His name is Mr Bell."

26   27

2D School

Step 4

1 Write.

Where's the bag? _____

Where's the pen? _____

Where's the rubber? _____

Where's the ruler? _____

Step 5

2 Ask and answer. Then write.

What colour's your _____ ?

object	me	friend 1	friend 2
pencil			
pen			
bag			
pencil case			

School 2D

3 Write.

Look at the picture on page 27 in your Coursebook.

Picture [1] The pink pencil is in the bag.
Picture [ ] _____
Picture [ ] _____
Picture [ ] _____
Picture [ ] _____

4 Listen, draw and colour.

34   35

77

2D Lesson 2

Main Language Items	Resource File	Materials Needed
Where's the pen in picture number 6? *Word order:* The blue pencil is under the chair.	19 21 35 35a	cassette/cassette player

Step 1 Action Game

a Divide the class into teams. Give each pupil a number from 1 to 20. Say '**You are Number 1**' etc. Teams need not be exactly equal (e.g. if there are more than twenty pupils in each team, allocate the same number to more than one team member). Give each team the name of a colour.

b Check pupils have understood. Say '**Stand up Number 1!**' etc. Then use any of the instructions or words introduced to date, in a team game, e.g.
Number 3, put your book under your chair.
Number 11, don't sit on your chair.
Pick up your pencil, number 19, etc. The first player to carry out the instruction wins a point for their team. However if the wrong player carries out the instruction, their team loses a point.

c Use any of the following:

Don't Point to …	a boy
Touch …	a girl
Stand on …	the floor
Sit on …	a chair
Stand up!	a/the table
Turn around!	the door
Walk to …	pen/pencil
Pick up …	Activity Book
Put down …	Coursebook
Open/Close your …	blackboard
Write …	chalk
Put your … on/under …	window

Step 2 Presentation

a Say '**Open your Coursebooks at page 27. Look at the pictures numbered 1 to 8.**'

b Play the tape. Pupils try to answer the questions. Stop the tape after each question to give pupils a chance to answer.

Tapescript:
Where's the book in picture 4?
Where's the ruler in picture 5?
What colour's the bag in picture 8?
Where's the pencil in picture 1?
What colour's the pencil case in picture 5?

Step 3 Pair work

a Divide the class into pairs. Pupils look at the pictures at the top of CB page 27 and ask and answer questions regarding location and colour, using the forms given in the Presentation.

b Pupils may refer to the picture by number, or less able pupils may simply point and ask.

c Pupils should then ask questions using any of the structures introduced to date. Encourage pupils to help and prompt one another.

Step 4 Write

a The first exercise on AB page 35 relates to the eight pictures on page 27 of the CB. Pupils write the number of one of the pictures in the box, then write a sentence describing that picture on the adjacent line. Use the example given as a model.

b Elicit further examples from pupils and write them on the blackboard. Erase these before pupils write their own.

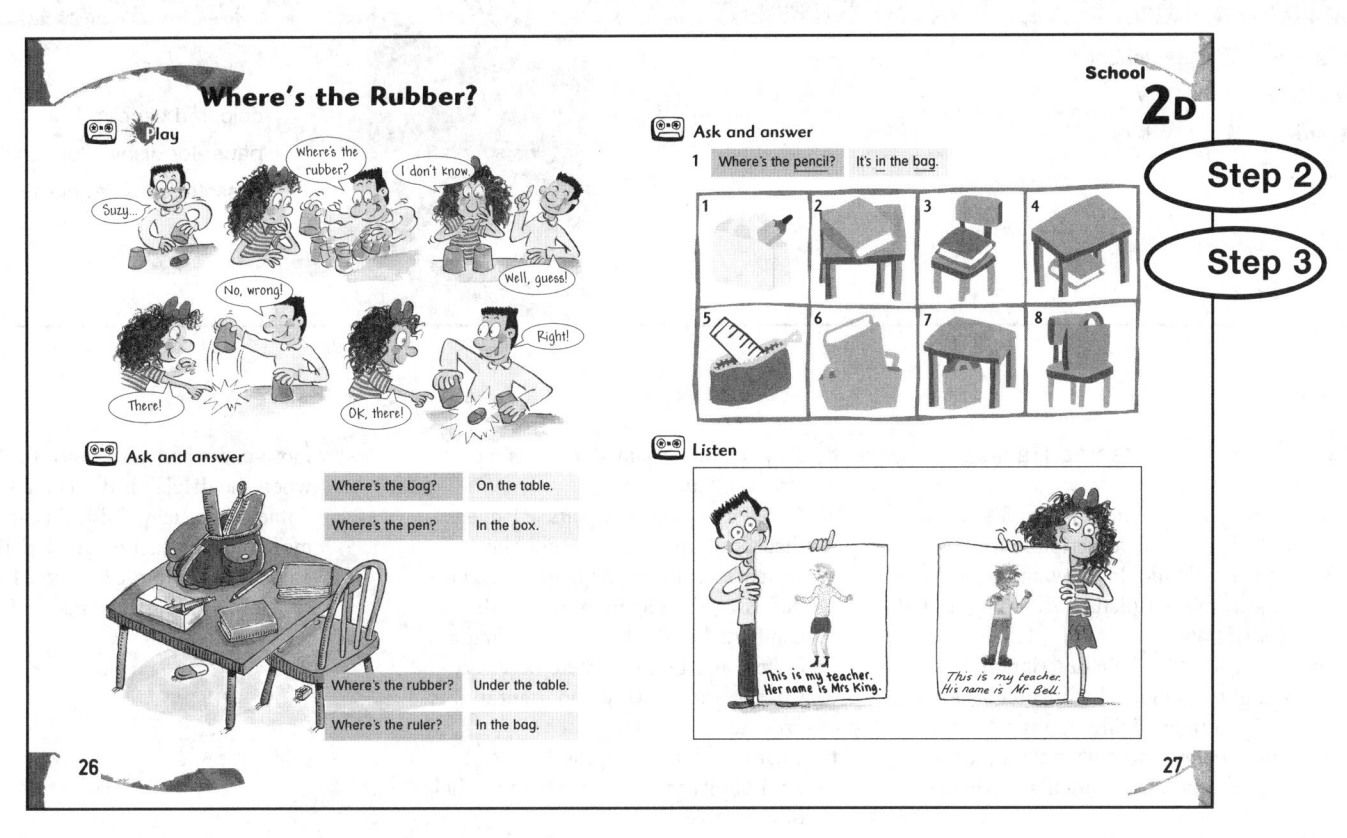

Where's the Rubber?

Play

Suzy... Where's the rubber? I don't know. Well, guess!

No, wrong! There! OK, there! Right!

Ask and answer

Where's the bag?	On the table.
Where's the pen?	In the box.
Where's the rubber?	Under the table.
Where's the ruler?	In the bag.

School 2D

Ask and answer

1. Where's the pencil? It's in the bag.

Step 2

Step 3

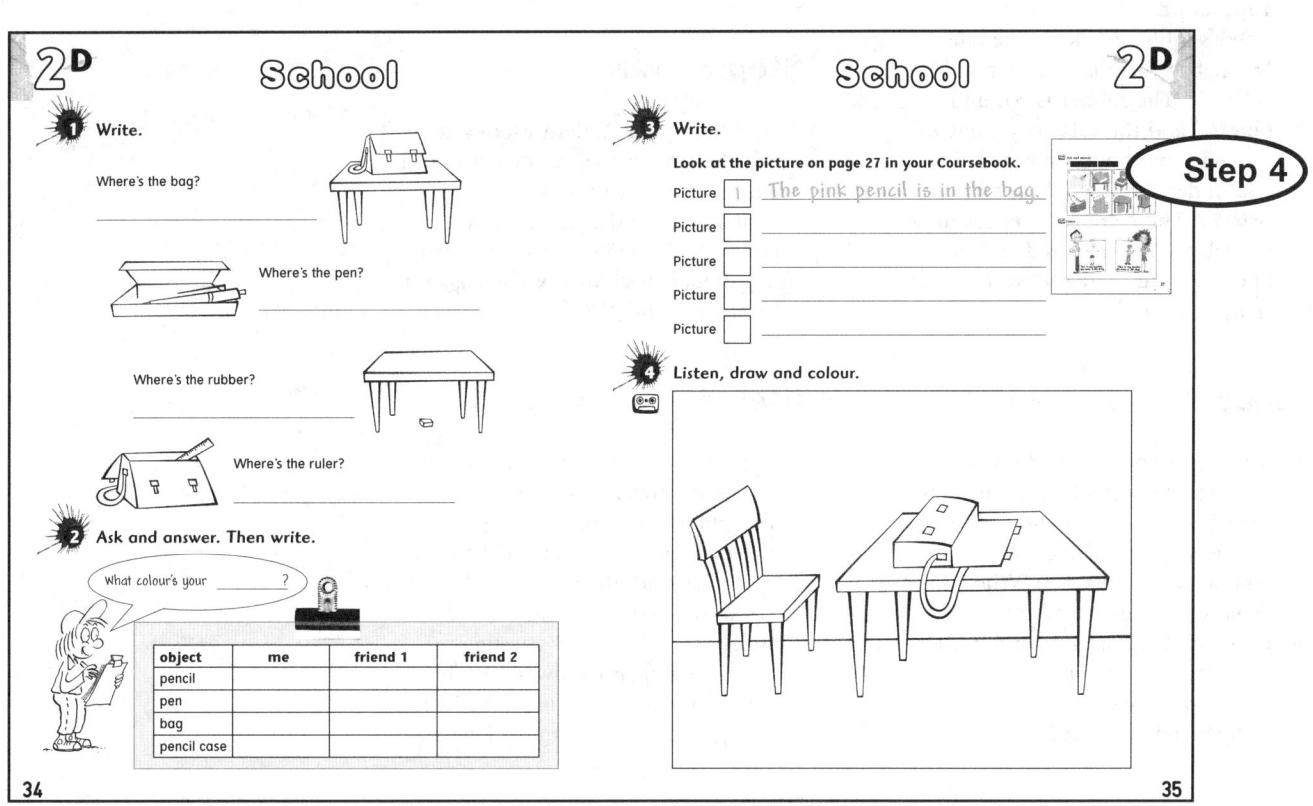

Listen

This is my teacher. Her name is Mrs King.
This is my teacher. His name is Mr Bell.

26 27

2D School

1 Write.

Where's the bag? _____

Where's the pen? _____

Where's the rubber? _____

Where's the ruler? _____

2 Ask and answer. Then write.

What colour's your _____ ?

object	me	friend 1	friend 2
pencil			
pen			
bag			
pencil case			

School 2D

3 Write.

Look at the picture on page 27 in your Coursebook.

Picture [1] The pink pencil is in the bag.
Picture [ ] _____
Picture [ ] _____
Picture [ ] _____
Picture [ ] _____

Step 4

4 Listen, draw and colour.

34 35

79

2D Lesson 3

Main Language Items		Resource File	Materials Needed
Her/His name is ...	teacher	1	coloured pencils
There is ...	Mr	2	paper for display (optional)
There are ...	Mrs		cassette/cassette player
Who is it ...?			
Is it me?			

Step 1   Listening (Task)

a   Look at the picture on page 35 of the AB. Listen to the description on the tape. Pupils should draw and colour objects in their picture according to the description.

b   First play the whole description straight through. Then play it again a line at a time, giving pupils sufficient time to draw and colour their pictures. Repeat each line as often as necessary.

Tapescript:
There's a blue book on the table. // In the bag there is a rubber and a ruler. // The rubber is red and blue // and the ruler is yellow. // There's a red book on the chair, // and under the chair there's a blue pen. // There are two pencils under the table. // One is red and one is blue. // And there's a green pencil sharpener on the bag. //

Step 2   Presentation

a   Say 'Open your Coursebooks at page 27.' Hold your book up for the class. Very quickly ask some preliminary questions about the pictures at the bottom of the page. Use **'Who's this? What's his name?'**

b   Play the tape. Pupils listen to the tape, reading at the same time.

c   Then cover the words, look at the pictures and listen again.

d   Play the tape again. All pupils repeat after the tape twice.

e   Divide the class into pairs. P1 opens their book. P2 tries to recite the sentences without the help of the tape but using the picture in the book to contextualise the language. P1 must correct and prompt where necessary. Co-operation is very important in this exercise.

f   Change roles and repeat. Continue until pupils can recite without the help of the book.

Step 3   Write

a   Say 'Open your Activity Books at page 36.' Pupils look at the unfinished sentences in activity 5.

b   Pupils complete the sentences, writing in their AB. When they have finished they should check their version against the model in the CB.

Step 4   Personal file

a   Pupils draw a picture of their teacher in the box provided and write a description of the picture alongside. Encourage pupils to compare their description with the models in the CB.

b   This work makes excellent wall displays and it is very motivating for pupils to see their own work exhibited in the classroom. Individual work to be displayed in this way can be done on loose paper and stuck into the AB when the display is dismantled.

c   Some classes may finish this activity more quickly than others. Use the colours song from CB page 21 for revision, as a possible final activity.

Where's the Rubber?

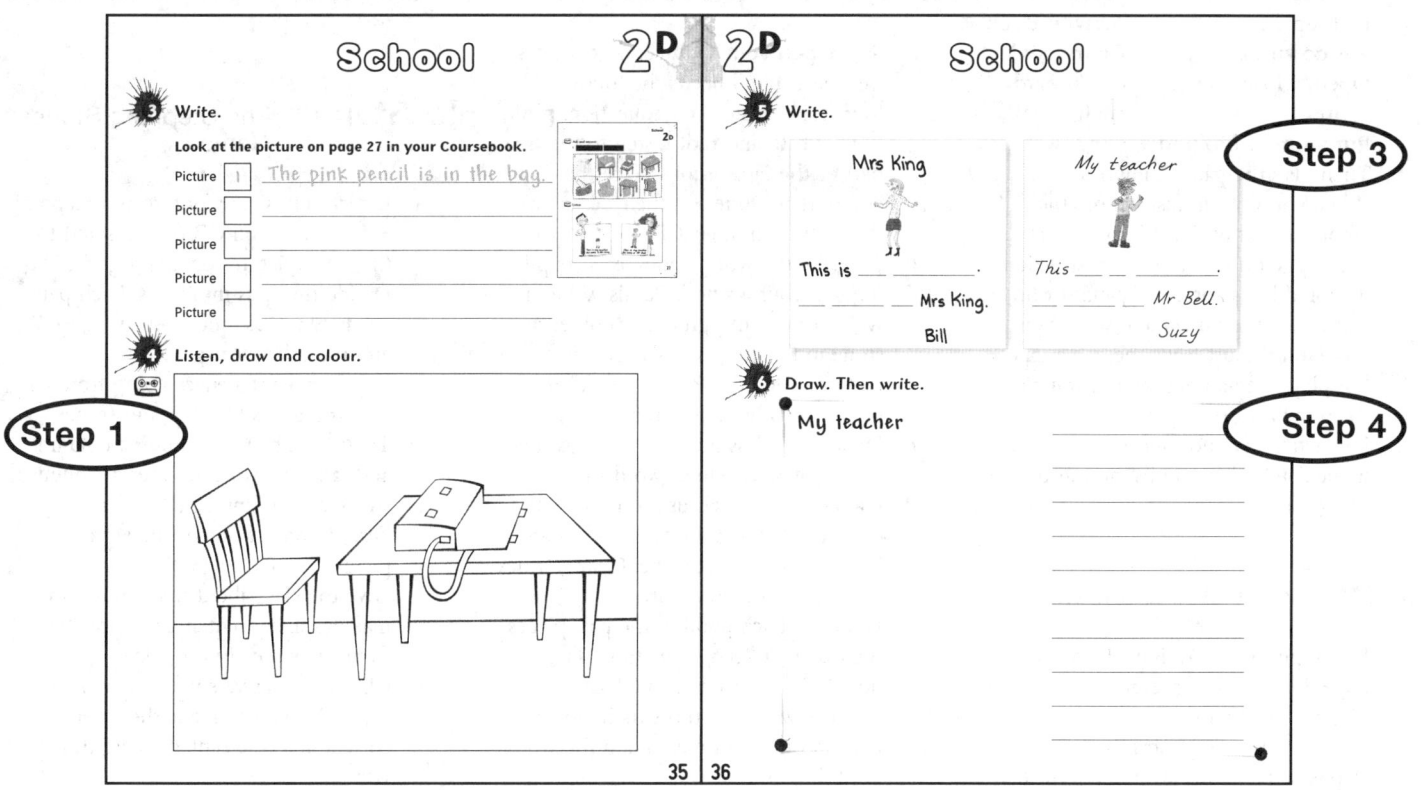

Play

Suzy... Where's the rubber? I don't know. Well, guess!
No, wrong! There! OK, there! Right!

Ask and answer

Where's the bag?	On the table.
Where's the pen?	In the box.
Where's the rubber?	Under the table.
Where's the ruler?	In the bag.

School 2D

Ask and answer

1 Where's the pencil? It's in the bag.

Listen

This is my teacher. Her name is Mrs King.
This is my teacher. His name is Mr Bell.

26 27

School 2D

3 Write.

Look at the picture on page 27 in your Coursebook.

Picture [1] The pink pencil is in the bag.
Picture [ ] _____
Picture [ ] _____
Picture [ ] _____
Picture [ ] _____

4 Listen, draw and colour.

2D School

5 Write.

Mrs King
This is _____.
_____ Mrs King.
Bill

My teacher
This _____.
_____ Mr Bell.
Suzy

6 Draw. Then write.

My teacher

35 36

81

Step 1 — Step 2 — Step 3 — Step 4

2ᴱ Lesson 1

Main Language Items		Resource File	Materials Needed
big	colours		cassette/cassette player
pig	in	21	materials to make word stones
snake	on		word stone collections
plane	under		
number			
cup			

Step 1 Action Game

a Briefly revise a variety of instructions used to date, selecting from the following:

Point to …	a boy
Touch …	a girl
Stand on …	the floor
Sit on …	a chair
Stand up!	a/the table
Turn around!	the door
Walk to …	pen/pencil
Pick up …	Activity Book
Put down …	Coursebook
Open/Close your …	blackboard
Write …	chalk
Put your … on/under	window

b Then play the game 'Simon Says'. When you give an instruction, the whole class should act it out. When you say **'Don't'** before the instruction it should be ignored. Any pupil who carries out the instruction when you say **'Don't'** must leave the game. The last player remaining is the winner. Keep the action very brisk. If instructions are not obeyed immediately then pupils must also leave the game.

Step 2 Listen and match

a Say **'Open your Activity Books at page 37.'** Point to the phrases and pictures in activity 1.
b Play the tape, one phrase at a time. Pupils listen and draw a line to match the phrase and picture.
c Play the tape again, pausing for pupils to repeat.
d Play the tape again. Pupils repeat the phrases as quickly as they can.
e Pupils practise saying the phrase as fast as they can.
f Ask volunteers to say the phrases as fast as they can in front of the class.

Step 3 Word stones

a Say **'Open your Coursebooks at page 28.'** Each pupil needs the following four stones from their collection: **pink, blue, white** and **red**. Listen to the first part of the tape. Pupils place the appropriate stones on their desks or on the pictures in their CBs.
b To make the word stones, each pupil requires four 'stones'. Pupils write one word (**kite, sink, glue, bed**) on each stone in felt-tip pen, as shown in the pictures. Play the second part of the tape. Pupils listen and repeat.
c Divide the class into pairs. Pupils then play games with their word stones.
d **Game 1:** Each pair uses one collection of stones face up. P1 says a word and P2 find the correct stone. Change roles and repeat the procedure.
e **Game 2:** Each pupil in the pair places their own collection of stones face down. P1 turns one stone face up and says the word. P2 turns their stones face up one at a time, saying the words, until they find the matching one. P1 counts the number of turns this takes. Change roles and repeat the procedure. The winner is the one who takes the least number of turns.
f **Game 3:** P1 places their collection of stones face down. P2 places their collection face up. P1 turns one stone over and says the word, e.g. **pink**. P2 finds a stone which rhymes and says the word, e.g. **sink**. Change roles and repeat.
g Pupils then store their stones for future use.

Step 4 The Stepping Stones Game

a Direct pupils' attention to the Stepping Stones Game on CB page 28 and to the eight pictures on CB page 27. Divide the class into pairs. Each pair needs two CBs: one open at page 27 and the other at page 28.
b Pupils make sentences going from left to right across the stepping stones. They must begin in the first column and take one word from each column.
c All sentences must be correct descriptions of one of the eight pictures on CB page 27.
d Give the class about ten minutes to make as many sentences as possible from the words in the book.
e Check the answers with the whole class. The pair to make the most correct and true sentences are the winners.

Words and Sentences

Word Stones

Use
pink   blue   white   red

Make
glue   sink   bed   kite

The Stepping Stones Game

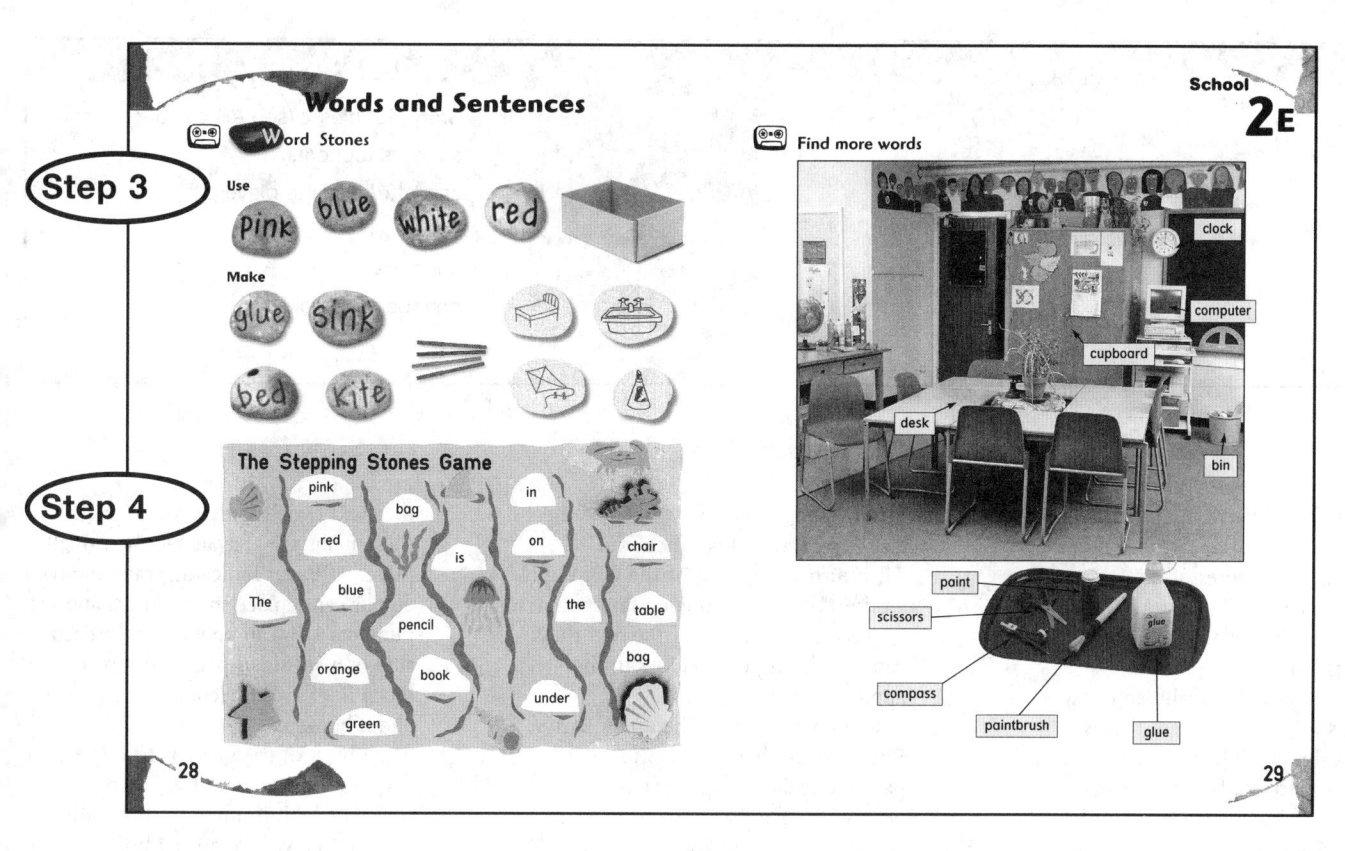

pink, red, The, blue, orange, green, bag, is, pencil, book, in, on, the, under, chair, table, bag

Find more words

clock, computer, cupboard, desk, bin

paint, scissors, compass, paintbrush, glue

Step 3
Step 4

School 2D

5 Write.

Mrs King — This is _____. _____ Mrs King. Bill

My teacher — This ___ _____. _____ Mr Bell. Suzy

6 Draw. Then write.

My teacher

School 2E

1 Listen and match.

A number under a cup
A snake in a plane
Six big pink pigs

2 Draw and say. Then listen and draw.

My picture   My friend's picture

Step 2

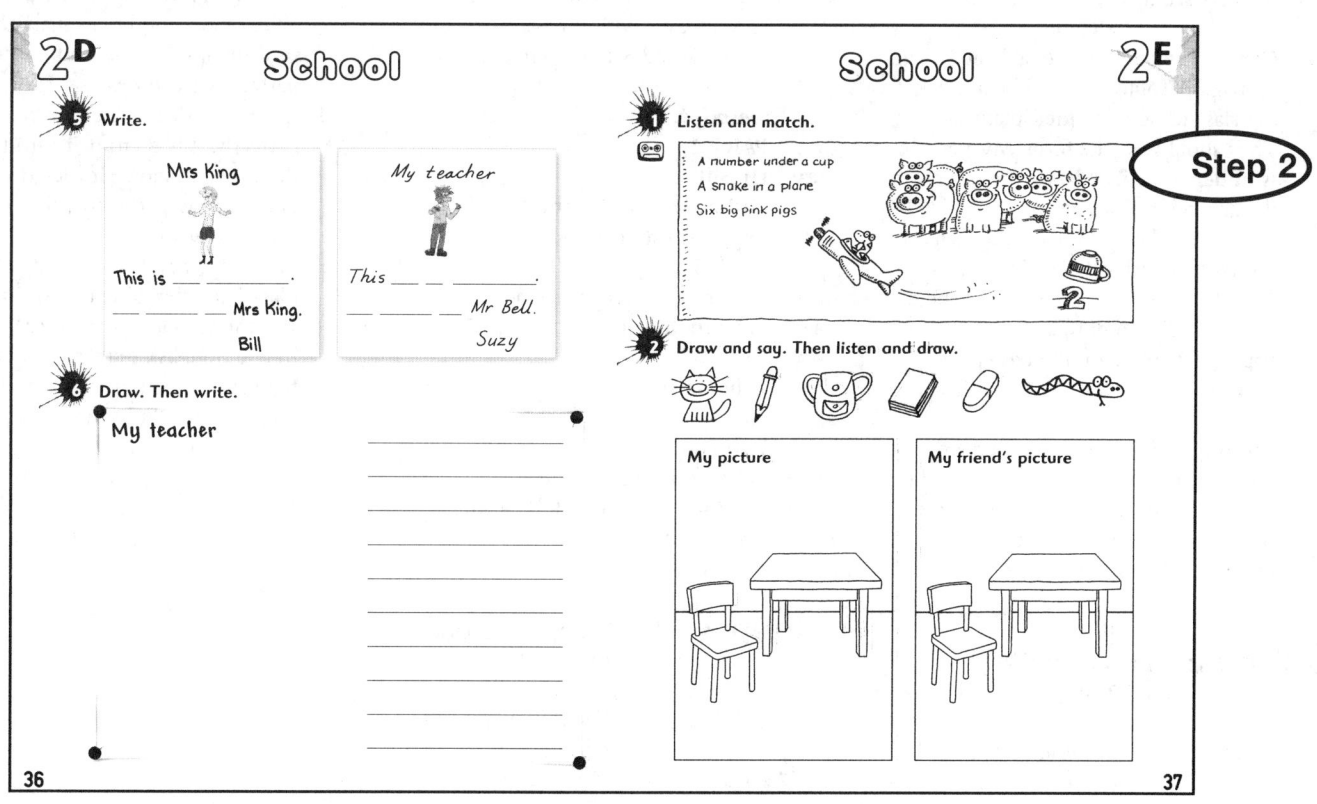

28   29   36   37   83

2ᴇ Lesson 2

Main Language Items	Resource File	Materials Needed
What's this? Is he … in/under/on …?	19 35	Story Bubbles 2 (see AB cut-outs section) scissors (optional) cassette/cassette player dice counters pen, pencil, book

Step 1 Draw and say

a Look at the pictures of the table and chair on page 37 of the AB. Above this are six smaller pictures of objects/animals.

b Pupils work individually and draw these six items anywhere that is physically possible in their pictures, i.e. objects must not be drawn suspended in mid air. Pupils must not let their partners see their pictures. Faster pupils can colour their pictures.

c Copy one picture of the table and chair on page 37 onto the blackboard. Ask the class to describe their pictures. They should use the form: **My pencil is under the chair**. Draw the objects in the appropriate place.

d Divide the class into pairs. Pupils must not look at each other's pictures. P1 describes their picture using the above form. P2 tries to draw the items in the appropriate place on the base picture on page 37 of their AB. Then change roles

e When pupils have finished drawing each other's pictures they compare the finished products, i.e. **My pencil is on the table. Your pencil is under the table.**

Step 2 Listening (Task)/Reading

a The cut-out *Story Bubbles 2* in the centre of the AB form the text of the introductory story on page 18 of the CB. Pupils should cut them out.

b Then turn to page 18 of the CB. Pupils work in pairs. Give them a few minutes to piece together any of the text they can, by placing the bubbles in the appropriate places.

c Play the whole text. Then play Part 1. Pupils check their answers to the first part and make changes where necessary. Give them two minutes to compare answers. Play Part 1 again. Check answers with the whole class.

d Do Parts 2 and 3 in the same way.

Tapescript:
PART 1
KEV: Hi Bill!
BILL: Hi Kev! … What's this?
KEV: Look! My mouse.
PART 2
KEV: Oh no! He isn't in the box!
BILL: Is he in your bag?
KEV: No.
BILL: Is he on the floor?
KEV: No.
PART 3
BILL: Is he under your chair?
KEV: No. Oh no! Look! He's on the teacher's table!

Step 3 The Stepping Stones Action Game 2

a Ideally the game should be played in pairs. Each pair needs one copy of the AB between them, open at page 38, a dice and two coloured counters. (If these items are unavailable then small pieces of paper indicating each pupil's colour can replace the counters and the numbers 1–6 can be written on each side of a six-sided pencil to replace the dice.) Pupils also need a pen, a pencil and a book.

b The object of the game is to make your way from the start to the finish.

c Players take it in turns to throw the dice and move around the board. When they land on a square they must read the instructions and tell their partner what to do.

d If their partner carries out the action correctly, it is then their turn to throw the dice and move. If they do not carry out the action correctly, the first player has another turn.

e Encourage pupils to use English as they play. They should count in English and use phrases such as 'Your/My turn.'

f In addition, ask pupils questions about the game as you monitor their progress, e.g. 'Is it your turn?', 'What's your colour?'

2 School

STORY

Where's Wow?

| 1 | 2 | 3 | 4 |
| 5 | 6 | 7 | 8 |

18 | 19

School 2ᴱ

1 Listen and match.

A number under a cup
A snake in a plane
Six big pink pigs

2 Draw and say. Then listen and draw.

| My picture | My friend's picture |

2ᴱ School

THE STEPPING STONES ACTION GAME 2

START

1 Put your pencil under your book!
2 Point to a pencil!
3 Pick up a pen and a pencil!
4 Touch three boys!
5 Pick up a pen!
6 Don't stand up!
7 Touch a pencil!
8 Put your pen and pencil under your book!
9 Go to 12!
10 Touch the window!
11 Touch the blackboard!
12 Pick up a pencil!
13 Open the door!
14 Put your pen under your book!
15 Put your book on the floor!
16 Point to the window and touch the blackboard!
17 Open your book!
18 Point to your teacher!
19 Open your book!
20 Go to 16!
21 Touch two girls!
22 Put your book under your chair!
23 Put your pencil in your book!

FINISH

37 | 38

Step 1 / Step 2 / Step 3

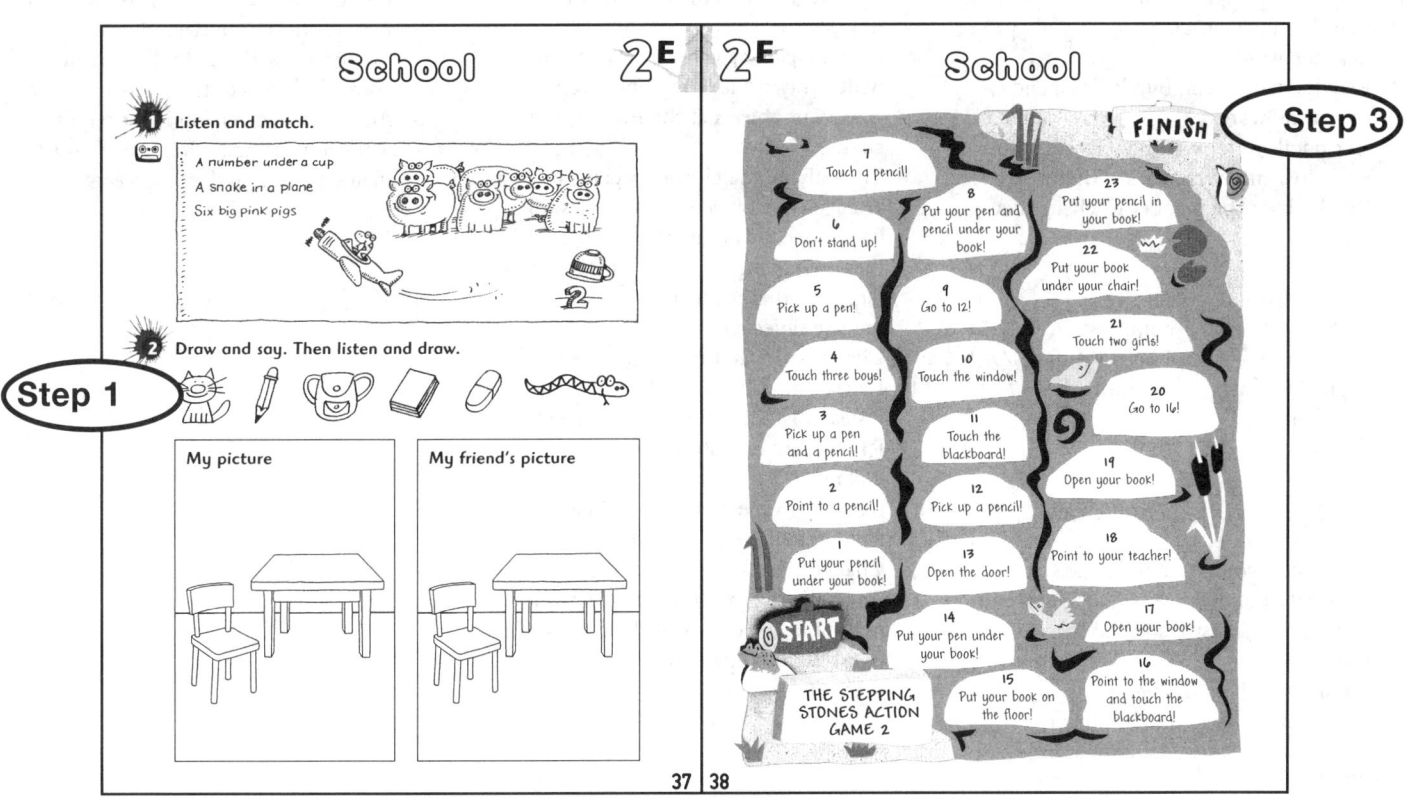

85

2E Lesson 3

Main Language Items		Resource File	Materials Needed
bin	compass		tray (optional)
clock	glue	24	classroom objects: scissors, pens, rulers, etc.
cupboard	paint		cassette/cassette player
computer	paintbrush		card for labels
desk	scissors		

Step 1 Find more words

a Say 'Open your Coursebooks at page 29' and look at the photos. Ask pupils in their L1 if any of them can see something that is not in their own classroom. Then ask them if they can see anything in their own classroom that is not in the photos.
b Play the tape and listen to the words while looking at the pictures.
c Play the tape again. This time pupils point to the appropriate place as they hear the word.
d Play the tape again. Pupils listen and repeat the words
e Ask pupils to look at the pictures and ask 'How many chairs are there?' etc. Pupils count the number of chairs they can see.

Tapescript:
bin // clock // compass // computer // cupboard // desk // glue // paint // paintbrush // scissors //

Step 2 Write. Then draw

a Say 'Open your Activity Books at page 39.' Pupils solve the anagrams and write the answers in the spaces provided.
b Pupils then draw the objects.
c When pupils have finished they can check their work by looking at page 29 of their CB.

Step 3 Pair work (Kim's Game)

a Say 'Open your Coursebooks at page 29' and look at the tray with five objects on. Tell pupils to study the picture and try to remember what they are. They only have 30 seconds to look at the picture.
b When 30 seconds have passed, all books must be closed. Then ask pupils to tell you what objects were on the tray.
c Play the game again in the classroom with a tray or table top and five real classroom objects at the front of the class.
d Then divide the class into pairs. P1 arranges five objects on their desk. P2 has 30 seconds to memorise them. P1 then covers the objects (or P2 turns to face the other way) and P2 must name the five objects.
e Change roles and repeat the procedure.
f Repeat the game as in d above, but instead of P2 naming all the objects, P1 removes one object while P2 is not looking. P2 then looks at the remaining objects and has to name the missing item.
g Change roles and repeat the procedure.
h An alternative version is for pupils to remember the colour of the objects. P1 then asks their partner **'What colour's the …?'**

Step 4 Classroom labels

a Divide the class into four groups and set up a display table for each group with a number of classroom objects, such as a pair of scissors, two red pens, a ruler, three books and a pencil sharpener.
b Pupils have 30 seconds to look at their table of objects. Then give pupils five minutes to make a label for each item.
c Pupils then put the labels on their table next to the appropriate objects.
d The group with the highest number of correctly labelled items is the winner.
e An alternative version is for pupils to work in pairs as in Step 3 and to label their partners' desk top objects.

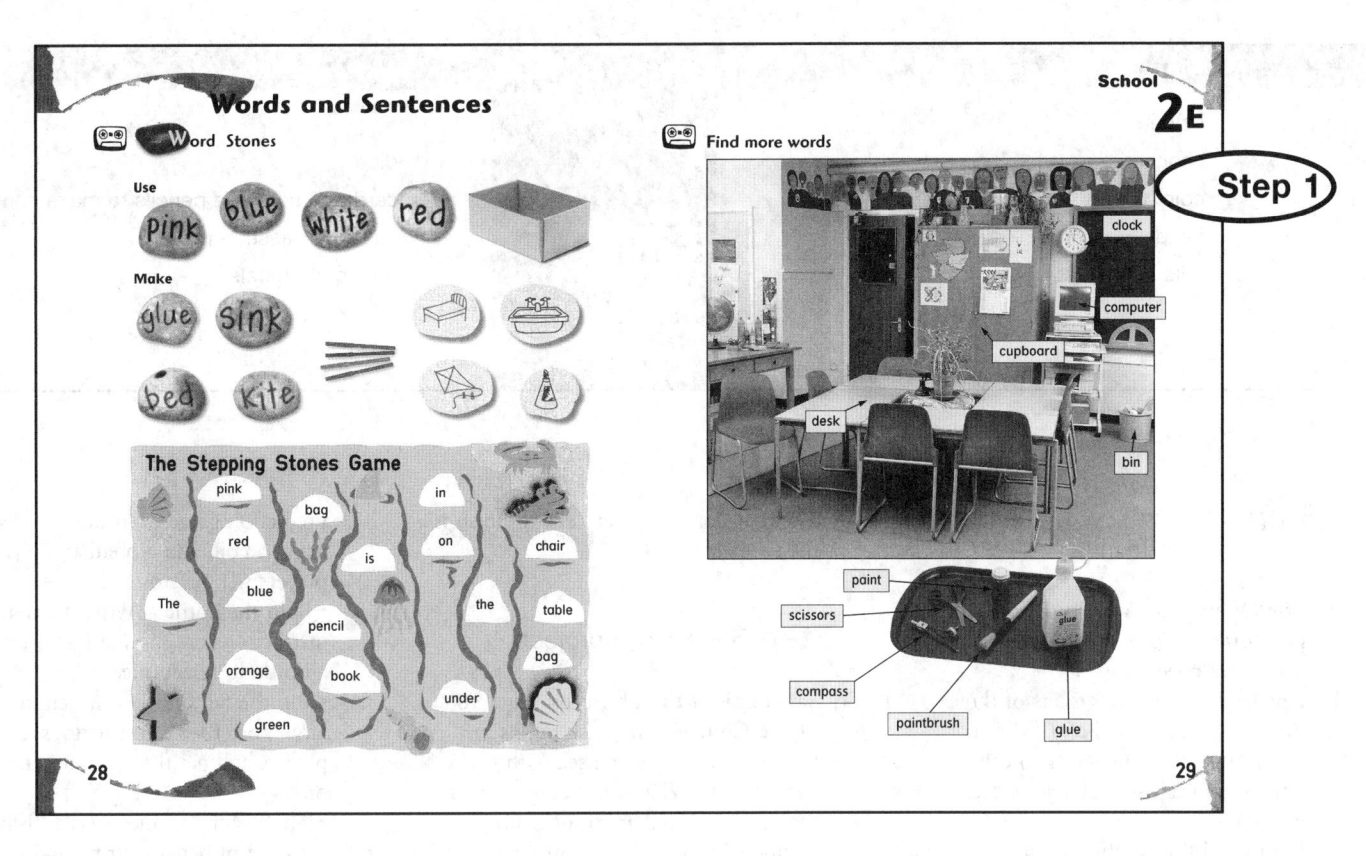

Words and Sentences

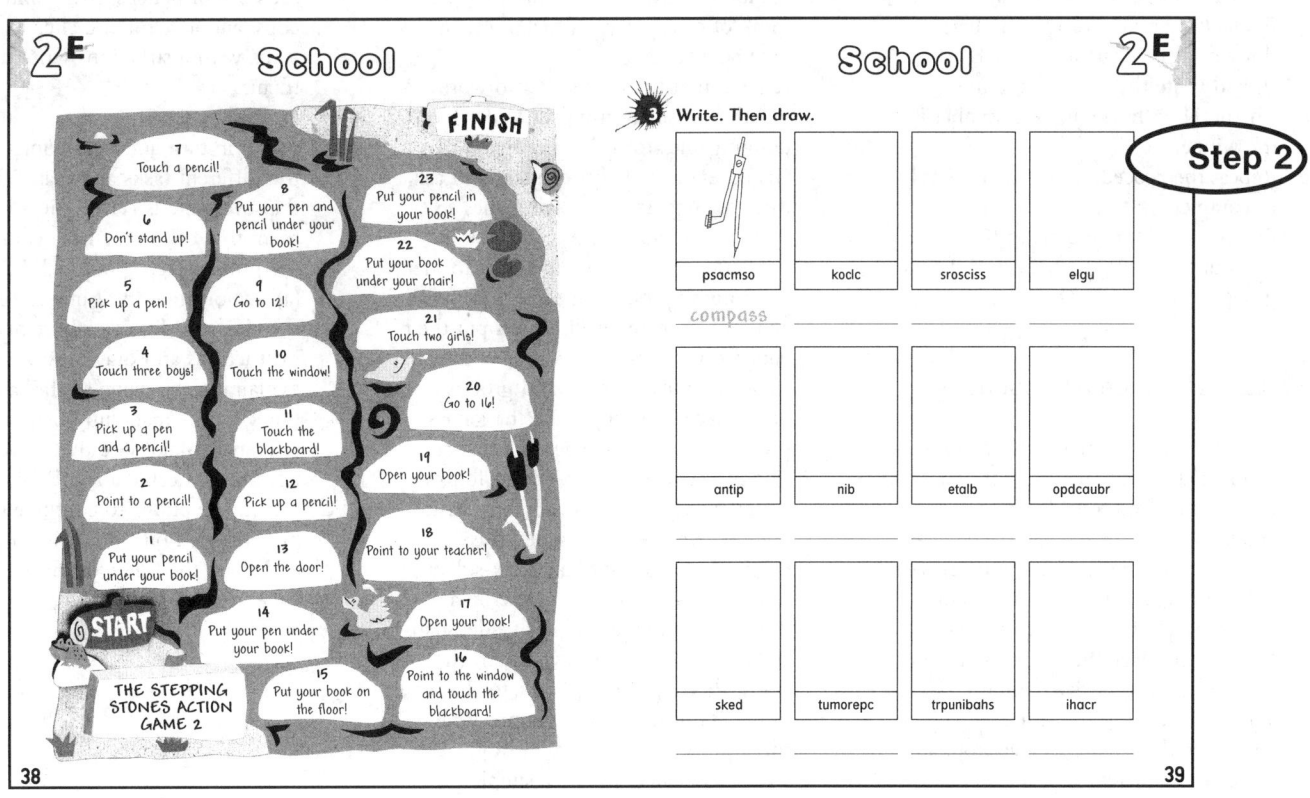

Word Stones

Use

pink blue white red

Make

glue sink bed kite

The Stepping Stones Game

The pink bag in
red is on chair
blue the table
pencil bag
orange book under
green

Step 1

Find more words

clock, computer, cupboard, desk, bin

paint, scissors, compass, paintbrush, glue

28 29

School

THE STEPPING STONES ACTION GAME 2

1. Put your pencil under your book!
2. Point to a pencil!
3. Pick up a pen and a pencil!
4. Touch three boys!
5. Pick up a pen!
6. Don't stand up!
7. Touch a pencil!
8. Put your pen and pencil under your book!
9. Go to 12!
10. Touch the window!
11. Touch the blackboard!
12. Pick up a pencil!
13. Open the door!
14. Put your pen under your book!
15. Put your book on the floor!
16. Point to the window and touch the blackboard!
17. Open your book!
18. Point to your teacher!
19. Open your book!
20. Go to 16!
21. Touch two girls!
22. Put your book under your chair!
23. Put your pencil in your book!

FINISH

School

3 Write. Then draw.

Step 2

psacmso	koclc	srosciss	elgu
compass			

antip	nib	etalb	opdcaubr

sked	tumorepc	trpunibahs	ihacr

38 39

87

2F Lesson 1 – Project

Main Language Items		Resource File	Materials Needed
numbers	colours		dice
dice	chancer	4	card and coloured pencils to make counters
winner	coin		cassette/cassette player
counter	heads		project materials
start	tails		
finish			

Step 1 Throw a dice and write

a Say '**Open your Activity Books at page 40**' and look at the chart at the top of the page.
b Divide the class into groups of three. Each group needs a dice. (If dice are unavailable, the numbers 1–6 can be written on each side of a six-sided pencil.)
c Each pupil throws the dice in turn. Pupils keep a note of the number thrown in the chart in their AB. They should write their score in letters.
d The pupil with the highest number is the winner.
e Repeat the procedure two more times to complete the chart.
f Pupils can continue playing the game without the chart, possibly in different groups.

Step 2 Dice and counters

a This game can be played alone, in pairs or in groups. Each player or group needs a dice and four different coloured counters: red, yellow, blue and green. Players decide what type of race it is and make counters out of card accordingly, e.g. tortoises, cars, etc.
b Pupils then place the counters at the start on the appropriate colour.
c Throw the dice in turn for each colour and move the counter the appropriate number of squares.
d The first 'tortoise', 'car', etc. to finish is the winner.

Step 3 Start a project

a Say '**Look at the photo on page 30 of the Coursebook.**' Ask pupils in their L1 what they can see with numbers on. What other objects can they think of that are to do with numbers in their classroom? Can they think of other ways of making their own chancers?
b Explain that they are going to work together in small groups in order to design games for other groups to play. Give them a short list of ideas and ask them to suggest additional games so that you can add them to the list. Encourage originality. This list can then be written up on a large sheet of paper and affixed to the wall. Pupils put their names down next to the project they want to be involved in, and groups can be formed accordingly. All the games should include an element of chance. The players can be required to follow an instruction, identify a colour, write a number, etc. Here are some ideas:
• Six-sided roller – Make a six-sided roller out of cardboard and write a different instruction on each side, such as **Point to the window, Touch the floor, Pick up a pen, Walk to the door, Stand up, Turn around, Draw three pens, Draw a brown dog, …**
• Heads or tails – Make a simple prediction game of 'heads or tails', using a coin and a prediction grid that players tick or cross.
• Spin the bottle – Write different instructions on a round mat, then spin a bottle to select one.
• Pin the tail on the instruction – Fill a large poster with instructions, blindfold players and get them to pin a tail on one.
• The Fishing Game – Make fishing rods out of pencils, string and paper clips, and attach more clips to small cards with instructions written on them.
c Before they start, sit down with each group in turn and help pupils organise the different tasks and materials, so that everyone is actively involved. Tell them that once they have completed the project each group will be asked to (a) demonstrate the game to the rest of the class and (b) contribute one page of instructions and drawings or sketches explaining the game so that a class book can be made up for future reference. Make sure they have the necessary vocabulary in English.
d Encourage pupils to continue their project work outside their English class and share their new games with friends.

Step 3

START A PROJECT

School 2F

SUPERSNAKE

This is the worm school.

2F School

Step 1

1. Throw a dice and write.

	Game 1	Game 2	Game 3
me			
friend 1			
friend 2			

Step 2

2. Throw a dice and move the counters.

START — yellow — red — green — blue — FINISH

School 2F

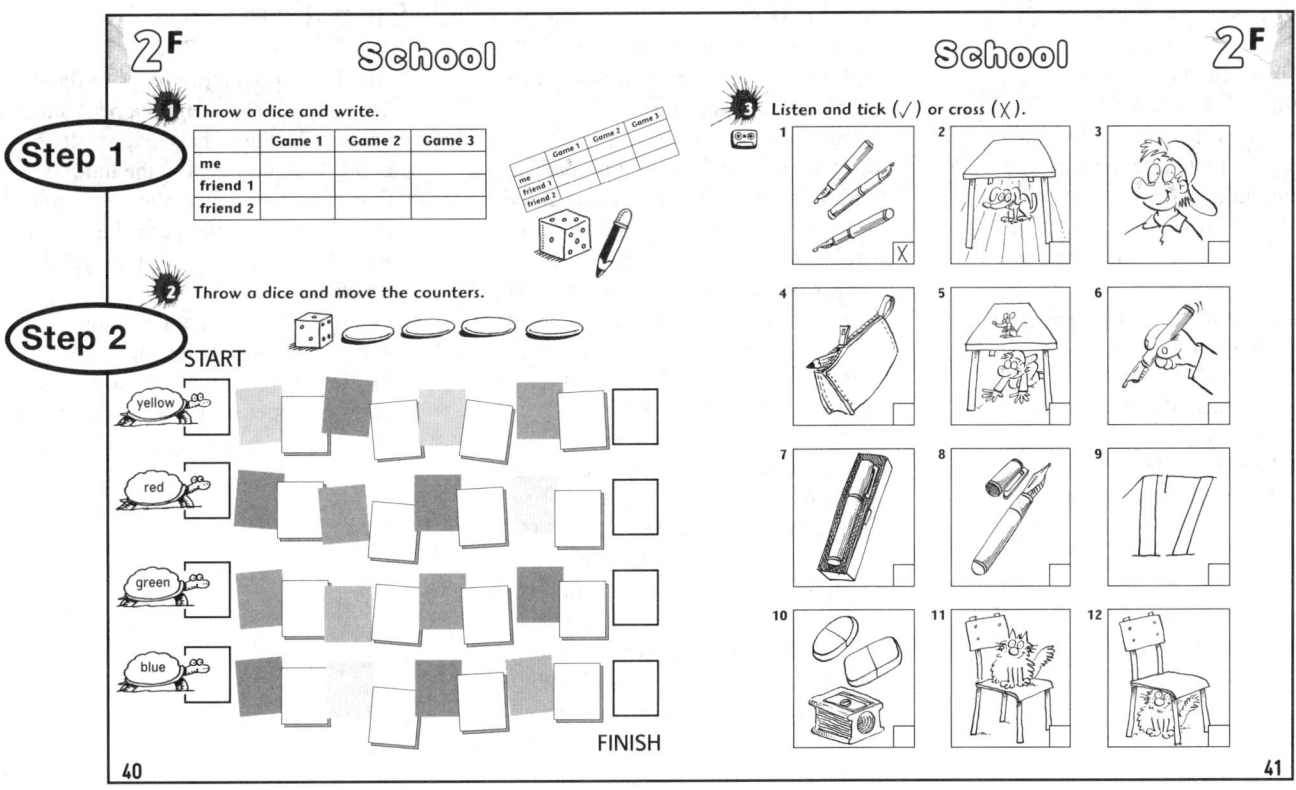

3. Listen and tick (✓) or cross (✗).

2F Lesson 2 – Evaluation

Main Language Items		Resource File	Materials Needed
What's four and five?	number		Test cards 2F (see photocopy masters on p.174)
That's very difficult.	school	27	scissors (optional)
I don't know.	worm	33	Supersnake puppets
Thanks.			cassette/cassette player
Goodbye.			

Step 1 Listening (Test)

a Look at the pictures on AB page 41. There is a short dialogue or sentence about each of the pictures. Pupils must decide if the dialogue or sentence is appropriate to the picture. If it is appropriate, they should put a tick in the corresponding box, if not, a cross. Play each one three times.

Tapescript (with answers):
1 How many pens are there? ~ Four (✗)
2 The cat is on the table. (✗)
3 Who's this? ~ Kev. (✓)
4 The pencil is in the pencil case. (✓)
5 Kev is on the table and Wow is under the table. (✗)
6 What's this? ~ It's a pencil. (✗)
7 Where's the pen? ~ Under the box. (✗)
8 Is this a pencil? ~ No, it's a pen. (✓)
9 What number's this? ~ Number sixteen. (✗)
10 How many pencil sharpeners are there? ~ One. (✓)
11 Where's the cat? ~ On the chair. (✓)
12 Where's the cat? ~ Under the table. (✗)

Step 2 Test yourself

a Photocopy one set of Test Cards 2F for each pupil (see photocopy master on TG page 174).
b Say 'Open your Activity Books at page 42 and look at the pictures.' Hand out the test card sheets and ask pupils to cut out the cards. Alternatively, give each pupil a set of cards already cut out. Pupils fold the ten cards along the dotted line, as shown in the picture.
c To do Test 1, pupils place all their cards in front of them with the pictures showing, following the visual instructions. Demonstrate.
d You can read the first word in the list, 'a book'. Pupils find the card with the picture of a book, and turn it over to read the word on the other side, to check whether they were correct. Then they put a tick or a cross in the box in their AB, according to whether they were right or wrong. Pupils then repeat for the other words.
e To do Test 2, pupils place all their cards in front of them with the words showing, following the visual instruction. Demonstrate.
f Pupils then look at the first picture, which is of a pen. Pupils must find the card with 'a pen' written on it, turn it over and look at the picture to check. They then put a tick or a cross in the box, according to whether they were right or wrong. Pupils then repeat for the other pictures.

g Pupils add up their scores out of ten for each test and total them. Finally, they circle the appropriate comment.

Step 3 Supersnake

a Look at the Supersnake cartoon on page 31 of the CB. Listen to the dialogue, reading at the same time.

Step 4 Role play

a Divide the class into groups of three. Two pupils need worm puppets and one pupil a Supersnake puppet. If pupils have no puppets, the index finger can be used for the worms and the whole arm for Supersnake.
b Play the tape again. This time pupils repeat.
c Pupils practise the puppet show without the help of the tape.
d Ask for one group to volunteer to act out the puppet show for the rest of the class.

START A PROJECT

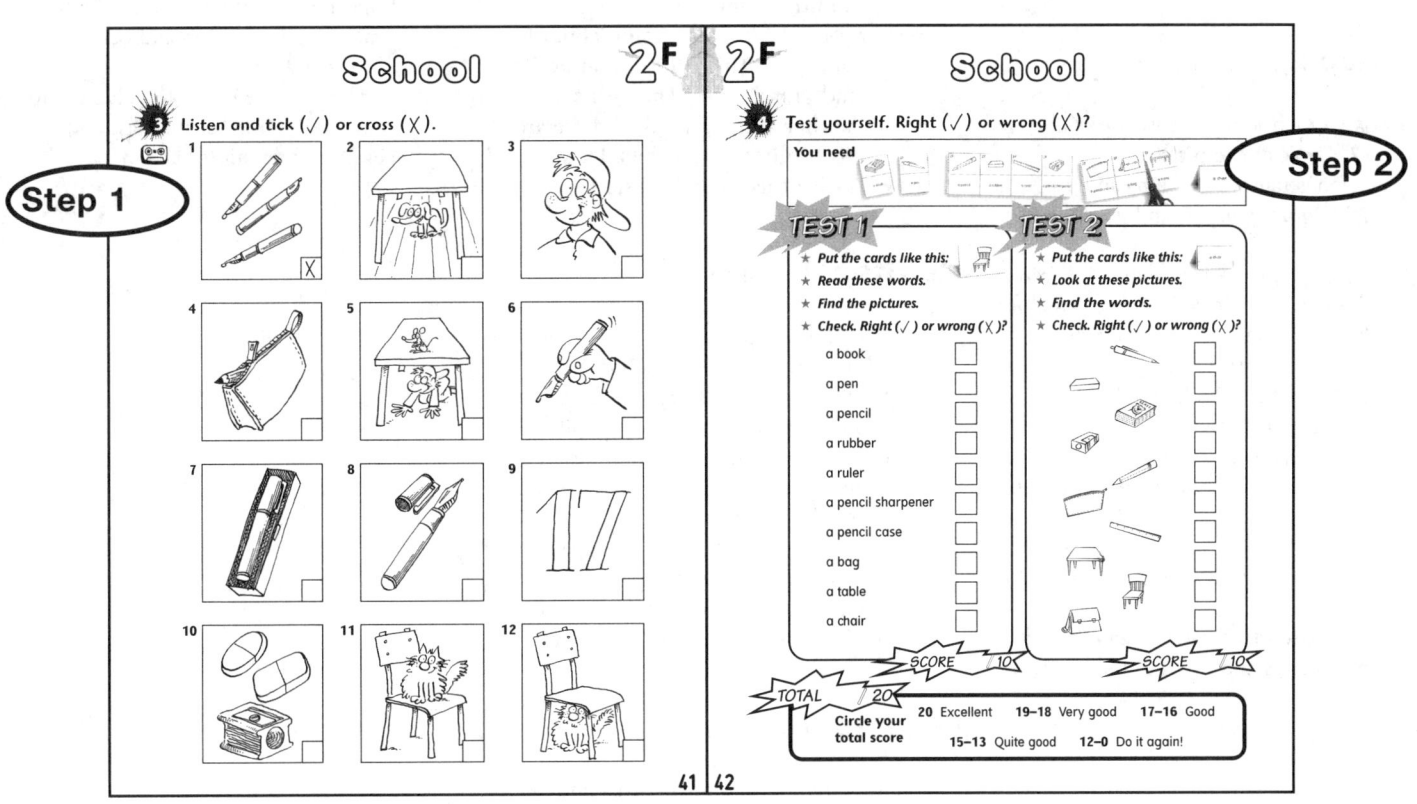

School 2F

SUPERSNAKE

This is the worm school.

Oh, dear! What is four and five?

Willy, what's four and five?

That's very difficult. I don't know.

Hey, look! There's Supersnake.

Look. A number!

It's number nine.

Four and five is nine.

Thanks, Supersnake. Goodbye.

Step 3

School 2F

3 Listen and tick (✓) or cross (✗).

Step 1

2F School

4 Test yourself. Right (✓) or wrong (✗)?

You need

Step 2

TEST 1
- Put the cards like this:
- Read these words.
- Find the pictures.
- Check. Right (✓) or wrong (✗)?

a book
a pen
a pencil
a rubber
a ruler
a pencil sharpener
a pencil case
a bag
a table
a chair

SCORE /10

TEST 2
- Put the cards like this:
- Look at these pictures.
- Find the words.
- Check. Right (✓) or wrong (✗)?

SCORE /10

TOTAL /20

Circle your total score
- 20 Excellent
- 19–18 Very good
- 17–16 Good
- 15–13 Quite good
- 12–0 Do it again!

3 Story lesson

Main Language Items				Resource File	Materials Needed
Who's that!	That's ...	my	sister		
Who are they?	This is ...	his	brother	34	
Is that...?	He's got ...	me	mother	46	cassette/cassette player
		photographs	father	45a	
		family	grandmother		
		friend	grandfather		

Step 1 Topic warm-up

a Tell pupils in their L1 that they are going to continue their English lessons by looking at families and friends. Introduce the words **family** and **friend** at this point.

b Then ask pupils what words they think they might learn. Can pupils tell you any words for members of the family in English?

Step 2 Story prediction

a Say 'Open your Coursebooks at page 32. Look at the pictures.' Demonstrate what you mean by holding up your CB and pointing to the pictures.

b Ask pupils in their L1 what they can see. Who are the children and what is their relationship? Where do they think they are?

c Ask what they think is going to happen in the story.

d Ask pupils if they can see anything in the pictures they can name in English.

Step 3 Story listening

a Say '**Listen to the tape.**' Pupils look at the pictures and listen to the tape at the same time.

b Play the tape again.

Tapescript:
BILL: Hey Kev, come here! Look at my photographs.
KEV: Who's that?
BILL: My sister, Suzy.
KEV: And is that Suzy?
BILL: No. That's my brother, Gary ... This is my mother and father. It's good, isn't it?
KEV: Mmm. It's OK ... Who are they?
BILL: My grandmother and grandfather. And this is me.
NARRATOR: Wow is dreaming about his family ... This is his grandmother and grandfather. This is his mother and father. And these are his brothers and sisters. He's got 21 brothers and 19 sisters.

Step 4 Story task

a Play the first part of the dialogue and point to Bill as he is speaking.

b Play the complete story on tape again and demonstrate the task to pupils: point to each character in turn as he is speaking. Pupils listen to the tape and watch the demonstration.

c Then play the complete story again. Pupils listen, look at the pictures and point to each character in turn as he or she is speaking.

Step 5 Story mime

a Allocate the roles of Bill, Kev and Wow to volunteers. Ask them to stand up as their character speaks/appears. Play the tape.

b Play the tape again. This time pupils stand up and perform actions as appropriate, miming the movements of the characters, e.g. Bill shows Kev some photos as he says '**Look at my photographs.**' Pupils can also mouth the words as they listen to the tape.

c Now divide the class into groups of three and allocate roles. Play the tape again. Pupils stand up and perform actions as appropriate.

d Finally, ask one group to volunteer to come to the front of the class and perform, listening to the tape.

3 Families

STORY

Family Photographs

Step 2
Step 3
Step 4

32

33

3A Lesson 1

Main Language Items		Resource File	Materials Needed
Who's this?	Mr Mills	5	
Is this ...?	Mrs Mills	23	
Is this ... or ...?	Mr Kay	41	cassette/cassette player
	Mrs Kay	45a	
	Gary	46	

Step 1 Action Game

a Revise the following instructions and words with individuals and the whole group:

Don't	a boy
Point to ...	a girl
Touch ...	the floor
Stand on ...	a chair
Sit on ...	a/the table
Stand up!	the door
Turn around!	pencil
Walk to ...	pen
Pick up ...	Activity Book
Put down ...	Coursebook
Open your ...	blackboard
Close your ...	window
Put your ... on ...	chalk
Put your ... under ...	

b Play a game contrasting the words **boys** and **girls**. Divide the class into two teams. One of the teams should be made up of all the boys in the class, the other all the girls. Do not physically separate the two teams, since this will detract from the game. Write the words **BOYS** and **GIRLS** on the blackboard for scoring purposes.

c Use combinations of the above instructions, preceded or followed by the words **boys** or **girls**. Only members of the appropriate team must follow the instructions.
e.g. **Boys, touch the floor.**
Girls, don't stand up.
Don't pick up your pencil, boys.
Open your Activity Books, girls.

d Points are awarded for the following reasons: if any member of the opposing team fails to obey an instruction; if a member of the opposing team carries out an instruction not directed at their team; if a member of the opposing team carries out an instruction preceded by 'Don't'.

Step 2 Presentation

a Say 'Open your Coursebooks at page 32 and look at the pictures.' Play the whole story on tape.

b Then say 'Open your Coursebooks at page 34' and ask pupils to look at the first two frames of the story. Ask pupils to tell you in their L1 what the language in the speech bubbles means.

c Play the story extract and point to the characters.

d Divide the class into pairs. All pairs work simultaneously. Play the tape again. P1 repeats Bill's words and P2 repeats Kev's words.

e Change roles and repeat the procedure.

Tapescript:
BILL: Hey Kev, come here! Look at my photographs.
KEV: Who's that?
BILL: My sister, Suzy.

Step 3 Presentation

a Look at the picture of Bill's family at the bottom of page 34.

b Listen to the tape and read the passage at the same time.

c Then pupils cover the words. Hold up your book and ask the class some simple questions about the picture. Use 'Who's this?', 'What his/her name?', etc.

d With the words still covered, pupils listen to the tape again, this time repeating line by line.

Step 4 Pair work

a Divide the class into pairs. Pupils ask and answer questions about the picture of Bill's family at the bottom of CB page 34. Use the structure '**Who's this?**' Begin by asking a few sample questions to the whole class, then write the question form on the blackboard.

b Continue briefly until the pupils are familiar with the names and then revise the question forms '**Is this Mr Kay?**' and finally '**Is this Mr Kay or Mrs Kay?**'

c Pupils then practise a variety of questions using all three structures.

Step 5 Match and write

a Say '**Open your Activity Books at page 43.**' Look at activity 1. Pupils draw a line to connect the characters to the appropriate photographs.

b Pupils write the names of the characters on the lines provided.

Step 6 Write

a Pupils read the questions and write the answers on the lines provided on page 43 of the AB. Use the information in the CB to help.

b Pupils then swap books with their partners and check and correct each other's answers.

Who's That?

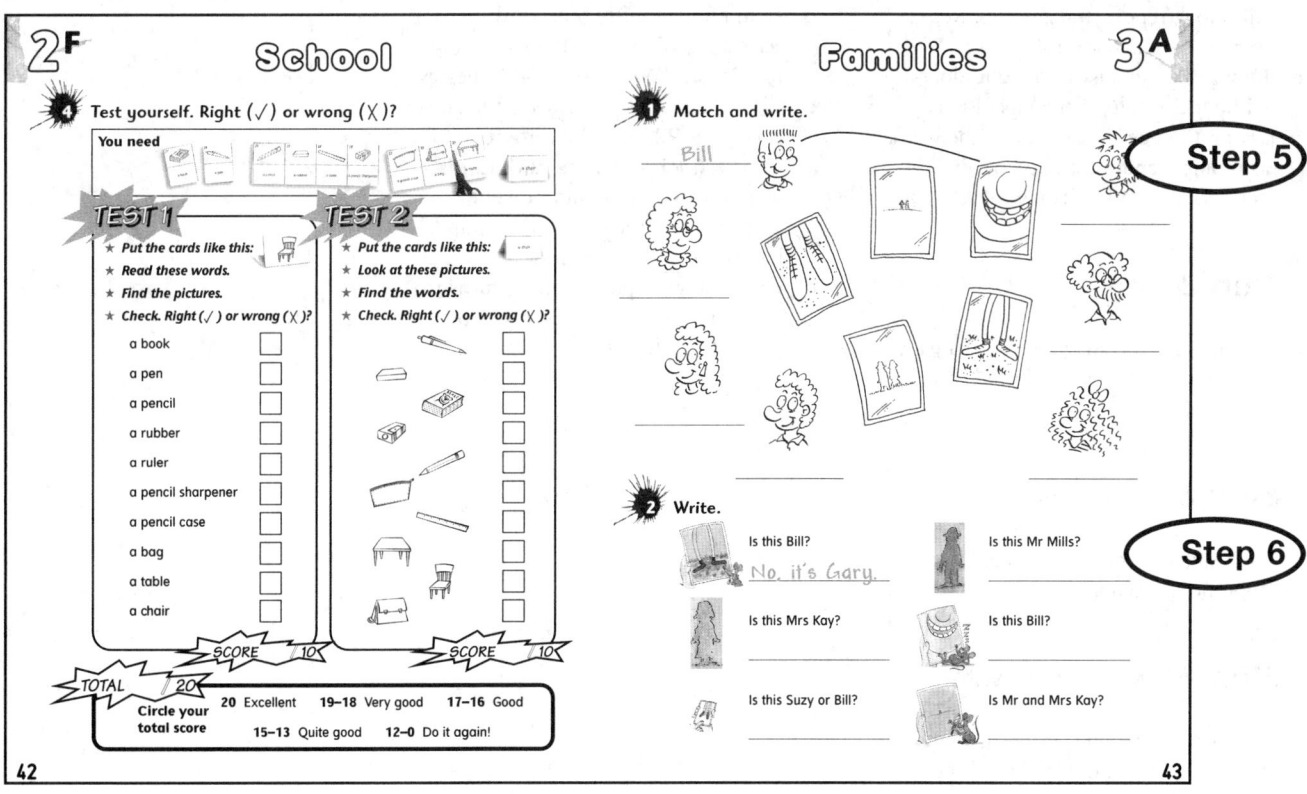

Listen

Hey Kev, come here! Look at my photographs!

Who's that?

My sister, Suzy.

Listen

This is my family. I've got one brother and one sister. My brother is called Gary and my sister is called Suzy. My father and mother are called Mr and Mrs Kay. My grandfather and grandmother are called Mr and Mrs Mills.

Families 3A

Ask and answer

my family

me — my brother — my sister — my father — my mother — my grandfather — my grandmother

Say the rhyme

How Many?

How many people live at your house?
One, my father.
Two, my mother.
Three, my sister.
Four, my brother.
There's one more. Now let me see.
Oh yes, of course. It must be me!

2F School

4 Test yourself. Right (✓) or wrong (✗)?

You need...

TEST 1
★ Put the cards like this:
★ Read these words.
★ Find the pictures.
★ Check. Right (✓) or wrong (✗)?

- a book
- a pen
- a pencil
- a rubber
- a ruler
- a pencil sharpener
- a pencil case
- a bag
- a table
- a chair

SCORE /10

TEST 2
★ Put the cards like this:
★ Look at these pictures.
★ Find the words.
★ Check. Right (✓) or wrong (✗)?

SCORE /10

TOTAL /20
Circle your total score
20 Excellent   19–18 Very good   17–16 Good
15–13 Quite good   12–0 Do it again!

Families 3A

1 Match and write.

Bill

2 Write.

Is this Bill? No, it's Gary.

Is this Mr Mills?

Is this Mrs Kay?

Is this Bill?

Is this Suzy or Bill?

Is Mr and Mrs Kay?

95

3A Lesson 2

Main Language Items		Resource File	Materials Needed
Who's this?	mother me	16a	
It's me.	father	29	character cards (9–15)
It's my ...	brother	47	coloured pencils
	sister	8a	cassette/cassette player
	grandfather	26a	
	grandfather	52	

Step 1 Pair work

a Divide the class into pairs, with one CB between each pair, open at page 35. Say 'Cover the words. Look at Bill's pictures.' One pupil in each pair plays the role of Bill and answers the questions. All pairs work simultaneously.
b Pupils repeat after the tape. P1 repeats the question 'Who's this?', pointing at the appropriate picture. P2, playing Bill's role, repeats the answers. Repeat four times, changing roles.
c Pupils ask and answer the questions without the help of the tape. Pupils asking the questions may use the words as prompts and must check their partners' answers. Change roles.

Step 2 Write

a Pupils solve the anagrams on AB page 44 and write the words in the spaces provided.

Step 3 Read and colour

Pupils colour the 'photograph' with the appropriate colours.

Step 4 Match and write

Pupils trace the lines from the numbers to the pictures and write the names of the appropriate characters in the spaces provided.

Step 5 Character card game

As pupils finish the puzzles in the AB, let them move on to the following simple card game in pairs.

a Use character cards 9–15 of the family. Pupils work in pairs. They need one pack of seven cards each.
b Both pupils shuffle their cards. P1 selects a card and, without showing it to P2, asks 'Who's this?' P2 guesses.
c Then P1 reveals the card. If the answer is correct, P2 wins the card; if incorrect, P1 keeps the card. Cards won in this way should be kept separate from the cards in the pupils' hands, for scoring purposes.
d Continue with pupils taking turns to ask and answer the questions. The player to collect the most cards is the winner.

Who's That?

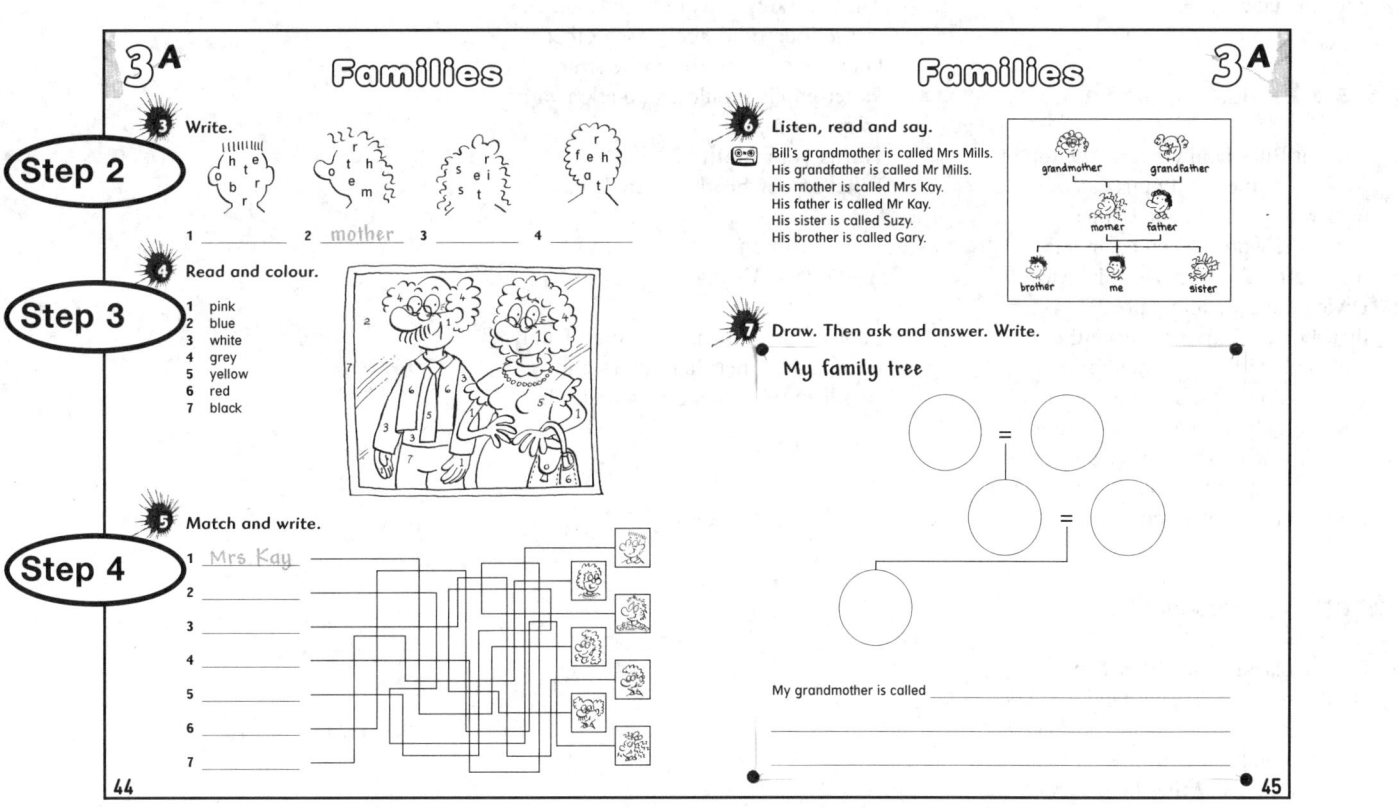

Listen

Hey Kev, come here! Look at my photographs!

Who's that?

My sister, Suzy.

Listen

This is my family. I've got one brother and one sister. My brother is called Gary and my sister is called Suzy. My father and mother are called Mr and Mrs Kay. My grandfather and grandmother are called Mr and Mrs Mills.

Families 3A

Ask and answer

my family

me — my brother — my sister
my father — my mother — my grandfather — my grandmother

Say the rhyme

How Many?

How many people live at your house?
One, my father.
Two, my mother.
Three, my sister.
Four, my brother.
There's one more. Now let me see.
Oh yes, of course. It must be me!

34

35

3A Families

3 Write.

1 _____ 2 mother 3 _____ 4 _____

4 Read and colour.
1 pink
2 blue
3 white
4 grey
5 yellow
6 red
7 black

5 Match and write.
1 Mrs Kay
2 _____
3 _____
4 _____
5 _____
6 _____
7 _____

44

Families 3A

6 Listen, read and say.

Bill's grandmother is called Mrs Mills.
His grandfather is called Mr Mills.
His mother is called Mrs Kay.
His father is called Mr Kay.
His sister is called Suzy.
His brother is called Gary.

grandmother — grandfather
mother — father
brother — me — sister

7 Draw. Then ask and answer. Write.

My family tree

○ = ○
  ○ = ○
○

My grandmother is called _____

45

97

3A Lesson 3

Main Language Items	Resource File	Materials Needed
My ... is called ... What's your *father's* name? What's your ... called? Is this your *mother*?	1 2 3 4	cassette/cassette player paper for display (optional)

Step 1   Rhyme

a   Say 'Open your Coursebooks at page 35. Look at the picture at the bottom of the page.'
b   Then listen to the rhyme on the tape, reading at the same time.
c   Listen again line by line with books closed and repeat the words. Do each line in the same way.
d   Play the rhyme again and sing along with the tape.

Step 2   Listen, read and say

a   Look at Bill's family tree at the top of page 45 in the AB. Pupils listen to the tape, reading at the same time.
b   Cover the words, listen again and repeat after the tape. Do this twice.
c   Divide the class into pairs. P1 takes their book. P2 tries to recite the sentences without the help of the words but using the picture in the book to help. P1 must correct and prompt where necessary. (Co-operation is very important in this exercise.) Then pupils change roles and repeat.

Step 3   Personal file

a   On the blackboard, either draw a family tree of your own family or ask one of the pupils to name the members of their family, and draw their family tree as a model. Write the names of family members alongside the pictures.
b   Pupils then draw their own family tree in the space provided on AB page 45, using Bill's family tree as a model.

Step 4   Pair work

a   Ask pupils the names of their family members to introduce the structure:
    What's your father's name?
b   Then working in pairs, pupils ask and answer questions about each other's family tree, using the above structure.
c   Faster pupils should try to ask a variety of questions, i.e.
    Is this your mother?
    What's your brother called? etc.

Step 5   Write

Pupils write the names of their family members on their family tree and complete the sentences underneath.

Who's That?

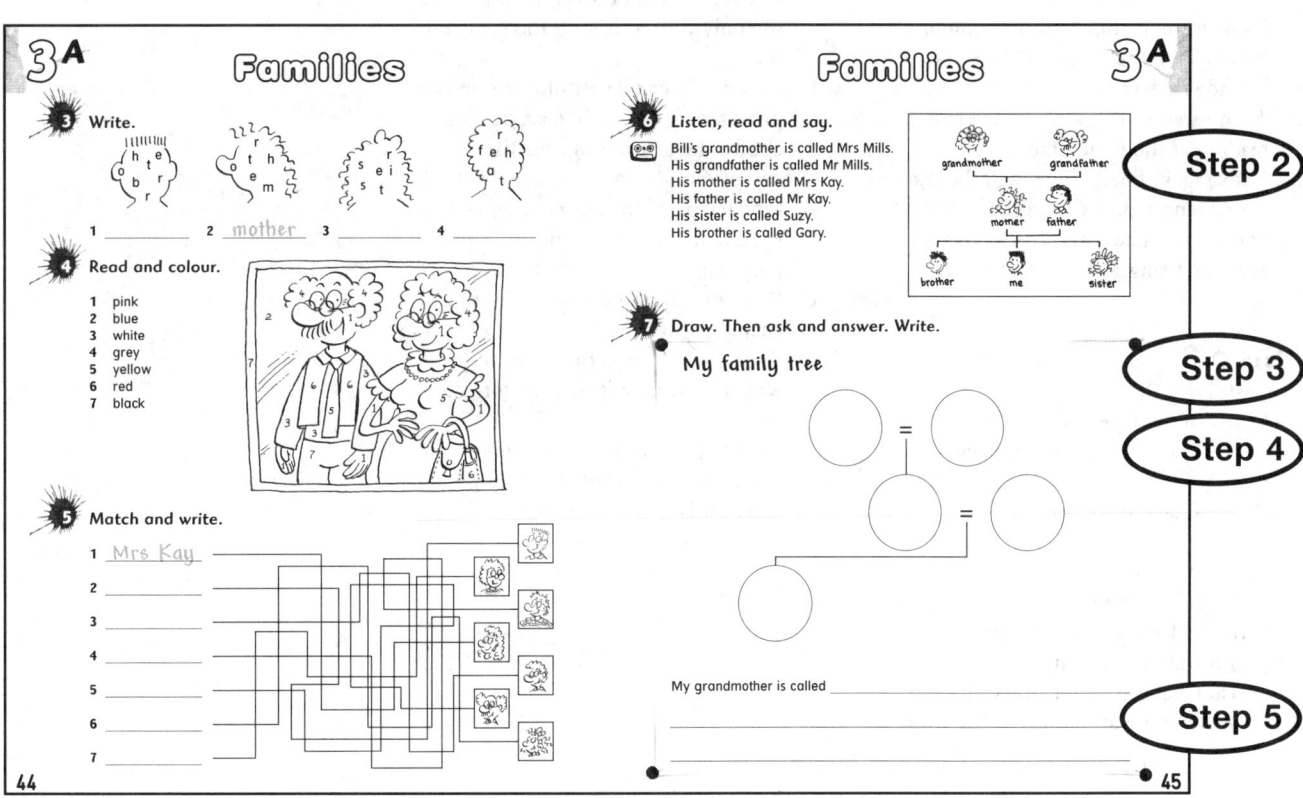

Listen

"Hey Kev, come here! Look at my photographs!"

"Who's that?"

"My sister, Suzy."

Listen

"This is my family. I've got one brother and one sister. My brother is called Gary and my sister is called Suzy. My father and mother are called Mr and Mrs Kay. My grandfather and grandmother are called Mr and Mrs Mills."

Families 3A

Ask and answer

my family

me — my brother — my sister
my father — my mother — my grandfather — my grandmother

Say the rhyme

How Many?

How many people live at your house?
One, my father.
Two, my mother.
Three, my sister.
Four, my brother.
There's one more. Now let me see.
Oh yes, of course. It must be me!

Step 1

34 / 35

3A Families

3 Write.

1. _____ 2. _mother_ 3. _____ 4. _____

(letters: h t e o b r r / r t h o m e / s r i e s t / r f e h a t)

4 Read and colour.

1 pink
2 blue
3 white
4 grey
5 yellow
6 red
7 black

5 Match and write.

1 Mrs Kay
2 _____
3 _____
4 _____
5 _____
6 _____
7 _____

Families 3A

6 Listen, read and say.

Bill's grandmother is called Mrs Mills.
His grandfather is called Mr Mills.
His mother is called Mrs Kay.
His father is called Mr Kay.
His sister is called Suzy.
His brother is called Gary.

grandmother — grandfather
mother — father
brother — me — sister

Step 2

7 Draw. Then ask and answer. Write.

My family tree

Step 3

Step 4

My grandmother is called _____

Step 5

44 / 45

99

3B Lesson 1

Main Language Items		Resource File	Materials Needed
How old are you?	Happy Birthday		
I'm/He's/She's 6 (years old)	birthday card	7	coloured pencils
Colour ...	badge	32	cassette/cassette player
Write ...	today		character cards 9–15

Step 1 Presentation

a Say 'Open your Coursebooks at page 36. Look at the pictures at the top of the page.'
b Play the tape. Pupils follow the dialogue looking at the pictures at the same time.

Step 2 Song

a Look at the picture and the song on page 36. Tell the class '**This is Gary's birthday party.**'
b Then listen to the song on the tape reading at the same time.
c Listen again line by line, with books closed, and repeat the words. Do each line in the same way. Play the song again and sing along with the tape.

Step 3 Listen and write

a Listen to the tape and write the ages of the children in the grid on page 46 of the AB.
b Play the tape three times.

Tapescript:
I'm Bill. I'm nine years old. My friend Kev is also nine years old and our friend Julie is ten. My sister Suzy is eight years old and her friend Kate is seven. My little brother Gary is five.

Step 4 Read and colour

a Working individually, pupils read the passage and colour the birthday card appropriately. This exercise may be finished for homework.

Step 5 Character card game

a Pupils work in pairs with two sets of character cards between each pair. They use only the cards with the six children on.
b P1 turns over one set of cards and gives the age of each character. P2 checks the answers against the completed grid on AB page 46. Each time P1 gives the correct age, they keep that character card for scoring purposes.
c P2 goes through the second set of character cards in the same way, giving the ages. P2 keeps the character card which corresponds to each correct answer.
d Each pupil counts up the number of cards they have kept. The pupil with most cards is the winner.

Step 1

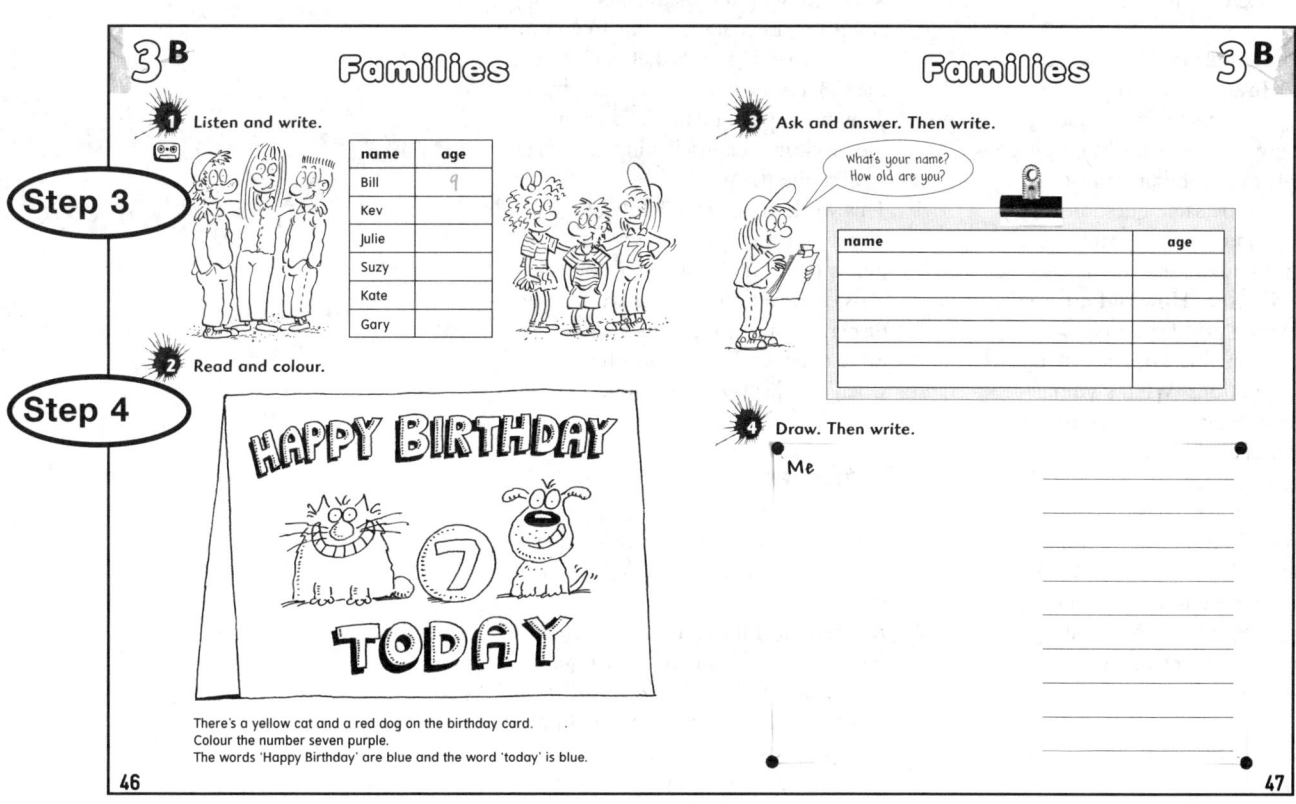

Happy Birthday

Listen

- What's that?
- A badge. It's my birthday today.
- How old are you?
- I'm five.
- Happy Birthday!
- Thank you.

Step 2

Sing

Happy Birthday to You!

Happy Birthday to you,
Happy Birthday to you,
Happy Birthday dear Gary,
Happy Birthday to you.

Listen

My name is Suzy.
I am eight years old.

Play

Snakes and Ladders

The winner!

100 a hundred

Families 3B

91	92	93	94	95	96	97	98	99
90 ninety	89	88	87	86	85	84	83	82
73	74	75	76	77	78	79	80 eighty	81
72	71	70 seventy	69	68	67	66	65	64
55	56	57	58	59	60 sixty	61	62	63
54	53	52	51	50 fifty	49	48	47	46
37	38	39	40 forty	41	42	43	44	45
36	35	34	33	32	31	30 thirty	29	28
19	20 twenty	21	22	23	24	25	26	27
18	17	16	15	14	13	12	11	10 ten
1	2	3	4	5	6	7	8	9

START HERE

36 / 37

3B Families

Step 3

1. Listen and write.

name	age
Bill	9
Kev	
Julie	
Suzy	
Kate	
Gary	

2. Read and colour.

HAPPY BIRTHDAY
7
TODAY

There's a yellow cat and a red dog on the birthday card.
Colour the number seven purple.
The words 'Happy Birthday' are blue and the word 'today' is blue.

Step 4

Families 3B

3. Ask and answer. Then write.

What's your name?
How old are you?

name	age

4. Draw. Then write.

Me

46 / 47

101

3ᴮ Lesson 2

Main Language Items	Resource File	Materials Needed
How old are you? How old is …? What's your name? My name is … I'm *ten* years old.	1 2 19 35 35a	coloured pencils paper for display (optional) cassette/cassette player

Step 1   Presentation

a Say 'Open your Coursebooks at page 36. Look at the pictures at the top of the page.'
b Play the tape. Pupils follow the dialogue looking at the pictures at the same time.

Step 2   Groupwork: Questionnaire

a Ask various pupils in the class the question 'How old are you?'
b When pupils understand the question and can answer satisfactorily, encourage individuals to ask the person sitting next to them the same question.
c Set up a chain of such questions and responses going around the whole class, i.e. 'I'm ten. How old are you?'
d Then copy the grid from page 47 of the AB onto the blackboard. Ask one pupil the questions 'What's your name?' and 'How old are you?' Write the responses in the grid. Give one or two more examples.
e Pupils repeat the exercise, asking their friends and filling in the chart on page 47 of their AB.
f When pupils have finished, round up the exercise by asking the pupils the ages of other class members, i.e. '**How old is *Maria*?**'

Step 3   Presentation

a Look at the picture of Suzy at the bottom of CB page 36. Pupils listen to the tape and read at the same time.

Step 4   Personal file

a Pupils draw a picture of themselves in the box provided on AB page 47 and write a description of the picture alongside. Encourage pupils to compare their description with that of Suzy's in the CB. (You could demonstrate by drawing a quick picture of a pupil on the blackboard and eliciting sentences to describe the picture.)
b This work makes excellent wall displays and it is very motivating for pupils to see their own work on the classroom wall. Individual work to be displayed in this way can be done on loose paper and stuck into the AB when the display is dismantled.

Optional   Game

a If there is time, use this quick game to end the lesson. Tell the pupils to close their books.
b Ask several children **How old are you?** Insist on the full answer. **I'm *eight*.**
c Ask other children the age of their classmates. **How old is *Maria*?** In most classes only two or three ages will be represented, so try to jump rapidly between the ages, in order to keep pupils attentive.

Happy Birthday

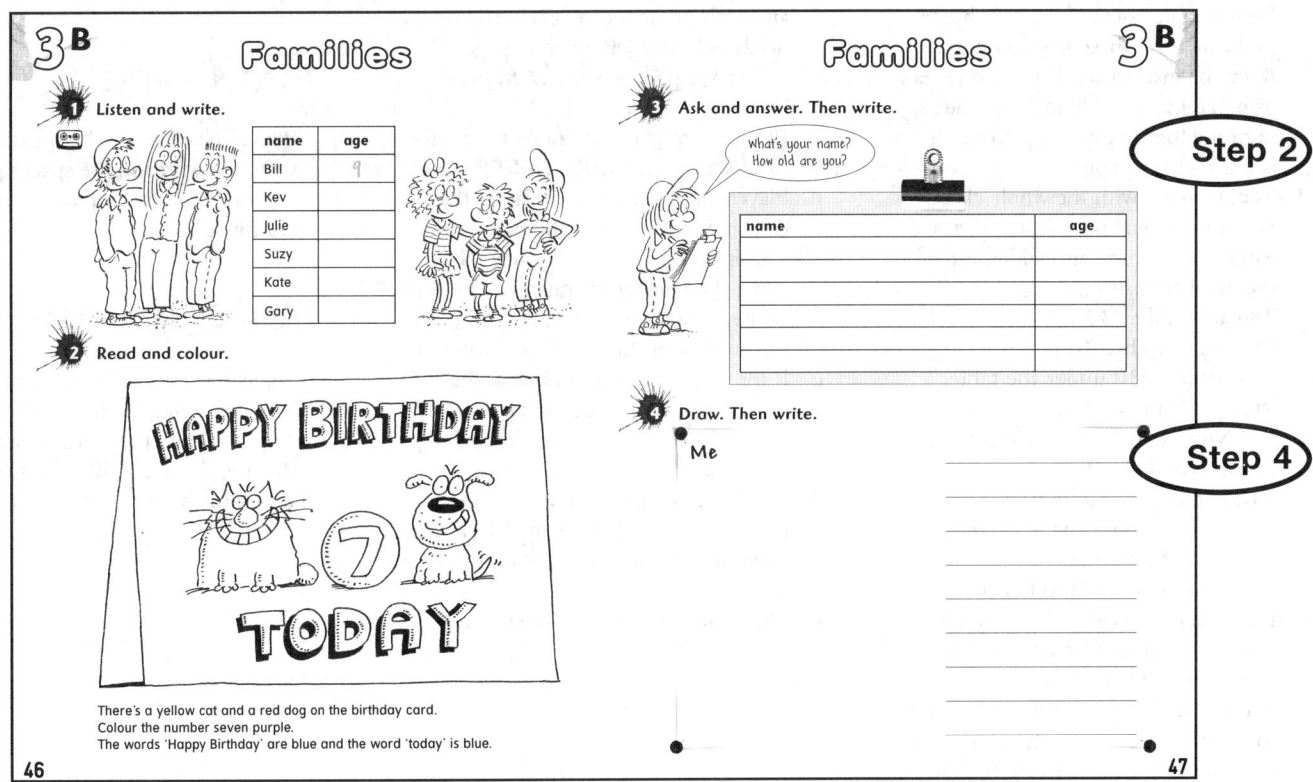

Step 1

Listen

- What's that?
- A badge. It's my birthday today.
- How old are you?
- I'm five.
- Happy Birthday!
- Thank you.

Sing — Happy Birthday to You!

Happy Birthday to you,
Happy Birthday to you,
Happy Birthday dear Gary,
Happy Birthday to you.

Step 3

Listen

My name is Suzy. I am eight years old.

36

Families 3B

Play — Snakes and Ladders

The winner! 100 a hundred

91	92	93	94	95	96	97	98	99
90 ninety	89	88	87	86	85	84	83	82
73	74	75	76	77	78	79	80 eighty	81
72	71	70 seventy	69	68	67	66	65	64
55	56	57	58	59	60 sixty	61	62	63
54	53	52	51	50 fifty	49	48	47	46
37	38	39	40 forty	41	42	43	44	45
36	35	34	33	32	31	30 thirty	29	28
19	20 twenty	21	22	23	24	25	26	27
18	17	16	15	14	13	12	11	10 ten
1	2	3	4	5	6	7	8	9

START HERE

37

3B Families

1 Listen and write.

name	age
Bill	9
Kev	
Julie	
Suzy	
Kate	
Gary	

2 Read and colour.

HAPPY BIRTHDAY 7 TODAY

There's a yellow cat and a red dog on the birthday card.
Colour the number seven purple.
The words 'Happy Birthday' are blue and the word 'today' is blue.

46

Families 3B

3 Ask and answer. Then write.

What's your name?
How old are you?

Step 2

name	age

4 Draw. Then write.

Me

Step 4

47

103

3B Lesson 3

Main Language Items	Resource File	Materials Needed
numbers 30–100 snakes ladders up down	20 31 32 32a 26a	numbers flashcards counters/dice

Step 1 Action Game

a Number flashcards are required for this game. The numbers 30, 40, 50, 60, 70, 80, 90, 100 should be written, one number on each card. Display the cards around the classroom. (Or write the numbers well apart on the blackboard.)

b Bring four pupils to the front. Use instructions '**Stand up! Walk! Stop!**'

c Say '**Point to Number 30. Point to Number 70. Point to Number 50.**' Demonstrate yourself if pupils have any problems with these new numbers. Keep the instructions brisk and repeat, using all the new numbers at random, until the four pupils can perform the actions without your help.

d Repeat step **c** with the whole class.

e Select individual pupils and practise a variety of instructions making use of the number flashcards, e.g.
Touch Number 30.
Pick up Number 30.
Put Number 30 under the table.
Pick up Number 70.
Put Number 70 on your chair.
Sit on Number 70. etc.

f Divide the class into four teams. Give each team a colour and write the team names on the blackboard.

g One member of each team comes to the front of the class. Tell them each to '**Pick up a piece of chalk.**' Then say '**Write number 68 on the blackboard.**' The first player to write the number (numeral only) on the blackboard wins a point for their team.

The second player then comes forward. Practise any number from 1–100. Continue until all players have had at least one go.

Step 2 Snakes and Ladders

A traditional board game to be played in groups of 2, 3 or 4. The game practises numbers and **up** and **down**. Each pupil needs a coloured counter and each group a dice. Each group needs only one CB, open at page 37. Encourage phrases such as '**My turn**', '**Pass the dice**', etc.

a Place the counters on the bottom left-hand square (1: START HERE).

b Players take it in turns to throw the dice and move around the board the appropriate number of squares. They count the number of squares in English as they move (one to six) and they say the number of the square they land on.

c If the square they land on is at the bottom of a ladder, e.g. square 4, they go up to the top of the ladder and say '**Up to 21**'.

d If the square they land on is at the head of a snake, e.g. square 13, they go down to the tail of the snake and say '**Down to 7**'.

e The winner is the first player to reach number 100.

Step 3 Add the numbers

a Say '**Open your Activity Books at page 48.**' Pupils add up the numbers that make up each head and write the age of the person on the line below. The written forms of the numbers occur on pages 24 and 37 of the CB. Encourage the use of referencing skills to complete this puzzle.

b Pupils can make their own number faces.

Step 4 Write

Pupils solve the number puzzles and write the words in the spaces provided. Use the *Words* section at the end of the CB for reference.

Step 5 Match and write

Pupils trace from the pets to the balloons above, to find out how old they are. Then they write a sentence about each animal, like the sentence about Butch.

Happy Birthday

Listen

- What's that?
- A badge. It's my birthday today.
- How old are you?
- I'm five.
- Happy Birthday!
- Thank you.

Sing — Happy Birthday to You!

Happy Birthday to you,
Happy Birthday to you,
Happy Birthday dear Gary,
Happy Birthday to you.

Listen

My name is Suzy. I am eight years old.

Families 3B — Snakes and Ladders

Play

The winner — 100 a hundred

91	92	93	94	95	96	97	98	99
90 ninety	89	88	87	86	85	84	83	82
73	74	75	76	77	78	79	80 eighty	81
72	71	70 seventy	69	68	67	66	65	64
55	56	57	58	59	60 sixty	61	62	63
54	53	52	51	50 fifty	49	48	47	46
37	38	39	40 forty	41	42	43	44	45
36	35	34	33	32	31	30 thirty	29	28
19	20 twenty	21	22	23	24	25	26	27
18	17	16	15	14	13	12	11	10 ten
1	2	3	4	5	6	7	8	9

START HERE

3B Families

5 Add the numbers. Then write.

How old is he? — thirty-one

How old is she? ___

How old is she? ___

How old is he? ___

6 Write.

| 10 | 20 | _thirty_ | 40 | 50 | 60 |

| 20 | 22 | 24 | 26 | __ | 30 |

| 50 | 55 | 60 | __ | 70 | 75 |

| 87 | 88 | __ | 90 | 91 | 92 |

7 Match and write.

5 4 3 6 13

Butch is five.
___
___
___

Families 3C

1 Write.

grandmother mother grandfather
father sister brother friend

1 Who's this? — Bill's sister.
2 Who's this? ___
3 Who's this? ___
4 Who's this? ___
5 Who's this? ___
6 Who's this? ___
7 Who's this? ___
8 Who's this? ___

2 Make word stones.

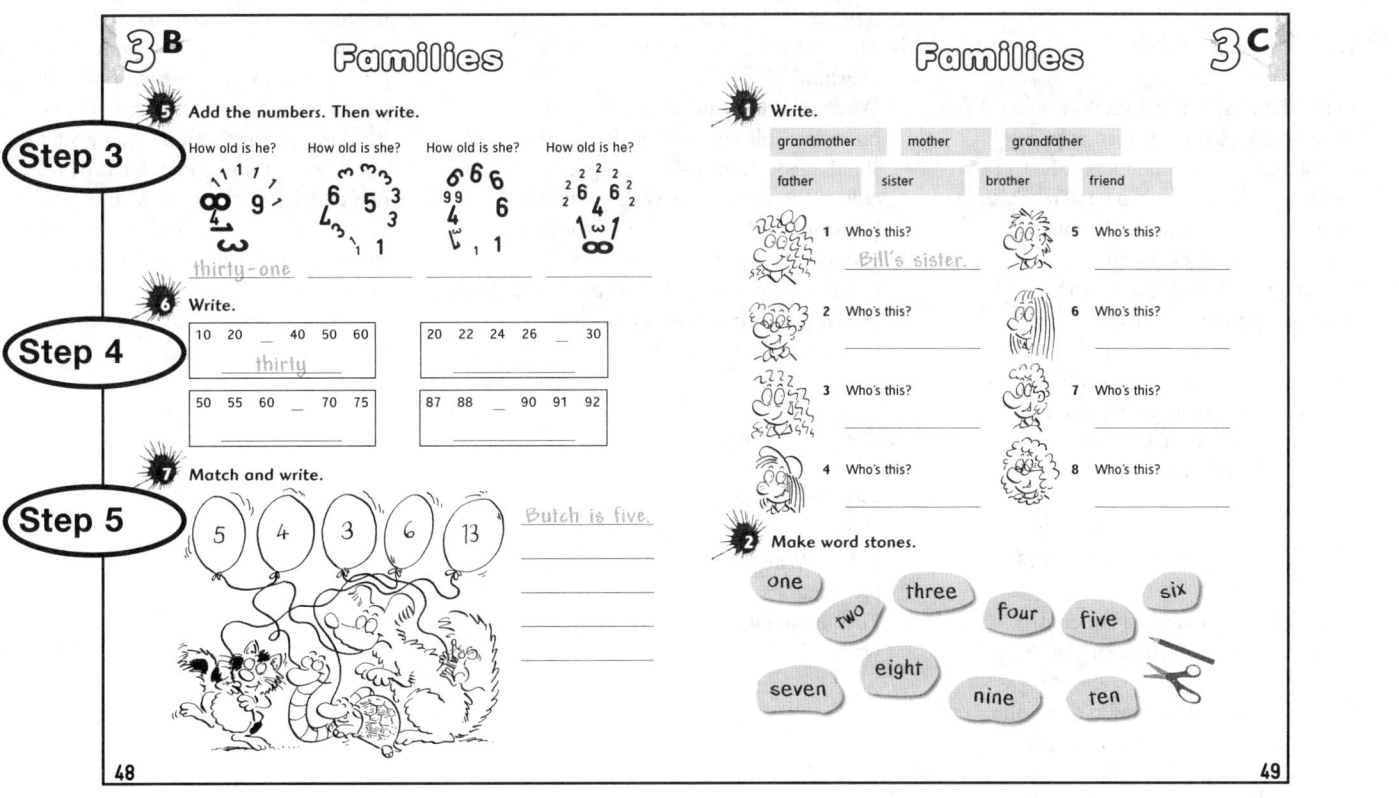

one two three four five six
seven eight nine ten

3c Lesson 1

Main Language Items		Resource File	Materials Needed
POSSESSIVE 's'	friend		
This is my friend	quickly	48	cassette/cassette player
isn't	slowly	47	character cards (6–15)
How are you?			materials to make word stones
Fine, thanks!			

Step 1 Presentation

a Say 'Open your Coursebooks at page 38.' Hold your book up for the class. Very quickly ask some preliminary questions about the pictures at the top of the page. Use **Who's this? Where's …? What's his/her name? Is this …?**

b Play the tape. Pupils follow the dialogue looking at the pictures at the same time.

Step 2 Pair work

a Divide the class into pairs. With one CB between each pair, open at page 38. All pairs work simultaneously.

b Pupils repeat after the tape. P1 repeats the questions. P2 repeats the answers. Repeat four times changing roles.

c Then pupils ask and answer the questions without the help of the tape. P1 asks the questions using the book to help. P2 answers without the help of the book. P1 should prompt and correct his/her partner's answers. Change roles and repeat

Step 3 Character card game

a Use the character cards numbered 6–15 from the AB centre cut-outs section.

b Pupils work in pairs. They require one pack of ten cards between each pair.

c Demonstrate the game with two pupils. Shuffle the cards. Lay the cards face down in a pile. P1 selects the top card, shows it to their partner and asks **'Who's this?'** P2 must answer, not giving the name of the character but their relationship to another character (i.e. pupils may describe Kate as **Kev's sister** or **Suzy's friend**, etc.). If P2 answers correctly, giving a true relationship, they win the card. If the answer is wrong, the card goes to the bottom of the pack.

d Then P2 selects a card and asks the question.

e When the class understand the procedure, all pupils play the game simultaneously in pairs. The player to collect the most cards is the winner.

f (Optional) Play the game as above but give points for each correct and possible relationship. Pupils may give as many possible answers as they can to each question.

Step 4 Write

a Read the questions on AB page 49 and choose the correct answers from the boxes. Write the answers in the spaces provided.

b Encourage pupils to check each other's work.

Step 5 Make word stones

a Pupils add ten more word stones to their collection.

b Say 'Open your Activity Books at page 49.' Point to the word stones. Check pupils are familiar with their meaning: say one of the numbers. Pupils hold up the same number of fingers.

c To make the word stones, each pupil requires ten 'stones' (either real stones or stone-shaped pieces of card, as before). Pupils write one word (numbers 1 to 10) on each stone in felt-tip pen, as shown in the pictures.

d Working in pairs, pupils play a simple word-recognition game. Each pair uses one collection of stones face up. P1 says a word and P2 finds the correct stone. Change roles and repeat the procedure.

e Pupils then store their stones for future use.

Bill's Friend

Listen

- This is my friend, Kev.
- Hello, Kev. How are you?
- Fine, thanks.
- Hi, Mum. Where's Duffy?
- Here! She's on the table.
- Oh, dear! Duffy isn't Wow's friend.

Ask and answer

	Who's Kev?	Bill's friend.
	Who's Gary?	Suzy's brother.
	Who's Mr Kay?	Bill's father.
	Who's Kate?	Kev's sister.
	Who's Mr Mills?	Gary's grandfather.

Families 3c

Listen and match

1. 2. 3. 4.

Listen

I'm Bill Kay. I've got one brother and one sister. My sister's name is Suzy. She's eight years old. My brother's name is Gary. He's five years old.

I'm Suzy Kay. I've got two brothers. Their names are Bill and Gary. Bill is nine and Gary is five.

38

39

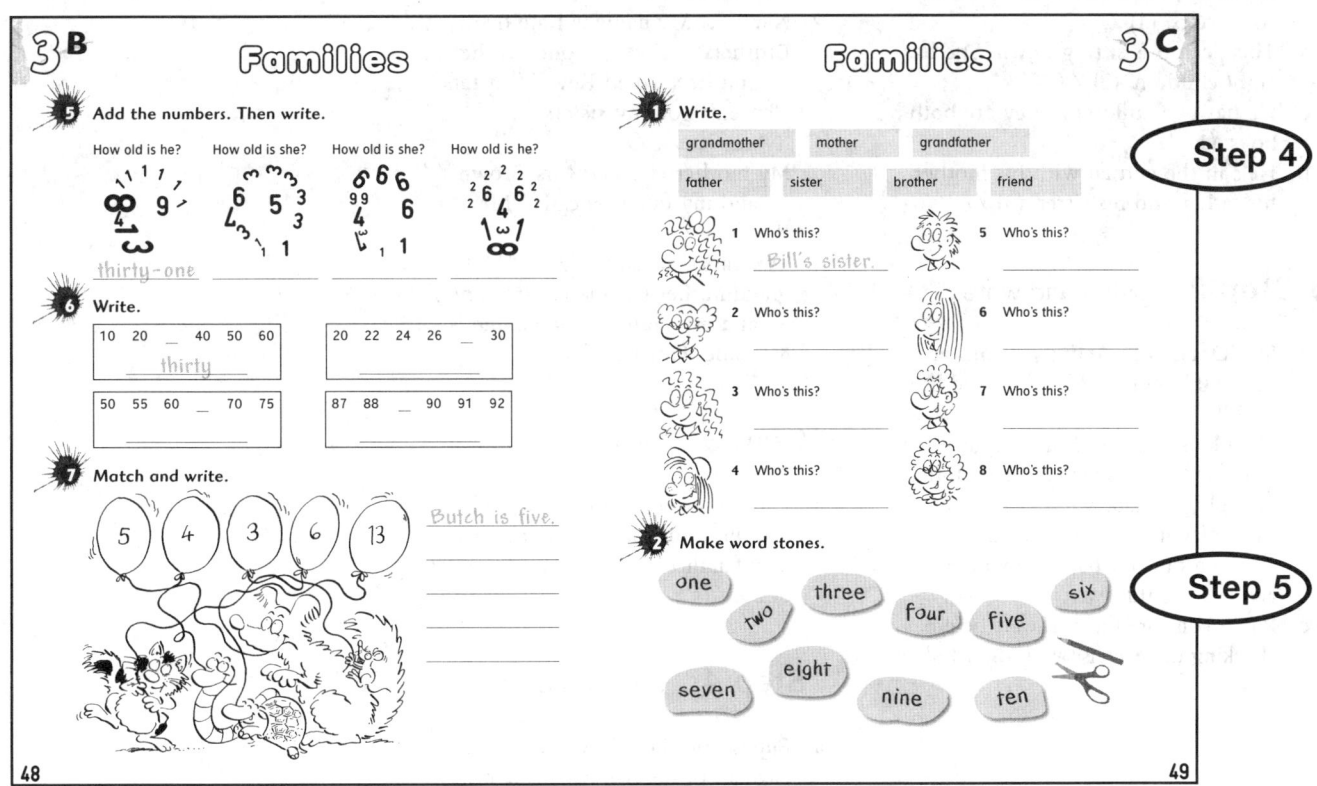

3B Families

5 Add the numbers. Then write.

How old is he? — thirty-one
How old is she? ___
How old is she? ___
How old is he? ___

6 Write.

| 10 | 20 | _ | 40 | 50 | 60 |
thirty

| 20 | 22 | 24 | 26 | _ | 30 |

| 50 | 55 | 60 | _ | 70 | 75 |

| 87 | 88 | _ | 90 | 91 | 92 |

7 Match and write.

5 4 3 6 13

Butch is five.

Families 3C

1 Write.

grandmother   mother   grandfather
father   sister   brother   friend

1 Who's this? — Bill's sister.
2 Who's this? ___
3 Who's this? ___
4 Who's this? ___
5 Who's this? ___
6 Who's this? ___
7 Who's this? ___
8 Who's this? ___

2 Make word stones.

one   two   three   four   five   six
seven   eight   nine   ten

48

49

3c Lesson 2

Main Language Items		Resource File	Materials Needed
What's your *brother's* name?	children	35	family photographs
I've got ...		45a	glue
He's/She's called ...		46	cassette/cassette player
I've haven't got any ...			

Step 1 Listen and match

a Say 'Look at the photographs at the top of page 39.' Play the first description on the tape. Pupils identify which family is described.
b Repeat the same procedure with the other descriptions.

Tapescript (with answers):

A He's in the garden with his mother, his father, his little brother and his two sisters. (4) //
B This person is sitting down. She has eight children. (2) //
C He has two children. They are both boys. (1) //
D He's in the garden with his mother, his father and his sister. (3) //

Step 2 Listen and write

a Say 'Open your Activity Books at page 50.' Look at Bill's form and listen to Bill.
b Then look at Kate's form. Pupils listen to the tape and complete Kate's form. First play the tape without stopping. Then play it again, line by line, allowing time for pupils to write the answers. Do this twice.
c Pupils compare their answers before checking the exercise with the whole class.

Tapescript:

1 Name. That's easy ... Bill Kay. //
Brothers. How many brothers have I got? //
Just one ... and his name is Gary. //
Now ... Sisters ... I've got one sister ... called ... Suzy. // Mother. She's called Mrs Kay. // And my father is called Mr Kay. //
Grandmother and grandfather // ... that's Mrs Mills and ... Mr Mills. Finished. //
2 Name ... My name is Kate Brown. //
Brothers ... I've got one brother // ... and he's called Kev. // Sisters ... I haven't got any sisters ... so that's ... no sisters. //
My mother is called Mrs Brown // ... and my father is called Mr Brown. //
Two more questions. // My grandmother's name is Mrs Lane // ... and my grandfather's name is ... Mr Lane. Finished. //

Step 3 Write

a Pupils draw a picture of themselves and fill in the information about their own families on the form on page 50 of the AB.

Step 4 Crossword

a Pupils read the crossword clues on page 50 of the AB. Each clue has a word missing. Write the missing words in the crossword grid.
b This exercise may be done for homework.

108

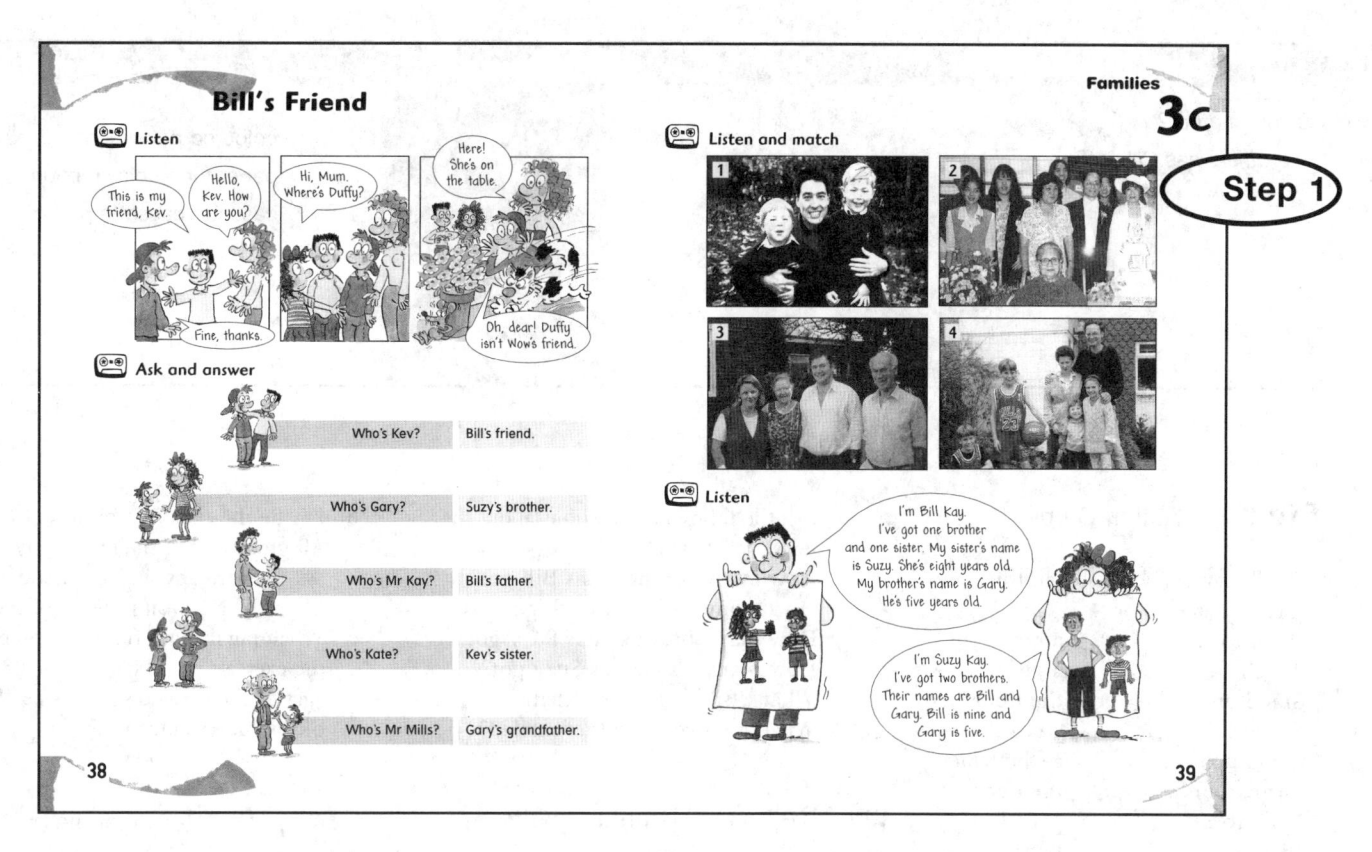

Bill's Friend

Listen

This is my friend, Kev.
Hello, Kev. How are you?
Fine, thanks.
Hi, Mum. Where's Duffy?
Here! She's on the table.
Oh, dear! Duffy isn't Wow's friend.

Ask and answer

Who's Kev?	Bill's friend.
Who's Gary?	Suzy's brother.
Who's Mr Kay?	Bill's father.
Who's Kate?	Kev's sister.
Who's Mr Mills?	Gary's grandfather.

38

Families 3c

Step 1

Listen and match

1 2 3 4

Listen

I'm Bill Kay. I've got one brother and one sister. My sister's name is Suzy. She's eight years old. My brother's name is Gary. He's five years old.

I'm Suzy Kay. I've got two brothers. Their names are Bill and Gary. Bill is nine and Gary is five.

39

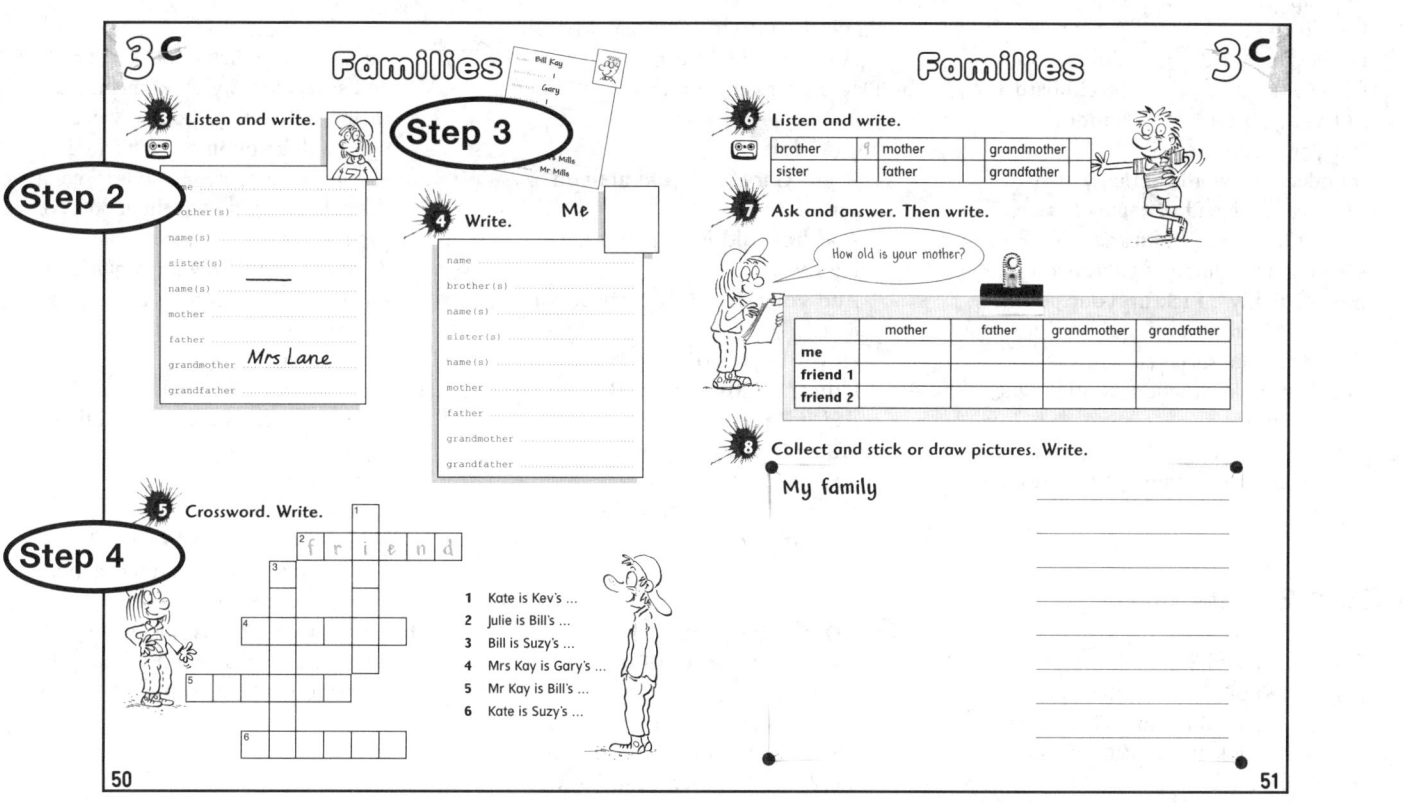

3c Families

Bill Kay
Gary
Mrs Mills
Mr Mills

3 Listen and write.

Step 3

me
brother(s) ....
name(s) ....
sister(s) ....
name(s) ___
mother ....
father ....
grandmother Mrs Lane
grandfather ....

4 Write. Me

name ....
brother(s) ....
name(s) ....
sister(s) ....
name(s) ....
mother ....
father ....
grandmother ....
grandfather ....

Step 2

5 Crossword. Write.

²f r i e n d

Step 4

1 Kate is Kev's ...
2 Julie is Bill's ...
3 Bill is Suzy's ...
4 Mrs Kay is Gary's ...
5 Mr Kay is Bill's ...
6 Kate is Suzy's ...

50

Families 3c

6 Listen and write.

| brother | mother | grandmother |
| sister | father | grandfather |

7 Ask and answer. Then write.

How old is your mother?

	mother	father	grandmother	grandfather
me				
friend 1				
friend 2				

8 Collect and stick or draw pictures. Write.

My family

51

3c Lesson 3

Main Language Items	Resource File	Materials Needed
How old is your *mother*? How many *brothers* has *Bill* got?	1 2 3 4	coloured pencils paper for display (optional) cassette/cassette player

Step 1 Action Game

a Briefly revise a variety of instructions used to date:

Point to …	a boy
Touch …	a girl
Stand on …	the floor
Sit on …	a chair
Stand up!	a/the table
Turn around!	the door
Walk to …	pencil
Pick up …	pen
Put down …	Activity Book
Open your …	Coursebook
Close your …	blackboard
Put your … on …	window
Put your … under …	

b Introduce the words 'quickly' and 'slowly' at the end of some of these instructions, and demonstrate the meaning accordingly, e.g. 'Touch the floor, quickly,' 'Pick up your pencil, slowly,' 'Turn around, quickly.' Exaggerate the speed at which you carry out the instructions to highlight the meaning.

c Practise with the whole class until they understand the meaning of the new words.

Step 2 Presentation

a Look at Bill and Suzy's drawings on page 39. Pupils listen to the tape, reading at the same time. Then cover the words, look at the pictures and listen again.

b Ask the following questions about the texts:
How many brothers has Bill got?
How many sisters has Bill got?
How many brothers has Suzy got?
How many sisters has Suzy got?
What's Bill's brother called?
What are Suzy's brothers called?

Step 3 Listen and write

a Pupils listen to the tape and write the ages in the grid on page 51 of the AB.
b Play the tape three times.

Tapescript:
Right Gary. How old are you? //
I'm 5. //
And how old is your brother? //
He's 9. //
And your sister? // Suzy … she's 8. //
How old are your mother and father? // My mum is 32 and my dad is 34. //
How old is your grandmother? //
She's 68. //
How old is your grandfather? //
He's 65. //

Step 4 Groupwork: Questionnaire

a Ask various pupils in the class the question 'How old is your mother/father/grandmother/grandfather?' If pupils don't know, ask them to 'guess'.

b Divide the class into groups of three. All groups work simultaneously. Pupils ask their friends similar questions and fill in the chart on page 51 of their AB.

c When pupils have finished, complete the exercise by asking the pupils the ages of their friend's family, i.e. 'How old is *Maria's* mother?'

Step 5 Personal file

a Pupils draw a picture of their brothers and sisters (or any other members of their family) in the box provided and write a description of the picture alongside. Encourage pupils to compare their description with the models on page 39 of the CB. (You could demonstrate by drawing a quick picture of your brothers and sisters on the blackboard and writing a description alongside.)

b Working in pairs, pupils ask and answer questions about each other's pictures. Use structures such as:
Who's this?
Is this your mother?
What's your brother's name?

c Then pupils change partners and ask other class members.

d This work makes excellent wall displays and it is very motivating for pupils to see their own work in this way.

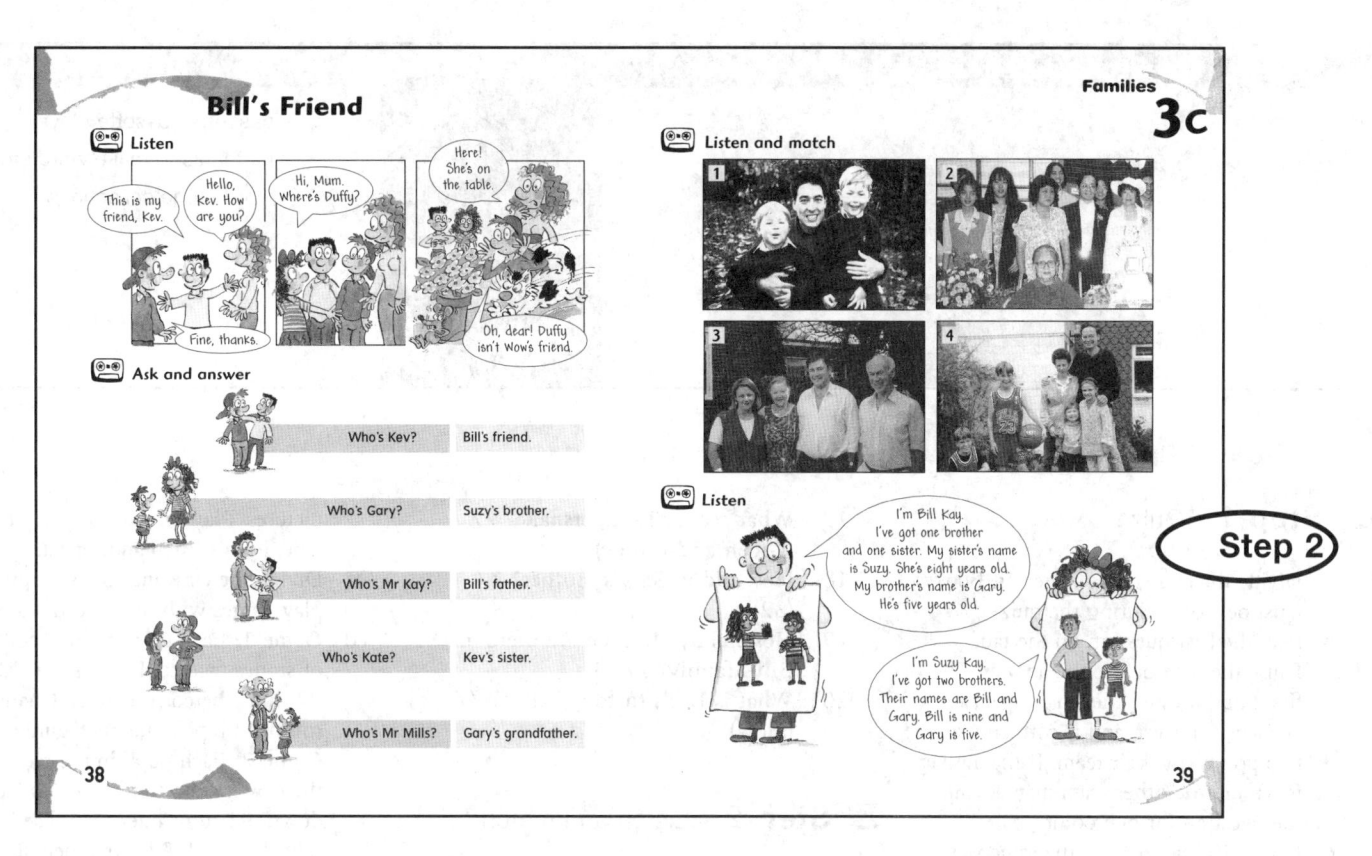

Bill's Friend

Listen

- This is my friend, Kev.
- Hello, Kev. How are you?
- Fine, thanks.
- Hi, Mum. Where's Duffy?
- Here! She's on the table.
- Oh, dear! Duffy isn't Wow's friend.

Ask and answer

Who's Kev?	Bill's friend.
Who's Gary?	Suzy's brother.
Who's Mr Kay?	Bill's father.
Who's Kate?	Kev's sister.
Who's Mr Mills?	Gary's grandfather.

Families 3c

Listen and match

1 2 3 4

Listen

I'm Bill Kay. I've got one brother and one sister. My sister's name is Suzy. She's eight years old. My brother's name is Gary. He's five years old.

I'm Suzy Kay. I've got two brothers. Their names are Bill and Gary. Bill is nine and Gary is five.

Step 2

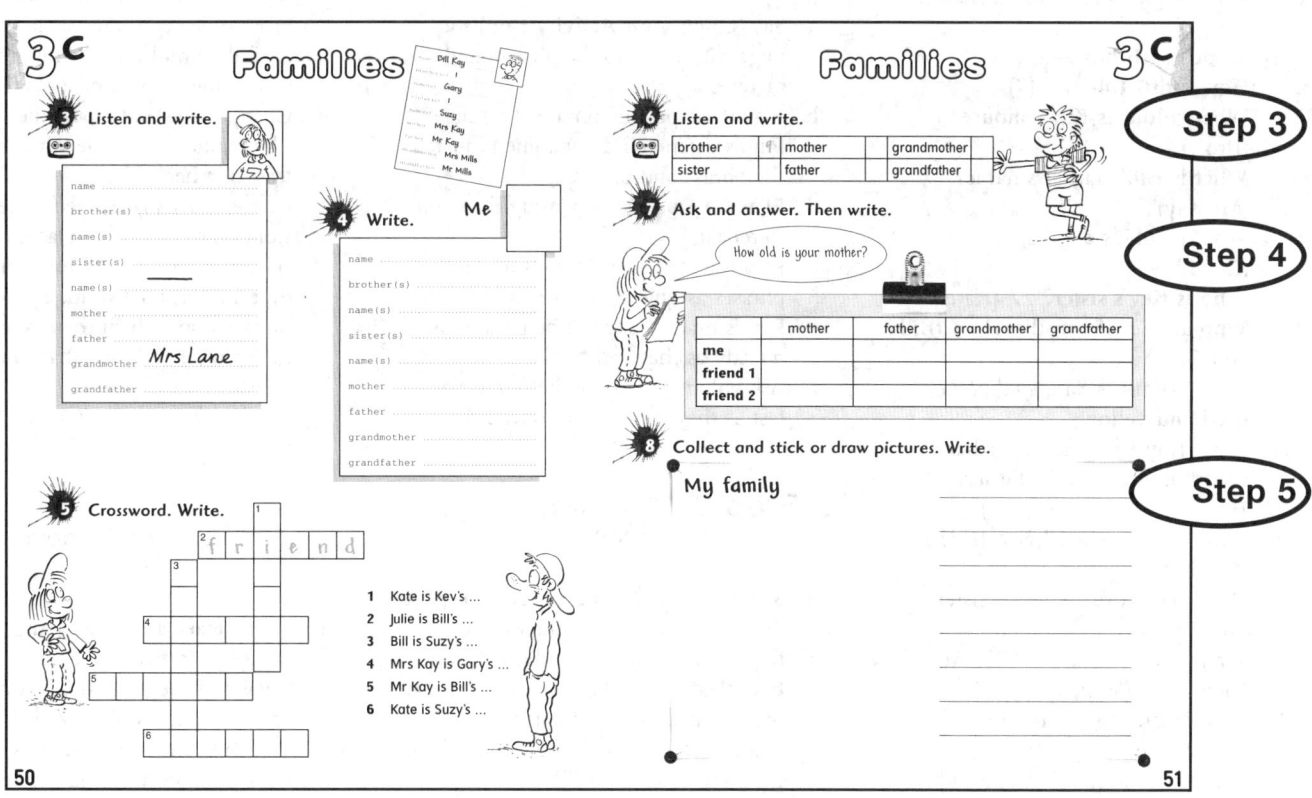

3c Families

3 Listen and write.

name ....
brother(s) ....
name(s) ....
sister(s) ....
name(s) ....
mother ....
father ....
grandmother Mrs Lane
grandfather ....

Bill Kay
|
Gary
|
Suzy
Mrs Kay
Mr Kay
Mrs Mills
Mr Mills

4 Write. Me

name ....
brother(s) ....
name(s) ....
sister(s) ....
name(s) ....
mother ....
father ....
grandmother ....
grandfather ....

5 Crossword. Write.

2 f r i e n d

1 Kate is Kev's ...
2 Julie is Bill's ...
3 Bill is Suzy's ...
4 Mrs Kay is Gary's ...
5 Mr Kay is Bill's ...
6 Kate is Suzy's ...

Families 3c

6 Listen and write.

| brother | mother | grandmother |
| sister | father | grandfather |

Step 3

7 Ask and answer. Then write.

How old is your mother?

	mother	father	grandmother	grandfather
me				
friend 1				
friend 2				

Step 4

8 Collect and stick or draw pictures. Write.

My family

Step 5

3D Lesson 1

Main Language Items	Resource File	Materials Needed
Revision	41 50	cassette/cassette player materials to make word stonesr word stone collections

Step 1 Quiz

a Divide the class into two teams. Books must be closed during the quiz.
b Play the first question on the tape. Pause the tape before the answer! The first pupil to raise their hand gets a chance to answer, and if correct, wins two points for their team. If the answer is wrong, the other team may attempt the question for one point.
c Do all 20 questions in the same way.

Tapescript (with answers):
1 How old is Bill? // (9)
2 What colour is Kev's mouse? // (Brown)
3 What is Bill's father's name? // (Mr Kay)
4 What is Julie's dog called? // (Butch)
5 Who is Kev's sister? // (Kate)
6 Who are Suzy's brothers? // (Bill and Gary)
7 What colour is Sam snake? // (Red and yellow)
8 Is Mr Kay Bill's father or his grandfather? // (His father)
9 How old is Slow? // (13)
10 What is Suzy's teacher called? // (Mr Bell)
11 How many brothers and sisters has Wow got? // (40)
12 What is the name of Willy worm's friend? // (Wendy)
13 Who is Bill's grandmother? // (Mrs Mills)
14 Is Duffy a dog? // (No, a cat)
15 How many brothers has Kate got? // (1)
16 What is 17 and 22? // (39)
17 What colour is Supersnake? // (Green and yellow)
18 How old is Gary's mother? // (32)
19 How many children are there in Bill's family? // (3)
20 What is Bill's tortoise called? // (Slow)

Step 2 Listen and match

a Say 'Open your Activity Books at page 52.' Point to the phrases and pictures.
b Play the tape, one phrase at a time. Pupils listen and draw a line to match the phrase and picture.
c Play the tape again, pausing for pupils to repeat.
d Play the tape again. Pupils repeat the phrases as quickly as they can.
e Pupils practise saying the phrases as quickly as they can.
f Ask volunteers to say the phrases as fast as they can in front of the class.

Step 3 Make and play word stones

a Say 'Open your Coursebooks at page 40.' Each pupil needs the following four stones from their collection: **one, two, three, four**. Listen to the first part of the tape. Pupils place the appropriate stones on their desks or on the pictures in their CBs.
b To make the word stones, each pupil requires four 'stones'. Pupils write one word (**tree, door, sun, shoe**) on each stone in felt-tip pen, as shown in the pictures. Play the second part of the tape. Pupils listen and repeat.
c Divide the class into pairs. Pupils then play games with their word stones.
d **Game 1:** Each pair uses one collection of stones face up. P1 says a word and P2 finds the correct stone. Change roles and repeat the procedure.
e **Game 2:** Each pupil in the pair places their own collection of stones face down. P1 turns one stone face up and says the word. P2 turns their stones face up one at a time, saying the words, until they find the matching one. P1 counts the number of turns this takes. Change roles and repeat the procedure. The winner is the one who takes the least number of turns.
f **Game 3:** P1 places their collection of stones face down. P2 places their collection face up. P1 turns one stone over and says the word, e.g. **four**. P2 finds a stone which rhymes and says the word, e.g. **door**. Change roles and repeat.
g Pupils then store their stones for future use.

Step 4 The Stepping Stones Game

a Pupils make sentences going from left to right across the stepping stones. They must begin in the first column and take one word from each column.
b Work in pairs. Give the class ten minutes to make as many sentences as possible from the words on the stones.
c Check the answers with the whole class. The pair to get the most correct and true sentences are the winners.

112

Words and Sentences

Families 3D

Step 3

Word Stones

one two three four

Make

tree door
sun shoe

Step 4

The Stepping Stones Game

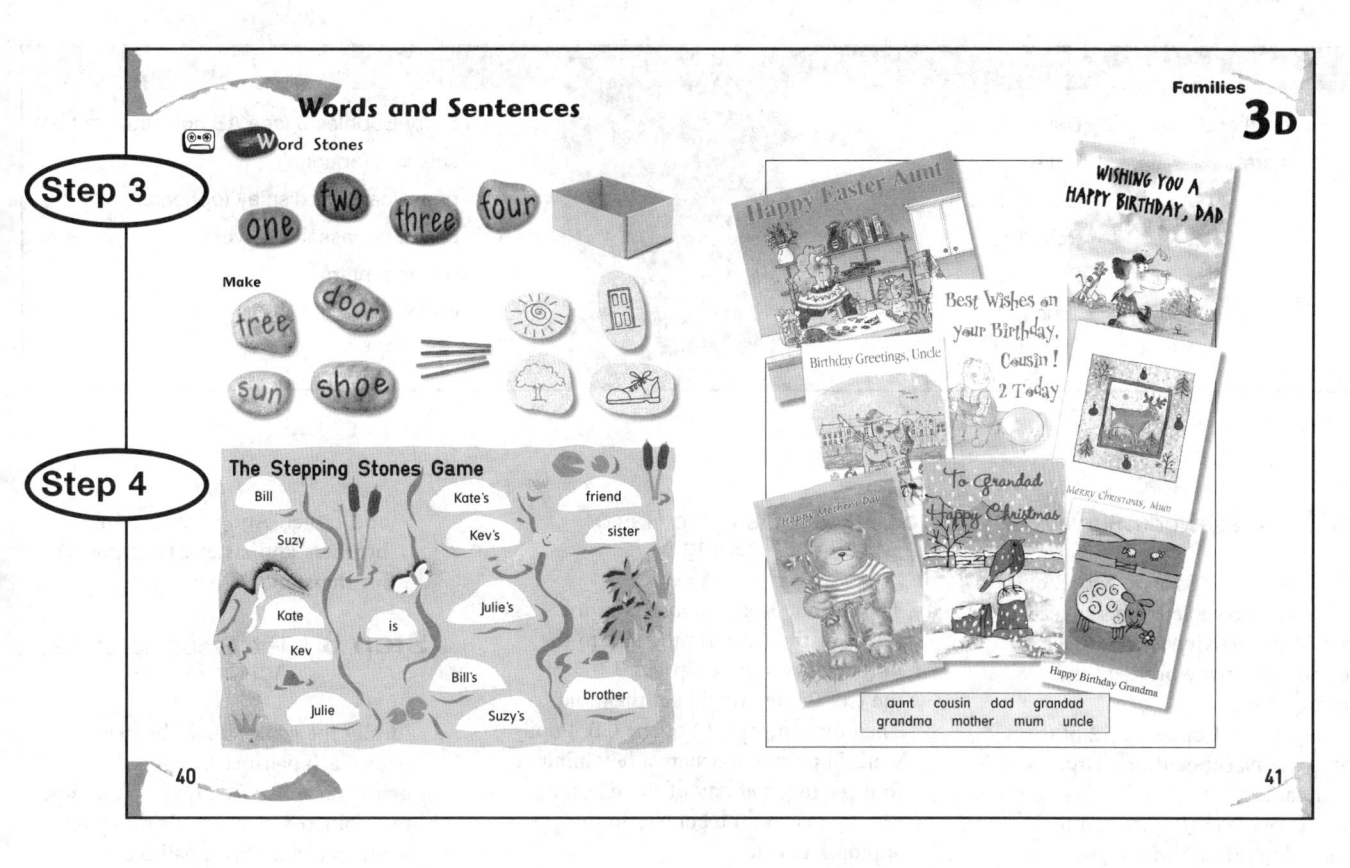

Bill   Kate's   friend
Suzy   Kev's   sister
Kate   is   Julie's
Kev
       Bill's   brother
Julie Suzy's

Happy Easter Aunt
WISHING YOU A HAPPY BIRTHDAY, DAD
Best Wishes on your Birthday, Cousin! 2 Today
Birthday Greetings, Uncle
To Grandad Happy Christmas
Merry Christmas, Mum
Happy Mother's Day
Happy Birthday Grandma

| aunt | cousin | dad | grandad |
| grandma | mother | mum | uncle |

40

41

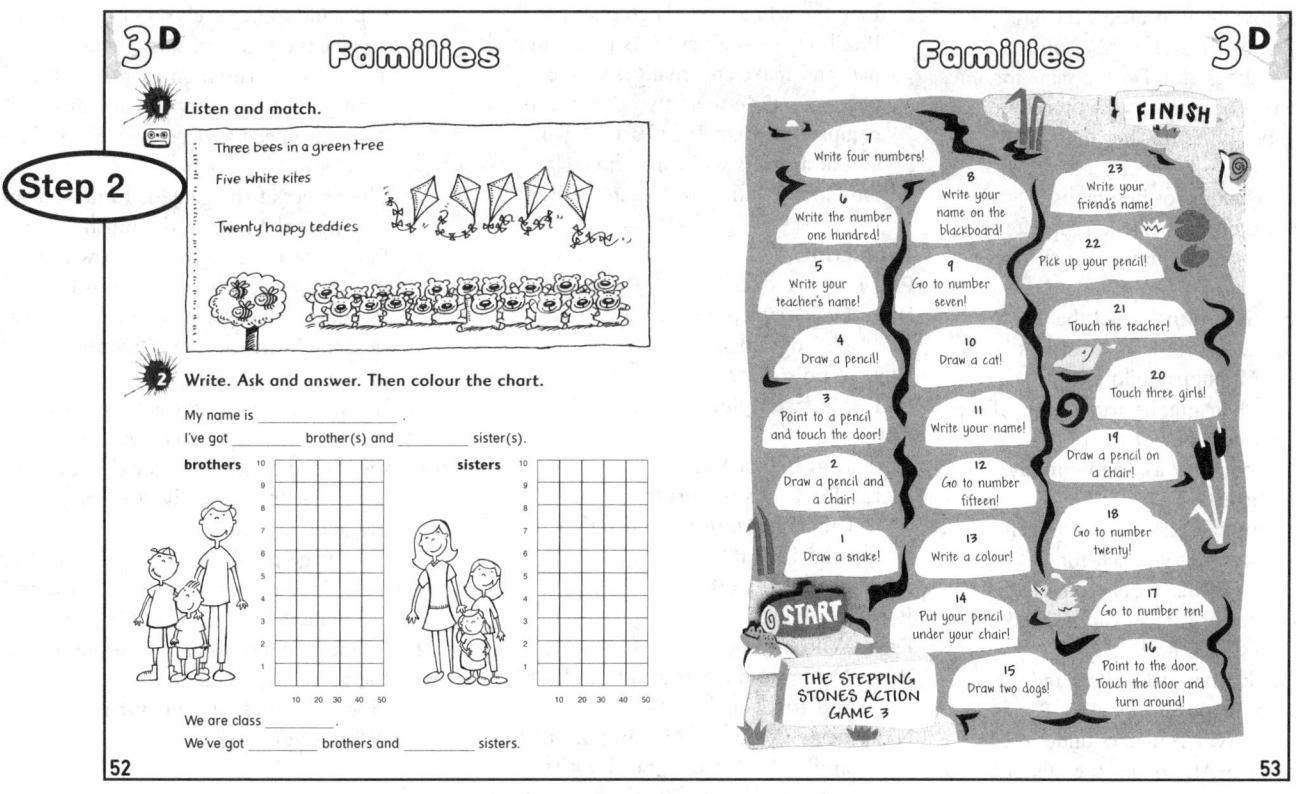

3D Families

1 Listen and match.

Step 2

Three bees in a green tree

Five white kites

Twenty happy teddies

2 Write. Ask and answer. Then colour the chart.

My name is _____ .
I've got _____ brother(s) and _____ sister(s).

brothers   sisters

        10 20 30 40 50   10 20 30 40 50

We are class _____ .
We've got _____ brothers and _____ sisters.

52

Families 3D

FINISH

7 Write four numbers!
6 Write the number one hundred!
5 Write your teacher's name!
4 Draw a pencil!
3 Point to a pencil and touch the door!
2 Draw a pencil and a chair!
1 Draw a snake!

START

8 Write your name on the blackboard!
9 Go to number seven!
10 Draw a cat!
11 Write your name!
12 Go to number fifteen!
13 Write a colour!
14 Put your pencil under your chair!
15 Draw two dogs!

23 Write your friend's name!
22 Pick up your pencil!
21 Touch the teacher!
20 Touch three girls!
19 Draw a pencil on a chair!
18 Go to number twenty!
17 Go to number ten!
16 Point to the door. Touch the floor and turn around!

THE STEPPING STONES ACTION GAME 3

53

3D Lesson 2

Main Language Items			Resource File	Materials Needed
I've got …	brothers	Draw		Story Bubbles 3 (see AB cut-outs section)
PLURAL 's'	sisters	Write	4	scissors (optional)
How many?		Go to …	44	paper/card for display (optional)
Their names …		Point to		cassette/cassette player
		Pick up		dice/counters
		Touch		paper/pencil

Step 1 Classwork: Survey

a Pupils open their ABs at activity 2 on page 52. They complete the sentence at the top of the activity, writing their name and how many brothers and sisters they have.

b Copy the graphs from page 52 of the AB onto the blackboard or a large piece of card.

c Ask for a volunteer (P1) to read their sentence aloud to the whole class. Ask the class how many brothers P1 has. Shade the appropriate number of squares on the graph. Do the same for P1's sisters. Then repeat this procedure with another pupil reading their sentence.

d Then direct pupils to the graphs in their AB. Pupils copy the appropriate number of shaded squares in their own AB.

e Pupils take it in turns to tell the whole class how many brothers and sisters they have. All pupils build up the answers on their graphs accordingly. If they do not hear one of their classmates they may ask '**How many brothers/sisters?**'

f Continue until all pupils have spoken.

g Record the answers yourself for confirmation. If this is done on a large sheet of paper or card, it can be used later as part of a wall display.

h Count the number of brothers and sisters of the pupils in the class. Pupils complete the two sentences under the graphs in their AB, giving the number of their class in the first one.

Step 2 Listening (Task)/ Reading

a The cut-out Story Bubbles 3 in the centre of the AB form the text to the introductory story on pages 32–3 of the CB. Pupils should cut them out.

b Then turn to page 32 of the CB. Pupils work in pairs. Give them a few minutes to piece together any of the text they can, by placing the bubbles in the appropriate places.

c Play the whole text. Then play Part 1. Pupils check their answers to the first part and make any changes where necessary. Give them two minutes to compare answers. Play Part 1 again. Check answers with the whole class.

d Do Parts 2 and 3 in the same way.

Tapescript:
PART 1
BILL: Hey Kev, come here! Look at my photographs.
KEV: Who's that?
BILL: My sister, Suzy.
PART 2
KEV: And is that Suzy?
BILL: No. That's my brother, Gary. This is my mother and father. It's good isn't it?
KEV: Mmm. It's OK.
PART 3
KEV: Who are they?
BILL: My grandmother and grandfather. And this is me.
NARRATOR: Wow is dreaming about his family. This is his grandmother and grandfather. This is his mother and father. And these are his brothers and sisters. He's got 21 brothers and 19 sisters.

Step 3 The Stepping Stones Action Game 3

a Ideally the game should be played in pairs. Each pair needs one copy of the board game between them, a dice and two coloured counters. (If these items are unavailable then small pieces of paper indicating each pupil's colour can replace the counters, and the numbers 1–6 can be written on each side of a six-sided pencil to replace the dice.) They also need a piece of paper and a pencil.

b The object of the game is to make your way from the start to the finish.

c Players take it in turns to throw the dice and move around the board. When they land on a square they must read the instructions and tell their partner what to do.

d If their partner carries out the action correctly, it is then their turn to throw the dice and move. If they do not carry out the action correctly, the first player has another turn.

e Encourage pupils to use English as they play. They should count in English and use phrases such as '**Your/My turn**'.

f In addition, ask pupils questions about the game as you monitor their progress, e.g. '**Is it your turn?**', '**What's your colour?**'

3 Families

Step 2

STORY

Family Photographs

1 2 3 4
5 6 7 8

32 33

3D Families

Step 1

1 Listen and match.

Three bees in a green tree
Five white kites
Twenty happy teddies

2 Write. Ask and answer. Then colour the chart.

My name is _____ .
I've got _____ brother(s) and _____ sister(s).

brothers   sisters

We are class _____ .
We've got _____ brothers and _____ sisters.

52

3D Families

Step 3

FINISH

7 Write four numbers!
8 Write your name on the blackboard!
23 Write your friend's name!
6 Write the number one hundred!
22 Pick up your pencil!
5 Write your teacher's name!
9 Go to number seven!
21 Touch the teacher!
4 Draw a pencil!
10 Draw a cat!
20 Touch three girls!
3 Point to a pencil and touch the door!
11 Write your name!
19 Draw a pencil on a chair!
2 Draw a pencil and a chair!
12 Go to number fifteen!
18 Go to number twenty!
1 Draw a snake!
13 Write a colour!
17 Go to number ten!
START
14 Put your pencil under your chair!
16 Point to the door. Touch the floor and turn around!
15 Draw two dogs!

THE STEPPING STONES ACTION GAME 3

53

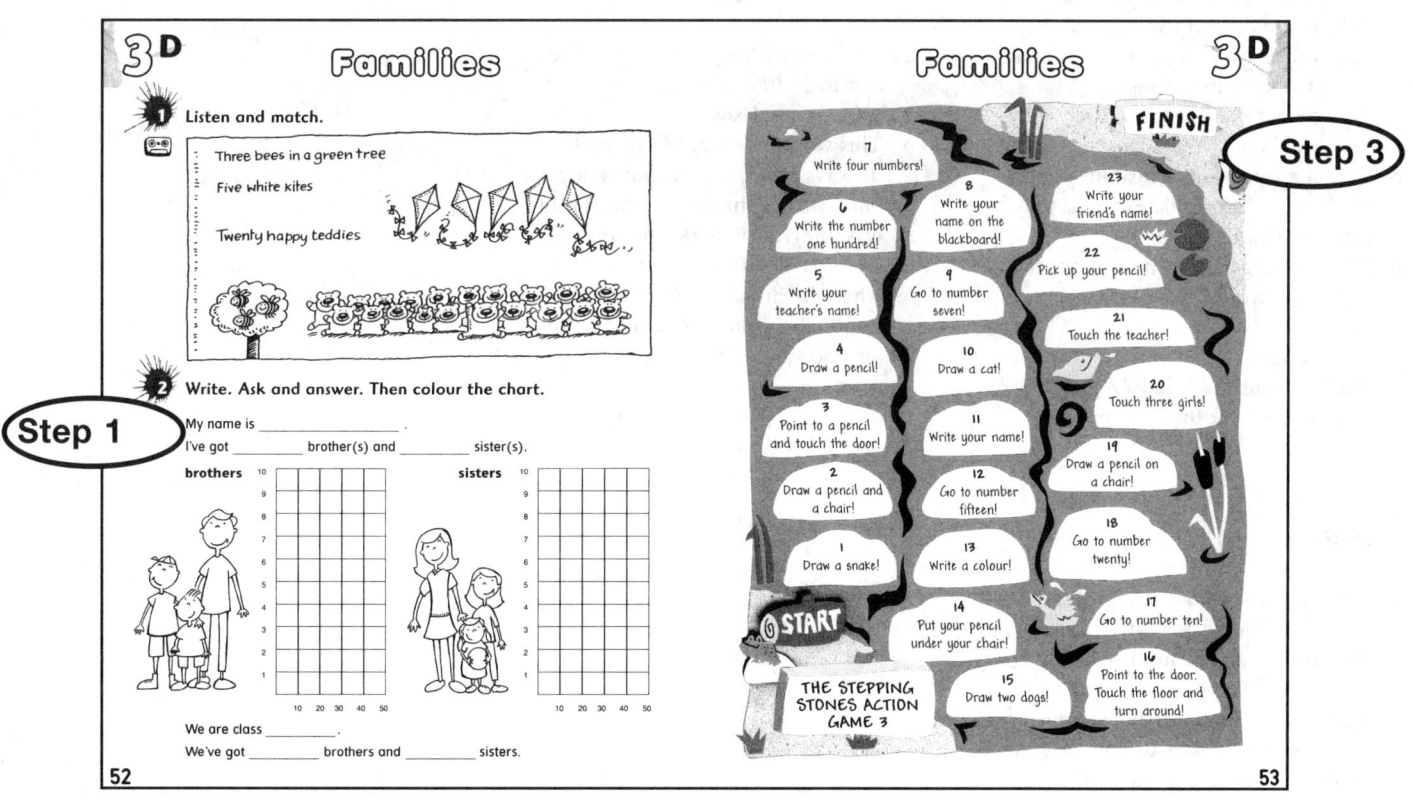

115

3D Lesson 3

Main Language Items		Resource File	Materials Needed
family	aunt		
mother	uncle		
mum	cousin	3	cassette/cassette player
dad			coloured pencils
grandma			
grandad			

Step 1   Find more words

a Say 'Open your Coursebooks at page 41' and look at the photos. Ask pupils in their L1 if any of them can see a card for **mothers**. Explain that '**mum**' is a familiar term for children to call their mother. Smaller children often say '**mummy**'. Then ask them to find a card for **fathers**. Explain the use of **dad** and **daddy**. Repeat this procedure for **grandma** and **grandad**. Ask pupils if there are different words that they use in their own L1 for their parents and grandparents.
b Play the tape and listen to the words while looking at the pictures.
c Play the tape again. This time pupils point to the appropriate card as they hear the word.
d Play the tape again. Pupils listen and repeat the words.

Tapescript:
aunt // cousin // dad // grandad // grandma // mother // mum // uncle //

Step 2   The Name Game

a Say a popular name for a girl in the pupils' L1. Pupils say '**my sister**' etc., if they have someone in their family with that name.
b Repeat with a popular boys' name.
c Then ask a volunteer to say a popular name. The first person to answer 'my …' says the next name.

Step 3   Crossword

a Pupils write the words in the appropriate places in the puzzle and tick them off on the list.

Step 4   Write, draw and colour

a Pupils write the greeting on the card and then draw and colour an appropriate design.
b This work makes excellent wall displays and it is very motivating for pupils to see their own work in this way. Individual work can be done on loose paper and stuck into the AB when the display is dismantled.
c Pupils can make real cards for other members of their family.

Words and Sentences

Word Stones

one two three four

Make

tree door
sun shoe

The Stepping Stones Game

Bill · Suzy · Kate · Kev · Julie
Kate's · Kev's · Julie's · Bill's · Suzy's
is
friend · sister · brother

Families 3D

Step 1

aunt cousin dad grandad
grandma mother mum uncle

40 · 41

3D Families

Step 3

3 Crossword. Write.

me
sister
brother
mother
father
mum
dad
grandma
grandad
aunt
uncle
cousin

Step 4

4 Write, draw and colour.

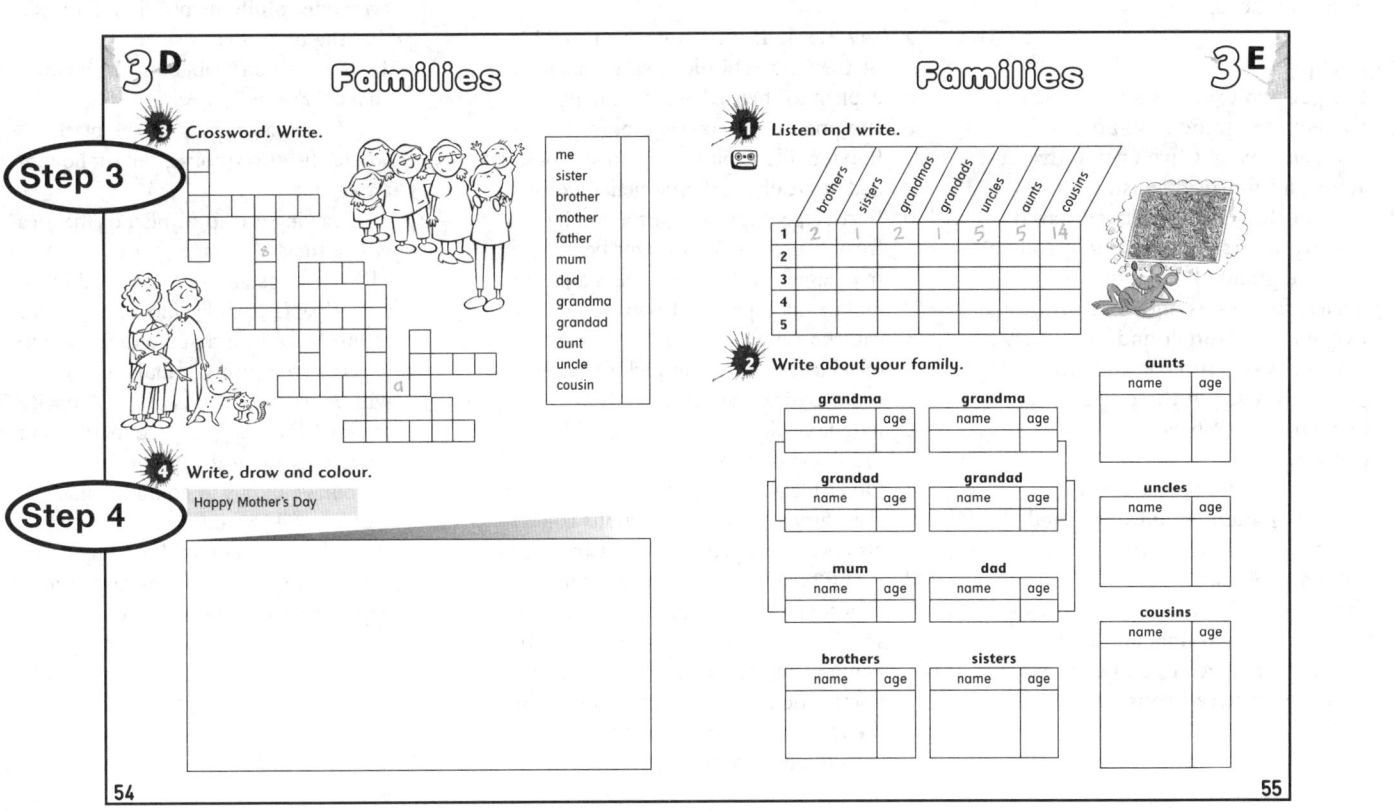

Happy Mother's Day

Families 3E

1 Listen and write.

	brothers	sisters	grandmas	grandads	uncles	aunts	cousins
1	2	1	2	1	5	5	14
2							
3							
4							
5							

2 Write about your family.

grandma — name | age
grandma — name | age
grandad — name | age
grandad — name | age
mum — name | age
dad — name | age
brothers — name | age
sisters — name | age
aunts — name | age
uncles — name | age
cousins — name | age

54 · 55

3E Lesson 1 – Project

Main Language Items			Resource File	Materials Needed
family	grandma	age	1	
brother	grandad	family tree	2	cassette/cassette player
sister	aunt		3	project materials
mother	uncle		4	
mum	cousin		45	
dad	name			

Step 1   Listen and write

a Say 'Open your Activity Books at page 55.' Play the five descriptions of children's families, pausing after each one. Pupils listen to the tape and write the appropriate number of brothers, sisters, etc. the child has got on the chart in activity 1.

b Play the tape three times. Allow pupils to compare their answers before replaying the tape.

Tapescript:
1 I've got two brothers and one sister. I've got two grandmas and one grandad. I've got five uncles, five aunts and fourteen cousins.
2 I've got three brothers but I haven't got any sisters. I've got one grandma and one grandad. I've got two uncles, four aunts and six cousins.
3 I've got one brother and one sister. I've got two grandmas and two grandads. I've got three uncles and two aunts but I haven't got any cousins.
4 I've got no brothers and sisters. I've got two grandmas and one grandad. I've got four uncles, five aunts and sixteen cousins.
5 I've got four brothers and two sisters. I've got one grandma and two grandads. I've got two uncles, two aunts and thirteen cousins.

Step 2   Write about your family

a In activity 2 on AB page 55, pupils collect the information they will need to make a family tree.

b Pupils complete the boxes as appropriate with the names and ages of members of their family.

Step 3   Start a project

a Say 'Look at the photo on page 42 of the Coursebook.' Ask pupils to explain in their L1 what a family tree is supposed to represent, both horizontally (siblings, cousins, spouses) and vertically (different generations).

b Encourage pupils to start a 'family and friends' project. This might be a family tree based on their AB charts and the mobile on page 42 of their CB. Pupils can choose which members/branches of their family tree to include. They can copy the idea of a family-tree mobile or design their own, perhaps in the shape of a tree.

c Other ideas for projects could be a class survey on families. Pupils could also do a personal file: '**My Family**'.

d If you prefer to make the project a collective effort, organise the class into small groups and explain that they are going to represent the family details of a set of fictional characters. Give them the reading list you have drawn up with the help of the L1 language teacher and make sure it features a variety of stories. Pupils can also suggest additional titles. The list can then be affixed to the wall and the books displayed in the classroom. Pupils write their names down next to the story they want to read and groups are formed accordingly.

e Before they start, sit down with each group in turn and help pupils organise the different tasks and materials so that everyone is fully involved. Tell them that the project consists in
1 Drawing and labelling the main character's family tree.
2 Making a drawing of the place where they live (house, hut, hollow of a tree, etc.).
3 Drawing a map or plan of the area where the action takes place.
The drawings are then mounted on poster paper and displayed around the room. Make sure that children have the necessary English vocabulary, as they will be reading stories in L1. A pocket edition of a bilingual dictionary could be very useful at this point.

f Encourage pupils to continue their project work outside their English class; the story books should remain available for some time in case other pupils want to read more tales.

Step 3

START A PROJECT

Families
3E

SUPERSNAKE

42

43

3D Families

3 Crossword. Write.

me
sister
brother
mother
father
mum
dad
grandma
grandad
aunt
uncle
cousin

4 Write, draw and colour.

Happy Mother's Day

Families **3E**

1 Listen and write.

	brothers	sisters	grandmas	grandads	uncles	aunts	cousins
1	2	1	2	1	5	5	14
2							
3							
4							
5							

Step 1

2 Write about your family.

grandma: name, age
grandma: name, age
grandad: name, age
grandad: name, age
mum: name, age
dad: name, age
brothers: name, age
sisters: name, age
aunts: name, age
uncles: name, age
cousins: name, age

Step 2

54

55

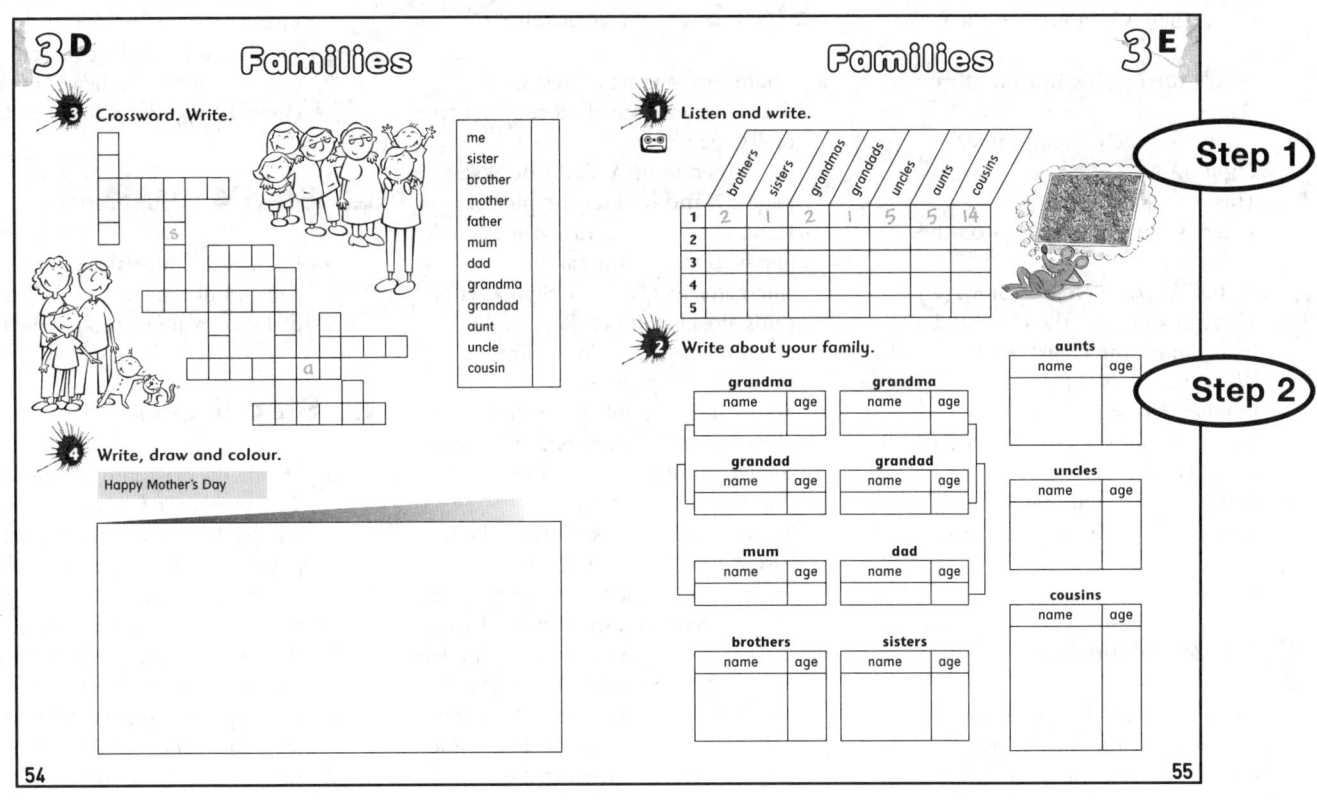

119

3E Lesson 2 – Evaluation

Main Language Items		Resource File	Materials Needed
What's that?	birthday		Test Cards 3E (see photocopy master on TG p.175)
How old is …?	card	33	scissors (optional)
I don't know.	idea		Supersnake puppets
Oh dear!			cassette/cassette player
I've got …			
I haven't got …			

Step 1 Listening (Test)

a Look at the pictures on page 56 of the AB. There is a short dialogue or sentence about each of the pictures. Pupils must decide if the dialogue or sentences is appropriate to the picture. If it is appropriate, they should put a tick in the corresponding box, if not, a cross. Play each one three times.

Tapescript (with answers):
1. Look, there's a mouse on the table. (✓)
2. Who's this? ~ It's Bill's mother. (✗)
3. How many pencils are there? ~ Eight. (✗)
4. This is Bill's sister. (✓)
5. Where's the pencil? ~ It's on the table. (✓)
6. Is this Wow? ~ No, it's Slow. (✓)
7. There is a pen on the chair and a book under the chair. (✗)
8. What number's that? ~ It's number 38. (✓)
9. What's under the table? ~ It's a dog. (✗)
10. Is this a pencil sharpener or a pencil case? ~ It's a pencil case. (✓)

Step 2 Writing (Test)

a Working individually, pupils read the questions and write the answers.

b If the exercise is being done as a test then answers can be written on a piece of paper to be collected in and marked by the teacher.

c The tests are designed to test communication as much as accuracy and should be marked accordingly. Therefore credit should be given for answers which show that pupils have understood the meaning of the questions and where their answers are comprehensible and appropriate.

Step 3 Test yourself

a Photocopy one set of Test Cards 3E for each pupil (see photocopy master on TG page 175).

b Say 'Open your Activity Books at page 57 and look at the pictures.' Hand out the test card sheets and ask pupils to cut out the cards. Alternatively, give each pupil a set of cards already cut out. Pupils fold the six cards along the dotted line as shown in the picture.

c To do Test 1, pupils place all their cards in front of them with the pictures showing, following the visual instruction. Demonstrate.

d You can read the first word in the list, 'sister'. Pupils look at the picture of Bill's family at the top of the page and find the card with the picture of Bill's sister (Suzy). They turn it over and read the word on the other side, to check whether they were correct. They then put a tick or a cross in the box in their AB, according to whether they were right or wrong. Pupils then repeat for the other words.

e To do Test 2, pupils place all their cards in front of them with the words showing, following the visual instruction. Demonstrate.

f Pupils then look at the first picture, which is of Bill's brother (Gary). Pupils must find the card with 'brother' written on it, turn it over and look at the picture to check. They then put a tick or a cross in the box in their AB according to whether they were right or wrong. Repeat for the other pictures.

g Pupils add up their scores out of six for each test and total them. Finally, they circle the appropriate comment.

Step 4 Supersnake

a Look at the Supersnake cartoon on page 43 of the CB. Pupils listen to the dialogue, reading at the same time.

Step 5 Role Play

a Divide the class into groups of three. Two pupils need worm puppets and one pupil a Supersnake puppet. If pupils have no puppets then the index finger can be used for the worms and the whole arm for Supersnake.

b Play the tape again. This time pupils repeat.

c Pupils practise the puppet show without the help of the tape.

d Ask for one group to volunteer to act out the puppet show for the rest of the class.

START A PROJECT

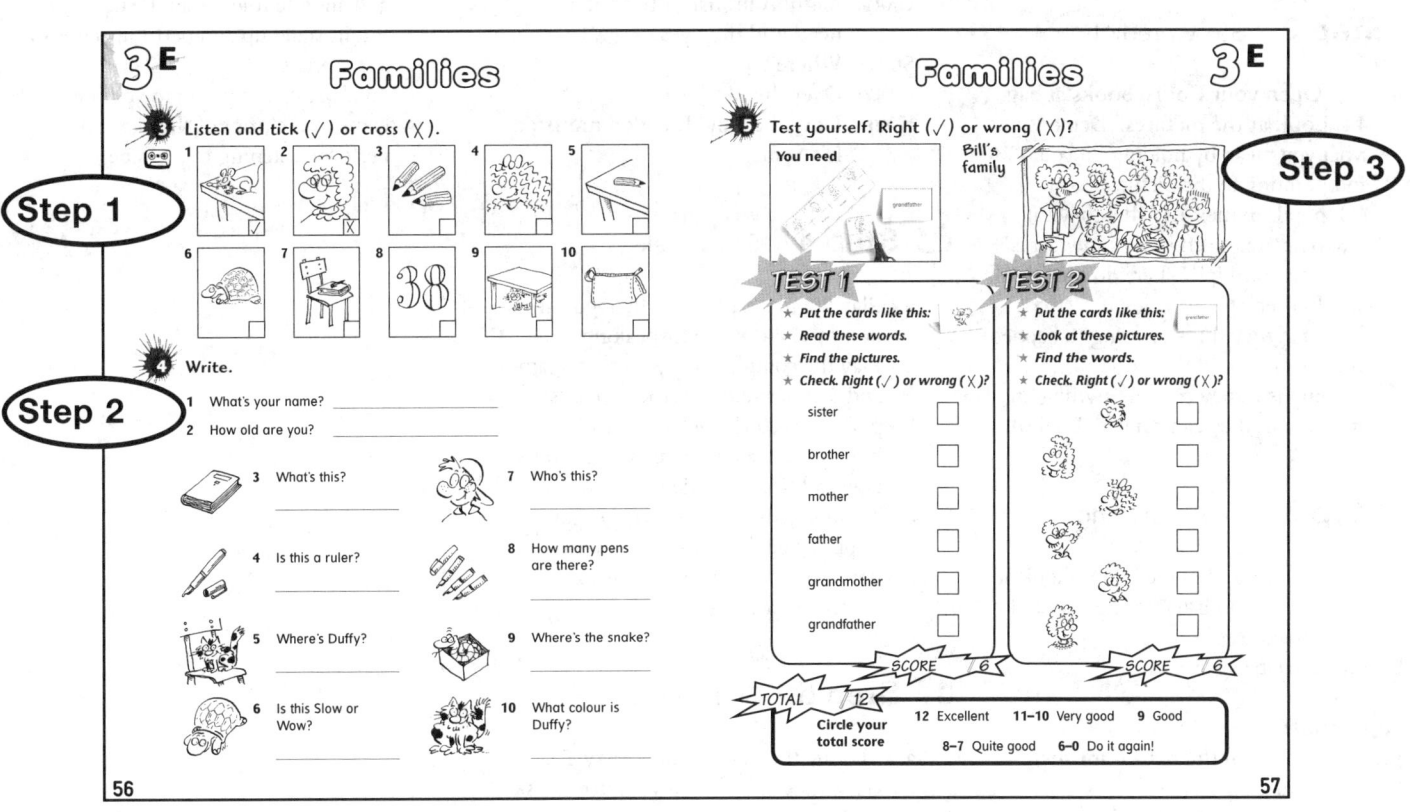

Families 3E

Step 4

SUPERSNAKE

What's that? — A card. It's Supersnake's birthday. — How old is he? — I don't know.

Oh, dear! I haven't got a card for Supersnake. — I've got an idea!

HAPPY BIRTHDAY

3E Families

Step 1

3 Listen and tick (✓) or cross (✗).

1 2 3 4 5
6 7 8 9 10

4 Write.

Step 2

1 What's your name? _____
2 How old are you? _____
3 What's this? _____
4 Is this a ruler? _____
5 Where's Duffy? _____
6 Is this Slow or Wow? _____
7 Who's this? _____
8 How many pens are there? _____
9 Where's the snake? _____
10 What colour is Duffy? _____

Families 3E

5 Test yourself. Right (✓) or wrong (✗)?

You need — Bill's family

Step 3

TEST 1
★ Put the cards like this:
★ Read these words.
★ Find the pictures.
★ Check. Right (✓) or wrong (✗)?

sister ☐
brother ☐
mother ☐
father ☐
grandmother ☐
grandfather ☐

SCORE 6

TEST 2
★ Put the cards like this:
★ Look at these pictures.
★ Find the words.
★ Check. Right (✓) or wrong (✗)?

☐
☐
☐
☐
☐
☐

SCORE 6

TOTAL 12
Circle your total score

12 Excellent   11–10 Very good   9 Good
8–7 Quite good   6–0 Do it again!

121

4 Story lesson

Main Language Items				Resource File	Materials Needed
Let's …	thin	hair	legs		
Come on!	big	body	eyes		
Over there!	small	head	monster	45a	cassette/cassette player
Don't be silly!	fat	nose		43	
hall of mirrors	long	ears			
tall	short	arms			

Step 1 Topic warm-up

a Tell pupils in their L1 that they are going to continue their English lessons by looking at the **body**. Introduce the word '**body**' at this point.
b Then ask pupils what words they think they might learn. Can pupils tell you any words for parts of the body in English?

Step 2 Story prediction

a Say 'Open your Coursebooks at page 44. Look at the pictures.' Demonstrate what you mean by holding up your CB and pointing to the pictures.
b Ask pupils in their L1 what they can see. Who are the children and what is their relationship? Where do they think the children are?
c Ask what they think is going to happen in the story.
d Ask pupils if they can see anything in the pictures they can name in English.

Step 3 Story listening

a Say '**Listen to the tape.**' Pupils look at the pictures and listen to the tape at the same time.
b Play the tape again.

Tapescript:
JULIE: Let's go in the hall of mirrors.
SUZY: Yeah! Come on!
BILL: Ha, ha! Look at Gary. He's tall and thin.
JULIE: Ooo! I'm small and fat and my hair is short.
KEV: Aagh! Where's my body?
JULIE: What a big head!
BILL: Oh no! Look at my nose!
GARY: Ha, ha! And look at those big ears!
SUZY: Look at me! Long arms and short legs.
GARY: Aagh! A monster! It's got a big head and big eyes.
SUZY: Where?
GARY: Over there!
KATE: Don't be silly! It isn't a monster. It's Sam.

Step 4 Story task

a Play the first part of the dialogue and point to Julie as she is speaking.
b Play the complete story on tape again and demonstrate the task to pupils: point to each character in turn as he/she is speaking. Pupils listen to the tape and watch the demonstration.
c Then play the complete story again. Pupils listen, look at the pictures and point to each character in turn as he/she is speaking.

Step 5 Story mime

a Allocate the roles of Julie, Suzy, Bill, Gary, Kate and Sam to volunteers. Ask them to stand up as their character speaks/appears. Play the tape.
b Play the tape again. This time pupils stand up and perform actions as appropriate, miming the movements of the characters, e.g. Bill points and laughs as he says '**Ha, ha. Look at Gary. He's tall and thin.**' Pupils can also mouth the words as they listen to the tape.
c Now divide the class into groups of six and allocate roles. Play the tape again. Pupils stand up and perform actions as appropriate.
d Finally, ask one group to volunteer to come to the front of the class and perform, listening to the tape.

4 Body

STORY

Hall of Mirrors

Step 2
Step 3
Step 4

44 45

4A Lesson 1

Main Language Items		Resource File	Materials Needed
What colour is/are …?	nose		
Who are you pointing to?	eyes		
	ear	48	coloured pencils
	hair	5	cassette/cassette player
	mouth		
	blonde		

Step 1 Action Game

a Introduce the names of various parts of the body. Demonstrate with the whole class. First, say '**Touch your nose. Touch your mouth. Touch one eye. Touch two eyes. Touch your ears. Touch your hair.**'

b Use the instructions '**Touch …**' and '**Point to …**' at random with the new words, until pupils can understand the instructions without your help. Practise with individuals and pairs.

c Then add the instructions '**Open …**' and '**Close …**' in combination with the words '**eye/eyes**' and '**mouth**'.

d When pupils are completely familiar with the new words, they can be combined with previous instructions to make new and amusing structures. Try the following:
Close your eyes and point to the door!
Close your eyes. Turn around. Don't open your eyes.
Now point to *Maria*. Open your eyes. Who are you pointing to?
Test pupils with similar instructions and questions.

Step 2 Presentation

a Say '**Open your Coursebooks at page 44 and look at the pictures.**' Play the whole story on tape.

b Then say '**Open your Coursebooks at page 46**' and ask pupils to look at the two frames of the story. Ask pupils to tell you in their L1 what the language in the speech bubbles means.

c Play the story extract and point to the characters.

d Divide the class into pairs. All pairs work simultaneously. Play the tape again. P1 repeats Bill's words and P2 repeats Julie's words.

e Change roles and repeat the procedure.

Tapescript:
BILL: Ha, ha! Look at Gary. He's tall and thin.
JULIE: Ooo! I'm small and fat and my hair is short.

Step 3 Pair work

a Divide the class into pairs. All pairs work simultaneously, with one CB between each pair, open at page 46. Say '**Cover the words. Look at the picture of Julie.**'

b Pupils repeat after the tape. P1 repeats the questions, P2 repeats the answers. Repeat four times, changing roles.

c Then pupils ask and answer the questions without the help of the tape. P1 asks similar questions about all the children.

d Change roles and repeat the procedure.

Step 4 Groupwork: Questionnaire

a Ask various pupils in the class the questions '**What colour are your eyes?**' and/or '**What colour's your hair?**'

b When pupils are familiar with the question form, direct them to the grid on page 58 of their ABs.

c All pupils work simultaneously in groups of three, asking other class members the same questions, and fill in the chart in their ABs.

d Finish the exercise by asking pupils about other class members, i.e. '**What colour are *Maria's* eyes?**' etc.

Step 5 Read and colour

a Working individually, pupils read the description of the boy and the girl on page 58 and colour their hair and eyes accordingly.

Optional

Ask pupils questions about their families.
What colour's your mother's/ father's hair?
Have you got a brother/sister?
If yes: **What's his/her name? What colour's his/her hair?**
What colour are his/her eyes?
How many brothers/sisters have you got?

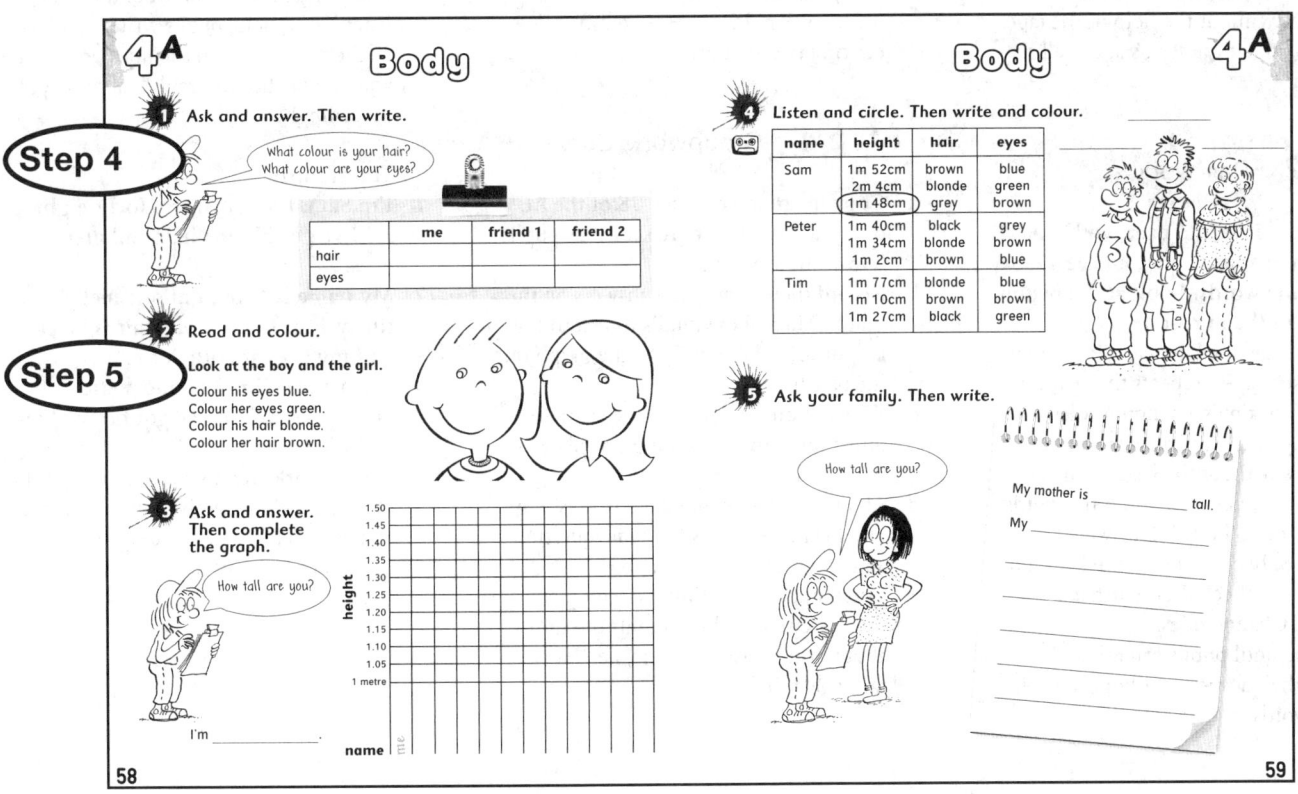

He's Tall and Thin

Step 2

Listen

"Ha, ha! Look at Gary. He's tall and thin."

"Oooh! I'm small and fat and my hair is short."

Ask and answer

| How tall is Suzy? | 1 metre 26 cm. |
| How tall is Kev? | 1 metre 34 cm. |

Step 3

Ask and answer

| What colour is Julie's hair? | Blonde. |
| What colour are Julie's eyes? | Green. |

Ask and answer

Look at Julie in the mirror.

Is Julie small?	Yes.
Is Julie's hair long?	No, it's short.
Is Julie thin?	No, she's fat.

Body 4A

Step 4

1. Ask and answer. Then write.

What colour is your hair?
What colour are your eyes?

	me	friend 1	friend 2
hair			
eyes			

Step 5

2. Read and colour.

Look at the boy and the girl.

Colour his eyes blue.
Colour her eyes green.
Colour his hair blonde.
Colour her hair brown.

3. Ask and answer. Then complete the graph.

How tall are you?

I'm _____

(graph: height 1 metre to 1.50, name)

4. Listen and circle. Then write and colour.

name	height	hair	eyes
Sam	1m 52cm	brown	blue
	2m 4cm	blonde	green
	1m 48cm	grey	brown
Peter	1m 40cm	black	grey
	1m 34cm	blonde	brown
	1m 2cm	brown	blue
Tim	1m 77cm	blonde	blue
	1m 10cm	brown	brown
	1m 27cm	black	green

5. Ask your family. Then write.

How tall are you?

My mother is _____ tall.

My _____

125

4^A Lesson 2

Main Language Items		Resource File	Materials Needed
How tall is/are ...?	tall	4	tape measure
Have you got ...?	centimetres	27	chart
			coloured pencils
			cassette/cassette player

Step 1 Pair work

a Divide the class into pairs. All pairs work simultaneously, with one CB between each pair, open at page 47. Say 'Cover the words. Look at the pictures.' Point to the first exercise on page 47.

b Pupils repeat after the tape. P1 repeats the questions. P2 repeats the answers. Repeat four times changing roles.

c Then pupils ask and answer the questions without the help of the tape. P1 asks similar questions about all six children.

Step 2 Pair work

a Divide the class into pairs, with one CB between each pair, open at page 47. Say 'Cover the words. Look at the picture of Julie in the mirror.'

b Pupils repeat after the tape. P1 repeats the questions, P2 repeats the answers. Repeat four times, changing roles.

c Then pupils ask and answer the questions without the help of the tape. P1 asks the questions, using the words in the book to help. P2 answers, looking only at the picture. P1 should prompt and check their partner's answers. Change roles.

d Continue until pupils can ask and answer the questions without the help of the words.

Step 3 Measuring activity

a You will need a tape measure or a chart fixed to the wall, marked off at 5 cm intervals. Two pupils should measure the other members of the class in turn, and each pupil should make a record of their own height on page 58 of the AB.

b Revise structures and vocabulary during the activity:
Guess how tall *Maria* **is.**
Are you right or wrong?
Maria **is 1m 25cm. How many centimetres is that?**

Step 4 Groupwork: Survey

a Copy the graph on page 58 of the AB onto the blackboard. Ask various pupils 'How tall are you?'

b Record their names and answers on the graph. Then allow pupils to record the heights of other pupils on the graph on the blackboard.

c When pupils understand the exercise, direct them to the graph on page 58 of their ABs.

d All pupils work simultaneously, asking other class members the same question and completing their graph.

e When pupils have finished, complete the exercise by asking pupils questions about other class members, i.e. '**How tall is** *Maria*?' etc.

Step 5 Listen and circle

a Pupils listen to the tape and look at AB page 59. For each of the three children, they must circle the appropriate word to indicate their height, hair colour and eye colour.

b Play the tape three times. Allow pupils to compare their answers before replaying the tape to focus their listening.

c Using the information from the listening to help, pupils write the name of each character on the lines provided and colour the children's hair and eyes accordingly.

Tapescript:

1 I'm Sam. I'm one metre forty-eight. // I've got blonde hair and green eyes. //

2 My name is Peter. I'm one metre thirty-four tall. // My hair is black and my eyes are brown. //

3 My name's Tim. I'm one metre twenty-seven. // I've got brown hair and blue eyes. //

d (Homework) Pupils should find out the height of other members of their family and complete the sentences at the bottom of page 59 in their AB.

He's Tall and Thin

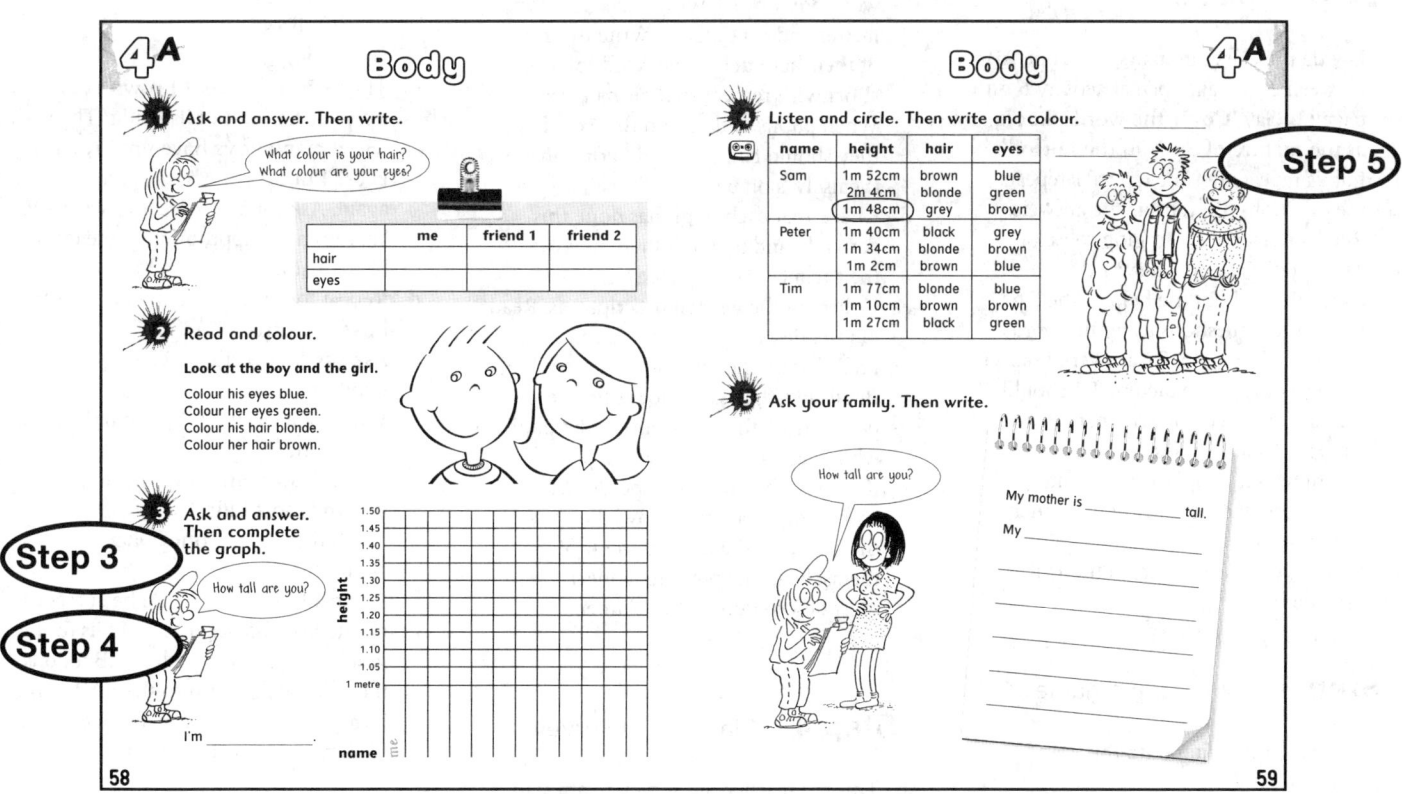

Body 4A

Listen

Ha, ha! Look at Gary. He's tall and thin.

Oooh! I'm small and fat and my hair is short.

Ask and answer

| How tall is Suzy? | 1 metre 26 cm. |
| How tall is Kev? | 1 metre 34 cm. |

Step 1

Ask and answer

| What colour is Julie's hair? | Blonde. |
| What colour are Julie's eyes? | Green. |

Ask and answer

Look at Julie in the mirror.

Is Julie small?	Yes.
Is Julie's hair long?	No, it's short.
Is Julie thin?	No, she's fat.

Step 2

46 47

4A Body

1 Ask and answer. Then write.

What colour is your hair?
What colour are your eyes?

	me	friend 1	friend 2
hair			
eyes			

2 Read and colour.

Look at the boy and the girl.

Colour his eyes blue.
Colour her eyes green.
Colour his hair blonde.
Colour her hair brown.

3 Ask and answer. Then complete the graph.

How tall are you?

I'm _____ .

Step 3
Step 4

height: 1.50, 1.45, 1.40, 1.35, 1.30, 1.25, 1.20, 1.15, 1.10, 1.05, 1 metre

name

Body 4A

4 Listen and circle. Then write and colour.

name	height	hair	eyes
Sam	1m 52cm	brown	blue
	2m 4cm	blonde	green
	1m 48cm	grey	brown
Peter	1m 40cm	black	grey
	1m 34cm	blonde	brown
	1m 2cm	brown	blue
Tim	1m 77cm	blonde	blue
	1m 10cm	brown	brown
	1m 27cm	black	green

Step 5

5 Ask your family. Then write.

How tall are you?

My mother is _____ tall.
My _____

58 59

127

4A Lesson 3

Main Language Items		Resource File	Materials Needed
Is ... *small*?	small		
Who's got ...?	tall	4	cassette/cassette player
Put up your hands!	short	45	
Count ...	long		

Step 1 Presentation

a Ask pupils questions relating to their homework exercise (AB page 59, activity 5). Use the following question forms.
How tall is your mother/father?
Have you got a brother/sister?
If yes: How tall is he/she?

Step 2 Pair work

a Divide the class into pairs, with one AB between each pair, open at activity 6 on page 60. Say 'Cover the words. Look at the picture of Suzy in the mirror.'
b Pupils repeat after the tape. P1 repeats the questions. P2 repeats the answers. Repeat four times changing roles.
c Then pupils ask and answer the questions without the help of the tape. P1 asks the questions using the words in the book to help, P2 answers, looking only at the picture. P1 should prompt and check his/her partner's answers. Change roles.
d Continue until pupils can ask and answer the questions without the help of the words.
e Pupils write the answers in the spaces provided.

Step 3 Writing and game

a Copy the following onto the blackboard:

> GUESS WHO?
> I'm a boy/girl. I'm ___ tall
> I've got ___(colour) eyes and
> long/short ___(colour) hair.

b Ask for a volunteer to complete the sentences giving a description of him/herself. Pupils must delete the word **boy** or **girl**; write their height in metres and centimetres; write the colour of their hair; delete the word **long** or **short** with respect to their hair.
c When pupils understand the exercise, they should complete a description of themselves on paper.
d Check that each pupil has done this correctly and then tell them to write their names on the paper.
e Collect in the written descriptions. Read out the descriptions one at a time preceded by the question 'Guess who!'
f Pupils must guess the identity of the person from the description. The pupil who guesses correctly wins a point. (Give out the piece of paper to keep score.) Pupils are not allowed to give the answer if the description is of themselves. The pupil to 'collect' the most descriptions is the winner.

Step 4 Classwork: Survey

a This is a teacher-led survey relating to hair and eye colour and hair length of pupils in the class.
b Copy the following information onto the blackboard:

	BOYS	GIRLS
Eyes – brown		
blue		
green		
grey		
Hair – brown		
black		
blonde		
short		
long		

c Then say 'Who's got brown eyes? Put up your hand!' Pupils count. Then ask 'How many boys have got brown eyes? Put up your hand!' Pupils count again. Ask for a volunteer to write the answer in the appropriate place on the blackboard.
d Repeat for other eye colours for both **boys** and **girls**.
e Ask similar questions relating to the pupils' hair, i.e.
Who's got brown/short hair? Put up your hands!
Count how many boys have got brown/short hair.
Teach the word '**None**' where applicable.
f When all the figures have been recorded on the blackboard, direct pupils to the graphs on page 60 of their AB. Pupils transfer the figures into their AB in the form of block graphs, using one colour for boys and another for girls.

4A Body

6 Listen and ask and answer. Then read and write.

Look at Suzy in the mirror.

Step 2

Is Suzy small? _____
Is Suzy's hair short? _____
Is Suzy thin? _____

7 Complete the graph.

Step 4

Our class   = boys   = girls

Eyes colour	Hair colour	Hair length
brown blue green grey	brown black blonde	short long

60

4B Body

1 Listen and make a face.

She's got long blonde hair and . . .

He's got short black hair and . . .

He's got short blonde hair and . . .

She's got long brown hair and . . .

61

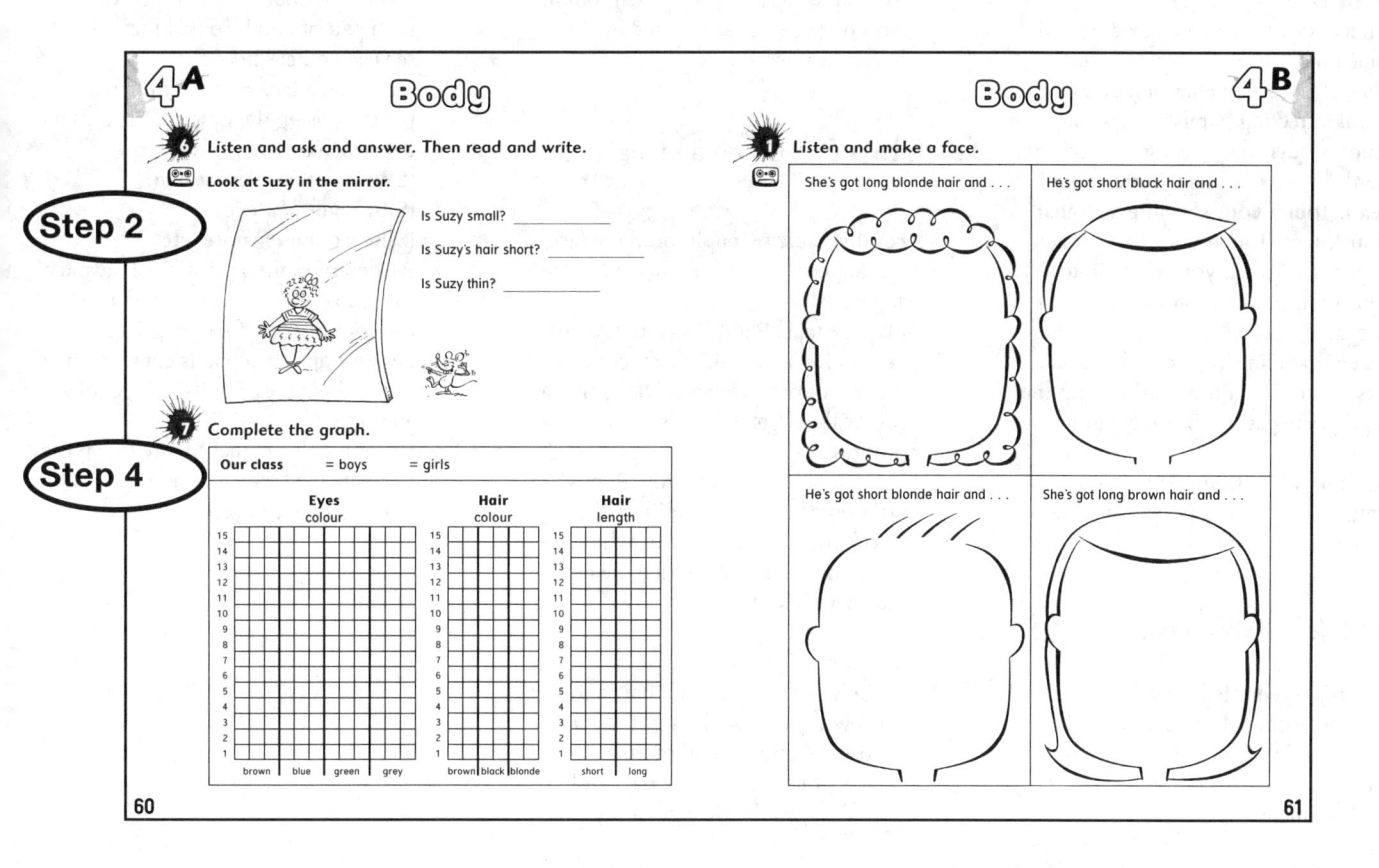

129

4ᴮ Lesson 1

Main Language Items			Resource File	Materials Needed
Has she/he got …?	ears	head		card/paper
Are his *eyes green*?	mouth	shoulders	24	scissors (optional)
She's/He's got …	nose	knees		coloured pencils
	big	toes		cassette/cassette player
	small			

The song and the making activity may take longer than you think. Be prepared to postpone the follow-up activities until the next lesson.

Step 1 Song

a Say 'Look at the song and pictures on page 48 of your Coursebook. Listen to the tape.'
b Pupils listen to the song, reading at the same time.
c Then check comprehension of the words, directing pupils through an action sequence in the same order as the words in the song. Say '**Touch your head. Touch your shoulders. Touch your knees. Touch your toes. Touch your eyes. Touch your ears. Touch your mouth. Touch your nose.**' Repeat.
d Listen again line by line with books closed and repeat the words. Touch the appropriate part of the body at the same time.
e Play the whole song again and sing along with the tape, performing the actions at the same time.

Step 2 Make a face

This is a teacher-led Task Reading exercise. Although pupils may understand the written instructions, these are intended only as reinforcement.

a Each pupil requires seven small rectangular pieces of card measuring 6 x 2 cm. You may find it useful to cut out and prepare the card in advance for pupils.
b Pupils then draw three pairs of eyes, two noses and two mouths according to the descriptions on page 48 of the CB.
c These 'face pieces' are then to be used with the face outlines on page 61 of the AB. Pupils must colour the hair on the faces on page 61, as directed by the sentences in each box.

Step 3 Listen and make a face

For this exercise, pupils need the face pieces from Step 2, and their ABs, open at page 61.
a Play the tape. Pupils listen to the first description and build up a picture on the appropriate 'face base'. Play the tape two or three times. Pupils compare their pictures.
b Play the second description. Pupils make another face on a different base.
c Check the answers with the whole class by asking pupils to describe the faces they have built up.

Tapescript:
1 She's got long blonde hair and brown eyes. // She's got a small nose // and a small mouth.
2 He's got short blonde hair and green eyes. // He's got a big mouth and a small nose.

Step 4 Pair work

Pupils need the face pieces for this exercise.
a Divide the class into pairs. Each pupil places their AB (open at page 61) and face pieces in front of them. A book should be stood up on end between each pair of pupils so that they cannot see each other's books.
b P1 makes a face on one of the base pictures, using their pieces. Then using the structures
(S)he's got *long blonde* hair.
(S)he's got *blue* eyes.
(S)he's got a *big* nose, etc.
P1 describes their picture. P2 must try to reconstruct an identical picture on the correct 'base' following P1's description. Then pupils compare their finished pictures. Pupils change roles and repeat.
c Faster pupils can make more face pieces to create more possibilities (e.g. big/small green eyes).

Step 1

Faces and Monsters

Sing

Head and Shoulders ...

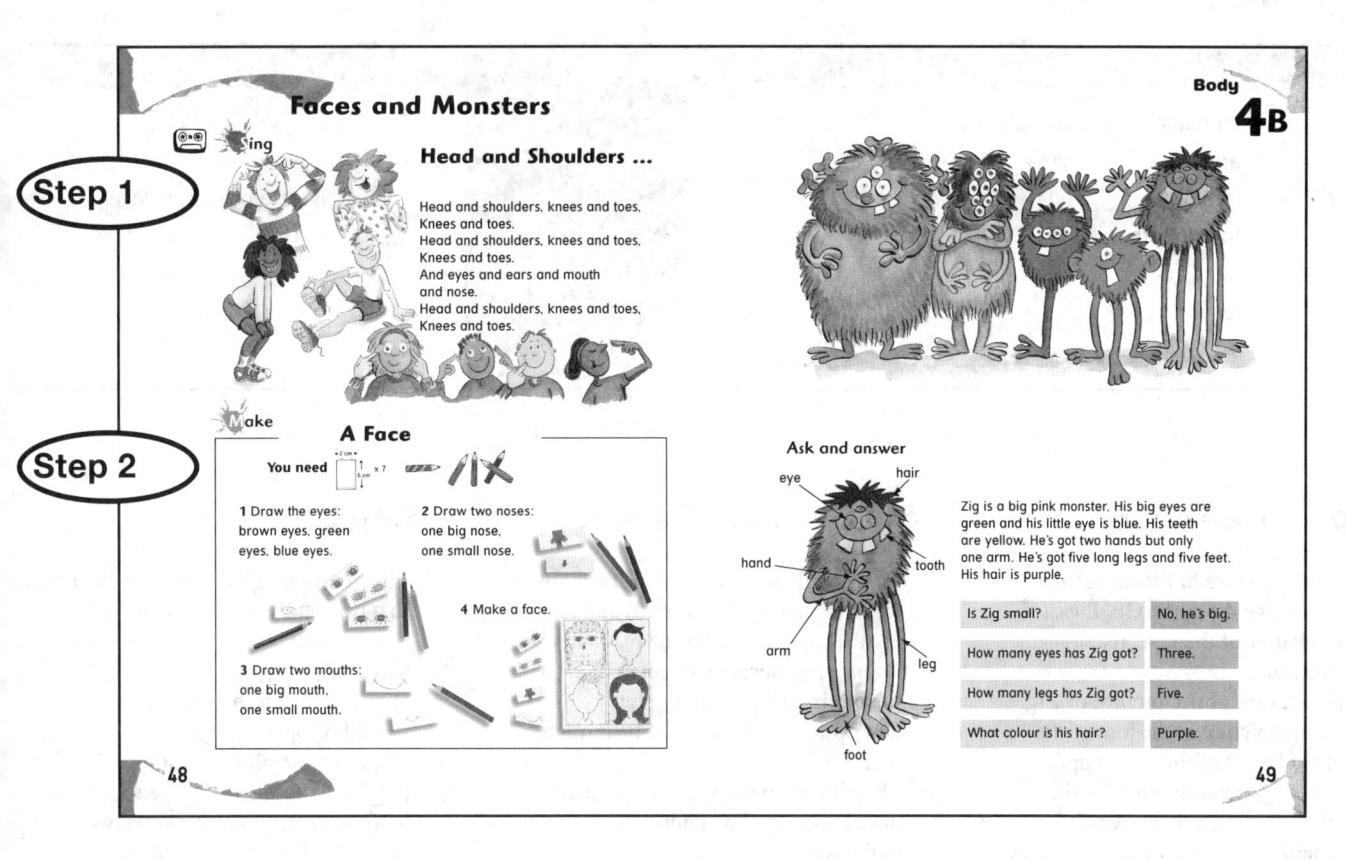

Head and shoulders, knees and toes,
Knees and toes.
Head and shoulders, knees and toes,
Knees and toes.
And eyes and ears and mouth and nose.
Head and shoulders, knees and toes,
Knees and toes.

Step 2

Make

A Face

You need ...

1 Draw the eyes: brown eyes, green eyes, blue eyes.

2 Draw two noses: one big nose, one small nose.

3 Draw two mouths: one big mouth, one small mouth.

4 Make a face.

Body 4B

Ask and answer

eye — hair
hand — tooth
arm — leg
foot

Zig is a big pink monster. His big eyes are green and his little eye is blue. His teeth are yellow. He's got two hands but only one arm. He's got five long legs and five feet. His hair is purple.

Is Zig small?	No, he's big.
How many eyes has Zig got?	Three.
How many legs has Zig got?	Five.
What colour is his hair?	Purple.

48 — 49

4A Body

6 Listen and ask and answer. Then read and write.

Look at Suzy in the mirror.

Is Suzy small? _____
Is Suzy's hair short? _____
Is Suzy thin? _____

7 Complete the graph.

Our class ■ = boys □ = girls

Eyes colour	Hair colour	Hair length
brown blue green grey	brown black blonde	short long

Body 4B

1 Listen and make a face.

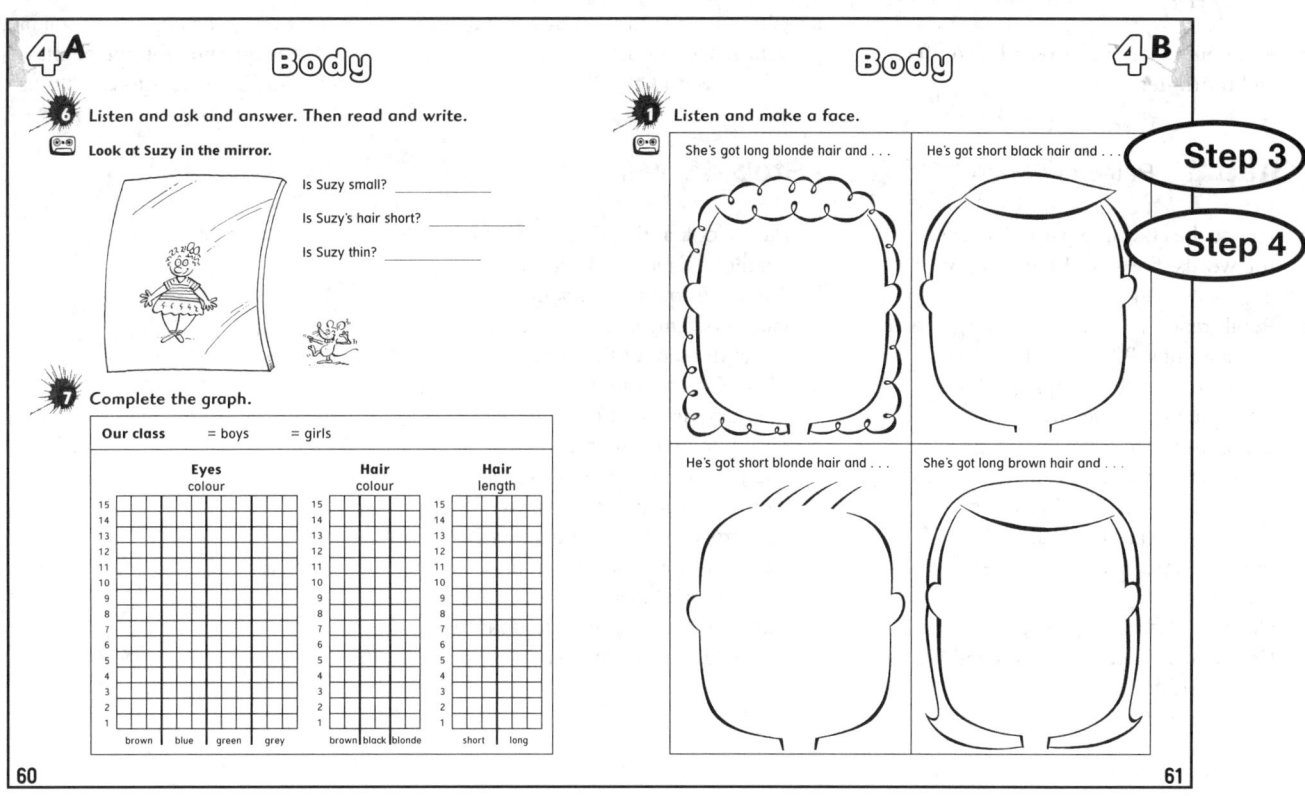

She's got long blonde hair and ...   **Step 3**

He's got short black hair and ...   **Step 4**

He's got short blonde hair and ...

She's got long brown hair and ...

60 — 61

131

4B Lesson 2

Main Language Items			Resource File	Materials Needed
Is ...?	monster	very ugly	29	cassette/cassette player
How many ...?	arms	hairy	32a	
What colour ...?	foot/feet	body		
	tooth/teeth			
	hands			
	legs			

Step 1 Presentation

a Look at the picture of the monsters at the top of page 49 in the CB. Pupils listen to Part 1 of the tape, reading at the same time.
b Then say '**Look at the picture of Zig.**' Point to the picture at the foot of the page. Play Part 2 of the tape. Pupils listen to the passage and read at the same time. Say '**Cover the words.**' Then pupils listen again with the words covered.
c Point out the irregular plurals **foot–feet** and **tooth–teeth**.

Step 2 Pair work

a Divide the class into pairs. Say '**Cover the words. Look at the picture of Zig.**'
b Pupils repeat after the tape. P1 repeats the questions, P2 repeats the answers. Repeat four times changing roles.
c Then pupils ask and answer the questions without the help of the tape. P1 asks the questions using the words in the book to help. P2 answers, looking only at the picture. P1 should prompt and check their partner's answers.
d Change roles and repeat the procedure.
e Continue until pupils can ask and answer the questions without the help of the words.

Step 3 Read. Then write

a Pupils look at the picture of the monster family on page 62 of the AB and read the descriptions under the picture.
b Pupils must decide the names of each of the monsters by studying the descriptions and using the pictures in both books to help.
c They should write the name of each monster on the line under each picture in the AB.
d Check pupils' answers by holding up your AB, pointing to the monsters and asking 'Who's this?'

Step 4 Writing

a Pupils look at the picture of the monster family on page 49 of the CB.
b Ask pupils questions about the monsters, similar to those relating to Zig at the foot of the page.
c Then elicit questions from pupils that they can ask about the monsters.
d Each pupil must then write two questions of their own choice about the monsters. The questions relating to Zig may prove useful as models. Each question should be written on a separate small piece of paper.
e Collect in each pupil's questions to use in the quiz which follows.

Step 5 Quiz

The questions for the quiz are the ones that the pupils have just written. Correct grammatical inaccuracies as you read them out.

a Divide the class into two teams. CBs should be open at page 49.
b Read out one of the questions. The first pupil to raise their hand gets a chance to answer, and if correct wins two points for their team. If the answer is wrong, the opposing team may attempt the question for one point.
c Do all the questions in the same way.

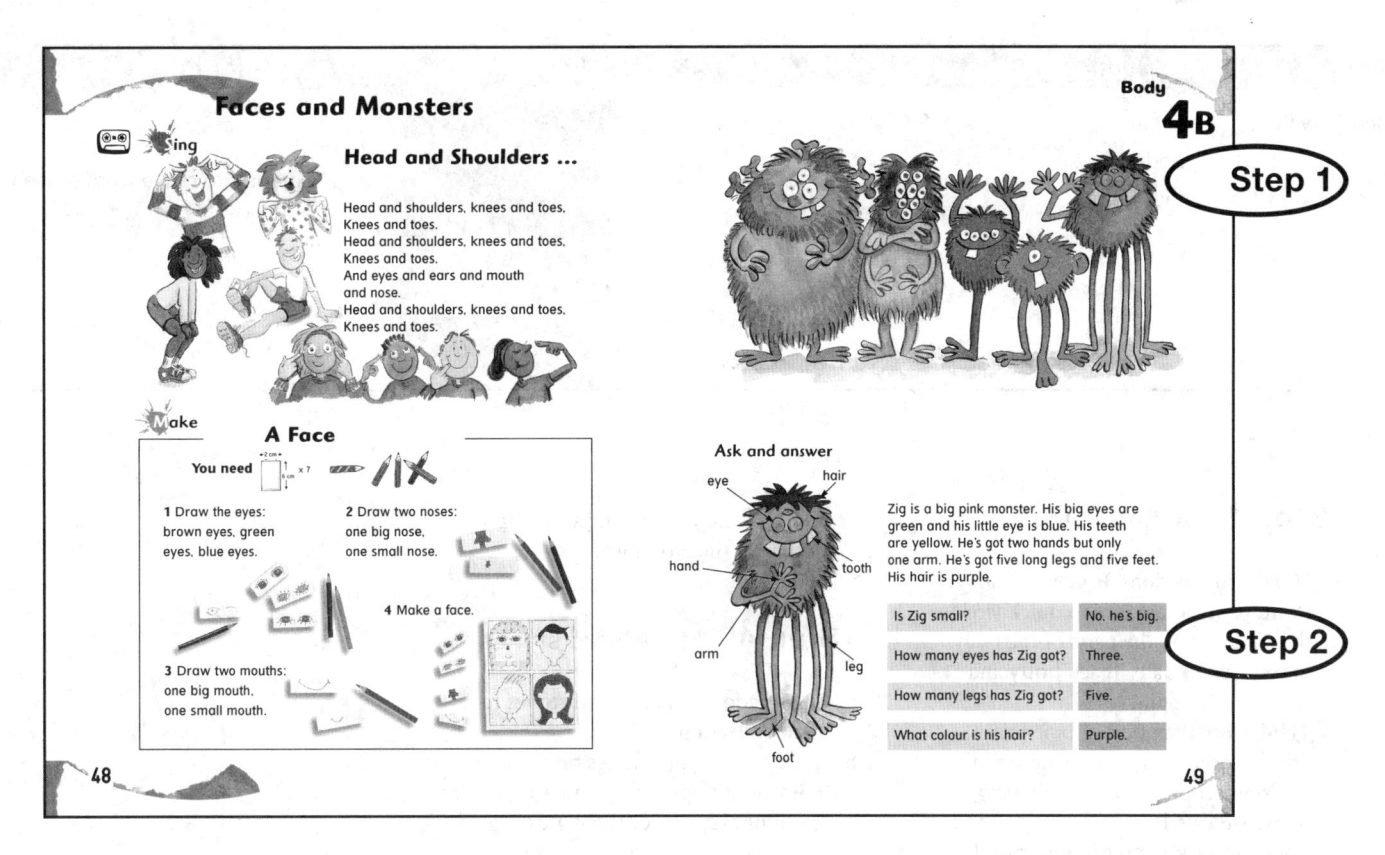

Faces and Monsters

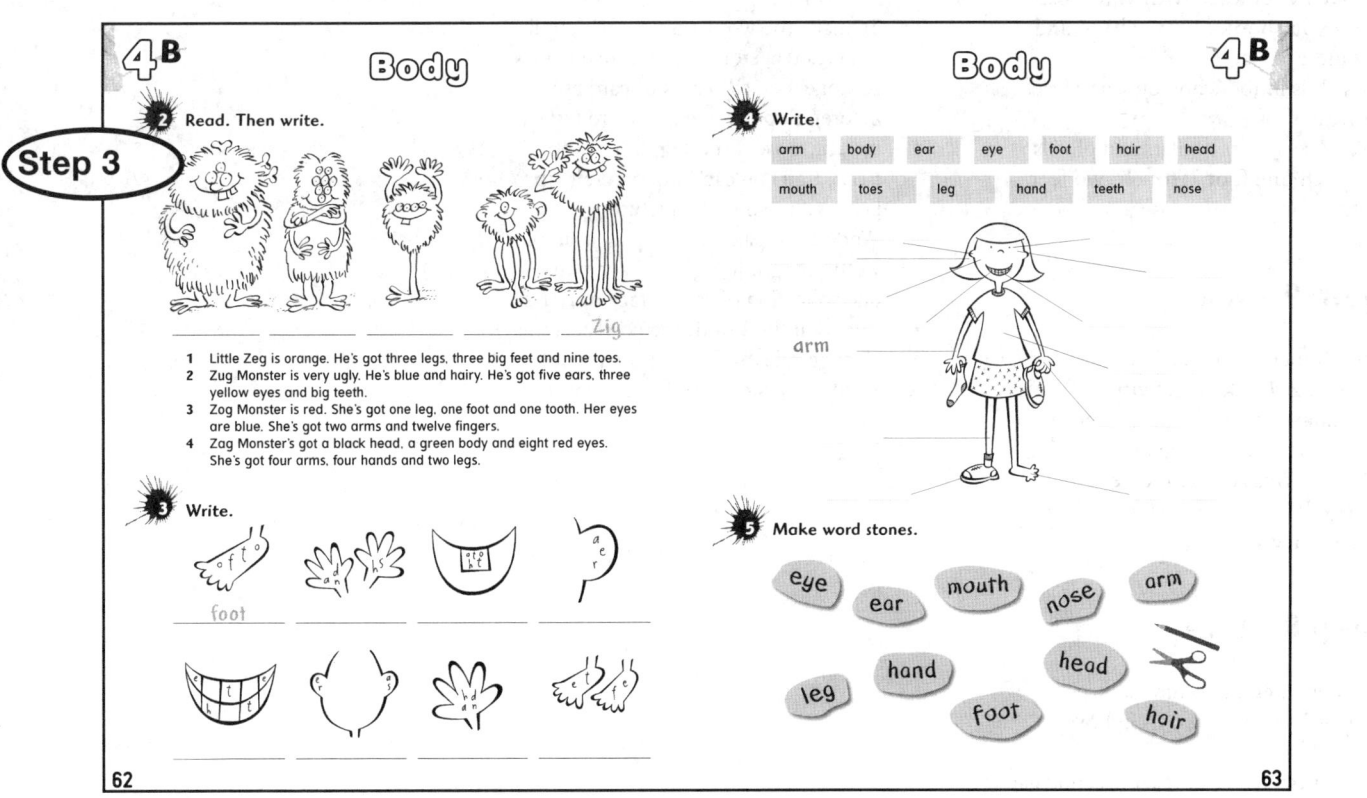

Sing

Head and Shoulders ...

Head and shoulders, knees and toes,
Knees and toes.
Head and shoulders, knees and toes,
Knees and toes.
And eyes and ears and mouth and nose.
Head and shoulders, knees and toes,
Knees and toes.

Make — A Face

You need — ... ×7

1 Draw the eyes: brown eyes, green eyes, blue eyes.
2 Draw two noses: one big nose, one small nose.
3 Draw two mouths: one big mouth, one small mouth.
4 Make a face.

48

Body 4B — Step 1

Ask and answer — Step 2

eye, hair, hand, tooth, arm, leg, foot

Zig is a big pink monster. His big eyes are green and his little eye is blue. His teeth are yellow. He's got two hands but only one arm. He's got five long legs and five feet. His hair is purple.

Is Zig small?	No, he's big.
How many eyes has Zig got?	Three.
How many legs has Zig got?	Five.
What colour is his hair?	Purple.

49

4B Body — Step 3

2 Read. Then write.

Zig

1 Little Zeg is orange. He's got three legs, three big feet and nine toes.
2 Zug Monster is very ugly. He's blue and hairy. He's got five ears, three yellow eyes and big teeth.
3 Zog Monster is red. She's got one leg, one foot and one tooth. Her eyes are blue. She's got two arms and twelve fingers.
4 Zag Monster's got a black head, a green body and eight red eyes. She's got four arms, four hands and two legs.

3 Write.

foot

62

Body 4B

4 Write.

| arm | body | ear | eye | foot | hair | head |
| mouth | toes | leg | hand | teeth | nose |

arm

5 Make word stones.

eye, ear, mouth, nose, arm, leg, hand, head, foot, hair

63

133

4ᴮ Lesson 3

Main Language Items		Resource File	Materials Needed
Touch … with …	finger	13	materials to make word stones
	body	14	
	foot/feet	41	
	tooth/teeth	46	

Step 1 Action Game

a Use the instructions **Touch …** and **Point to …** at random to quickly revise the names of all the parts of the body introduced to date. Teach **body** and **finger** at this point.

b These words can be combined with other instructions to make new and amusing actions. Try the following:
Stand on one leg!
Touch your knee with your nose!
Put your book on your head and stand up! etc.

c Use this introduction only as a brief revision.

d Practise using singulars and plurals: 'Touch one foot,' 'Touch two feet.' etc.

Step 2 Write

a Say '**Open your Activity Books at page 62. Look at Activity 3**' Pupils unjumble the letters in each picture and write the word on the line provided.

b NOTE This activity focuses on the irregular plurals **foot–feet** and **tooth–teeth**.

Step 3 Write

a Pupils label the picture on page 63 of the AB using the words in boxes at the top of the page.

a Faster pupils can revise the action game in Step 1 in pairs, to allow all pupils sufficient time to finish.

Step 4 Make word stones

a Pupils add ten more word stones to their collection.

b Point to the word stones on AB page 63. Check pupils are familiar with their meaning: say one of the words, e.g. **nose**. Pupils point to their noses.

c To make the word stones, each pupil requires ten 'stones' (either real stones or stone-shaped pieces of card as before). Pupils write one word (**eye, ear, mouth, nose, arm, leg, hand, foot, head, hair**) on each stone in felt-tip pen, as shown in the pictures.

d Working in pairs, pupils play a simple word-recognition game. Each pair uses one collection of stones face up. P1 says a word and P2 finds the correct stone. Change roles and repeat the procedure.

e Pupils then store their stones for future use.

Faces and Monsters

Sing

Head and Shoulders ...

Head and shoulders, knees and toes,
Knees and toes.
Head and shoulders, knees and toes,
Knees and toes.
And eyes and ears and mouth and nose.
Head and shoulders, knees and toes,
Knees and toes.

Make

A Face

You need

1 Draw the eyes: brown eyes, green eyes, blue eyes.
2 Draw two noses: one big nose, one small nose.
3 Draw two mouths: one big mouth, one small mouth.
4 Make a face.

Body 4B

Ask and answer

eye, hair, hand, tooth, arm, leg, foot

Zig is a big pink monster. His big eyes are green and his little eye is blue. His teeth are yellow. He's got two hands but only one arm. He's got five long legs and five feet. His hair is purple.

Is Zig small?	No, he's big.
How many eyes has Zig got?	Three.
How many legs has Zig got?	Five.
What colour is his hair?	Purple.

48 / 49

4B Body

2 Read. Then write.

_____ _____ _____ _____ Zig

1. Little Zeg is orange. He's got three legs, three big feet and nine toes.
2. Zug Monster is very ugly. He's blue and hairy. He's got five ears, three yellow eyes and big teeth.
3. Zog Monster is red. She's got one leg, one foot and one tooth. Her eyes are blue. She's got two arms and twelve fingers.
4. Zag Monster's got a black head, a green body and eight red eyes. She's got four arms, four hands and two legs.

3 Write.

foot

Body 4B

4 Write.

| arm | body | ear | eye | foot | hair | head |
| mouth | toes | leg | hand | teeth | nose |

arm

5 Make word stones.

eye, ear, mouth, nose, arm, leg, hand, head, foot, hair

62 / 63

Step 2 · Step 3 · Step 4

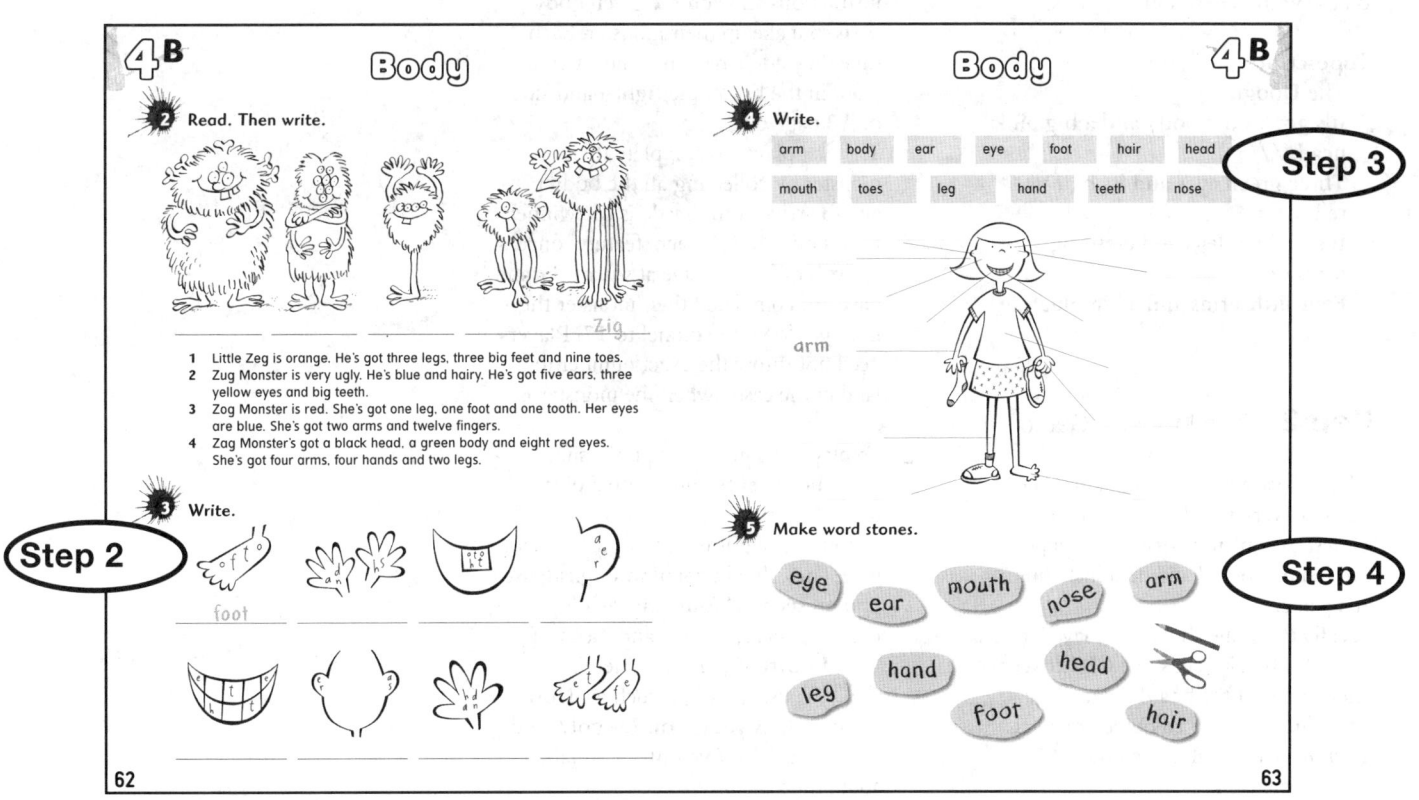

135

4c Lesson 1

Main Language Items		Resource File	Materials Needed
How many …?	ghost	friendly	
Can I borrow …?	hairy	spiders	counters/dice
Give …	bad	angry	13a	coloured pencils
Draw …	crocodile		36	cassette/cassette player
Go to …			

Step 1 Listen and write

a Pupils listen to the poem and write down how many eyes, legs, toes and arms the monster has in the boxes alongside the words at the top of AB page 64. Play the tape two or three times.
b Then pupils write the numbers out in full within the body of the poem.
c Finally pupils draw 'The Doogie' based on the written description.

Tapescript:
The Doogie
It's got a little body and a big pink head, //
Three green eyes and its hair is red. //
It's got two legs and eight big toes, //
Four little arms and a big blue nose. //

Step 2 The Monster Game

This is basically a reading game. The rules are very simple but it may be easiest to explain by gathering pupils around one board and demonstrating the game.

a Ideally the game should be played in pairs. Each pair needs one CB between them, open at the board game on page 50, a dice and two coloured counters. Each player will also need their AB open at page 64.
b The object of the game is to make your way from the start to the castle at the top. Along the way, players must 'collect' body parts and draw them to make a monster in the space provided on page 64 of the AB.
c Each player must draw a head and a body for their monster before they start.
d Players take it in turns to throw the dice and move around the board. When they land on a square they must read the instructions and add the given body parts to make up their monster. Each time they add a part they must tick the word in the list on the right-hand side of AB page 64.
e The first player to complete their monster by collecting all the body parts and to arrive at the castle is the winner.
f Pupils only collect each 'feature' once. However, if they arrive at square 37 and have not completed their monster they must go down the tunnel to 17. Players need not throw the exact number to land in the castle when the monster is complete.
g To play the game again pupils simply copy the list of features onto a piece of paper.
h Encourage pupils to use English as they play. They should count in English; use phrases such as 'Your/My turn'; request pencils, colours and dice using 'Can I borrow …?' or 'Where's the …?'; use questions such as 'How many … has your monster got?' and phrases such as 'I've got …' to talk about their pictures.
i In addition ask pupils questions about the game as you monitor their progress, e.g.
Whose turn is it?
How many … has your monster got?
Has your monster got legs? etc.

Two Big Ears

Body 4c

Step 2 — The Monster Game board (pages 50–51)

4c Body

Step 1

1. Listen and write. Then draw.

How many? | eyes | legs | toes | arms |

The Doogie

It's got a little body and a big, pink head.

_____ green eyes and its hair is red.

It's got _____ legs and _____ big toes.

_____ little arms and a big, blue nose.

Step 2

2. Play the game.

Look at the Monster Game on page 50 in your Coursebook.

Draw your monster here.

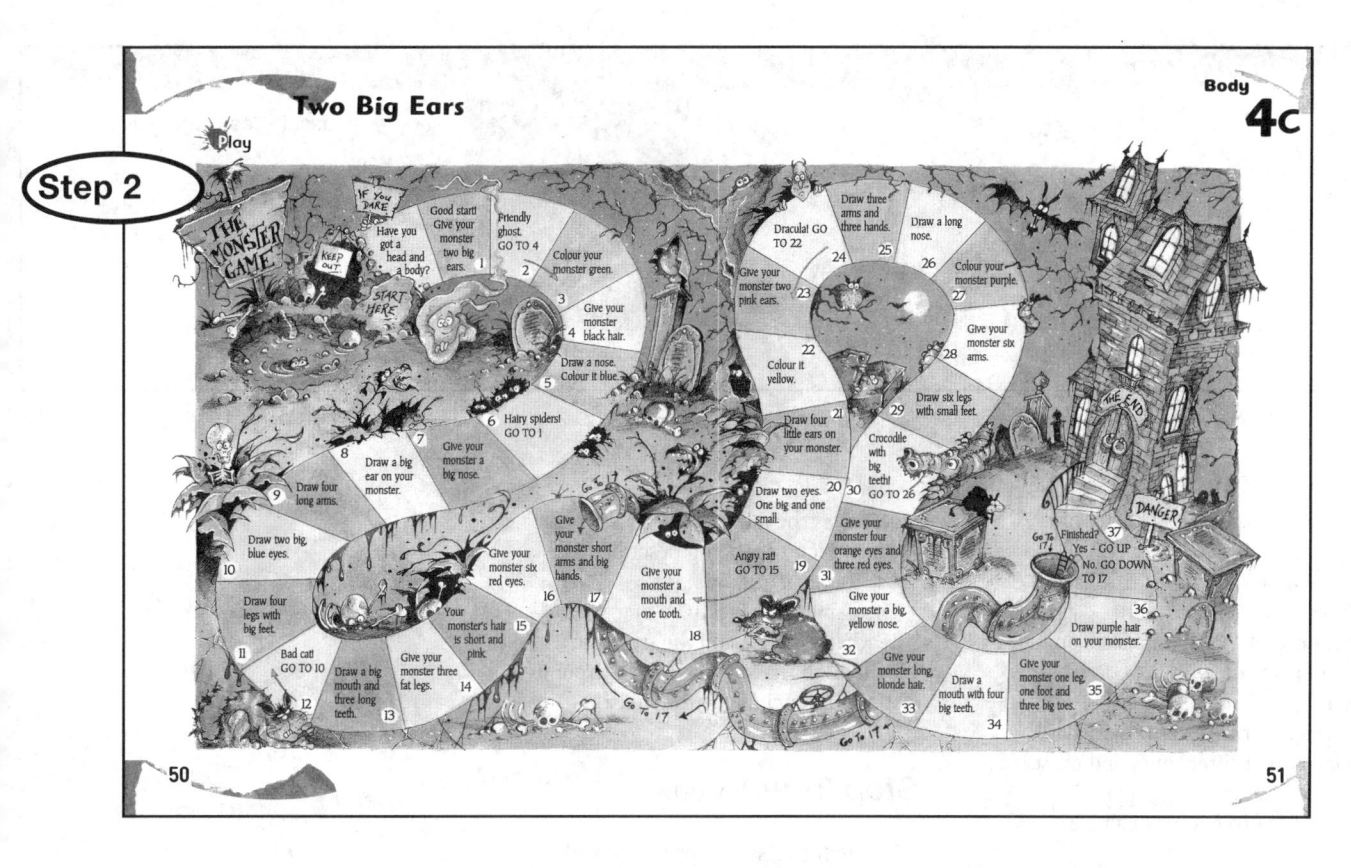

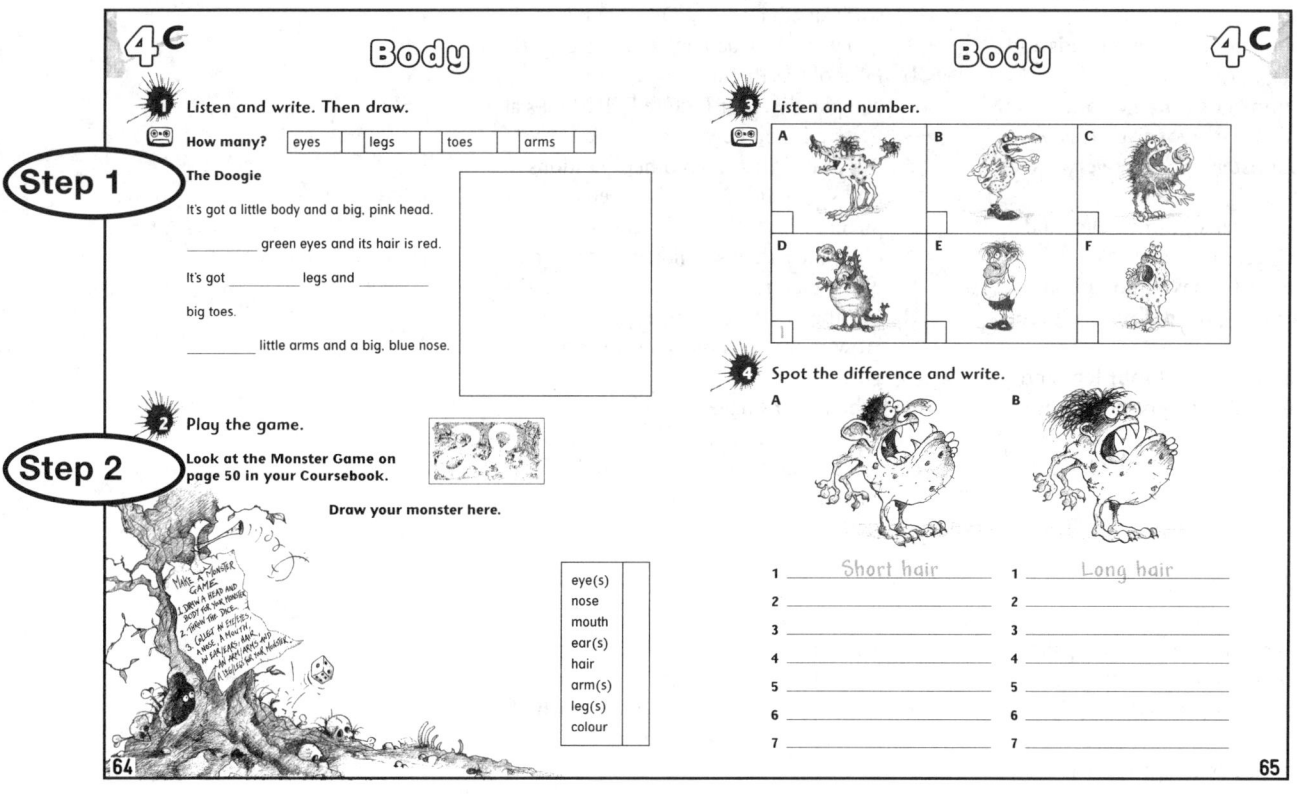

eye(s)
nose
mouth
ear(s)
hair
arm(s)
leg(s)
colour

Body 4c

3. Listen and number.

A | B | C
D | E | F

4. Spot the difference and write.

A | B

1. Short hair   1. Long hair
2. _____   2. _____
3. _____   3. _____
4. _____   4. _____
5. _____   5. _____
6. _____   6. _____
7. _____   7. _____

137

4c Lesson 2

Main Language Items	Resource File	Materials Needed
It's got … How many … has it got? hasn't got	50	cassette/cassette player

Step 1   Listen and number

a   Say 'Open your Activity Books at page 65.' Pupils listen to the descriptions of the six monsters on the tape and place them in the correct order by writing the number of each description in the boxes provided. Play the tape two or three times and pause after each description.

b   Number 1 is given as an example.

Tapescript:
1   This monster's got two heads and three legs. //
2   This monster's only got one leg. // But it's got five arms. //
3   This monster's got one very big eye and two big ears. //
4   This monster's got five eyes and two big teeth. //
5   This monster hasn't got a body. // It's got a big head, four arms and two legs. //
6   This monster's got four legs and long toes. // It's got no hands and no arms. //
    Answers: A = 6, B = 2, C = 5, D = 1, E = 3, F = 4.

Step 2   Pair work

a   Divide the class into pairs. All pairs work simultaneously. Use the six pictures at the top of page 65 of their AB.
b   P1 selects one of the pictures and describes the monster. P2 must guess which picture is being described.
c   Use the structure 'It's got …'
d   The game can quickly be practised Teacher → Class and the structure written on the blackboard if the pupils are experiencing any difficulty.

Step 3   Pair work

a   Divide the class into pairs. All pairs work simultaneously. Direct pupils to the two pictures in activity 4 on AB page 65.
b   P1 looks at Picture A and must completely cover Picture B. P2 looks at Picture B and covers Picture A.
c   Pupils must ask each other questions to find seven differences between the pictures. Each time they find a difference, they should circle that area of the picture.
d   Use the question form, e.g.
    How many legs has your monster got?
e   When pupils have found seven differences they should compare their pictures, and then move on to the writing exercise which follows.

Step 4   Writing

a   This exercise is based upon the Spot-the-Difference pictures.
b   Pupils list the difference under each of the two pictures. An example has been given.

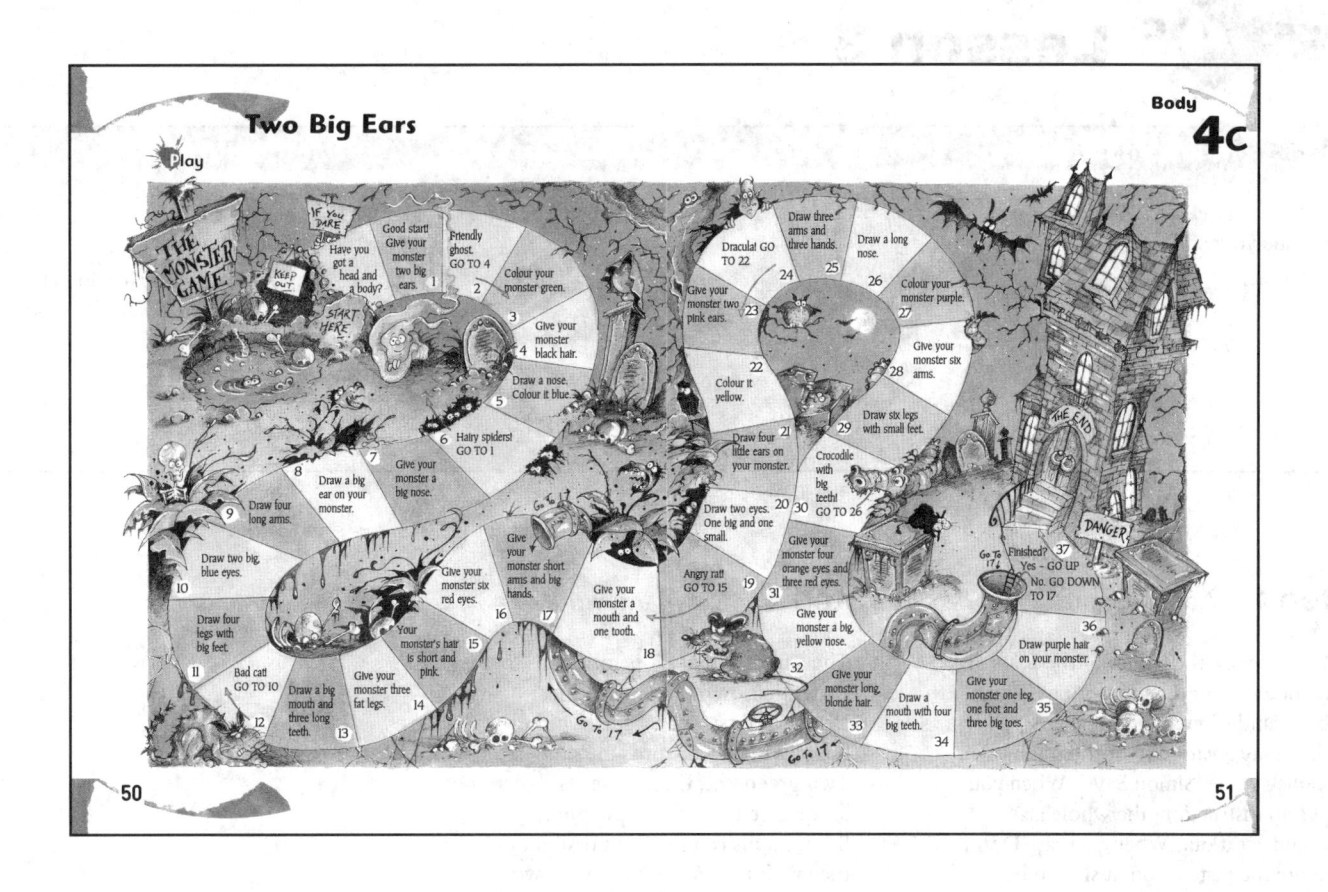

Two Big Ears

Body 4c

(The Monster Game board — numbered spaces 1–37)

1. Have you got a head and a body?
2. Good start! Give your monster two big ears.
3. Friendly ghost. GO TO 4
4. Colour your monster green.
5. Give your monster black hair.
6. Hairy spiders! GO TO 1
7. Draw a nose. Colour it blue.
8. Draw a big ear on your monster.
9. Draw four long arms.
10. Draw two big, blue eyes.
11. Draw four legs with big feet.
12. Bad cat! GO TO 10
13. Draw a big mouth and three long teeth.
14. Give your monster three fat legs.
15. Your monster's hair is short and pink.
16. Give your monster six red eyes.
17. Give your monster short arms and big hands.
18. Give your monster a mouth and one tooth.
19. Angry rat! GO TO 15
20. Draw two eyes. One big and one small.
21. Draw four little ears on your monster.
22. Colour it yellow.
23. Give your monster two pink ears.
24. Dracula! GO TO 22
25. Draw three arms and three hands.
26. Draw a long nose.
27. Colour your monster purple.
28. Give your monster six arms.
29. Draw six legs with small feet.
30. Crocodile with big teeth! GO TO 26
31. Give your monster four orange eyes and three red eyes.
32. Give your monster long, blonde hair.
33. Give your monster a big, yellow nose.
34. Draw a mouth with four big teeth.
35. Give your monster one leg, one foot and three big toes.
36. Draw purple hair on your monster.
37. Finished? Yes – GO UP TO 17 No. GO DOWN TO 17

Body 4c

1. Listen and write. Then draw.

How many? | eyes | legs | toes | arms |

The Doogie

It's got a little body and a big, pink head.

_____ green eyes and its hair is red.

It's got _____ legs and _____ big toes.

_____ little arms and a big, blue nose.

2. Play the game.

Look at the Monster Game on page 50 in your Coursebook.

Draw your monster here.

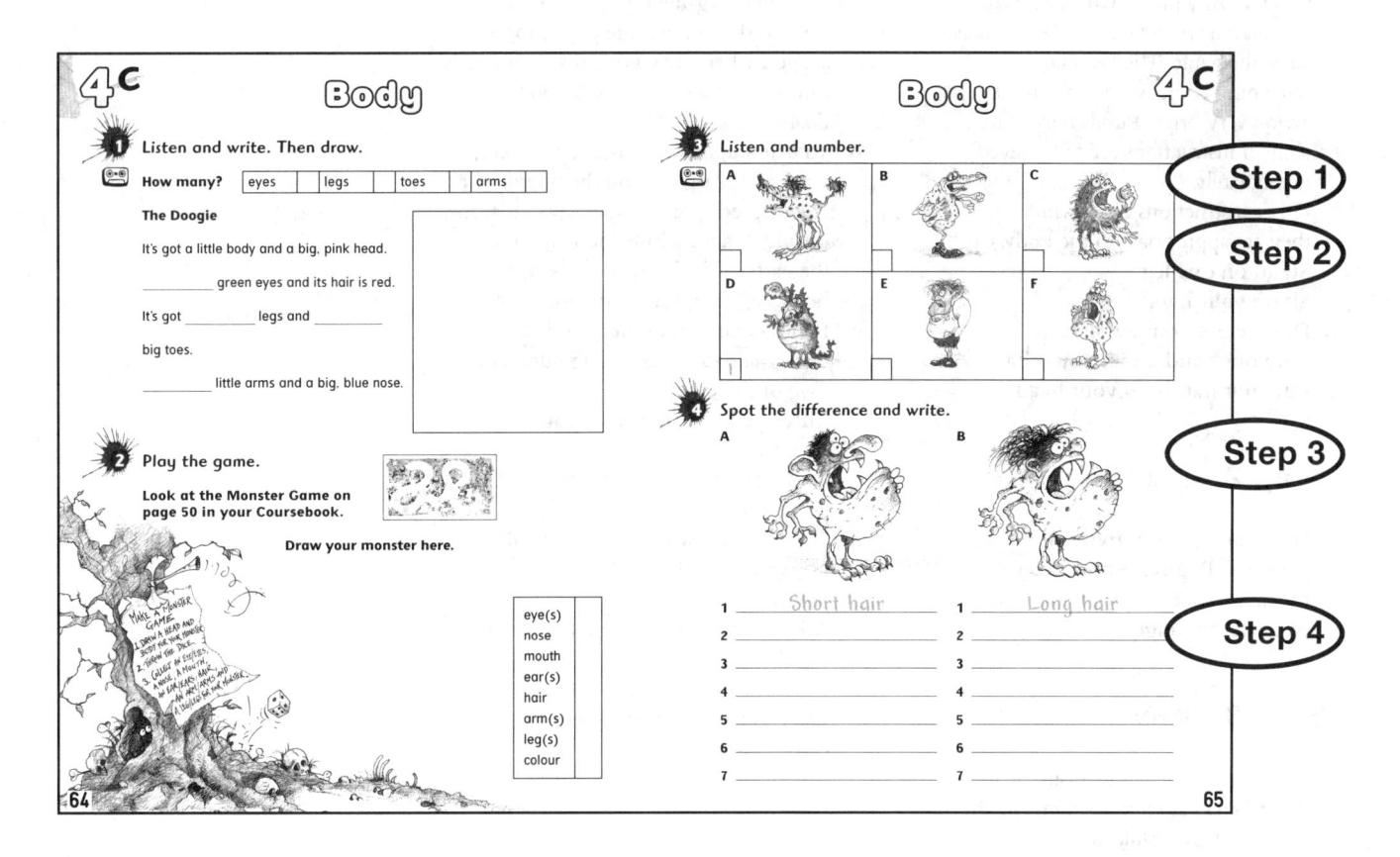

3. Listen and number.

A B C
D E F

4. Spot the difference and write.

A — Short hair B — Long hair

1. _____ 1. _____
2. _____ 2. _____
3. _____ 3. _____
4. _____ 4. _____
5. _____ 5. _____
6. _____ 6. _____
7. _____ 7. _____

eye(s)
nose
mouth
ear(s)
hair
arm(s)
leg(s)
colour

Step 1
Step 2
Step 3
Step 4

139

4c Lesson 3

Main Language Items	Resource File	Materials Needed
Don't … How many … has your …? witch spell cauldron	1 2 3 26a	coloured pencils paper for display (optional)

Step 1   Action Game

a   Briefly revise the names of the parts of the body using the instructions '**Point to …**' and '**Touch …**'.
b   Then play a variation of the traditional English game 'Simon Says'. When you give an instruction, the whole class should act it out. When you say '**Don't**' before the instruction, it should be ignored. Any pupils who carries out the instruction when you say '**Don't**' must leave the game. The last player remaining is the winner. Keep the action very brisk. Pupils must leave the game if instructions are not obeyed immediately.
c   Other instructions can be added where they are appropriate to the body, e.g.
Stand on one leg!
Sit on your hands!
Don't close your eyes!
Put your hand under your chair!
Put your hands on your head!

Step 2   Read and colour

a   Say '**Open your Activity Books at page 66**'. Pupils read the description of the monster in activity 5 and colour the picture accordingly.

Step 3   Write

a   Pupils select the words from the top of the Witch's cauldron to complete the spell inside the cauldron.

Step 4   Draw and write

a   The aim of activity 7 is for pupils to write their own spell inside the cauldron. First write a spell on the board with some words missing. e.g.
Two green …., three … eyes,
… orange toes, and a purple … .
See if pupils can suggest possibilities for the missing words. If not, write words at random alongside the spell – **ears, four, nose, red** – and get the pupils to suggest where they go. Individual pupils can come and write answers on the board.
b   To help pupils write their own spells, write all the options on the board. The colours, **red, green, blue, orange, pink, purple, black, white** and **brown**, and the parts of the body: **nose, ear, arm, head, leg, eye, toe, hand** and **foot**.
c   Pupils choose from these options to make their spell, also using numbers. Two or three items are enough, e.g.
Three yellow noses, one purple ear, two green toes.
Check that they are using the final -s for plurals, or the irregular plural, **feet**.
d   They then draw a picture round the cauldron as in the model on page 66 of the AB.
e   Ask for volunteers to read their spells to the class.
f   Pupils can make up and illustrate more spells to be displayed around the classroom.

4C Body

5 Read and colour.

This is Albert. He's got a big, purple head, a purple body and three blue legs. He's got two arms and six fingers. He's got four eyes. They are green. His ears are pink and his hair is orange.

6 Write.

red   nose   ears   Three

Six _____ eyes.
_____ long toes.
Four small pink _____.
One long black _____.

7 Draw and write.

Step 2
Step 3
Step 4

4D Body

1 Write.

How many can you see?

legs	
heads	
bodies	
eyes	
noses	
ears	
hands	
feet	

2 Crossword. Write.

Down   Across

1   1
2   2
3   3

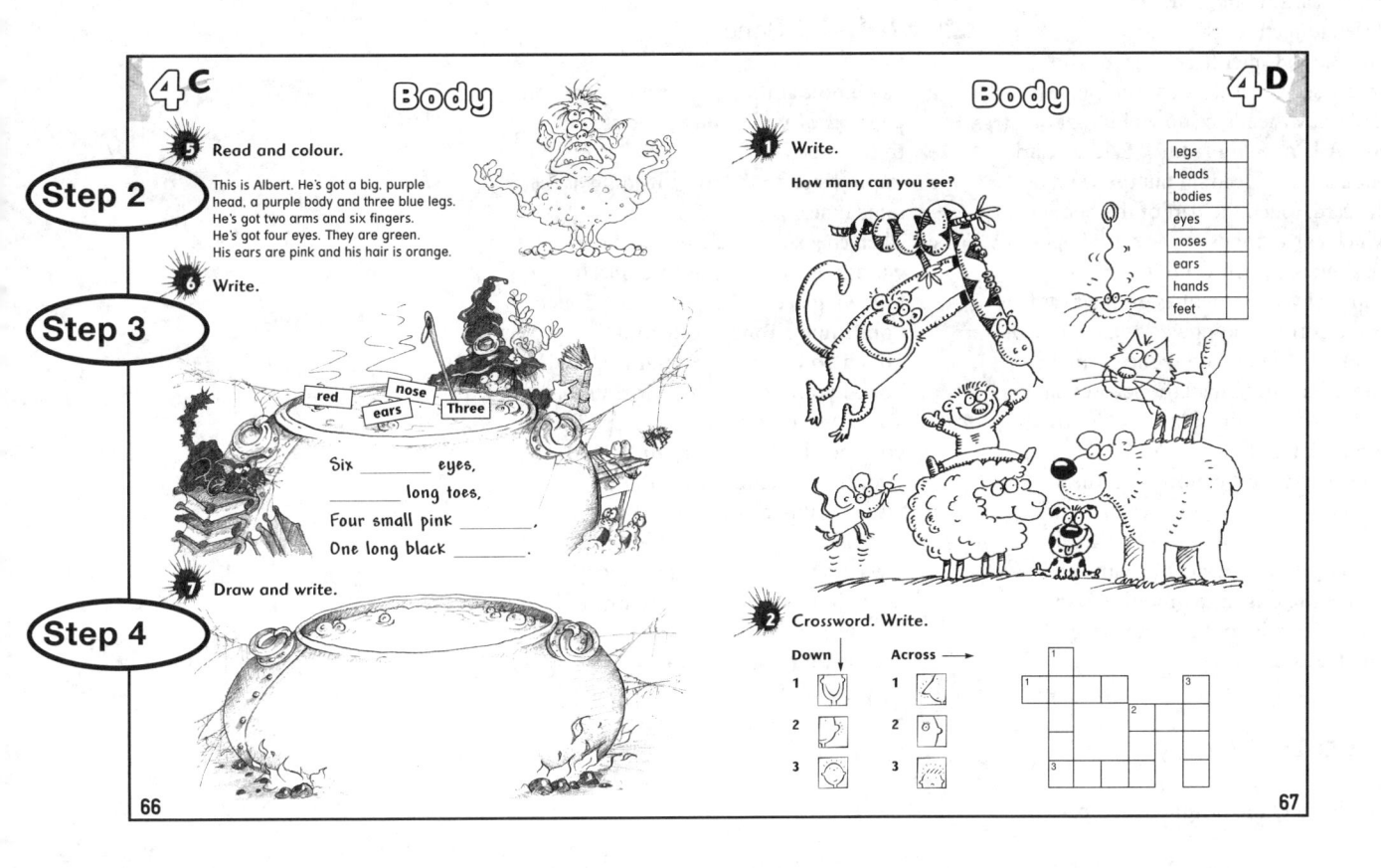

66   67

4D Lesson 1

Main Language Items		Resource File	Materials Needed
finger	*parts of the body* (revision)	38	Bingo cover cards
thumb			cassette/cassette player
keep moving			
nod of the head			
happy			
today			

Step 1   Bingo

a   To play Bingo each pupil will need to make twelve small cover cards, each with the name of one of the parts of the body clearly printed on it.

b   Instruct pupils to cover any six squares on their Bingo card on CB page 52 by placing the appropriate cover card face down over the picture. In this way each pupil's card should now have six different pictures showing.

c   The Bingo Caller (teacher) will also need a set of cover cards. Shuffle your cards. Lay them face down in front of you. Ask '**Are you ready?**' Select a card but instead of reading out the word on the card, touch the part of the body which corresponds to the card. Pupils must guess which word it is.

d   Pupils cover the pictures on their card as the corresponding words are selected.

e   Continue 'calling' until one of the pupils has covered all the squares on their card. The first player to do so shouts '**Bingo!**'

f   This player must confirm that their Bingo card is correct by reading back the names from the cards that are face up. If correct, they are the winner.

g   Divide the class into groups of 4–6 players. Pupils continue the game simultaneously in groups.

Step 2   Write

a   Pupils study the picture on AB page 67, count the different parts of the body, and write the appropriate number alongside each word in the list.

Step 3   Crossword

Pupils look at the picture clues and write the answers in the crossword.

Step 4   Song

a   Say '**Look at the song and pictures on page 52 of your Coursebook. Listen to the tape.**'

b   Pupils listen to the song, reading at the same time.

c   Then check comprehension of the words, directing pupils through the following action sequence. Say '**Touch your finger. Touch your thumb. Touch your arm with your finger. Touch your arm with your thumb. Touch your leg with your arm. Touch your head with your thumb. Nod your head. Stand up. Sit down.**'

d   Listen again line by line with books closed and repeat the words, performing the actions at the same time. (Pupils hold up their finger, thumb, arm and leg in sequence. They must move quickly to keep in time with the words.)

e   Play the whole song again and sing along with the tape, performing the actions at the same time.

142

Step 1

One Finger, One Thumb ...

B I N G O

Step 4

Sing

One Finger, One Thumb ...

One finger, one thumb, keep moving.
One finger, one thumb, keep moving.
One finger, one thumb, keep moving.
We'll all be happy today.

One finger, one thumb,
One arm, one leg, keep moving ...

One finger, one thumb, one arm, one leg,
One nod of the head, keep moving ...

One finger, one thumb, one arm, one leg,
One nod of the head,
Stand up, sit down, keep moving ...

52

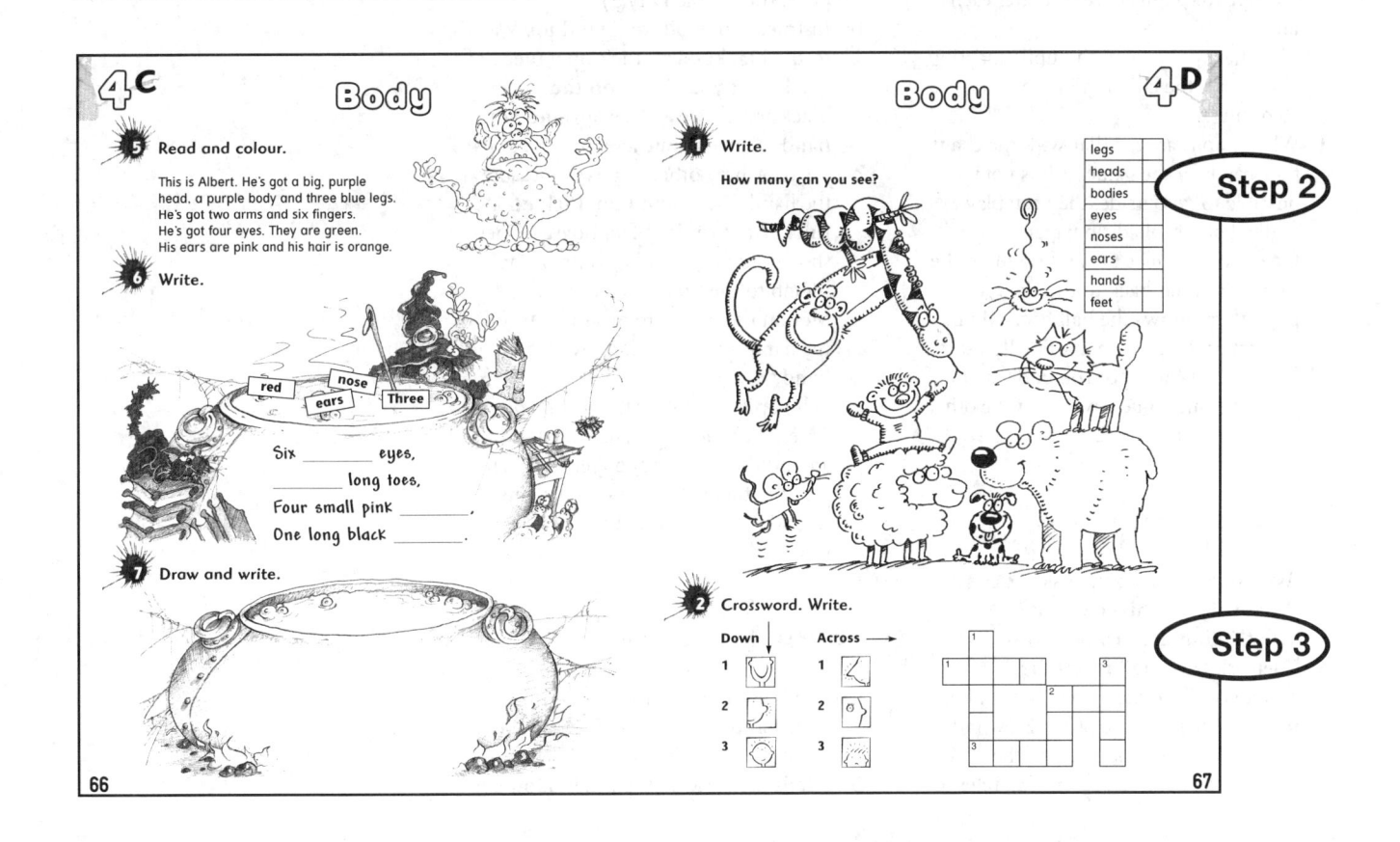

Play

Queenie

Queenie

Queenie, Queenie,
Who's got the ball?
Is she big or is she small?
Is she fat or is she thin?
Or is she like a rolling pin?

(= a rolling pin)

Listen

My Monster
by Kev Brown

This is my monster.
It's called Bulldog.
It's green, purple, red and blue.
It has got thirty eyes. It has
got three mouths. It has got
four long legs and five long
arms. It has got three noses.

Body 4D

53

4C Body

5 Read and colour.

This is Albert. He's got a big, purple
head, a purple body and three blue legs.
He's got two arms and six fingers.
He's got four eyes. They are green.
His ears are pink and his hair is orange.

6 Write.

red   nose
ears   Three

Six _____ eyes,
_____ long toes,
Four small pink _____ .
One long black _____ .

7 Draw and write.

66

Body 4D

1 Write.

How many can you see?

legs	
heads	
bodies	
eyes	
noses	
ears	
hands	
feet	

Step 2

2 Crossword. Write.

Down ↓   Across →

1   1
2   2
3   3

Step 3

67

143

4D Lesson 2

Main Language Items		Resource File	Materials Needed
Who's got the ball?	How tall is/are ...?	4	ball or rolled-up paper
big	How big is/are ...?	30	rulers
small			cassette/cassette player
fat			
thin			
rolling pin			

Step 1 Queenie

Queenie is a game that English children often play in the playground, using a ball.

a Say 'Open your Coursebooks at page 53 and look at the pictures.' Play the tape. Pupils listen and read at the same time.
b Listen again with books closed, pausing the tape for pupils to repeat after each line.
c Play the tape again with pupils chanting along with the children in the recording.
d When pupils are familiar with the chant, they can play the game. If it is not possible to go outside, they can play with a ball of rolled-up paper.
e One pupil is 'Queenie' and stands at the front with their back to the class. The pupil then throws the ball back while the rest of the class chant. Finally, ask 'Queenie' **'Who's got the ball?'** and 'Queenie' must guess which of the other pupils caught the ball.

Step 2 Presentation

a Ask a pupil to stand up. Ask the class: **What colour is his/her hair? What colour are his/her eyes?**
b Then ask **'How tall is he/she?'** Members of the class guess how tall the pupil is. Then ask the pupil **'How tall are you?'** and check if any of the guesses were correct. Pupils can refer to page 58 of their AB if they cannot remember how tall they are.
c Repeat the above procedure with other pupils.

Step 3 Measure your hands and feet

a Demonstrate the task illustrated on page 68 of the AB (activity 3).
b Instruct two pupils to **'Stand up. Walk to the blackboard. Pick up a piece of chalk. Put your hand on the blackboard. Now draw around your hand.'** Demonstrate along with pupils.
c Instruct three other pupils to measure the hands. Say **'Stand up. Pick up a ruler. Walk to the blackboard.'** They should measure from the end of the thumb to the tip of the little finger. Motion them each to measure one of the hands in turn. Ask **'How big is the hand?'**
d Tell pupils to look at the picture on page 68 of their AB. They should draw around their hands and feet and then measure them. These measurements should be recorded in the space provided.

Step 4 Pair work

a Pupils ask their partner **'How big is your hand?'** They record the answer in the space provided in their AB.
b Pupils then ask their partner **'How big is your foot?'** and record the answer in the space provided.

One Finger, One Thumb ...

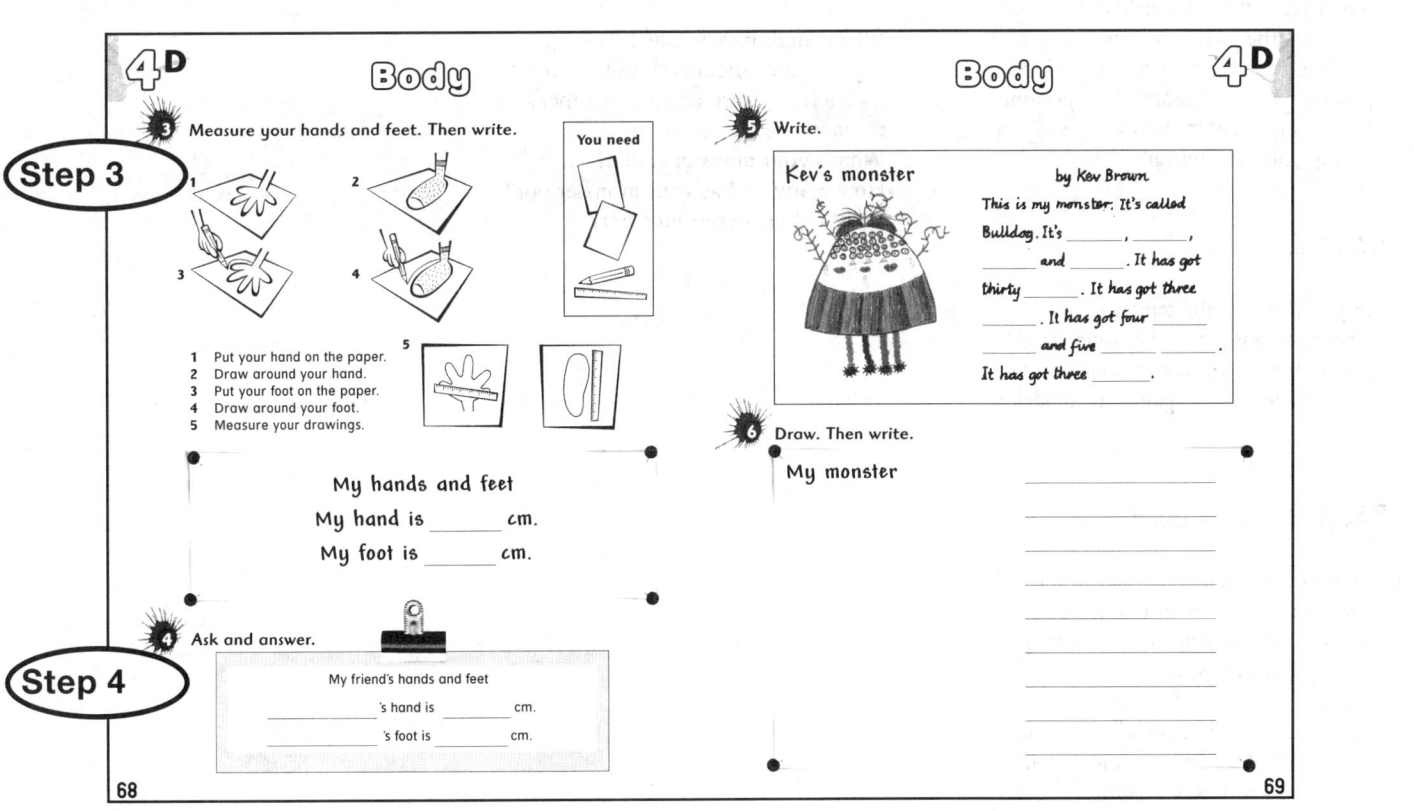

Body 4D

Step 1

Play — Queenie

Queenie, Queenie,
Who's got the ball?
Is she big or is she small?
Is she fat or is she thin?
Or is she like a rolling pin?

(= a rolling pin)

Sing — One Finger, One Thumb ...

One finger, one thumb, keep moving.
One finger, one thumb, keep moving.
One finger, one thumb, keep moving.
We'll all be happy today.

One finger, one thumb,
One arm, one leg, keep moving ...

One finger, one thumb, one arm, one leg,
One nod of the head, keep moving ...

One finger, one thumb, one arm, one leg,
One nod of the head,
Stand up, sit down, keep moving ...

Listen

My Monster
by Kev Brown

This is my monster.
It's called Bulldog.
It's green, purple, red and blue.
It has got thirty eyes. It has
got three mouths. It has got
four long legs and five long
arms. It has got three noses.

52   53

4D Body

Step 3

3 Measure your hands and feet. Then write.

You need

1 Put your hand on the paper.
2 Draw around your hand.
3 Put your foot on the paper.
4 Draw around your foot.
5 Measure your drawings.

My hands and feet
My hand is _____ cm.
My foot is _____ cm.

Step 4

4 Ask and answer.

My friend's hands and feet
_____'s hand is _____ cm.
_____'s foot is _____ cm.

68

Body 4D

5 Write.

Kev's monster   by Kev Brown

This is my monster. It's called
Bulldog. It's _____, _____,
_____ and _____. It has got
thirty _____. It has got three
_____. It has got four _____
_____ and five _____ _____.
It has got three _____.

6 Draw. Then write.

My monster

69

145

4D Lesson 3

Main Language Items	Resource File	Materials Needed
It has got …	1 2 3	coloured pencils paper for display (optional) cassette/cassette player

Step 1 Presentation

a Look at Kev's drawing of his monster on CB page 53. Pupils listen to the tape, reading at the same time. Then they cover the words, look at the picture and listen again.

b Play the tape again. All pupils repeat twice.

c Divide the class into pairs. P1 opens their book. P2 tries to recite the sentences without the help of the words but using the picture to contextualise the language. P1 must correct and prompt where necessary. (Co-operation is very important in this exercise.) Then change roles and repeat.

Step 2 Write

a Pupils complete the sentences in writing on AB page 69 (activity 5). When they have finished, they should check their version against the model in the CB.

Step 3 Personal file

a Pupils must invent a monster of their own, draw a picture of it in the box provided on AB page 69 and write a description alongside. They should think of a name for their monster and draw it in the habitat in which it would live. Encourage pupils to compare their description with Kev's monster above.

b This work makes excellent wall displays and it is very motivating for pupils to see their own work displayed in this way. Individual work can be done on loose paper and stuck into the AB when the display is dismantled.

c Faster pupils can invent, draw and write about their monster's family.

Step 4 Pair work

a When pupils have finished their monster, they should ask and answer questions, in pairs, about each other's pictures. Use the questions:
What's your monster called?
How many … has your monster got?
What colour's your monster?

Body 4D

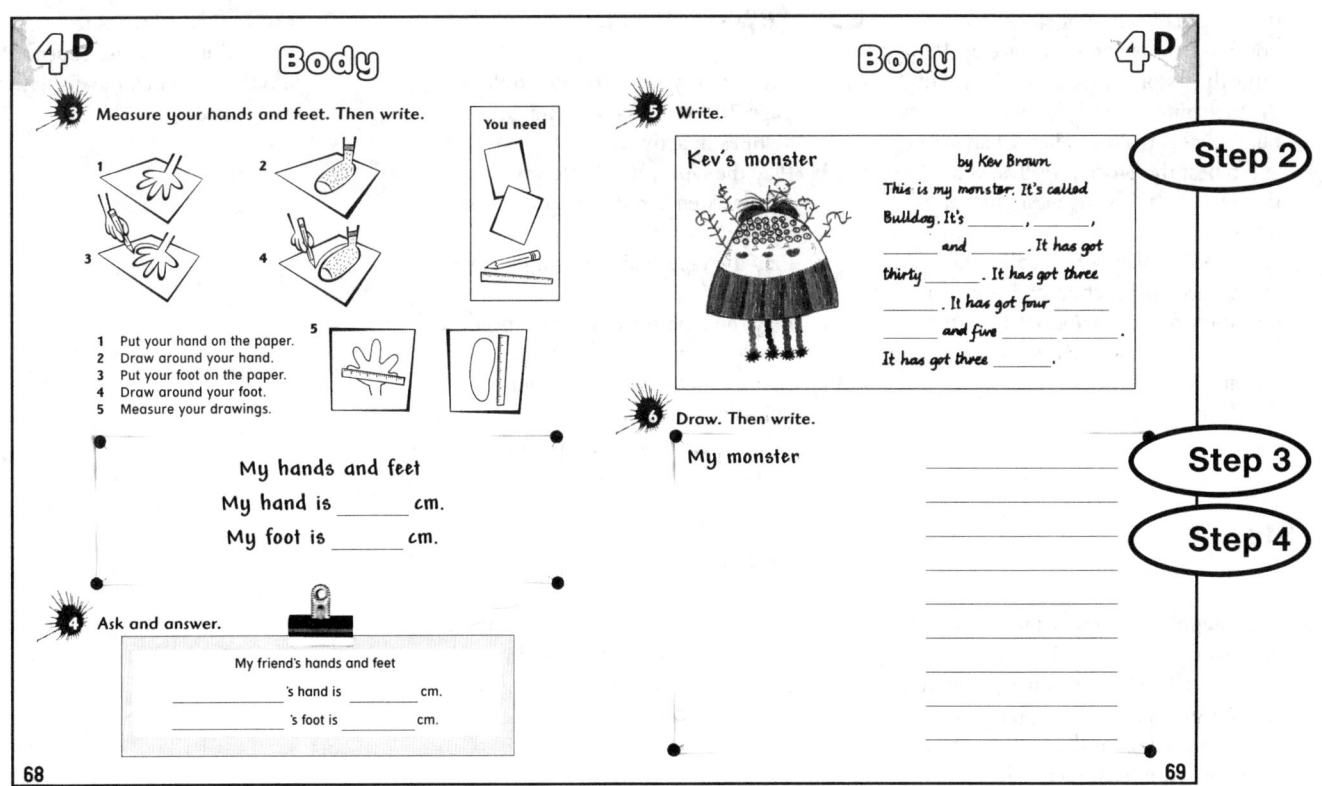

One Finger, One Thumb ...

Sing — One Finger, One Thumb ...

One finger, one thumb, keep moving.
One finger, one thumb, keep moving.
One finger, one thumb, keep moving.
We'll all be happy today.

One finger, one thumb,
One arm, one leg, keep moving ...

One finger, one thumb, one arm, one leg,
One nod of the head, keep moving ...

One finger, one thumb, one arm, one leg,
One nod of the head,
Stand up, sit down, keep moving ...

Play — Queenie

Queenie, Queenie,
Who's got the ball?
Is she big or is she small?
Is she fat or is she thin?
Or is she like a rolling pin?

(= a rolling pin)

Listen

My Monster
by Kev Brown

This is my monster.
It's called Bulldog.
It's green, purple, red and blue.
It has got thirty eyes. It has
got three mouths. It has got
four long legs and five long
arms. It has got three noses.

Step 1

4D Body

3 Measure your hands and feet. Then write.

You need

1. Put your hand on the paper.
2. Draw around your hand.
3. Put your foot on the paper.
4. Draw around your foot.
5. Measure your drawings.

My hands and feet
My hand is _____ cm.
My foot is _____ cm.

4 Ask and answer.

My friend's hands and feet
_____'s hand is _____ cm.
_____'s foot is _____ cm.

Body 4D

5 Write.

Kev's monster by Kev Brown

This is my monster. It's called
Bulldog. It's _____, _____,
_____ and _____. It has got
thirty _____. It has got three
_____. It has got four _____
_____ and five _____ _____.
It has got three _____.

Step 2

6 Draw. Then write.

My monster

Step 3

Step 4

4E Lesson 1

Main Language Items		Resource File	Materials Needed
Put	toes	1	word stone collections
foot	new	2	paper for display (optional)
back	shoe	3	cassette/cassette player
my			
your			
nose			

Step 1 Word stones

a Each pupil needs the sixteen stones from their collection, as shown on page 54 of the CB.
b Divide the class into pairs. Pupils then play games with their word stones.
c **Game 1:** Each pair uses one collection of stones, face up. P1 says a word and P2 finds the correct stone. Change roles and repeat the procedure.
d **Game 2:** Each pupil in the pair places their own collection of stones face down. P1 turns one stone face up. P2 turns their stones face up until they find the matching one. P1 counts the number of turns this takes. Change roles and repeat the procedure. The winner is the one who takes the least number of turns.
e **Game 3:** P1 places their collection of stones face up. P2 chooses a stone and says the word, e.g. **sink**. P1 finds the appropriate stone. Change roles and repeat.
f Pupils then store their stones for future use.

Step 2 The Stepping Stones Game

a This Stepping Stones Game refers to the six characters on page 46 of the CB. Pupils must make a sentence going from left to right across the stepping stones. They must begin in the first column and take one word from each column.

b Pupils work in pairs. All sentences must be correct descriptions of one of the children.
c Give the class about ten minutes to make as many sentences as possible from the words in the book.
d Check the answers with the whole class. The pair to come up with the most correct and true sentences are the winners.

Step 3 Listen and match

a Say '**Open your Activity Books at page 70.**' Point to the phrases and pictures in activity 1.
b Play the tape, one phrase at a time. Pupils listen and draw a line to match the phrase and picture.
c Play the tape again, pausing for pupils to repeat.
d Play the tape again. Pupils repeat the phrases as quickly as they can.
e Pupils practise saying the phrases as quickly as they can.
f Ask volunteers to say the phrases as fast as they can in front of the class.

Step 4 Write

Pupils look at Kev's photo of him and his sister on AB page 70 and complete the sentences in writing, using words from the boxes.

Step 5 Personal file

a Pupils stick a photo of themselves and one of their family in the space provided.
b Pupils write a description of their family photo. Encourage pupils to compare their description with the model above (Kev's family photo).
c This work makes excellent wall displays and it is very motivating for pupils to see their own work displayed in this way. Individual work to be displayed can be done on loose paper and stuck into the AB when the display is dismantled.

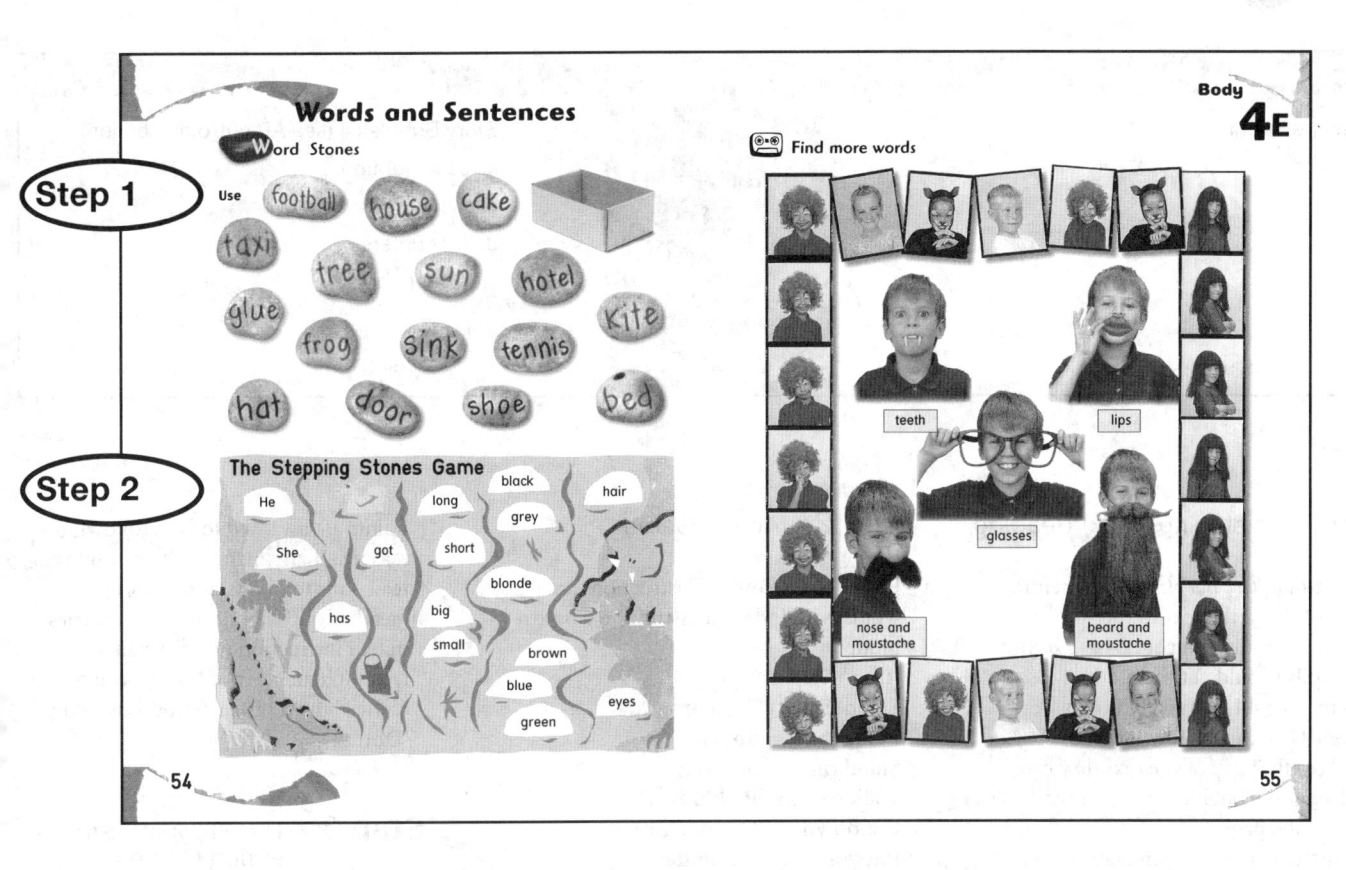

Words and Sentences

Word Stones

Use: football, house, cake, taxi, tree, sun, hotel, glue, kite, frog, sink, tennis, hat, door, shoe, bed

The Stepping Stones Game

He / She / got / has — long, short, big, small, black, grey, blonde, brown, blue, green — hair, eyes

Find more words

teeth, lips, glasses, nose and moustache, beard and moustache

Body
4E

54

55

Body

1 Listen and match.

Put your foot on the book
My nose, your toes
Two new blue shoes

2 Write.

blue   eyes   hair   long   short   sister

This is me and my _____ . I've got _____ brown hair and blue _____ Kate has got _____ brown _____ and _____ eyes.

Kev Brown

3 Write and stick.

My family photo

Stick photo here

THE STEPPING STONES ACTION GAME 4

START

1. Go to number four!
2. Stand on one leg and turn around!
3. Pick up a pencil and put it on your head!
4. Touch a boy on the arm!
5. Put your hand on your head!
6. Touch a girl's hair!
7. Go to number thirteen!
8. Touch your legs!
9. Write 'Hello' on the blackboard!
10. Touch your ears!
11. Put your book on your head!
12. Pick up a pencil sharpener!
13. Write three words on the blackboard!
14. Go to number eleven!
15. Pick up a pencil and put it on the floor!
16. Stand on your chair and touch your toes!
17. Walk to the teacher!
18. Stand on one leg and point to the door!
19. Touch your leg with your nose!
20. Point to your eyes and open your mouth!
21. Pick up three books!
22. Touch your hair!
23. Touch a blue pencil!

FINISH

70

71

149

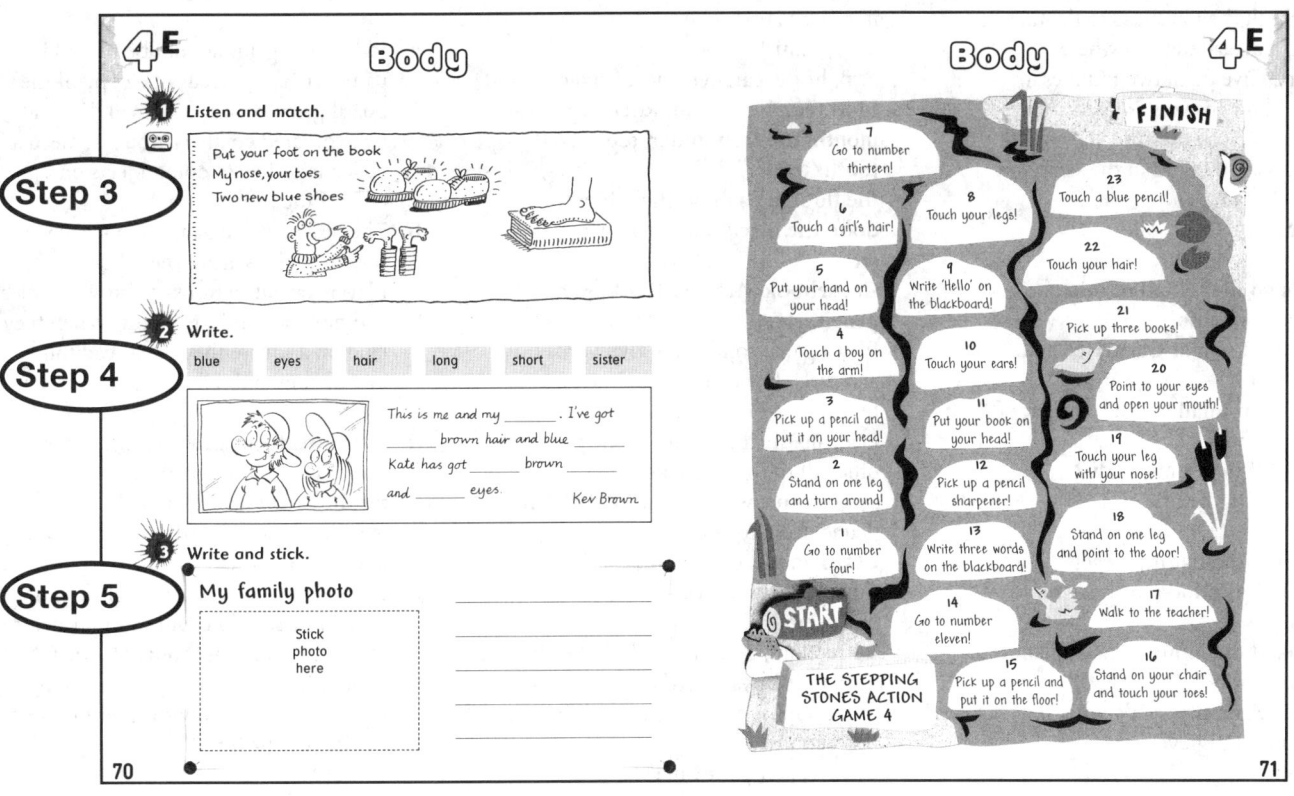

4E Lesson 2

Main Language Items	Resource File	Materials Needed
body vocabulary (revision)	17 29	Story Bubbles 4 (see AB cut-outs section) scissors (optional) cassette/cassette player dice/counters classroom objects

Step 1 Listening (Task)/Reading

a   The cut-out *Story Bubbles 4* in the centre of the AB form the text to the introductory story on pages 44–5 of the CB. Pupils should cut them out.

b   Turn to page 44 of the CB. Pupils work in pairs. Give them a few minutes to piece together any of the text they can by placing the bubbles in the correct place on the page.

c   Play the whole text. Then play Part 1. Pupils check their answers to the first part and make alterations where necessary. Give them two minutes to compare their answers. Play the first part again. Check the answers with the whole class. Do Part 2 in the same way.

Tapescript:
PART 1
JULIE: Let's go in the hall of mirrors.
SUZY: Yeah! Come on!
BILL: Ha, ha! Look at Gary. He's tall and thin.
JULIE: Ooo! I'm small and fat and my hair is short.
KEV: Aagh! Where's my body?
JULIE: What a big head!
PART 2
BILL: Oh no! Look at my nose!
GARY: Ha, ha! And look at those big ears!
SUZY: Look at me! Long arms and short legs.
GARY: Aagh! A monster! It's got a big head and big eyes.
SUZY: Where?
GARY: Over there!
KATE: Don't be silly! It isn't a monster. It's Sam.

Step 2 Action Game

a   Revise the following instructions and words with individuals and the whole group:
(Don't …)
Stand up!   Turn around!
Point to …   Touch …
Stand on …   Sit on …
Walk to …   Pick up …
Put down …   Open/Close your …
Put you're … on/under …
in combination with
a boy, a girl
arm, body, ear, eye, face, finger, foot/feet, hair, head, knee, leg, mouth, nose, shoulder, toe, tooth/teeth
the floor, a chair, a/the table, the door, the blackboard, the window, etc.
Cousebook, Activity Book, pen, pencil, etc.

b   Play a game contrasting the words **boys** and **girls**. Divide the class into two teams. One of the teams should be made up of all the boys in the class, the other all the girls. Do not physically separate the two teams since this will detract from the game. Write the words **BOYS** and **GIRLS** on the blackboard for scoring purposes.

c   Use combination of the above instructions, preceded or followed by the words **boys** or **girls**. Only members of the appropriate team must follow the instructions, e.g.
Boys, touch your knees.
Girls, don't stand up.
Don't pick up your pencil, boys.
Close your eyes, girls.

d   Points are awarded for the following reasons: if any member of the opposing team fails to obey a instruction; if a member of the opposing team carries out an instruction not directed at their team; if a member of the opposing team carries out an instruction preceded by 'Don't'.

Step 3 The Stepping Stones Action Game 4

a   Ideally the game should be played in pairs. Each pair needs one copy of the board game between them, a dice and two coloured counters. You also need a collection of classroom objects on a table at the front.

b   The object of the game is to make your way from the start to the finish.

c   Players take it in turns to throw the dice and move around the board. When they land on a square they must read the instructions and tell their partner what to do.

d   If their partner carries out the action correctly, it is then their turn to throw the dice and move. If they do not carry out the action correctly, the first player has another turn.

e   Encourage pupils to use English as they play. They should count in English and use phrases such as '**Your/My turn.**'

f   In addition ask pupils questions about the game as you monitor their progress, e.g. '**Is it your turn?**', '**What's your colour?**'

(Homework) Ask pupils to bring magazine pictures of faces to the next class.

150

4 Body

STORY

Hall of Mirrors

Step 1

4E Body

1. Listen and match.

Put your foot on the book
My nose, your toes
Two new blue shoes

2. Write.

| blue | eyes | hair | long | short | sister |

This is me and my _____ . I've got _____ brown hair and blue _____ Kate has got _____ brown _____ and _____ eyes.
— Kev Brown

3. Write and stick.

My family photo

Stick photo here

Body 4E

Step 3

THE STEPPING STONES ACTION GAME 4

START

1. Go to number four!
2. Stand on one leg and turn around!
3. Pick up a pencil and put it on your head!
4. Touch a boy on the arm!
5. Put your hand on your head!
6. Touch a girl's hair!
7. Go to number thirteen!
8. Touch your legs!
9. Write 'Hello' on the blackboard!
10. Touch your ears!
11. Put your book on your head!
12. Pick up a pencil sharpener!
13. Write three words on the blackboard!
14. Go to number eleven!
15. Pick up a pencil and put it on the floor!
16. Stand on your chair and touch your toes!
17. Walk to the teacher!
18. Stand on one leg and point to the door!
19. Touch your leg with your nose!
20. Point to your eyes and open your mouth!
21. Pick up three books!
22. Touch your hair!
23. Touch a blue pencil!

FINISH

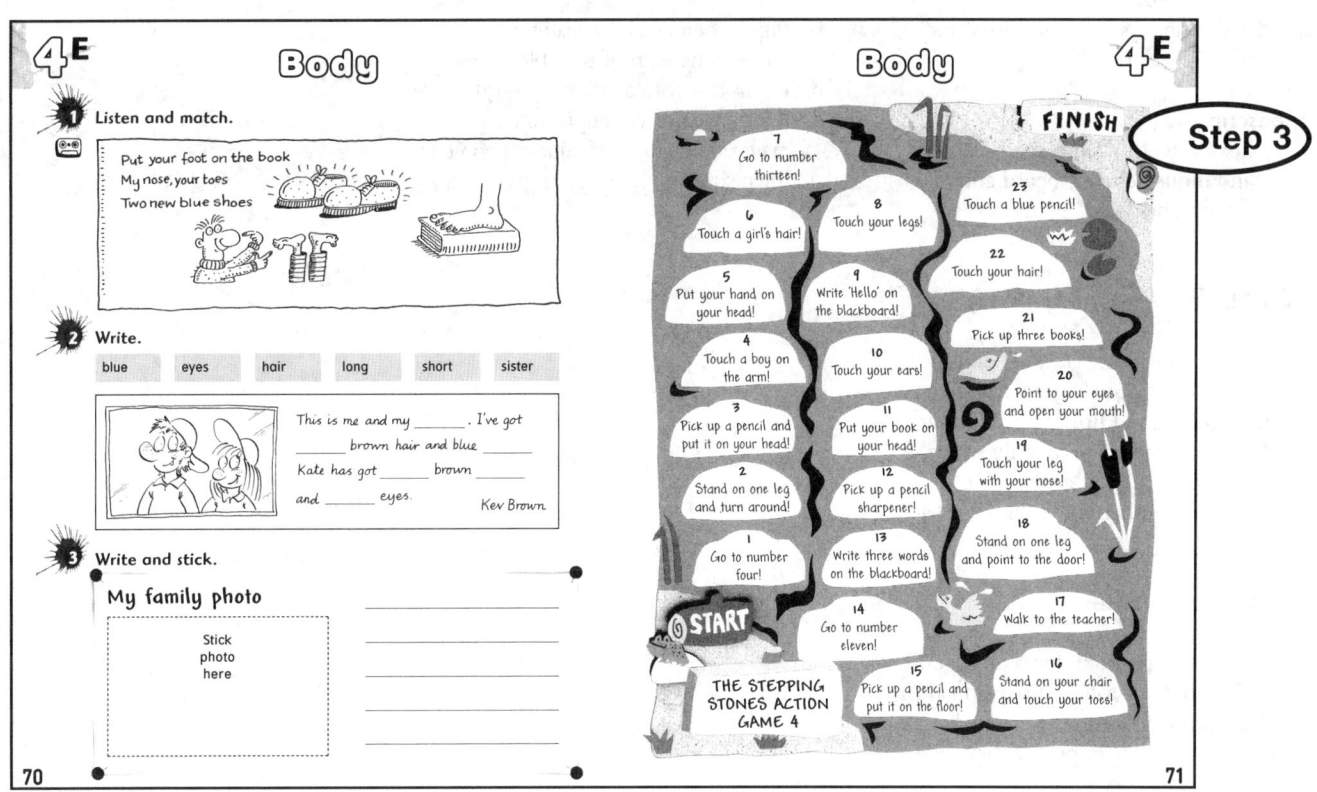

151

4E Lesson 3

Main Language Items			Resource File	Materials Needed
beard	curly/straight hair	hair		cassette/cassette player
glasses	freckles	eyes	5	magazine pictures of faces
lips	eyelashes	ears		scissors (optional)
moustache		nose		
teeth		mouth		
whiskers				

Step 1 Find more words

a Say '**Open your Coursebooks at page 55**' and look at the photos. Ask pupils in their L1 what they can see. Discuss the features they can see. Which disguise would they choose and why?
b Play the tape and listen to the words while looking at the pictures.
c Play the tape again. This time pupils point to the appropriate child as they hear the word.
d Play the tape again. Pupils listen and repeat the words.

Tapescript:
lips // teeth // glasses // nose and moustache // beard and moustache

Step 2 Listening (Task)

a Describe one of the children on page 55 of the CB, e.g. '**She's got curly green hair and big red lips.**' Pupils look at the photos and try to identify which child it is.
b Repeat with other photos.

Step 3 Write

a Look at the 'photofit' faces on page 72 of the AB. Have a class discussion in L1 about how the pictures were made and how many different people they think make up each face.

b Pupils solve the anagrams and write the words in the appropriate spaces to label the features.

Step 4 Make a face

a Pupils make their own 'photofit' faces by cutting out facial features from different magazine photos and sticking them down on paper to create a new face.
b Pupils then label the features.
c Display the work if possible.
d Pupils can vote on their 'favourite' face.
e **(Homework)** Ask pupils to bring two magazine pictures of famous people to the next class.

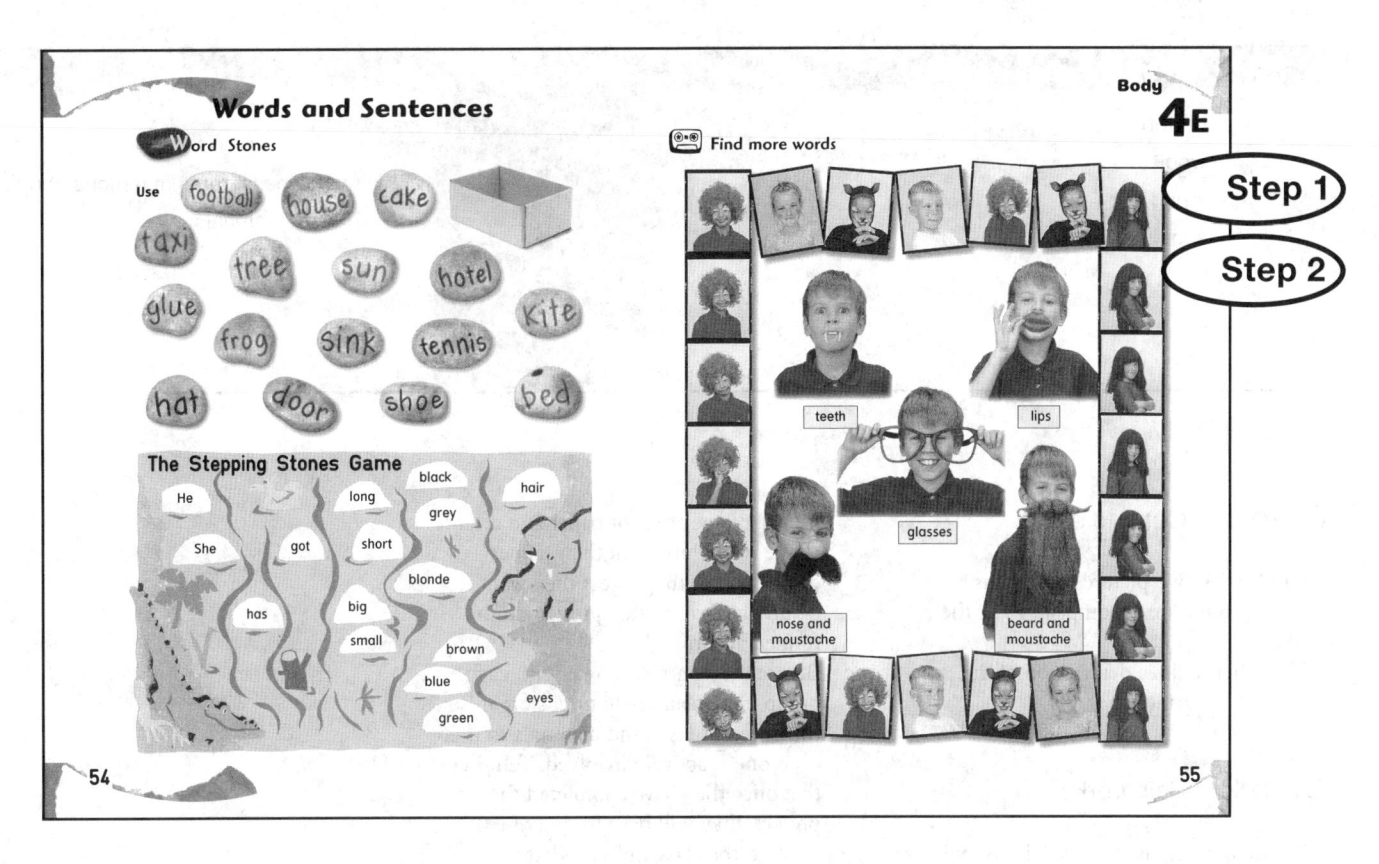

Words and Sentences

Word Stones

Use: football, house, cake, taxi, tree, sun, hotel, glue, frog, sink, tennis, kite, hat, door, shoe, bed

The Stepping Stones Game

He, She, got, has, long, short, big, small, black, grey, blonde, brown, blue, green, hair, eyes

Body
4E

Find more words

teeth, lips, glasses, nose and moustache, beard and moustache

Step 1
Step 2

54   55

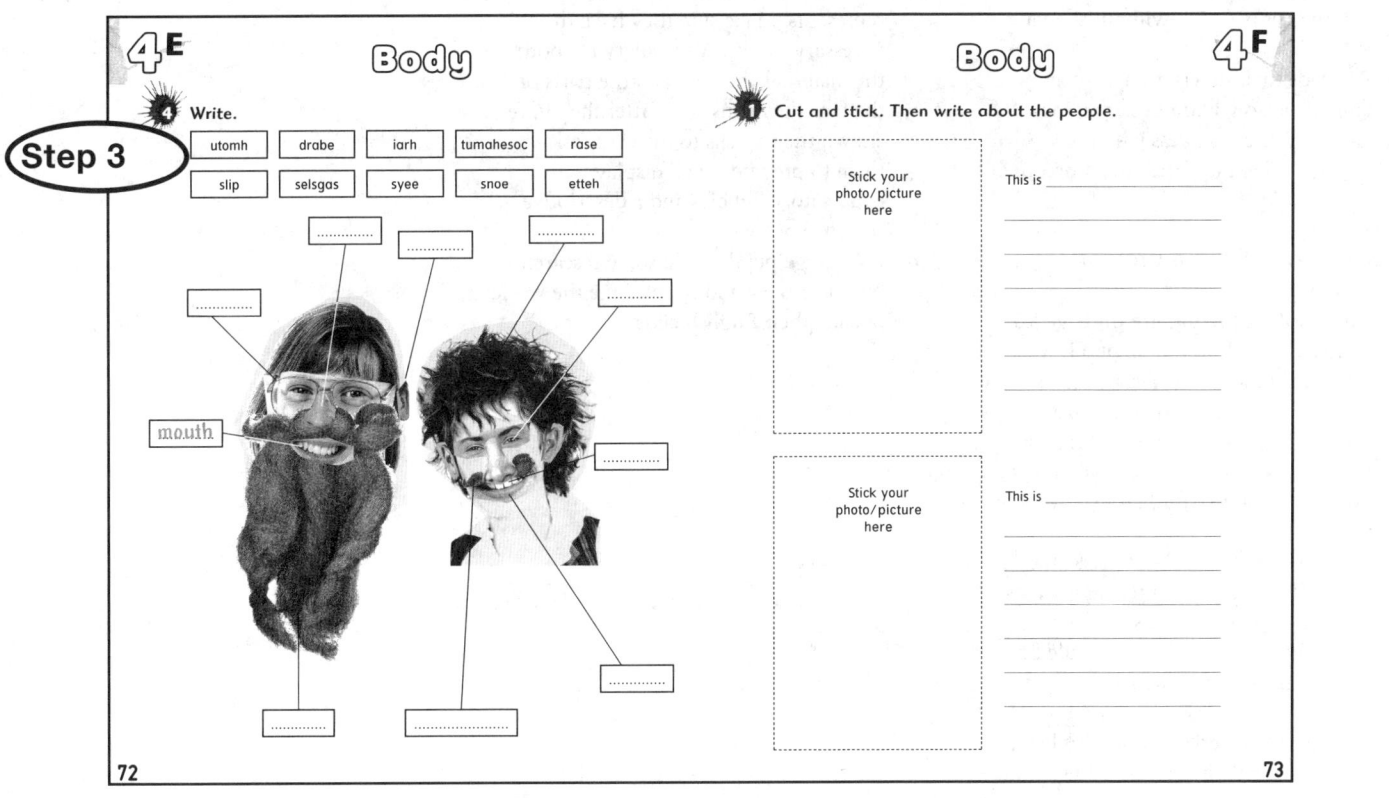

4E Body

4 Write.

utomh, drabe, iarh, tumahesoc, rase
slip, selsgas, syee, snoe, etteh

mouth

Step 3

Body **4F**

1 Cut and stick. Then write about the people.

Stick your photo/picture here

This is _____

Stick your photo/picture here

This is _____

72   73

153

4F Lesson 1 - Project

Main Language Items		Resource File	Materials Needed
eyes	button	37	
hair	wool	47	magazine pictures of famous people
face	string	48	project materials
mask	sequin		

Step 1 Cut and stick

a Pupils stick two pictures of famous people in the spaces on page 73 of their AB.
b They then write a description of the people alongside.

Step 2 Pair work

a Divide the class into pairs. P1 has their AB open at page 73, without showing P2.
b P1 reads their description of their famous person, without saying the name. P2 tries to guess who it is.
c Change roles and repeat the procedure.

Step 3 Start a project

a Say 'Look at the picture on page 56 of the Coursebook.' Ask pupils what they can see and have a class discussion about masks in L1. When are masks used (e.g. at carnival-time)? What can they be made of? What can you use for eyes (e.g. buttons), for hair (e.g. wool or string)?
b Ask pupils to think about masks they would like to create. Offer suggestions of your own: animal masks, robot masks, etc. Groups of masks could be made: a troupe of clowns, a family from Mars, etc. Start class collection boxes for appropriate materials a few days before pupils tackle their project. Write up the list on a large sheet of paper and affix it to the wall. Pupils put their names down next to the project they want to be involved in, so that groups can be formed accordingly.
c Before they start, sit down with each group in turn and help pupils organise the different tasks and materials so that everyone is actively involved. Tell them that once they have completed the project, they will have to describe their mask to the class and say what it represents. Make sure they have the necessary English vocabulary for both the materials they use and the parts of the face they construct. After they have shown their masks to the class, ask them to prepare a wall display with explanatory bubbles and a descriptive sentence or two.
d Encourage pupils to do some research on this project and to continue the work outside their English class.

Step 3

START A PROJECT

Body
4F

SUPERSNAKE

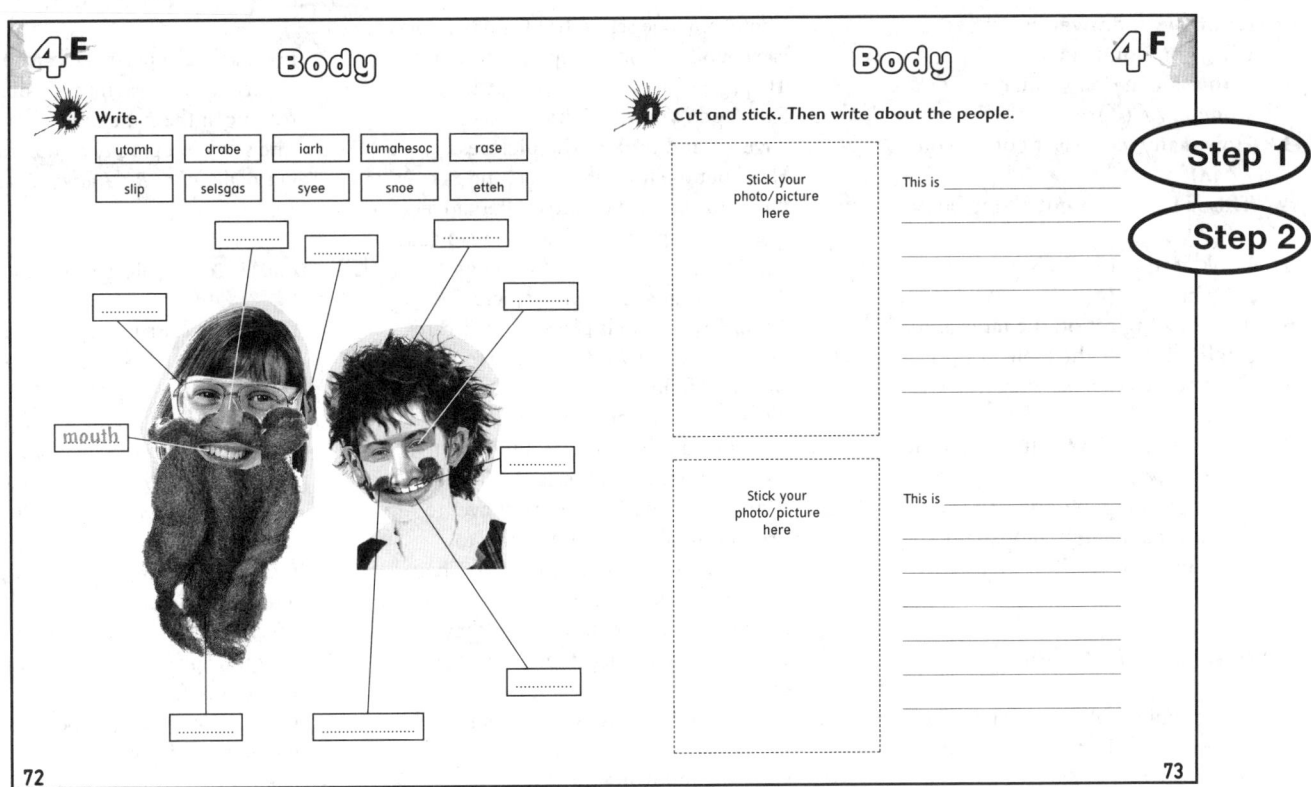

Hello, Little Red Worm. What's that? / A basket for my grandmother.

Let's go! Quickly!

Over there. There's my grandma's house.

Aha! A rat. Wait here, Little Red Worm.

Hello, Grandma.

What a big nose you've got!

What big teeth you've got!

You're not a worm. You're a rat!

And I'm not a worm.

Aagh! It's Supersnake!

Thank you, Supersnake.

56 / 57

4E Body

4. Write.

utomh | drabe | iarh | tumahesoc | rase
slip | selsgas | syee | snoe | etteh

mouth

Body 4F

1. Cut and stick. Then write about the people.

Stick your photo/picture here

This is _____

Step 1

Step 2

Stick your photo/picture here

This is _____

72 / 73

155

4F Lesson 2 – Evaluation

Main Language Items	Resource File	Materials Needed
What a big nose you've got! What big teeth you've got! You aren't a … You're a …	17	Test cards 4F (see photocopy master on TB p.175) Supersnake puppets scissors (optional) cassette/cassette player

Step 1 Listening (Test)

a Look at the pictures on page 74 of the AB. There is a short dialogue or sentence referring to each of the pictures. Pupils must decide if the dialogue or sentence is appropriate to the picture. If it is appropriate, they should put a tick in the corresponding box; if not, put a cross. Play each one three times.

Tapescript (with answers):
1 Bill's got blonde hair. // (✗)
2 Is this a man or a woman? ~ It's a woman. // (✓)
3 How many legs has it got? ~ Four. // (✗)
4 This is Fred. He's got a long body. // (✓)
5 Look at the girl. She's got very long hair. // (✗)
6 There's a big cat on the table and a small cat under the table. // (✗)
7 How many arms has it got? ~ One. // (✓)
8 Where's the ruler? ~ It's under the table.// (✓)
9 Julie's got long, blonde hair. // (✓)
10 Aagh! What an ugly monster! It's got four eyes. // (✗)

Step 2 Write (Test)

a Working individually, pupils read the questions and write the answers on a sheet of paper.
b If the exercise is being done as a test then these should be collected in and marked by the teacher.

c The tests are designed to test communication as much as accuracy and should be marked accordingly. Therefore credit should be given for answers which show that pupils have understood the meaning of the questions and where their answers are comprehensible and appropriate.

Step 3 Test yourself

a Photocopy one set of Test Cards 4F for each pupil (see photocopy master on TG page 175).
b Say 'Open your Activity Books at page 75 and look at the pictures.' Hand out the test card sheets and ask pupils to cut out the cards. Alternatively, give each pupil a set of cards already cut out. Pupils fold the ten cards along the dotted line as shown in the picture.
c To do Test 1, pupils place all their cards in front of them with the pictures showing, following the visual instruction. Demonstrate.
d You can read the first word in the list, 'a mouth'. Pupils find the card with the picture of a mouth, and turn it over to read the word on the other side, to check whether they were correct. Then they put a tick or a cross in the box in their AB, according to whether they were right or wrong. Pupils then repeat for the other words.
e To do Test 2, pupils place all their cards in front of them with the words showing, following the visual instruction. Demonstrate.
f Pupils then look at the first picture, which is of a nose. They must find the card with 'a nose' written on it, turn it over and look at the picture to check. They put a tick or a cross in the box in their AB, according to whether they were right or wrong. They then repeat for the other pictures.
g Pupils add up their scores out of ten for each test and total them. Finally, they circle the appropriate comment.

Step 4 Supersnake

a Look at the Supersnake cartoon on page 57 of the CB. Listen to the dialogue, reading at the same time.
b The story is a parody of the traditional fairy tale, *Little Red Riding Hood*.

Step 5 Role play

a Divide the class into groups of three. One pupil needs a worm puppet and one a Supersnake puppet. The pupil playing the rat should act the part without a puppet to give proportion to the size of the features. (If time allows, rat sock-puppets can be made in the same way as the puppets on page 17 of the CB.) If pupils have no puppets, the index finger can be used for the worm and the whole arm for Supersnake.
b Play the Supersnake dialogue again. Pupils repeat.
c Pupils practise the puppet show without the help of the tape.
d Ask for one group to volunteer to act out the puppet show for the rest of the class.

START A PROJECT

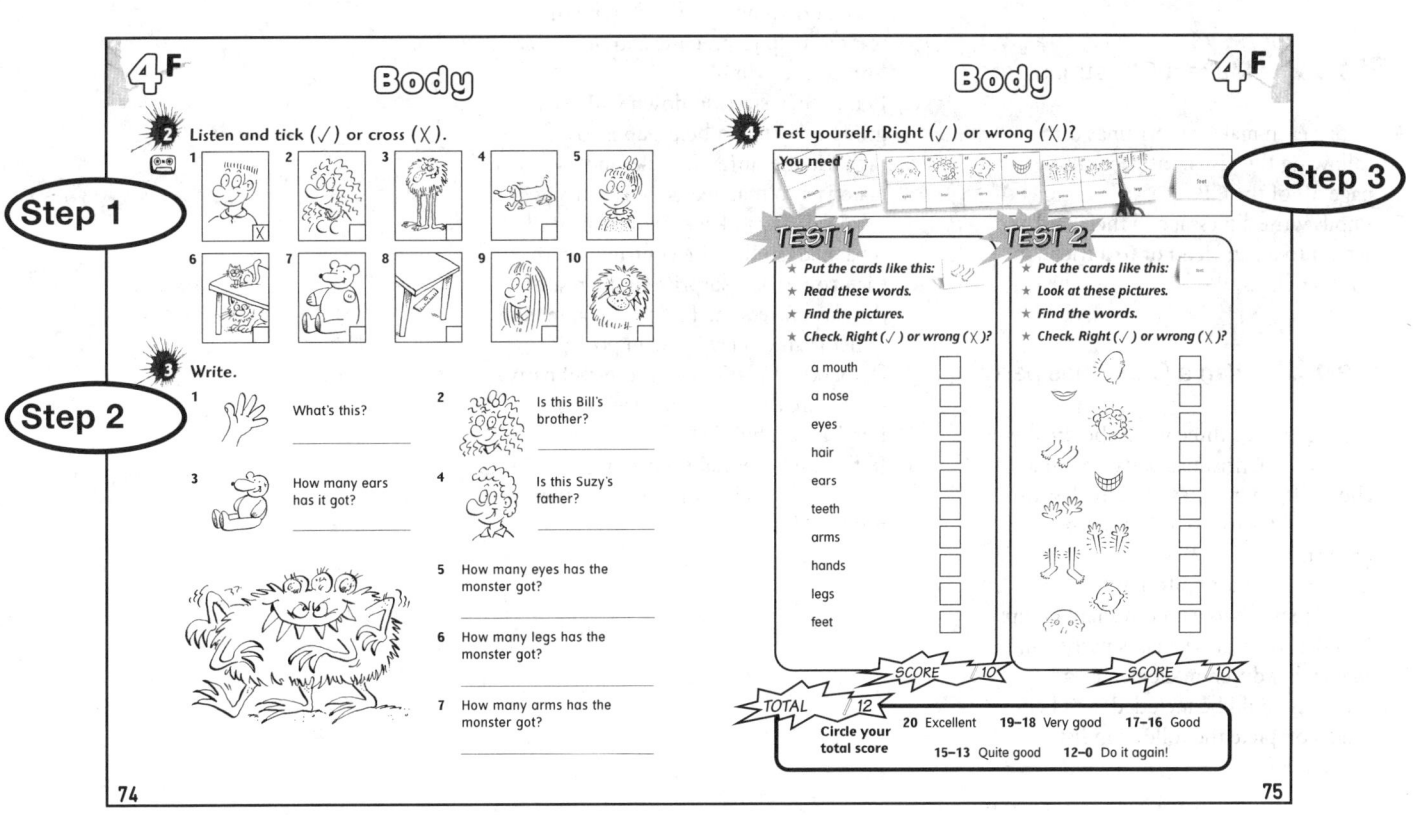

SUPERSNAKE

Body
4F

Step 4

- Hello, Little Red Worm. What's that?
- A basket for my grandmother.
- Let's go! Quickly!
- Over there. There's my grandma's house.
- Aha! A rat. Wait here, Little Red Worm.
- Hello, Grandma.
- What a big nose you've got!
- What big teeth you've got!
- You're not a worm. You're a rat!
- And I'm not a worm.
- Aagh! It's Supersnake!
- Thank you, Supersnake.

56 / 57

4F **Body**

Step 1

2 Listen and tick (✓) or cross (✗).

1 2 3 4 5
6 7 8 9 10

Step 2

3 Write.

1. What's this?
2. Is this Bill's brother?
3. How many ears has it got?
4. Is this Suzy's father?
5. How many eyes has the monster got?
6. How many legs has the monster got?
7. How many arms has the monster got?

Body 4F

Step 3

4 Test yourself. Right (✓) or wrong (✗)?

You need

TEST 1
★ Put the cards like this:
★ Read these words.
★ Find the pictures.
★ Check. Right (✓) or wrong (✗)?

- a mouth
- a nose
- eyes
- hair
- ears
- teeth
- arms
- hands
- legs
- feet

SCORE /10

TEST 2
★ Put the cards like this:
★ Look at these pictures.
★ Find the words.
★ Check. Right (✓) or wrong (✗)?

SCORE /10

TOTAL /12

Circle your total score
20 Excellent   19–18 Very good   17–16 Good
15–13 Quite good   12–0 Do it again!

74 / 75

157

Festivals – Christmas

Main Language Items			Resource File	Materials Needed
We wish you …	carol singers	turkey	card	cassette/cassette player
Merry Christmas/Xmas	Christmas tree	Christmas pudding	message	card
Happy New Year	presents	snow	7a	paper
Glad Tidings	Father Christmas	holly	33	coloured pencils
bring	sleigh	robin		glue
kin (= family)	reindeer	Season's Greetings		scissors (optional)

Step 1 Sing

A Listen to the whole Christmas carol on the tape. Follow with the words and pictures in the CB.
B Listen to the carol again with the book closed.
C Then listen again line by line, and repeat the words.
D Play the whole song again. Sing along with the tape.

Step 2 Make a Christmas card

A Pupils each make a Christmas card following the visual instructions on page 59 of the CB.
B Pupils write a message in their card and send it to a penfriend or to a friend in another class.

Step 3 Plan a Christmas party

NOTE Two or three weeks before the date of the Christmas party, set aside about fifteen minutes of each class to allow groups to work on their particular project.

a Explain to your pupils that they are going to work together in small groups in order to organise a class party. Ask them what different elements and activities could be included, and help them complete the following list of preparations:

food
games
prizes
music
decorations
Nativity Play
invitations

b Ask pupils to suggest additional activities if they wish, write up the complete list on a large sheet of paper and affix it to the wall. Pupils put their names down next to the activity they want to help to prepare, and groups are formed accordingly.

c Before they start, sit down with each group in turn and help pupils to organise the different tasks and materials so that everyone is actively involved. Try to keep the groups well separated, so that the contribution of each comes as a surprise to the rest of the class. Stress the fact that imagination rather than money is the important factor when planning a successful party. Make sure they have the necessary English vocabulary.

d In this case especially, encourage pupils to continue their project outside their English class.

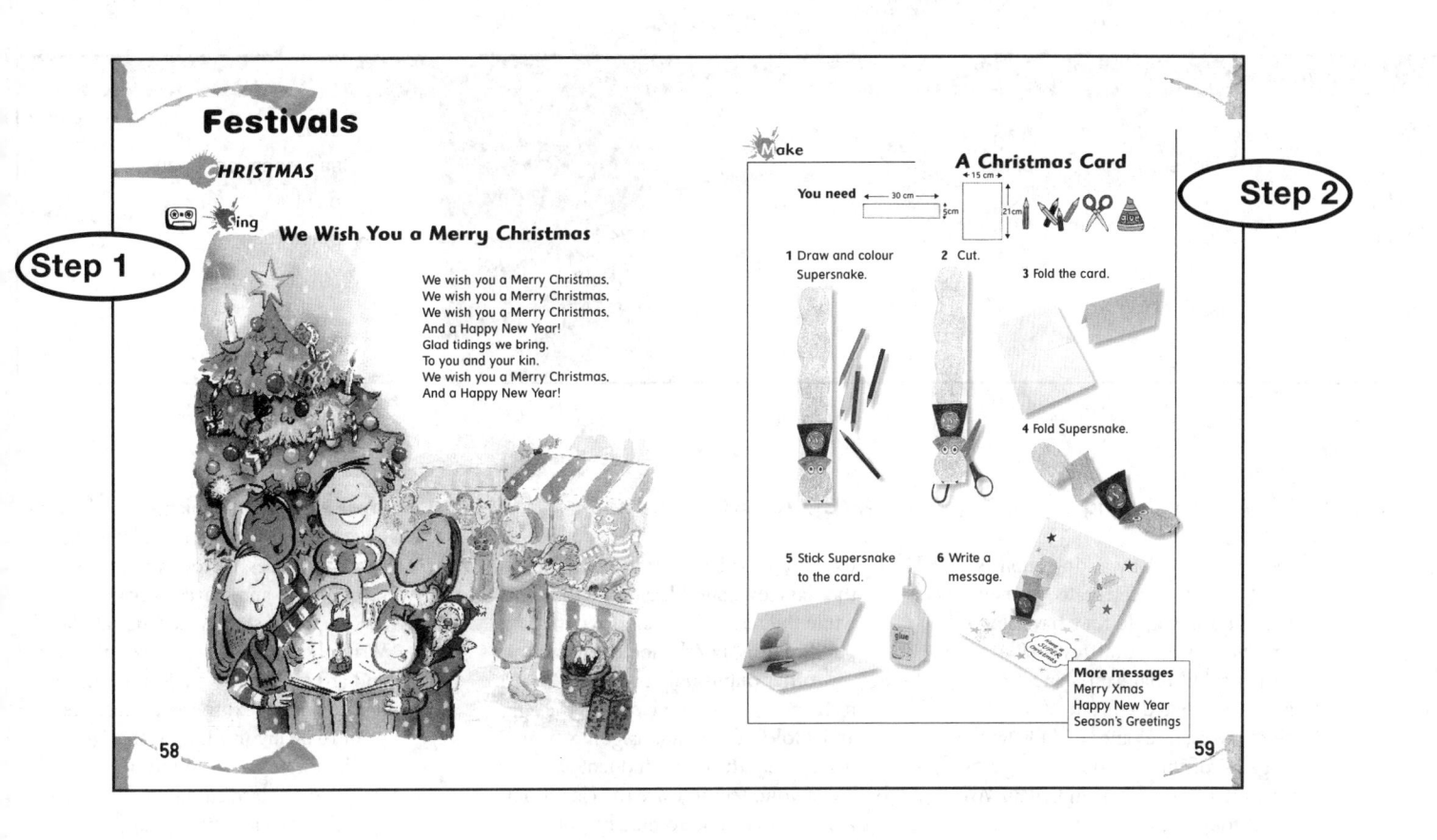

Festivals

CHRISTMAS

We Wish You a Merry Christmas

We wish you a Merry Christmas.
We wish you a Merry Christmas.
We wish you a Merry Christmas.
And a Happy New Year!
Glad tidings we bring.
To you and your kin.
We wish you a Merry Christmas.
And a Happy New Year!

Step 1

Make

A Christmas Card

You need — 30 cm — 5cm 15 cm 21cm

1 Draw and colour Supersnake.
2 Cut.
3 Fold the card.
4 Fold Supersnake.
5 Stick Supersnake to the card.
6 Write a message.

More messages
Merry Xmas
Happy New Year
Season's Greetings

Step 2

159

Festivals - Easter

Main Language Items			Resource File	Materials Needed
Easter	break	water	28	eggs
egg	winner	pattern	41	saucepan (optional)
rolling	hide			paint
painted	seek			paintbrush
hill	find			
last	boil			

Step 1 Egg rolling

a Introduce the topic by asking pupils in their L1 if Easter is celebrated in their country. If it is not, do they have any other kind of springtime festival? Are there any traditional games and activities associated with this festival?

b Look at the pictures and read the text on page 60 of the CB about egg rolling, a traditional Easter game in Britain. Ask pupils if they know of any similar races.

Step 2 Look and find

a Pupils work individually or in pairs. Ask pupils to look at the picture on page 60 and find the eggs that are hidden in it.

b Give pupils five minutes and then ask 'How many eggs are there?' (20)

c Ask the class to tell you where the eggs are hidden.

Step 3 Make a painted egg

a Pupils each make a painted egg following the visual instructions on page 61 of the CB. You may prefer to bring eggs into class that have already been hard-boiled.

b Pupils paint faces or patterns on the eggs.

Step 4 Hide and seek

a Explain the rules of Hide and Seek to the class: one pupil leaves the room while the rest hide an egg. When the pupil returns, he/she looks for the egg. The other pupils help by saying 'Warm' if the pupil is getting closer to the egg, and 'Cold' if the pupil is going away from where the egg is hidden.

b Ask a volunteer to leave the classroom. Ask another pupil to hide his/her painted egg somewhere in the classroom.

c Ask the volunteer to return to the classroom and tell him/her to 'Find the egg!'

d The other pupils watch and say 'Warm' or 'Cold' as appropriate, until the pupil finds the egg.

e Repeat the game with another volunteer.

Optional Start an Easter project

a Explain to your pupils that they are going to celebrate the coming of spring by growing plants for the classroom. Working in groups, they will have to find the base materials and containers they need, and gather observations about the development of their plants for presentation to the rest of the class. This can be done through drawings and growth charts.

Some easy-to-grow plants that do not have to be purchased include lentils, beans, potatoes, carrot and pineapple tops, onions and cloves of garlic.

b Ask pupils to suggest additional plants. Write the list on a large sheet of paper and affix it to the wall. Pupils put their names down next to the project they want to be involved in, so that groups can be formed accordingly.

c Before they start, sit down with each group in turn and help pupils to organise the different task materials, so that everyone is actively involved. Remind them that the completed projects are meant to decorate the classroom, so the containers are important too! Make sure they have the necessary English vocabulary.

d Encourage pupils to continue their project work outside their English class, perhaps by growing more plants for members of their family or friends.

Festivals

EASTER

Play
Egg Rolling

Find a hill. Everybody has a painted egg. Roll the eggs down the hill. The last egg to break is the winner!

Look and find

How many eggs are there?

Make — A Painted Egg

You need

1 Boil an egg for 5 minutes.

Ask an adult to help!

2 Put the egg in cold water for 10 minutes.

3 Paint a face or a pattern on the egg.

Step 1

Step 2

Step 3

Resource File

The **Resource File** contains over 60 ideas for the classroom and includes ideas for Project Work, ways of handling mixed-ability classes, how to prepare extra material, as well as many games and other activities not included elsewhere in the course.

These ideas can be used at any time, although the range and variety of activities in **New Stepping Stones** makes the use of this material optional. All the activities in the **Resource File**, however, are linked to the material in the Coursebook. Each of the activities in the 'file' has a number. This number is used for reference purposes in the Lesson Notes to indicate when a particular **Resource File** activity is helpful or suitable.

Display/charts and follow-up activities

The topic-based nature of **New Stepping Stones** provides an ideal basis for project work: wall displays, classroom charts and other follow-up activities.

Wall displays serve a number of purposes. They are attractive and create a pleasant atmosphere in the classroom. They provide extra motivation when they are created by the pupils and especially when they are about the pupils themselves. Much of the work in **New Stepping Stones** can be expanded to relate even more closely to the pupils and their surroundings.

1 Wall displays

Work created in the **Personal File** section of the course makes very good displays. The work can be mounted on paper and a display made which relates to the topic itself. (For example, in *School* the individual work can be stuck on a large cut-out background in the shape of a school building.) These displays can be followed up with spoken or written work which relates to the pupils themselves.

2 Pupils' files

Pupils can be encouraged to keep a file of work about themselves and the work they do in their English lessons. This is more flexible than an exercise book since all work done on paper can then be easily stored. Work from wall displays can also be kept in the files after the displays have been taken down. This can also add another dimension to the **Personal File** activities. Work from these can genuinely form part of a 'Personal File'. Pupils can practise the drawing and writing in their AB and, after correction, display finished pieces of work in their file.

3 Comprehension cards

If work from the Personal File is displayed on the walls then Comprehension cards make ideal follow-up work. Make worksheets by creating questions based upon the information provided by the pupils, e.g. for *Families*.

> **FAMILIES**
> 1. How many brothers has Anna got?
> 2. Who's Maria?
> 3. What's Paul's sister called?
> 4. Has Susan got a brother?

The cards can be used for oral and/or written work or form the basis for quizzes or even tests. They can be used for every topic and be graded in degree of difficulty to suit individual needs.

> **BODY**
> 1. How tall is Maria?
> 2. How tall is Paul?
> 3. How tall is Alex?
> 4. How tall is Anna?

> **BODY**
> 1. What colour is Maria's hair?
> 2. What colour are Paul's eyes?
> 3. How tall is Alex?
> 4. Is Anna's hair long?

The comprehension cards can be used individually or in small groups. Pupils can go to the display, read, make notes, sit down and write answers in full, then test their partners' knowledge of other class members.

4 Class surveys

The information gathered in **Surveys/Questionnaires** can be presented in wall charts, giving personal information in note form, e.g. for *Body* – at the start of the topic pin a chart to the wall:

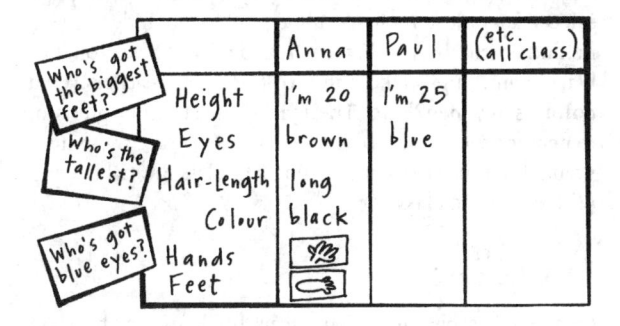

Gradually add the information to the chart as the topic progresses. Put questions around the display to add interest and focus attention on different aspects of the topic, e.g. **Who's got long hair? Who's got blue eyes?**

Such displays can relate to any of the topics in **New Stepping Stones**:

Pets – Name and colour of pets.
School – Survey on How many boys/girls/teachers/tables/chairs etc. in your classroom.
Families – How many brothers and/or sisters each pupil has; their ages, names, etc.
Body – Survey on eye and hair colour.

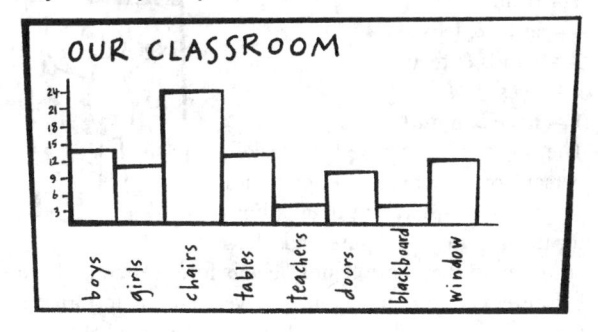

5 Class collage

Pupils collect and stick pictures related to the topic as the topic progresses, thereby building their own reference 'corner'. Displays could include:

a Topic Wall Dictionary, or
b Topic Dictionary Books – tie several blank sheets of paper together, stick pictures of various objects on the paper and write the names inside. Hang these Dictionaries on the wall for class use.

5a

Make a collage of cartoon characters to accompany the *Pets* topic. Many cartoon characters are universal and can reinforce vocabulary in a familiar way and help pupils see that language is international, e.g. Mickey Mouse, Snoopy, Donald Duck, Bugs Bunny, etc.

6 Colour collage

Similar in style to the class collage above, colour collages differ in that they are not restricted to a topic or the particular words in the course. Pupils collect pictures of anything of a given colour and affix them to a display. The teacher provides the English words and pupils label their pictures.

One or more such collages can be on the wall at any one time. They can be used for simple oral presentation or demonstration, and in games.

7 Display Card

Each pupil will need a sheet of paper folded in half to make a 'birthday card' or 'computer screen' upon which they draw a design of something they can name in English, or write an English word. These can then be displayed hanging from a 'washing line'. This is good for revision of vocabulary.

Games

In general the games in this section are oral games though some involve reading and writing.

8 Silent games

If you require a bit of peace and quiet, it is possible for pupils to respond silently to the questions you ask. These games are a form of listening comprehension which do not put pupils under pressure to speak in front of their peers.

8a

Each pupil requires two pieces of paper. On one piece they must write **Yes** and on the other **No**. The teacher asks questions relating to the Topic or a picture in the book. Pupils respond by holding up the appropriate card.

8b

Alternatively, the whole game can be silent. The teacher holds up written question cards and pupils respond using their written answer cards.

8c

Alternatively, the teacher can ask questions and pupils quickly write the answer on a piece of paper and hold it up. (Restrict to one-word answers.)

9 Memory tray

Place several objects on a tray. Let pupils look for ten seconds, then cover the objects with a cloth. Pupils write down the objects they can remember. This can be either an individual challenge or co-operative teamwork. Start with a few items, then make the game progressively more challenging by adding more items each time.
(T-led, whole class, Individuals/teams)

10 I-spy

The game can be played in pairs or groups though initially it is best to play with the whole class. Referring either to objects in the classroom or pictures in the pupils' books, say **'I can see something beginning with B.'** (NOTE Use the sound of the letter only, not its name.) The class then try to guess the object. The winner thinks of the next object.
(T-led, pupil-led, whole class, teams or pairs)

11 Test the Teacher

A quick game to turn the tables on the teacher. Each pupil selects an object (pencil, rubber, etc.) and hides it (e.g. behind their back). Write **'Teacher v Class'** on the blackboard. Pupils take it in turn to ask the teacher **'What colour's my pen?'** etc. The teacher must either guess or remember the colour. If the teacher is correct she wins a point, if not the class wins a point. The class invariably wins!
(T-led. Whole class)

12 Who am I?

One pupil is blindfolded or turns his back on the class. Another pupil comes out and says something in English (perhaps disguising his voice) or touches the first player on the back. The player at the front must guess the identity of the mystery person. Using the question form **'Is it *Maria*?'**, P1 continues to guess until he is correct.
(T-led, whole class, guessing game)

13 Body Building

You will need one dice per group of four. Write the following code on the blackboard:
6 = **body**
5 = **head**
4 = **arms & legs**
3 = **hands & feet**
2 = **eyes**
1 = **nose & mouth**
The object of the game is to make a person or a monster. Pupils must throw a six to start and draw a body for their figure. The figures must have arms before they have hands, legs before feet and a head before eyes, nose and mouth. Players take it in turns to throw the dice and draw their figure. The first player in each group to complete their figure is the winner.
(Groups, game of chance)

13a

By adding other lists to the blackboard more vocabulary can be practised.
i.e. 1 = **red**, 2 = **blue**, 3 = **yellow** etc.
Each pupil has two throws. One to decide the part of the body, one the colour.

13b

Alternatively, the game can be used as a basis for guided written work. In *School* the following list could be used

1 = bag	1 = red
2 = book	2 = blue
3 = pen	3 = pink
4 = pencil	4 = brown
5 = rubber	5 = white
6 = ruler	6 = orange

Pupils 'win' classroom items, record what they collect, then write a description. **'I've got a red pen'** etc.
(Groups, individual writing practice)

14 Lip reading

One pupil comes to the front (clearly visible to the class) and silently 'says' a word. The class have to guess the word using the movement of the lips as their clue. The first pupil to guess correctly takes the next turn. The game can also be played in pairs or groups, depending on size of class, to avoid the problem of the class being unable to see the lips clearly. Words can be:

a completely guided – using word cards (Bingo counters). Pupils pick cards at random, read the words, and perform the appropriate lip action;
b partially guided – using word cards (collective nouns: A COLOUR. A PET, etc.). Pupils pick a card, think of a relevant noun, show the card to the group as a clue and then silently say the word.

(Whole class, groups, pairs)

15 Colour words

Divide the class into teams. Each team elects a 'writer'. The teacher says the name of a colour (e.g. **red**) and pupils have three minutes to write down as many items as they can see in the classroom which are that particular colour (e.g. **a door, a pencil, a coat, socks**). At the end of the time limit, ask each team **'How many words have you got?'** Start with the team with the most words and check the answers. Write the words on the blackboard so pupils can check their spelling. Give points: 4 for biggest list, 3 for the second, 2 for the third and 1 for the fourth. Repeat with another colour.
(T-led, co-operative group work, vocabulary game)

16 Mind reading

One pupils comes to the front of the class and thinks of a word. Use collective nouns to prompt pupils (e.g. **'Martin, think of a number.'**). Once he has thought of a word he must 'transmit' it to the class. The rest of the class write down the word they 'receive' on a sheet of paper. When all pupils have written down what they think the word is, P1 reveals the word he was thinking of. If anyone has the right answer, they show their paper to the class. This pupils then takes over as 'transmitter'.
(T-led, whole class, guessing game)

16a

Picture flashcards can be used, with pupils 'transmitting' pictures. P1 gives a clue, e.g. **'It's a pet'**.

17 What is it?

One pupil comes to the front of the class. The teacher whispers the name of an object or shows the pupil a flashcard (word or picture). The pupil then starts to draw the object on the blackboard. As soon as other members of the class think they know what it is, they raise their hand. The teacher immediately tells the drawer to **'Stop'** drawing and requests the answer.
If the answer is correct then that pupil takes over as 'drawer'. If not, the original drawing is continued until it is guessed.

17a

This can be played as a team game. Divide the class into two teams. Members of each team take it in turns to draw. An incorrect answer loses a point for the team.
(T-led, whole class, teams, guessing game)

18 Find your partner

You will need two identical sets of flashcards (pictures or words). Each card will show a picture or a word which pupils know in English. You will need as many cards in total as there are pupils in the class.
Give each pupil a card. They must not show their card to anyone else. The object of the game is for each pupil to find someone with an identical card by asking other players **'Have you got a ...?'** until they find someone with the same item.

18a

The above game can be made more challenging by limiting the number of different objects on the cards but changing the details, such as the number or colour of the objects. Pupils would then have to ask more than one question, e.g. **'Have you got a door?' 'Yes.' 'What colour is it?' 'Pink.'** etc.
(NOTE This is a good way of moving students into new pairs or groups, if required. When they have found their new partner they sit down together and do the next task.)
(Whole class, speaking)

19 Battleships

Divide the class into pairs. Each pupil requires an identical grid to his partner.
E.g. for *Pets*

	cat	dog	tortoise	snake	mouse
Jim		✓		✓	
Tina	✓		✓		
Tom		✓		✓	✓
Jane	✓			✓	✓

There can be any number of names and pets on the grid. A total of about twenty squares is recommended. Each pupil places ten ticks at random on their grid. Pupils must not look at each other's grids. Players take it in turns to ask questions to find the location of their opponent's ticks.
e.g. **'Has Tom got a snake?'** etc.
The first player to find all their opponent's ticks is the winner.
This type of exercise can be adapted to any topic:
E.g. for *School*

	on the table	under the chair	in the bag
pen	✓		
ruler		✓	
chalk			✓
book			✓
box	✓	✓	

For this grid use the question form, **'Is the pen in the bag?'** or **'Is there a pen in the bag?'**
(Pairs, game of chance)

20 Dice Bingo

A simple adaptation of the Bingo game in the CB, to be played in pairs or groups. Each pair/group requires six dice. On a sheet of paper, pupils draw a Bingo grid (e.g. a square containing nine smaller squares) and write random numbers (in words) from 6 to 36.

fifteen	ten	seven
thirty four	eighteen	nine
twenty two	thirty	twenty four

Players take turns to throw the six dice and add up the numbers. Any player having that number on their Bingo card crosses off the word. The first player to cross off all their numbers is the winner.
(Groups/pairs, game of chance)

21 Hidden objects

Ask one or more pupils to leave the room for a moment. The class hides an object (rubber, book, etc.) somewhere in the classroom. When the pupils return they must find out the location of the hidden object by asking questions to the rest of the class, e.g. **'Is it in your bag?'** Then repeat with other pupils. This game can also be played as a team challenge.

21a

Alternatively, pupils need not actually hide an object, but using the pictures in the CB simply imagine where the object could be hidden. Their partners then ask questions to find the location.
(Whole class, pairs)

22 Touch and guess

Divide the class into two teams. You will need a bag and a selection of miscellaneous objects. Place an object in the bag without showing the class. A representative from each team comes to the front and tries to guess what is hidden in the bag by feeling the object. For each correct answer, pupils win a point for their team. Repeat the procedure with other players.
(T-led, teams)

23 Blind guess

A very simple guessing game to be played in pairs using pictures in the CB. One pupil closes his eyes and points to something in the picture, then tries to guess the object without looking. Pupils can have two guesses. If pupils guess correctly they win a point; if not, their opponent wins a point.
(Pairs, guessing game)

24 Repeat after me

This is a game involving the teacher against the class. Hold up a picture of a cat, for example, and say **'This is a cat.'** If the statement is correct the class must repeat the sentence. If it is incorrect the class must not repeat. Award points to yourself or the class, depending upon the appropriateness of their responses.
(T-led, whole class)

Reading and writing practice

25 Perfect Pets

A co-operative writing exercise for pairs or groups. Pupils make a list of 'perfect pets' they could give to their family and/or friends. The information can be gathered into a survey or wall display. Ask pupils, '**What is your 'perfect pet' for Maria?**' etc.

26 Messages

A writing game to be played in pairs. Pupils write an instruction on a small piece of paper and pass it to their partner, e.g.

> Hello Ann,
> Draw a cat, please.
> Thank you
> Alex

Their partner then performs the task.

26a

This exercise can be used in conjunction with the language from the Action Games.

27 Question exchange

This is a writing exercise to be done in pairs. Each pupil needs a sheet of paper. Pupils write a question which may or may not be accompanied by a drawing, e.g.

| 1/ What's this? (mouse) A mouse ✓ | 1/ How old is Gary? Five ✓ |
| 2/ What's this? (car) A car ✓ | 2/ What's Julie's dog called? Wow ✗ Butch ✓ |

Then pupils exchange papers, write the answer to their partners' question and then return the paper. Each person then checks and corrects their partners' answer and writes another question. It is important to ensure that pupils are checking each other's work.

28 Coded messages

Working in pairs, pupils write each other coded messages which contain instructions. Pupils exchange message, decipher the code and perform the instruction.

Pupils can be given codes such as 1 = A, 2 = B etc. and then write messages of the form:

16 15 9 14 20   20 15   20 8 5   4 15 15 18

Alternatively, pupils can simply rearrange words within sentences, rearrange letters in words or make up their own codes.

29 Puzzles

Pupils exchange simple self-made puzzles with their partners, such as jumbled words, e.g.
This is a colour – edr
This is a pet – gdo

30 Measuring activities

The measuring activities in the topic on the *Body* can be extended to other parts of the body to give extra vocabulary (e.g. length of arm, waist, head, wrist, etc.). Pupils record their findings in writing. The information can be used as the basis for oral work, class surveys or wall displays.

31 Numbers

To practise the written form of the numbers, pupils can create their own random number dictations by using one or more dice as a cue to writing out the numbers in full. Can be done individually or in pairs.

32 Hidden numbers

This is a teacher-led, whole-class activity to practise the written forms of the numbers. Write a description on the blackboard which contains various numbers, e.g.
Tom is 8 years old. He's got 3 sisters and 4 brothers. Wendy is 7, Kathy is 12 and Alice is 2. His brother Jim is 14, Andy is 9 and Bob and Joe are 6.
Then ask questions. Pupils must respond by writing the numbers out in full.
e.g. **1 How old is Tom?**
2 How many sisters has Alice got?

32a

An alternative to using a written description is to use pages in the CB and to name objects which occur more than once on a page. Pupils count the objects and write the numbers out in full.

33 Quiz

Using selected pictures in the CB, pupils each write two questions of their choice relating to colour, location, number, etc. Then collect the questions. Divide the class into two teams and use pupils' own questions as the basis for the quiz.

34 Connect

This game can provide remedial reading practice and is particularly suitable for younger children. Each pupil will need two sets of flashcards. One set of pictures and one set of words. (The character cards from the AB cut-outs section can be used as the picture set.)
Spread the cards face up on the table. The task is to connect the correct word and picture. As pupils gain confidence, add a competitive element to the exercise. Pupils work in pairs. They place the cards face down and try to remember the positions of the cards and collect matching pairs.

35 Connections

Using pictures in the CB as cue cards, pupils write a number of questions, each on a separate piece of paper with the answers on other pieces. Their partners then have to match the questions and answers.

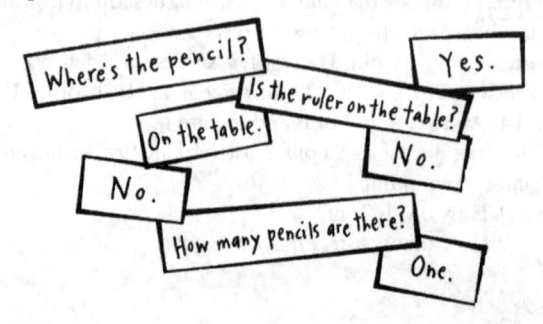

35a

The question and answer sheets can be prepared in advance by the teacher and used with mixed-ability classes. Grade exercises in degree of difficulty and use when faster pupils have finished the task in hand.

36 Jigsaw reading

Use a passage or dialogue from the book. Pupils copy out each of the sentences on a separate piece of paper, lay them face up and shuffle them around. The task is to put them together in the correct order, e.g. CB page 49.

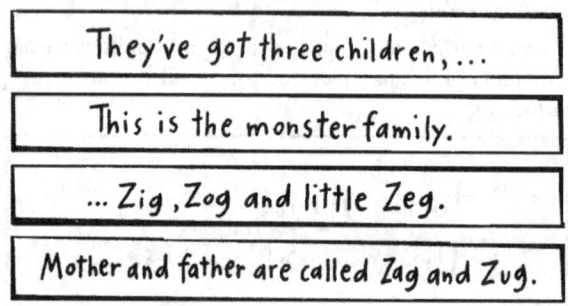

> They've got three children, …
> This is the monster family.
> … Zig, Zog and little Zeg.
> Mother and father are called Zag and Zug.

You can prepare the sheets in advance or simply write the sentences on the blackboard in the wrong order. The exercise can then be done individually, in pairs or as a whole class activity.

37 Memory test

You will need a number of flashcards with sentences clearly written on them, e.g. **Kev's got brown hair**. Show the card to the class for ten seconds then remove it. Pupils then have to write the sentence. Start off with very simple exercises: just one word and gradually increase length and complexity. This activity is very good for encouraging reading and silent repetition as pupils write.

38 River race

This is a spelling game to be played in pairs. Each pair will need two pieces of string for the river bank and twenty small cards (stepping stones) write on. Pupils take turns selecting a word for their partner to write on a 'stepping stone'. The pupil writing cannot look in his book. If the word is spelt correctly then it is placed in the 'river'. The first player to reach the opposite bank is the winner. Pupils must use ten cards to reach the opposite bank.

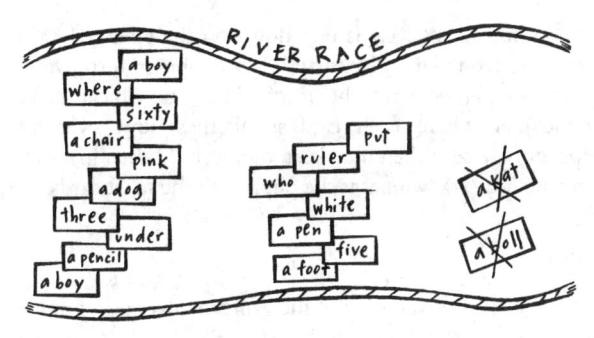

39 Sequences

To practise vocabulary or the spelling of words which cause difficulty. Affix pictures of objects etc. to the blackboard and number them. Read out a sequence of words, naming the objects in random order. Pupils have to write down the numbers of the pictures in the same order. The pupils write out the sequence in words in the correct order.

40 My pencil case

This is basically an additional piece of work for the **Personal File**. Pupils either write a list or a short paragraph about the contents of their pencil case or bag.

'Making' activities

Although making activities are time consuming, some teachers choose to expand topics into other areas of the curriculum or simply feel that there is sufficient scope to extend a particular theme further. Constructing three-dimensional wall displays, or making things which can be used as a focus for extra language practice, are two ways of doing this. Such activities are also very enjoyable. However, it is more rewarding if these activities are not simply an end in themselves, but a means to an end, or part of a larger-scale activity or project.

Therefore there should be a linguistic purpose either in the task itself or as a follow-up/extension of the making activity. This can take the form of a guided **Reading Task**, prepared in advance or written on the blackboard. Alternatively, objects made by the pupils can be used in **Role Plays** or as the basis for written descriptions, surveys, questionnaires, etc.

41a Make a puppet

Hand puppets can be made very cheaply and quickly and are very useful for pupils to use to speak 'through', either to practise question-and-answer routines or to act out role plays. They can be used for reinforcing vocabulary related to the *Body* or *Families*.

41b Make a mask

Masks can be useful in **Role Play** activities, particularly for the more reserved pupils. They also make good wall displays.

They can be made very quickly and cheaply out of paper plates, card, wool and any scrap materials.

Character cards (AB cut-outs)

This section contains further games and activities which can be used in conjunction with the character cards.

42 Yes-No game

Use character cards. Pupils work in groups of four. Each group needs only one pack of cards.

P1 takes a card and the group take it in turns to ask Yes/No type questions to determine the identity of the picture, e.g. P2 may ask 'Is it a boy?' If the reply is 'Yes,' he can ask a second question. If 'No' P3 asks a question, etc. When the character is correctly identified, that pupil keeps the card. The winner is the player with the most cards.

43 Who is it?

Use character cards. Pupils work in pairs. Each pair needs only one pack of cards. P1 takes a card and describes the character: e.g. 'His brother's called Bill. He's 5 years old.' or 'She's tall and she's got blonde hair.'

P2 must try to guess the identity of the card. If correct, he/she wins the card.

44 Reading game

Use character cards. Pupils work in pairs with one pack of cards between each pair. Each pair will need a brief description of each Playing Card on a separate piece of paper. These can be prepared in advance by the teacher or each pupil can make their own set. They will contain descriptions such as 'His brother's called Bill. He's 5 years old.' or 'She's tall and she's got blonde hair.'

44a

Lay all the cards face down on the table. P1 turns over a picture and a description. If they match, P1 keeps the card and repeats the task. When he/she turns over a pair which do not match they must be laid face down and it is P2's turn.

44b

P1 takes the descriptions and P2 the pictures. P1 reads one to the descriptions and P2 must try to select the correct card.
Award points.

44c

The above exercise can be done on an individual basis as a remedial reading exercise. Pupils match pictures and descriptions.

45 Search

Use character cards. Pupils work in pairs. Use only the cards with people on and not pets. Each pair needs only one set of cards.

Pupils spread their cards face down on the table. P1 says 'Find someone with black hair.' P2 attempts to turn over a card compatible with the instruction. The object is to remember where each card is. If they turn over an appropriate card then they keep the card. P2 then gives an instruction. The winner is the pupil with the most cards.

45a

An even simpler variation of the game involves using only the names of the characters. i.e. 'Find Bill.'

46 Snap

This is an adaptation of the traditional card game, Snap. Use the character cards. Pupils work in pairs, each with their own set of cards.

Each pupil shuffles his cards and then holds his pack face down. Players take it in turns to lay one of their cards face up on a new pile on the table. If a player turns over an identical card to the one his partner last turned over, then players must shout the name of the character. The first player to do so wins both sets of cards. When either player wins all cards the game is over. If either player turns over all his cards he picks up the pack and starts again.

47 Word Snap

Use character cards. Pupils work in pairs. One pupil requires a set of cards and his partner will need identical size pieces of paper or card on which the corresponding names should be written.

Pupils hold their cards face down in their hands. Then P1 puts a card face up on the table. P2 places a word-card on top. If word and picture correspond, the first player to say 'Snap' wins the cards. If they don't correspond then pupils continue to add cards until they find a match. The winner is the player to win most cards.

48 Happy Families

A game to be played in groups of four. Use the character cards. Each pupil needs a set of cards. Pupils take it in turns to ask the player on their left for any card. If this player hasn't got the card that is requested then he can give his opponent any card. The object is to collect matching sets of two, three and four of the same card. Set a time limit on the game. Points are awarded for each card in a set.
2 points for each card in a pair = 4 points
3 points for each card in a three set = 9 points
4 points for each card in a four set = 16 points
Players must give any card in their hand that they are asked for, even if it is part of a set they are collecting. However, at any time in the game a player may lay down a set in front of him. The value of this set is then his and he does not have

to relinquish these cards. The set cannot then be added to. The winner is the player with the highest total of points at the end of the game.

The game can practise the following structures:

Can I have Suzy, please.
I want Bill, please.
Have you got Bill?
Give me Suzy, please.
Suzy, please.

Creating extra materials

The character cards provide an added visual support to much language practice in **New Stepping Stones** and are used in a number of games and activities. If time allows, or pupils are having difficulties, then similar materials can be prepared for other CB topics.

49 Classroom cards

For revising and practising the vocabulary of the classroom, colours, and for use in **Role Plays**. Make picture cards using pictures or drawings of classroom objects, e.g. a ruler, rubber, pen, pencil.

50 Monster cards

Useful for practising the names of parts of the body, colours, numbers, plurality, giving simple descriptions and structures such as:

It's got …
How many …?

Organising your classroom

51 Returning work

When returning work or possessions to pupils, hold up objects or pieces of work and ask 'Whose is this?' Pupils have to answer 'It's mine'.

52 Storing materials

The logistics of storing cut-outs will be influenced by the availability of space, class size, and the number of classes you teach. The ideas below are intended only as suggestions:

1 **If space is limited:**

a Give each pupil a large envelope. Tell them to write their name and class clearly on the envelope. Put the pull-out sections from the AB inside. Collect the envelopes and store in a folder.

b When a Games Pack is used for the first time, hand out the envelopes. Pupils cut out their own cards. Give each pupil an elastic band or a small envelope for storing the cards after use. (The cutting-out can, of course, be done in advance.) Always return individual envelopes to the class folder for storage.

2 **If there is more space available the individual packs can be stored in separate folders.**

a Store the original pull-out sections as suggested in 1a above.

b Use a separate folder for each pack. You will need four small envelopes for each class member. Instead of returning all cut-out material to the large envelope, put them into small envelopes and store in separate folders. It is useful to colour-code the folders according to the topics in the CB. Use either coloured folders or attach coloured stickers to the folder.

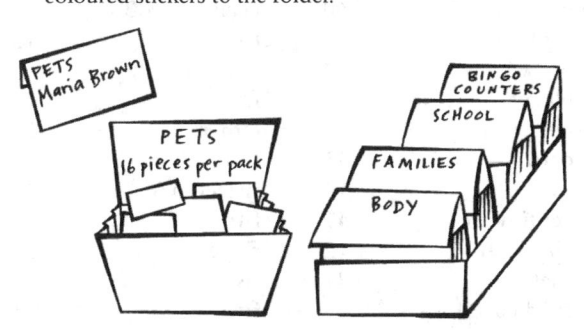

Encourage pupils to take care of the materials. To avoid the problem of misplaced items it is useful to get the pupils to count the pieces before putting them away. This activity is also useful for practising counting aloud in English.

171

Wordlist

This wordlist contains all the words presented in *New Stepping Stones*, Level 1, and gives the pages upon which they first appear. The letters AB indicate that the words are in the Activity Book. The words in **bold type** are used actively in production and the pupils should know these words. Pupils may have an active knowledge of other words, though it is not a requirement of the course that they are able to produce them.

a	12	colour	13	forty	37	knee	48
again	24	**come in**	24	four	3	**know**	31
airport	2	compass	29	fourteen AB	32	late	24
and	3	computer	8	friend	37	leg AB	63
angry	51	cousin	41	friendly	50	**like** (prep)	53
arm AB	63	cow AB	17	ghost	50	lip	55
aunt	41	crocodile	51	girl	12	live	35
bad	50	cup AB	37	glasses	55	long	47
badge	6	**cupboard**	29	glue	28	me	35
bag	20	cut	17	goodbye	31	measure AB	68
ball	53	**dad**	41	grandad	41	merry	58
basket	57	desk	29	grandfather	35	metre	47
beard	55	difficult	31	grandma	41	monkey	12
bed	28	**dog**	10	grandmother	35	monster	49
bees AB	52	don't AB	27	green	3	mother	35
big AB	37	door AB	15	grey	20	mouse	10
bin	29	duck AB	17	hair	46	moustache	55
bird	15	ear	48	hairy AB	62	mouth	48
birthday	36	Easter	60	hamster	15	moving	52
black	3	egg	60	hand AB	62	**mum**	41
blackboard AB	31	eight AB	11	happy	52	**my**	27
blonde	46	eighteen AB	32	have got AB	52	**name**	7
blue	3	eighty	37	head	48	new AB	70
body AB	63	eleven AB	32	**hello**	6	New Year	59
boil	61	eye	46	hen AB	17	nine AB	11
book	20	face	49	**her**	27	nineteen AB	32
boy	12	family	32	**hi**	6	ninety	37
break	60	family tree AB	45	hill	60	no	11
brother	35	farm	13	**his**	27	nod	52
brown	3	fast food	2	hotel	2	nose	48
budgie	16	fat	47	how many?	35	on	26
burger bar	2	father	35	how old ... ? AB	47	one	3
card	43	feet	49	how tall ... ? AB	59	orange	20
cat	10	fifteen AB	32	hundred	37	over there	57
centimetre	47	fifty	37	I	7	paint	29
chair AB	12	finger	52	idea	43	paintbrush	29
chalk AB	31	fish	15	in	26	painted	61
children	49	five	3	**is**	12	paper AB	68
Christmas	58	floor AB	15	isn't	38	pen AB	18
clock	29	foot AB	63	keep	52	pencil AB	18
cold	61	football	2	kite	28	pencil case	22

172

pencil sharpener	22	snake	10	wait	57		
people	35	spider	50	walk AB	8		
pet	4	spinning top	21	water	61		
photograph	34	sport	2	what	7		
pick up AB	18	stand on AB	15	where	26		
picture	37	stand up AB	6	white	3		
pink	20	stick	17	who	7		
plane	17	stop	2	worm	31		
point to AB	12	sun	40	write AB	31		
potato	3	supermarket	2	yellow	3		
purple	21	table AB	12	yes	11		
put AB	31	tall	47	you	12		
put down AB	18	taxi	2	your	7		
quickly	57	teacher	27				
rabbit	15	teddies AB	52				
rat	15	teeth AB	62				
red	3	ten AB	11				
restaurant	2	tennis	2				
roll	60	thanks	31				
rolling pin	53	that	8				
rubber	22	there	31				
ruler	22	thin	47				
school	24	thirteen AB	32				
scissors	29	thirty	37				
Season's Greetings	59	this	7				
seven	3	three	3				
seventeen AB	32	thumb	52				
seventy	37	time	24				
sheep AB	17	toe	48				
shoe	40	tooth AB	62				
short	47	tortoise	10				
shoulder	48	touch AB	12				
shut	24	tree	40				
sink	28	turn around AB	8				
sister	35	twelve AB	32				
sit down AB	6	twenty AB	32				
sit on AB	15	two	3				
six	3	ugly AB	62				
sixteen AB	32	uncle	41				
sixty	37	under AB	31				
small	47	very	24				

Photocopy master: Test cards 1F and 2F

1F	1F	1F	1F
a dog	a cat	a mouse	a tortoise
1F		2F	2F
a snake		a book	a pen
2F	2F	2F	2F
a pencil	a rubber	a ruler	a pencil sharpener
2F	2F	2F	2F
a pencil case	a bag	a table	a chair

©Addison Wesley Longman 1997

Photocopy master: Test cards 3E and 4F

3E	3E	3E	3E
sister	brother	mother	father

3E	3E	4F	4F
grandmother	grandfather	a mouth	a nose

4F	4F	4F	4F
eyes	hair	ears	teeth

4F	4F	4F	4F
arms	hands	legs	feet

©Addison Wesley Longman 1997

Addison Wesley Longman Limited,
Edinburgh Gate, Harlow,
Essex CM20 2JE, England
and Associated Companies throughout the world.

© John Clark and Julie Ashworth 1997

"The right of Julie Ashworth and John Clark to be identified as authors of this Work has been asserted by them in accordance with the Copyright, Designs and Patents Act 1988".

All rights reserved; no part of this publication may be reproduced, stored in a retrieval system, or transmitted in any form or by any means, electronic, mechanical, photocopying, recording or otherwise, without the prior written permission of the Publishers.

First published in this edition 1997
Second impression 1997

ISBN 0 582 31131 4

Set in 3.5mm Columbus

Printed in Spain by Graficas Estella

Cover illustration by Trevor Dunton

Illustrated by: Bernice Lum, Mérel, Trevor Dunton, Julie Ashworth, David Le Jars, Lisa Williams, Chris Mould, Emma Holt, Neil Layton, Lisa Smith.

Acknowledgements

Thanks to the following people who helped in the development of *New Stepping Stones*:

In Argentina: María Mónica Marinakis, Myriam Raquel Pardo Herrero.

In France: Christiane Fatien, Catherine Quantrell-Park, Jean-Pierre Top.

In Poland: Magdalena Dziob, Ilona Kubrakiewicz, Urszula Mizeracka.

In Spain: Ana Baranda, Mercé Barroetabeña, Maribel Cequier, Marisa Colomina Puy, Paloma Garcia Consuegra, Susana Garralda, Jordi Gonzalez, María Antonieta Millán Gómez, Immaculado Minguez, Mady Musiol, María Elena Pérez Márquez, María Angeles Ponce de León, Antonio Tejero.

In the UK: Viv Lambert, Sally McGugan.

and to those who contributed so much to the original edition:

Janet Ashworth, Sylvia Bakapoulou, Kathleen Chiacchio, Lety Dominguez, Marijke Dreyer, Peta Harloulakou, Gilbert Horobin, Mrs Ioannou, Anita Lycouri, Lucy McCullagh, John Oakley, Mr Proudfoot, Lorena Rosas, Gordon Slaven, Ray Tongue, Jo Walker.